Contents

UNIT 7: EDUCATING FOR HEALTH AND SOCIAL WELL-BEING

UNIT 8: RESEARCH PERSPECTIVES IN HEALTH AND SOCIAL CARE

GNVQ Advanced

Health and Social Care

SECOND EDITION

Liam Clarke • Bruce Sachs • Sue Ford

STANLEY
THORNES

First published in 1994 by:
Stanley Thornes (Publishers) Ltd
Ellenborough House
Wellington Street
CHELTENHAM
GL50 1YW

Reprinted 1994

Second edition published 1995

A catalogue record for this book is available from the British Library.
ISBN 0 7487 2225 4

Typeset by P & R Typesetters Ltd, Salisbury
Printed and bound in Great Britain at The Bath Press, Avon

Acknowledgements

We would like to thank all the students and clients who have taught us the real essence of care. We have listened!

Liam Clarke
Bruce Sachs
Sue Ford

The authors and publishers are grateful to the following for permission to reproduce material:

Age Concern, page 313; Alzheimer's Disease Society, page 188 (right); BNA, pages 70, 268 (bottom); British Diabetic Association, page 115; Butter Council, page 341; Gene Cox, pages 83, 84, 85; D.C. Thompson & Co., page 113; Daily Mail, page 344; Down's Syndrome Association, page 177; Educare for photographs from the *Caring for Mary* Video workbook, pages 29, 34, 46, 51, 57; Ken Fisher/Tony Stone Images, cover photo; Gloucestershire Royal Hospital Special Care Baby Unit, page 349; Gloucestershire Social Services Department, page 188 (left); Guardian News Service Ltd, page 247; John Harris, page 68; Health Education Authority, pages 3, 218, 220, 343, 352, 358; John Birdsall, 310/Age Concern, 269, 295, 297, 300; Kanga's Pouch Day Nursery, page 366; Chris Kelly, page 279; Jenny Matthews/Save the Children Fund, page 315; Milk Marketing Board, page 341; Multiple Sclerosis Society, page 337; National Osteoporosis Society, page 171; Nick Oakes/Age Concern, page 289; Tony Othen/Age Concern, page 71; Pharmacia Ltd, page 341; Sainsbury's plc, page 220; Stroud District Council, page 341; Sam Tanner/Age Concern, pages 268 (top), 319, 327; Terrence Higgins Trust, pages 335, 341; Ulrike Preuss/Age Concern, page 278; *Unison Magazine*, page 236; WRVS, pages 255–7.

Every effort has been made to contact copyright holders and obtain permission to reproduce material prior to publication. We apologise if anyone has been overlooked.

The authors and publishers gratefully acknowledge the contribution made to this book by Peter Waltham.

Introduction

Since publication of the highly successful first edition of this text, we have learned much about what health and social care students value in a book of this sort.

First, this book is written from a perspective of health and social care practitioners. The authors have had extensive first-hand experience working in the caring professions, and bring that perspective to each chapter. The GNVQ requirements are explored in relevant and realistic ways. Although much of our time is now spent externally verifying GNVQ courses, we are still care professionals first, and wouldn't want it any other way.

Second, we have provided a depth and detail of knowledge which the serious student requires. This is not a revision aid, but rather a useful reference source. It has been written to provide the student with more than just basic GNVQ knowledge. We would expect that this text will serve the student well in further, more advanced courses, such as HND level. In fact, HND students will find this text to be an invaluable resource.

Third, in providing depth, we have not departed from the basic GNVQ knowledge requirements, which are set out clearly and plainly. Depth of knowledge does not mean complex, difficult texts.

This book covers all of the mandatory units of the Advanced GNVQ in Health and Social Care, and as such will support students registered with any of the awarding bodies; BTEC, RSA or City & Guilds. It will also provide background reading and vital underpinning knowledge for candidates for NVQs in care at both Levels two and three.

Whilst this book comprehensively supports the structure and content of the mandatory units, we have developed the material beyond minimum requirements in order to put it clearly into a proper vocational context. Many of the case studies and perspectives expressed in this book come from the real experiences of the authors.

We have placed an emphasis on active learning with activities and case studies used to illustrate and expand upon the contents of each unit. How the book is used will to some extent be determined by the way in which the GNVQ is tackled. We suggest that the student makes extensive use of work placement opportunities in relation to all of the subjects covered in this book. Students should also be acquainted with the methods of assessment used for GNVQs, so that work may be planned with assessment in mind. A brief section on this topic is provided.

Each chapter concludes with revision questions and example assignments. The revision questions are based on the knowledge and understanding for the units. The assignment(s) at the end of each chapter have been designed to address some of the elements specified for each unit, and will provide suitable evidence for student portfolios, in line with the Evidence Indicators.

The Advanced GNVQ in Health and Social Care is a challenging and worthwhile achievement. It will provide the student with a thorough knowledge of Health and Social Care, and an opportunity to experience working in care settings. As a qualificiation, it may provide the means directly into employment for some. For most, it will provide access to higher education, including courses toward social work and nursing qualifications. The vocations and professions included within Health and Social Care are some of the most personally rewarding jobs there are. They require special people, willing to devote themselves to the well-being of others. The authors of this book have considerable direct professional experience in the Health and Social Care industry. We know how important this work is, and the devotion that one needs to possess in order to succeed. We dedicate this book to all those who use it, for the purpose of making a better, more caring world for all people. Good luck, and work hard!

Liam Clarke
Bruce Sachs
Sue Ford
August 1995

Assessment for GNVQ

What is a GNVQ?

A General National Vocational Qualification (GNVQ) is an alternative qualification to A levels or GCSEs and can be taken at three levels:

- **Foundation GNVQ:** equivalent to four GCSEs at grades D–G, these normally take one year of full-time study.
- **Intermediate GNVQ:** equivalent to four GCSEs at grades A–C, these normally take one year of full-time study.
- **Advanced GNVQ:** equivalent to two A levels (Advanced GNVQs are sometimes referred to as 'Vocational A levels'), these are normally taken over a two-year period of full-time study.

How is a GNVQ structured?

All GNVQ courses are made up of **units:**

- **mandatory vocational units** – these you must study
- **optional vocational units** – these you choose to study
- **mandatory core skills units** in Communication, Information Technology and Application of Number – not studied as separate units, but taught and tested in the activities and assignments in the vocational units.

What is in a unit?

Let us take Unit 5, Element 5.3 of the Advanced GNVQ in Health and Social Care as an example.

1 Unit title ⟶

2 Each unit is divided into **elements** (usually three – this is the third element in this unit)

4 The **range** explains the areas you will need to study in order to be able to provide evidence and demonstrate knowledge in the written tests.

UNIT 5: THE STRUCTURE AND DEVELOPMENT OF HEALTH AND SOCIAL CARE SERVICES

Element 5.3: Investigate the organisation of health and social care planning and provision

PERFORMANCE CRITERIA

A student must:

1 explain the **structure** of health and social care
2 describe the **role** of **purchasers** in meeting the needs of their population
3 explain the principle **changes** which provider services have had to make to meet the demands of purchasing and providing

RANGE

Structure: commissioning roles, purchasing roles, provider roles
Role: assessing the health and social care needs of the population, planning how to meet health and social care needs, stimulating service provision where it is missing, assessing service providers'

---

3 Each element is divided into **performance criteria**. These describe all the things for which you must be able to provide **evidence** that you can do them.

ability to deliver services, contracting with service providers, monitoring and evaluating services against contract

Purchasers: single agency, multi-agency; for individuals, for communities

Changes: structures, accountability, contracts, client involvement

EVIDENCE INDICATORS

A short report which:

- describes the role of a local purchaser
- describes the changes required of a local provider in meeting the needs of the purchaser
- includes examples of different agencies involved in health and social care.

5 The **evidence indicators** set out exactly what evidence you will need to supply to satisfy all the assessment requirements.

What is the Advanced GNVQ in Health and Social Care?

It is made up of eight mandatory units, each with three elements. Each of the awarding bodies providing the GNVQ also offer a number of optional units, from which four must be chosen.

The Advanced units and elements are:

- Unit 1: Equal opportunities and individuals' rights
    - Investigate legal rights and responsibilities in relation to equality of opportunity
    - Explore how individuals can be affected by discrimination
    - Examine ethical issues in health and social care practice
- Unit 2: Interpersonal interaction in health and social care
    - Explore interpersonal interaction
    - Demonstrate skills of interpersonal interaction
    - Analyse methods of interacting with clients in health and social care
- Unit 3: Physical aspects of health and social well-being
    - Investigate the organisation of structures within human body systems
    - Investigate the functions of the main organ systems
    - Investigate methods for monitoring and maintaining the healthy functioning of the human body
- Unit 4: Health and social well-being: psycho-social aspects
    - Investigate human growth and development
    - Analyse how individuals function in and are influenced by society
    - Investigate the effects of socio-economic factors on health and social well-being
- Unit 5: The structure and development of health and social care services
    - Investigate the provision of health and social care services and facilities
    - Explain why health and social care provision develops and changes
    - Investigate the organisation of health and social care planning and provision
- Unit 6: Health and social care practice
    - Investigate the planning of care and interventions for individual clients
    - Investigate methods for promoting and protecting health and social well-being
    - Evaluate how clients experience and influence health and social care provision
- Unit 7: Educating for health and social well-being
    - Investigate health education campaigns

  - Investigate the reasons for, sources of and methods used in health education campaigns
  - Evaluate the effectiveness of a health education campaign for a target population
- Unit 8: Research perspectives in health and social care
  - Investigate the research process
  - Plan research into health and social care and gather data
  - Produce and present health and social care research findings

How is a GNVQ assessed?

The GNVQ units are assessed **internally** and **externally**, and both assessments must be passed in order for that unit to be credited to the candidate.

External assessment

Written tests on seven mandatory units are set by either BTEC, RSA or City & Guilds (Unit 2 is not externally tested). These are either short answer or **multiple choice questions**. The tests assess the knowledge and skills that you have gained during the time you have been studying the unit. Each GNVQ written test paper lasts about one hour, and the pass mark is **70 per cent**.

External testing takes place a number of times each year and, if you do not pass, there is no restriction on the number of times that you can resit each test.

Internal assessment

This will take place within your school or college. Projects, assignments, tests that you complete are all organised into a **portfolio of evidence**. We will look a little later at what a portfolio of evidence is and what should go into it. Your teacher will support you in preparing your portfolio. Your **assessors** will probably be your teachers. Their assessments are checked **(verified)** by another experience teacher called an **internal verifier**. The internal verifier selects some of your work and checks that it has met the **national standards**. Verification will also ensure that all the assessment within a school or college is consistent with the national standards. The work of the internal verifier is also checked by an **external verifier** who is appointed by BTEC, City & Guilds or RSA to ensure that the assessments agree with national standards. The external verifier will visit your school or college at least twice a year and will usually see some of your work and talk to you about it.

Assessment for GNVQ is based on showing the assessor what you have achieved. Your teacher (assessor) will judge the evidence you have presented for each element of each unit, and ensure that your completed work meets the required national standard. You will need to compile a portfolio of relevant evidence of your achievements. Your assessor will advise whether you have provided enough evidence to pass a unit, and how to provide any missing evidence. Remember you can try as many times as you like to reach the required standard. No time limits can be put on you to complete work. GNVQs are designed so that you can work at your own pace. Some students may gather evidence in a short period, others may take longer.

What if I don't agree with an assessment?

Each school or college must have an appeals procedure which will deal effectively with any complaints that a student may have. You can appeal on the grounds that an assessment procedure was not properly carried out or an outcome (pass) was not carried out in a proper manner. **Ask your teacher or lecturer for a copy of the appeals procedure.** You are entitled to a copy at the beginning of the course.

Preparing for assessment

Your portfolio of evidence and the external tests for each mandatory unit will need to be complete and passed in order for the unit to be credited toward the full GNVQ award. Evidence may be obtained in a variety of ways including:

- **Practical tests** Be familiar with what you are going to be tested on, and have ready all equipment and materials you will need. Do not rush, and remember to work to health and safety guidelines. Always make sure what you are doing is safe both for you and any other person. Your assessor will have given you a clear guideline of what you have to do to reach the required standard.
- **Assignments and projects** Plan your time carefully, take time drawing up your action plan, discuss your work with your teacher or lecturer. Try to meet all the things you set yourself to do in your action plan. Make sure your work is neat and well presented. Each assignment or project will have clear written guidelines of what you have to do to achieve a pass. These guidelines will also have been discussed with your tutor and you will have had an opportunity to question them.
- **Observation** You may be observed by either one of your own classmates or a teacher. They will observe you to see if you carry out certain tasks. For example how you behave in groups, can you organise other people for instance. Try not to feel uncomfortable when being observed.
- **Oral questioning** This is a common way to explain to your assessor why you have done certain things. What you have written or done in groups may not be clear, your assessor will ask you questions to allow you to elaborate and clarify your evidence.
- **Written tests** Understand the process of revision and ask your teacher to explain the best way for you to revise. Start revising for written tests early. Revising is helped if you have clear and complete notes. Always read the instructions on the test papers carefully and remember to plan your time.

What grades are there?

Each GNVQ unit when completed to the national standard will be given a pass. To gain the Advanced GNVQ you must pass all the mandatory units. Individual units are not graded as merit or distinction; you can only formally obtain a pass for each unit individually.

To obtain a merit or distinction your work must show that you have consistently exhibited skills under the following two headings.

- **Process** – includes the three themes of:
  - planning
  - information seeking and information handling
  - evaluation.
- **Quality of outcomes** The award of a final grade for the four individual themes (planning, information seeking and information handling, evaluation and quality of outcomes) is based on the best third of the evidence you present for each theme. In order to get a merit or distinction you must achieve a third of the evidence in all four themes.

What is a portfolio?

Your portfolio will usually be kept in a large A4 ring binder. All your written evidence, assignments, projects, photographs and drawings will be kept in the binder. Also in the binder you must keep a list (index) of other evidence such as video tapes, sound recordings, large drawings etc. This is so that the assessor, internal verifier and external verifier can find this evidence.

A portfolio is a convenient way to keep a record and to present evidence that you have collected. It is a permanent record of the evidence of your achievements over the two years. The evidence that you have collected will allow you to demonstrate to your assessors that you have achieved the skills, knowledge and understanding to gain the Advanced GNVQ qualification.

Your portfolio should be organised into sections, each section containing evidence for each unit. The portfolio will also contain forms which will be completed by your assessor: these forms will contain basic information about the status of your evidence with respect to each unit.

Providing evidence for your portfolio

Evidence indicators in the specification (see the diagram) set out what is assessed and what evidence you will need to provide for your portfolio. You do not need to provide any evidence in your portfolio other than that described by the evidence indicator.

There are two types of evidence:

- **Performance evidence** Sometimes called direct evidence, this may consist of a report, assignment, a product (toy for example) or an assessor's written report of observation of something you have done.
- **Supplementary or indirect evidence** This may consist of photographs, videos, audio tapes, evidence of written or oral questioning, tests or references from workplace supervisors.

Evidence should arise as a result of the work you have been asked to do by your assessor and which you agreed to do after you had drawn up your action plan. How much and what evidence you require will be discussed with you and should form the basis of your **individual action plan** (IAP).

Remember

- A piece of work may provide evidence for more than one element or unit.
- Present your portfolio in a professional manner.
- All the evidence that you are providing should be **sufficient** (enough), **authentic** (your own work) and **relevant** (tests what the performance criteria asks to be tested).
- The assessor and verifiers should find the portfolio easy to read, understand and access. The index should identify what the evidence refers to.
- The documentation should be well organised and easy to read.
- Before you present, remember that you will be asked questions about it by the assessor and the internal and external verifier.
- You should know exactly what is in your portfolio as you could be asked to explain the evidence to the external verifier.

GNVQ Advanced health and social care: Summary of units and elements

This summary shows how the activities and assignments relate to the units and elements. By keeping a record of your work, many of these exercises will generate useful evidence for your portfolio.

		Activities	Assignments
1	**Equal opportunities and individuals' rights**		
1.1	Investigate legal rights and responsibilities in relation to equality of opportunity	1.1–1.7	1.1
1.2	Explore how individuals can be affected by discrimination	1.8–1.15	1.2
1.3	Examine ethical issues in health and social care practice	2.1–2.11	2.1
2	**Interpersonal interaction in health and social care**		
2.1	Explore interpersonal interaction	3.1–3.5	3.1
2.2	Demonstrate skills of interpersonal interaction	3.2–3.10	3.2
2.3	Analyse methods of interacting with clients in health and social care	4.1–4.9	4.1
3	**Physical aspects of health and social well-being**		
3.1	Investigate the organisation of structures within human body systems	5.1–5.3, 5.5–5.6	5.1
3.2	Investigate the functions of the main organ systems	5.4, 5.9–5.16, 6.3	5.2
3.3	Investigate methods for monitoring and maintaining healthy functioning of the human body	6.1–6.2, 6.4–6.5, 6.7–6.10, 6.14–6.16, 6.21, 6.23–6.25, 6.27–6.29	6.1
4	**Health and social well-being: psycho-social aspects**		
4.1	Investigate human growth and development	7.1-7.21	7.1
4.2	Analyse how individuals function in and are influenced by society	8.1–8.12	8.1
4.3	Investigate the effect of socio-economic factors on health and social well-being	8.13–8.22	8.1
5	**The structure and development of health and social care services**		
5.1	Investigate the provision of health and social care services and facilities	9.1–9.6, 9.8	9.1
5.2	Explain why health and social care provision develops and changes	9.5–9.13	9.2
5.3	Investigate the organisation of health and social care planning and provision	10.1–10.4	10.1
6	**Health and social care practice**		
6.1	Investigate the planning of care and interventions for individual clients	11.1–11.17	11.1
6.2	Investigate methods for promoting and protecting health and social well-being	12.1–12.5	12.1
6.3	Evaluate how clients experience and influence health and social care provision	12.6	12.1
7	**Educating for health and social well-being**		
7.1	Investigate health education campaigns	13.1–13.5	13.1
7.2	Investigate the reasons for, sources of and methods used in health education campaigns	13.6	13.2
7.3	Evaluate the effectiveness of a health education campaign for a target population	14.1–14.7	14.1
8	**Research perspectives in health and social care**		
8.1	Investigate the research process	15.1–15.14	15.1
8.2	Plan research into health and social care and gather data	16.1–16.11	16.1
8.3	Produce and present health and social care research findings		16.2

Core skills: Summary of units at level 3

This summary shows how the activities and assignments provide opportunities to provide evidence of the core skills. When planning a piece of work, think carefully about the core skills you can provide evidence for. For example, use information technology as often as possible when producing written work, leaflets, posters, charts and diagrams.

Core skills	Activities	Assignments
Communication		
3.1 Take part in discussions	1.3, 1.5, 1.7, 1.8, 1.9, 1.10, 1.12, 1.13, 1.15, 2.1, 2.2, 2.4, 2.5, 3.2, 3.4, 3.5, 3.6, 3.7, 3.8, 3.9, 4.3, 4.5, 4.7, 4.9, 5.1, 5.15, 7.1, 7.4, 7.7, 7.8, 7.10, 8.1, 8.2, 8.3, 8.8, 8.16, 9.1, 9.4, 9.13, 11.3, 11.11, 11.13, 12.2, 12.3, 13.1, 14.2, 14.3, 15.2, 15.9, 15.10, 16.2	3.2, 5.2, 7.1, 8.1, 9.1, 9.2, 11.1, 12.2, 15.1
3.2 Produce written material	1.2, 1.3, 2.3, 4.4, 4.5, 4.6, 7.10, 7.12, 7.13, 8.8, 8.14, 9.1, 9.2, 9.5, 9.8, 11.11, 11.13, 11.16, 13.5, 15.4	1.1, 1.2, 2.1, 3.1, 3.2, 4.1, 5.1, 6.1, 7.1, 8.1, 9.1, 9.2, 11.1, 12.2, 13.1, 13.2, 14.1, 15.1
3.3 Use images	6.11, 7.17, 7.18, 9.1, 11.7, 11.11, 11.16	1.2, 2.1, 5.1, 6.1, 7.1, 8.1, 9.1, 9.2, 11.1, 12.2, 13.1, 15.1
3.4 Read and respond to written materials	7.5, 7.16, 8.5, 8.8, 8.17, 9.1, 9.2, 9.3, 9.7, 9.8, 11.3, 11.7, 11.11, 11.13, 11.16, 13.3, 13.4, 13.5, 14.4, 14.5, 14.6, 14.7	1.1, 1.2, 2.1, 7.1, 8.1, 9.1, 9.2, 11.1, 12.2, 13.1, 13.2, 15.1
Information technology		
3.1 Prepare information	9.6, 16.8, 16.11	4.1, 15.1, 16.1
3.2 Process information	9.6, 9.11, 16.8, 16.11	15.1, 16.1
3.3 Present information	9.6, 9.11, 15.6, 16.8, 16.11	15.1, 16.1
3.4 Evaluate the use of information technology	9.6, 9.11, 16.8, 16.11	5.1, 6.1, 15.1, 16.1
Application of number		
3.1 Collect and record data	8.10, 9.11, 9.12, 15.6, 16.3, 16.6, 16.7, 16.8, 16.9, 16.10, 16.11	3.1, 14.1, 15.1, 16.1, 16.2
3.2 Tackle problems	8.9, 8.10, 8.11, 9.6, 9.12, 15.14, 16.3, 16.6, 16.7, 16.8, 16.9, 16.10, 16.11	15.1, 16.1, 16.2
3.3 Interpret and present data	3.3, 6.5, 6.6, 6.21, 6.22, 6.23, 6.25, 6.26, 6.27, 8.9, 8.10, 8.11, 8.18, 9.6, 9.12, 9.14, 15.6, 15.14, 16.3, 16.6, 16.7, 16.8, 16.9, 16.10, 16.11	14.1, 15.1, 16.1, 16.2

I   Legal rights and anti-discriminatory practice

What is covered in this chapter

- The principles underpinning equality of opportunity
- The responsibilities of individuals and organisations to promote anti-discriminatory practice
- Inconsistencies in equal opportunities
- Sources of advice and support in ensuring equality
- Legislation supporting anti-discriminatory practice
- The bases of discrimination
- The contexts in which discrimination may occur
- The effects of discrimination on society and individuals.

These are the resources you will need for your portfolio for element 1.1:

- A report, focusing on equality of opportunity legislation relating to one category in the range, which:
  - describes why the principles which underpin equality of opportunity legislation are important to health and social care practitioners
  - describes the responsibilities of individuals and organisations
  - describes consistencies and inconsistencies in equality of opportunity rights between the four UK countries
  - explains how individuals may seek redress under the law, providing examples of each of the four routes listed in the range
  - explains three of the factors which influence the formation of equality of opportunity legislation, giving one example for each.
- Notes on the responsibilities of individuals and organisations under equality of opportunity legislation relating to the remaining four categories in the range.

These are the resources you will need for your portfolio for element 1.2:

- A report which:
  - explains the bases of discrimination stated in the range
  - describes how discrimination may appear in individuals' behaviour and in society
  - describes some long-term and short-term effects of discrimination on individuals.

Finally:

- Your written answers to the activities, review questions and assignments in this chapter.

The principles underpinning equality of opportunity

It is the nature of the human mind to generalise and to infer conclusions. The mind is a huge sorting machine, which busies itself by constantly cataloguing our experiences. While this generalising may be necessary to maintain mental order, by its nature, it introduces significant errors into our perceptions of the world around us. These errors of perception may inadvertently result in discriminatory practices, either individually or culturally. Consequently, our perceptions need to be constantly monitored, questioned, and reconsidered.

The concept of equality is central to the practice of care, as we shall see in Chapter 2. Many of the individuals who receive care services have been marginalised and oppressed. They have been forced to the 'edge' of society, and are denied the status and life chances enjoyed by other groups. In extreme cases, this marginalisation has resulted in oppression, where the mistreatment of certain groups has been systematically adopted by society. Access to health care, social care, employment, education, housing, and leisure activities may be limited or denied.

There is legislation which should stop the extremes of inequality and discrimination. However, the legislation is restricted to only some forms of discrimination, and places the responsibility on the individual to pursue action. Though this legislation is important, the real fight against inequality and discrimination is attitude change. Because marginalisation and oppression are frequently experienced by users of health and social care services, it is a professional responsibility of care workers to understand and combat inequality and discrimination. This responsibility begins by ensuring that equal opportunity exists in health and social care services.

The responsibilities of individuals and organisations to promote anti-discriminatory practice

Care organisations employ, and provide services for, every conceivable type of individual. It is important that all people are responded to as essentially human. We are all far more alike than we are different. Negative discrimination is the cause of many problems and much suffering. Whatever else care workers may do, they must never add to the problems of those they seek to help. Discrimination must be challenged, but gently, as intolerance can creep in here also. The aim must be to change people's beliefs, and not just their superficial behaviour. This requires considerable skill, particularly that of managers, as all victims of discrimination should be given complete support. Most care organisations have established procedures to deal with problems.

Activity 1.1

Find out what procedures exist in your school or college for dealing with discriminatory behaviour. This should include both racism and equal opportunities.

Combating racial discrimination
Some positive steps which may be taken to eliminate ethnic and racial discrimination are:
- effective work with multi-racial community associations
- countering racist attitudes in the local community

Imran Khan says: Protect your children against childhood disease. Ask your doctor, health visitor or clinic about immunisation now.

इमरानखान कहते हैं कि बाल्यवस्था के रोगों के सामने अपने बच्चे की रक्षा किजीए। अभी रोधक्षमीकरण के विषय में अपने डाक्टर, हेल्थ विज़िटर या तो क्लिनिक से पूछें।

ইমরান খান বলেন, শৈশবের রোগ থেকে আপনার শিশুদের রক্ষা করুন। আপনার ডাক্তার, 'হেলথ ভিজিটার' অথবা 'ক্লিনিক' –এ প্রতিষেধক ব্যবহার কথা এখনই জিজ্ঞাসা করুন।

ઇમરાનખાન કહે છે કે બાળપણના રોગો સામે તમારા બાળકનું રક્ષણ કરો. હમણાં જ રોગથી ભયમુક્ત થવા વિષે તમારા ડૉક્ટર, હેલ્થ વિઝીટર અથવા ક્લિનિકને પૂછો.

ਇਮਰਾਨ ਖਾਨ ਦਾ ਕਹਿਣਾ ਹੈ ਅਪਣੇ ਬੱਚਿਆਂ ਨੂੰ ਬਚਪਨ ਦੇ ਰੋਗਾਂ ਤੋਂ ਬਚਾਓ। ਹੁਣੇ ਹੀ ਲੰਡੇ ਲਵਾਉਣ ਲਈ ਅਪਣੇ ਡਾਕਟਰ, ਹੈਲਥ ਵਿਜ਼ਿਟਰ ਜਾਂ ਕਲਿਨਿਕ ਨਾਲ ਸੰਪਰਕ ਪੈਦਾ ਕਰੋ।

ڈاکٹر، ہیلتھ وزیٹر یا کلینک سے حفاظتی تدابیر کے متعلق دریافت کیجیے۔
عمران خان کا کہنا ہے کہ اپنے بچوں کو بچپن کی بیماریوں سے محفوظ کیجیے۔ اپنے

We live in a multi-cultural society: health and social care services must reflect this fact

- creating alliances between different ethnic organisations which face common problems
- campaigning for adequate and non-discriminatory services for ethnic minorities
- educating staff in health and social care agencies, with the aim of changing both attitudes and behaviour.

Individual rights and entitlements in respect of discrimination

All users of health and social care services have basic rights. Some of these rights are established in law. Others are integral to the values which underpin health and social care work (see Chapter 2).

These rights have originated from a vast variety of sources. Pressure groups and independent national organisations have played major roles. In some instances, they have conducted campaigns to raise awareness of particular issues. In other instances, their contributions to Royal Commissions or to the government's consultative White Papers has been immensely influential. The media has played a very significant role as well, in highlighting scandalous conditions, problems and individual cases. Trade unions have also been very active in this area, lobbying Parliament for appropriate action where required. Needless to say, many of these issues have become highly political, and each of the major political parties has articulated and published its views and intentions.

Some issues concerning individual rights in health and social care, such as euthanasia, are highly emotive. The differences in law and practice among different European countries may eventually affect British law, through either challenges in the European Court of Human Rights or through the European Parliament. The discussion of such issues, and the media attention that they attract, may in time significantly affect social values.

One of the most essential rights is that no clients will be subjected to any form of discriminatory practice. Neither direct nor indirect discrimination has a place in health and social care. Caring services exist to empower the socially disadvantaged. The more direct forms of some discriminatory practices are prohibited in law.

Inconsistencies in equal opportunities

With some forms of inequality, legislation protects individuals from discrimination. However, with many forms of inequality, the law offers little or no protection. For example, individuals of different ethnic origin are accorded numerous rights under race relations legislation, while individuals with disabilities are denied the same rights in law. Recent attempts in Parliament to legislate for the rights of disabled people have met with defeat.

Some inconsistencies are the consequence of legislation. For example, the differing legal age of consent for homosexual and heterosexual people. In this section, we will examine some inconsistencies experienced within the field of health and social care.

Inequalities in access to health and social care services

One of the most serious consequences of discrimination is inequality in health. Reinforced initial prejudices are often reflected in service design. Major inequalities result from the comparatively low societal status of those who require services. The power structure which perpetuates these inequalities emphasises need rather than demand. *Need* is a professionally validated (i.e. defined by doctors, social workers, etc.) requirement of an individual or group. *Demand* is a lay defined requirement. Patient support groups are organised on a national scale, and exist to express the demands being made by service users. Examples are MIND (mental health), MENCAP (learning disabilities), and the ME Association (Myalgic Encephalomyelitis). For other support organisations see Appendix 2.

The Black Report

Many of the inequalities in health care were highlighted by the Black Report. This report provided evidence of a persistent social class structure in health provision. The Registrar General's definition of social class is given in Table 1.1.

You will note that classes are numbered from one to five. The terms 'upper class', 'middle class', and 'working class' are not actually used.

In general usage, upper class refers to social class I, middle class refers to social class II and part of social class III, and working class refers to part of social class III and classes IV and V. The Registrar General's Classification is based purely on socio-

Table 1.1 Social class: the Registrar General's Classification

Social class	Examples of occupations in each class
Class I Professional	Accountant, doctor, dentist, solicitor, university lecturer
Class II Managerial and technical	Manager, teacher, librarian, nurse, farmer
Class III (non-manual) Clerical and minor supervisory	Clerk, typist, shop assistant, policeman, draughtsman, sales representative
Class III (manual) Skilled manual	Electrician, tailor, bus driver, printer, cook
Class IV Semi-skilled manual	Agricultural worker, postman, telephone operator, fisherman, barman
Class V Unskilled manual	Railway porter, labourer, lorry driver's mate, window cleaner, office cleaner

economic status. An individual's perception of his or her own class may be quite different to what the official classification would indicate.

The Black Report revealed that middle-class people receive more preventative health treatment than do working-class people. The middle classes are also treated by more experienced doctors, and do not have to wait as long to be seen. The Committee set up to produce the Report reviewed evidence by gender, age, ethnicity, religion and occupational class. Some of the findings include the following:

- The mortality rates of men are higher than those for women, and the relative difference is increasing.
- There are rising mortality rates among the 'lower' classes.
- There is unequal access and take-up of health services in relation to the above categories.
- Poverty and unemployment are major causes of ill-health. Two-thirds of all serious health problems in Britain are caused by material deprivation. The consequences of unemployment include stress, bad diet and inadequate housing. Examples of illnesses that rise with the unemployment figures are alcoholism, heart disease, psychiatric illness, indigestion, arthritis and high blood pressure.
- If the mortality rate of social class I had been applied to classes IV and V during 1970–72, there would have been 74,000 fewer deaths among people under the age of 75, including 10,000 fewer children.

The recommendations of the Black Report include:
- improved facilities for the health of mothers and children
- priority for disabled people to improve the quality of their lives
- priority for preventative and educational action to encourage good health and to discourage bad habits, particularly smoking

- an increase in Child Benefit
- free school meals and milk
- more control over an independent source of income for women
- day care places for children
- development of a strategy involving the re-distribution of income towards women and ethnic minorities, as generally low-paid workers, and toward the disabled and people with children.

Activity 1.2

Discuss the following:

a How do the attitudes and values of different groups in our society inhibit access to services?

b How may the organisation of health and social care services inhibit access by certain groups?

The Black Report established definite links between the health of the nation and social policy. Improved housing and working conditions are as important to the nation's health as drugs. The establishment of a National Health Service (NHS) had not succeeded in meeting the health requirements of the nation with equanimity.

Unfortunately, the Black Report was commissioned by a Conservative government, who generally opposed the welfare state. Since most of the recommendations would be effective only within a government policy to reduce poverty and inequality, the government did not implement the recommendations. Thus, we have legislation addressing some areas of inequality, but not others. These inconsistencies are continuing to be addressed by various pressure groups.

(There is more about the Black Report in other chapters.)

Mental health

Mental health is an area which dramatically demonstrates social inequalities. A great deal of research has been done in this area, and some interesting findings have been as follows:

- **Social class** Treatment regimes tend to reflect the social status of the patient. 'Lower' class patients are more likely to have physical treatments (powerful drugs, electro-convulsive therapy, etc.), and generally have less contact with senior doctors. Middle-class patients receive more attention and are more likely to be offered psychotherapy.
- **Ethnicity** UK citizens of Afro-Caribbean origin:
  - have higher rates of diagnosed schizophrenia
  - are more likely to be involuntary patients
  - are more likely to see a junior doctor
  - are more likely to have ECT or powerful drugs.
- **Gender** More women are diagnosed as mentally ill than men. This is likely to be because of their low status, lack of material possessions and lack of power. They are also more likely to be referred to a psychiatrist and to be admitted to hospital. Identified vulnerability factors include having school-age children at home, lack of waged work, absence of a close and confiding relationship, social isolation and low self-esteem. The most likely individuals to experience the psychiatric services are

working class women who are full-time housewives with children under the age of six years.

The Mental Health Act 1983, while ensuring the rights of some patients, did not address the inequalities which still persist.

Activity 1.3

In small groups, make a list of the reasons why you believe that black and Asian patients perceived as psychotic are more likely to be detained involuntarily in a mental hospital (Littlewood and Lipsedge, 1981).

Health status

One of the most significant factors limiting access to health care is that there is not enough money to go around. The choice of who receives help is often left to the clinical judgement of doctors. Patients who are elderly, or chronically or terminally ill are often denied access to services. More recently, doctors have made controversial decisions to refuse services to perceived self-inflicted illnesses, for example, not treating a cancer patient unless he or she gives up smoking, or refusing treatment to drug addicts and alcoholics. Discrimination is now occurring in relation to lifestyle choices.

As medicine becomes more technologically oriented, patients who require care and support, as opposed to physical medical treatment, become more and more marginalised. Hospitals are closing to save money, and patients are meant to be cared for in the community. However, the resources required to achieve this are scarce, adding tremendous burdens onto cash-strapped local authorities. It has been estimated that by the year 2020, the number of disabled and dependent individuals in the UK will outnumber the able-bodied. If the will is not there to provide the support and resources needed, society will have to discriminate as to who is helped and who is not. Is there a fair or right way to do this? The shortage of resources is likely to result in continuing inconsistencies.

Activity 1.4

In this section, we have explored some of the inconsistencies in promoting equality. With reference to the section describing legislation supporting anti-discriminatory practice, identify and discuss:

a Any further inconsistencies you have discovered.

b Any examples of consistency among the various Acts and Charters.

Sources of advice and support in ensuring equality

Most illnesses and disabilities have organisations dedicated to the requirements of clients. Good sources of help in finding the appropriate group are the Citizens' Advice Bureaux and public libraries.

Many social services departments and health authorities or trusts have published statements and policies in relation to equality. Individual service organisations may be approached for advice and support. The Commission for Racial Equality (CRE) is a good source of information and support in relation to racial issues. The Equal Opportunities Commission (EOC) will assist with problems pertaining to gender. (See Appendix 2 for addresses.)

Presently, only women and ethnic minorities are covered by anti-discriminatory legislation. Clients have legal recourse when their rights in these areas are impinged. Recourse in other areas is largely in respect of published policies and codes of practice. Appropriate voluntary organisations, the Citizens' Advice Bureau or the Community Health Council may be able to help.

There is a significant variety in the routes through which individuals may seek redress. However, there are inconsistencies in the civil liberties of different groups. The differing age of consent for homosexuals and heterosexuals has already been cited. Access to legal redress is still rather limited, and the reductions in eligibility for Legal Aid is making it more so. Currently under consideration by Parliament is an adaptation of the American system, where the lawyer only gets paid if he or she wins the case. This may open up the possibilities of litigation to those who cannot now afford it.

Activity 1.5

Divide the class into working groups. Each working group will concentrate on a particular discriminated-against part of society. Identify the rights available to that group through legislation. When this is completed, each working group should present a summary of its findings, and the class will make notes of inconsistencies in rights, where they exist.

Legislation supporting anti-discriminatory practice

The following legislation is all relevant.

- **The Local Government Act 1966** provided money to local government to work with immigrants from the Commonwealth. Only recently has this money been more accountably targeted.
- **The Sexual Offences Act 1967** legalised consensual activity between men in private, provided that both parties were over 21 years of age (in England and Wales). Recently, this has been controversially lowered to 18 years of age, but still not providing equality for homosexuals with heterosexuals, for whom the age of consent is 16 years.
- **The Chronically Sick and Disabled Persons Act 1970** suggests a range of services to be made available to disabled and ill people, including the provision of telephones and functional adaptations to their homes. This Act only set out guidelines.
- **The Equal Pay Act 1975** makes it unlawful to discriminate between men and women doing the same jobs, in terms of their pay and conditions. Despite this landmark piece of legislation, statistical evidence shows that women still face discrimination in employment and pay. In addition, occupations such as nursing, which are perceived (wrongly!) as being largely women's work, remain extremely low paid.
- **The Sex Discrimination Act 1975 and 1986** sets out the rights of all individuals in issues regarding gender. It makes it illegal to discriminate on the grounds of gender or marital status in education and employment. The Act also allows for positive action in some cases, where being of a particular sex may be regarded as a genuine occupational requirement for a job. This Act set up the Equal Opportunities Commission to monitor and provide advice on promoting sexual equality.

- **The Race Relations Act 1976** makes it illegal to discriminate on the grounds of race, colour, ethnic origin and nationality. This Act is monitored by the Commission for Racial Equality (CRE), which the Act established, and to whom complaints may be brought. CRE carries out research, provides information and advice, and has the power to investigate complaints. The law allows positive action to ensure the involvement of all racial groups in society. Specific responsibilities are placed on local authorities, who have a duty to eliminate racial discrimination, and to promote equality. Nevertheless, racial discrimination still pervades British society.
- **The Education (Handicapped Children) Act 1980** intended to integrate children with special educational needs into mainstream provision where possible. This responsibility was placed on local authorities. Children with disabilities are to be assessed and 'statemented'. The 'statement' would define the specific educational needs of the child, which the local authority was to meet through mainstream provision. The massive resource implications of the Act meant that it could not be effectively implemented.
- **The Mental Health Act 1983** was implemented to safeguard the rights of patients compulsorily admitted under the Act to hospital. The Act ensured that the patient was made aware of his or her rights, and increased the role of the 'Approved' Social Worker, in recognition of balancing the importance of medical and social factors in psychiatric illness. The Act is monitored by the Mental Health Act Commission. The Act fails, however, to safeguard the rights of patients being treated 'informally'.
- **The Disabled Persons Act 1981 and 1986** increases the rights of disabled people by establishing the necessity for them to be informed about provision and consulted about their requirements.

  There are four main rights:
  - assessment of need is required by the local authority
  - resources must be provided which are appropriate to the individual, which helps him or her to live as independently as possible
  - representation is a right of all disabled people. (Where the ability to express one's own needs is limited, representation may be made by another person or an advocate.)
  - monitoring and review are necessary to reflect the changing needs of individuals with disabilities.

  The Act intended to involve disabled people and their carers fully. However, the effectiveness of the Act nationally has been limited, as it only set out guidelines and suggestions. No responsibilities were imposed on either the NHS or local authorities. Recent attempts to improve the rights of people with disabilities have been systematically defeated and discouraged by the government.
- **The National Health Service and Community Care Act 1990** ensures that individuals in need of care are appropriately assessed, and have rights of complaint. The Act allows for service-purchasing by authorities, and sets out responsibilities for all care agencies, both statutory and independent, to work collaboratively. It had been anticipated that an individual's needs and preferences could be better met through these provisions. However, inadequate funding and competition among agencies for money, have rendered the Act far less effective than it could have been. In addition, the Act restricted real choice for those individuals who could not wholly finance their care independently.
- **The Criminal Justice Act 1992** places a duty on those administering the criminal justice system to avoid discrimination on the grounds of race or gender. In addition,

its new sentencing structure was meant to provide more alternatives to prison. Since the introduction of the Act, prisons have been pushed beyond their capacities.

Activity 1.6

Choose either the Sex Discrimination Act or the Race Relations Act and identify what behaviours they describe as discriminatory.

The charters

In addition to legislation, there are a variety of government charters which indicate the rights and legitimate expectations of service users. These include:

- **The Citizen's Charter** – this charter outlines what all users of public services have a right to expect. If services do not meet the required standards, the procedures for complaint are made clear.
- **The Patient's Charter** – this charter (see pages 273–4) sets out the rights of all users of the NHS. It establishes minimum waiting times, and other quality criteria, and how to complain if standards are not met. The Patient's Charter only covers administrative standards. Concerns about GPs, opticians, pharmacists and dentists are expressed to the local Family Health Services Authority. Community health matters, including hospital closures and service cut-backs are dealt with by the Community Health Council. Concerns about hospital doctors are made through the Regional Health Authority (RHA). In addition, the service user always has recourse to his or her Member of Parliament (MP) or legal action.

Difficulties with local authority services should be expressed to local councillors, and those concerning independent organisations to the local social services department or health authority's inspection units.

Addressing emotional and spiritual needs of clients

While high quality in the provision of physical care must be maintained, the client's social, emotional and behavioural requirements must also receive skilled attention. Physical care is not enough on its own to maintain good health and happiness. The importance of skill in addressing the emotional and spiritual side of clients cannot be overstated. While some major problems may be addressed through legislation, it must be the interpersonal skill of the care worker, in his or her constant, intense involvement with service users, which promotes equality for all individuals.

Activity 1.7

a Individually or in groups, visit or contact some of the organisations referred to above, and collect leaflets describing their functions and services. Discuss in class the roles and responsibilities of the various organisations.

b Identify conflicts that may arise in some of the legislation described above between individuals, or between individuals and organisations.

The bases of discrimination

In this section we shall investigate and discuss some of the more prevalent forms of discrimination in our society.

In addition to discrimination in relation to health status and disability, the requirements of the UK's 2.5 million non-white population poses considerable problems for health and social care services. While 40 per cent of this group are UK-born, the others are not and they may experience considerable communication difficulties when insufficient regard is paid to language and cultural differences by care professionals. The easy response is to create specialist services and workers to deal with minority groups. However, while expedient, this response still leaves ethnic minorities outside of the mainstream, and does little to lessen the discrimination which exists. The needs of all minority groups should be met by generally more responsive and educated health and social care services.

Some forms of discrimination, such as racism and sexism, have received much public attention, but the types of discrimination go well beyond these, and particularly affect those vulnerable groups who are likely to use health and social care services. Discrimination results in inequality in access to services, and this in turn is reflected in statistics of the nation's health and social problems.

What is discrimination?

Making use of generalisations and stereotypes is part of human nature. It is how we make sense of the world. We put things into categories about which we may make general assumptions based on our previous experiences and education. Sometimes, however, generalisations and stereotypes may be based on ignorance and fear, resulting in prejudice, intolerance and discrimination, and hence oppression for other people.

> **Discrimination**
> The unfair treatment of a person based on prejudice and intolerance.

Where such discrimination is widespread in a society, it systematically undermines groups of people materially and psychologically. Their experiences become invalidated. Such discrimination results in exploitation and abuse. It disenfranchises groups of people from mainstream society. The dominant value system in a society often perceives the only worthwhile culture and attributes to be those positively valued by the majority of citizens. In the UK, this tends to be white, middle-class, Anglo-Saxon, Protestant, intelligent, young and healthy.

Discrimination is not restricted to particular groups in society. It is aimed at anyone who, for whatever reason, possesses attributes which are not culturally valued. On the basis of having such 'negative' attributes, assumptions are made about the individual. Such ignorance and intolerance is widespread throughout society. **All of us are likely to be both victims and perpetrators of discrimination.**

Activity 1.8

In small groups, discuss ways in which each of you has been discriminated against. Consider not just your race, but your age, sex, disability, etc.

Most of us will be acquainted with some forms of discriminatory practice, such as racism and sexism. There has been much media attention focused in these areas. However, the problem of discrimination is far more extensive. What links all forms of discrimination is the concept of intolerance. It is not unusual to be suspicious of those not like us in appearance, beliefs, background, and much more. The real challenge in developing anti-discriminatory practice in the caring services is in developing a more tolerant attitude to differences between people. If the underlying cause of intolerance is fear, then the objective of anti-discriminatory practice must be to remove the fear.

Activity 1.9

a In groups of three or four, discuss the sorts of ways in which individuals may be different from each other.

b When your group has agreed, write these differences down in a list. Decide what positive points and what negative points are associated with each difference.

Types of discrimination

Elderly people are largely written off as being of little use, and prone to disease and deterioration

In Activity 1.9, you may have listed some of the more common bases of discrimination:

- **Age** The culturally valued age to be in UK society appears to be between 18 and 35. The views of children tend to be disregarded. Much of the interaction between parents and children is corrective in nature. People over 35 will begin to experience the effects of discrimination in the job market. Elderly people are largely written off as being of little use, and prone to disease and deterioration.
- **Class** There is considerable evidence that discrimination on the basis of social class is widespread. Significant differences exist in educational opportunities, work and health care. A key indicator of class is the UK is accent. (See page 5 for a classification of social class.)

- **Culture** There are many sub-cultures in the UK based on race, religion, place of origin, lifestyle, and more. In fact, much discrimination is cultural discrimination. There is much intolerance of lifestyles which are not considered to be the 'norm'.
- **Gender** We are all aware of discrimination on the basis of gender. Women are still generally paid less than men, and are excluded from certain occupations. Both men and women are victims of sexual stereotyping, are expected to behave in certain ways, and fulfil particular roles.
- **Health status** Those in our society suffering from chronic, recurring or terminal health problems are often excluded from social and employment opportunities. They may also be perceived as 'problems' by health and social service agencies, and considered to be a burden on social security budgets.
- **HIV status** In recent years, we have seen much fear and ignorance about HIV and AIDS. Those who are HIV positive have been assumed to be homosexuals or drug addicts, and there is much irrational fear about having contact with them.
- **Marital status** Assumptions are still made about individuals on the basis of whether they are married or not. Married men are seen to be more conventional and trustworthy. Married women, on the other hand, may be perceived as an employment risk because they are likely to want or have children.
- **Cognitive ability** Those of low cognitive ability are often perceived as being unable to participate in society. If employable at all, they are often exploited on ridiculously low wages. Children of limited cognitive ability are frequently abandoned by the educational system, and are often removed from mainstream education into 'special' units.
- **Mental health** Those people experiencing mental health problems are frequently treated with suspicion. They are often perceived wrongly as being violent or dangerous. Attempts to house some individuals with mental health problems in the community sometimes results in protests and anger. Similarly, they are often denied decent employment opportunities.
- **Offending background** It is not uncommon to find that someone who has made a mistake, and has been in prison, is denied employment, and sometimes housing.
- **Physical ability** Those of limited physical ability are frequently denied access to public places, and suitable housing. Physically disabled children are sometimes denied mainstream education.
- **Place of origin** Those whose place of origin is other than the UK, often have different customs, beliefs and diet. Their experiences are often invalidated, and they are put under considerable pressure to appear to be British. Sometimes, they must disguise their accents and abandon their native dress in order to 'integrate'.
- **Political beliefs** Although the UK may be more tolerant of diverse political beliefs than some other nations, political allegiances are still frequently the basis on which many assumptions about individuals are made. Extremism, of any kind, is frowned upon.
- **Race** The colour of one's skin is still an overwhelming source of discrimination. The human species is racially diverse, but this is not always reflected in communities, education or employment. Racism remains one of the major sources of discrimination in the world.
- **Religion** Many different religious beliefs and practices can be witnessed throughout the UK. Rather than being a source of interest and education, religious differences are regarded with suspicion and hatred. Religious differences have been the cause of many wars throughout the world.
- **Responsibility for dependants** Discrimination exists, primarily in the employment

market, against those who have children to care for, as they are perceived to be less reliable. There is also some discrimination against men by the legal system in custody disputes.

- **Sensory ability** We live in a world that assumes everyone can see and hear. The needs of those who cannot are sometimes not considered in the provision of services.
- **Sexuality** We live in a society that is largely intolerant of anything other than heterosexual relationships. Homosexuals are treated with suspicion and sometimes violence. They were legally considered to be mentally ill until the 1960s. In addition, certain behaviours are perceived as promiscuous, or out of the ordinary, and are not tolerated by society in general. Those perceived to be sexually different from the 'norm' are denied both employment and social opportunities.

What are your assumptions?

The list above is not exclusive, but it is easy to see that there is a risk of discrimination wherever individuals or groups are perceived to be different from the 'norm', or what is commonly encountered and valued in mainstream society.

Activity 1.10

a In small groups, identify which groups of people are associated with HIV.
b Why does this association exist? Is it justified?

Direct and indirect discrimination

Discrimination may be *direct*, in that it is clearly articulated, public and obvious. For example, advertising for a job and stipulating that applicants should be under 40 years of age (ageism). Much direct discrimination is a societal problem and is legislated against. More often, however, discrimination is *indirect*, in that it is hidden and subtle.

Activity 1.11

Opposite are three examples of discrimination in the job market. Identify who is being discriminated against, and discuss your findings.

Example 1

WAREHOUSE PERSON

Due to recent company expoansion a further
person is required to assist in our fabric
warehouse.
Working within a team , the person we require
should be flexible, ages 23-35, and be able to
work on their won initiative. A knowledge of
goods in/despatch procedures would be
advantageious as well as the ability to work
well under pressure.
In return we offer an excellent salary, bonus
and pleasant working condition in the heart of
the Cotswolds.

Example 2

Production Manager c£ 27,000
Shift Manager c£20,000

A major brand leader in East Anglia requires two ambitious career minded managers for a
high volume 3 shift food packing operation.

You will have a degree or appropriate qualification and will be:

Production Manager

With 3 shifts reporting to you, you will be in your late 20's to early 30's and able to
demonstrate a track record of change management in a modern production enviornment.

Shift Manager

Aged early to late twenties, you are probably looking for you first major career move.

Both positions command an attractive salary and a relocation package.

Example 3

Case study

In September 1993 the press reported a case in which Mr Green, a black
insurance salesman, and his pregnant white girlfriend, Miss Jones, were awarded
£24,233 by an industrial tribunal after they had been simultaneously dismissed
from the sales department of the company for which they both worked.
The tribunal was told that when Miss Jones informed her employer that she was
pregnant, he swore at her and refused to allow her to attend ante-natal classes
(her right in law) saying, 'I ain't running a charity, I'm running a business.' He gave
her additional work to do at home, saying that if she had worked 'instead of playing
with that black', she would not have become pregnant. He referred to her as a
'slag' and a 'stupid cow', among other abusive terms. His business partner was
equally abusive towards her.

When Miss Jones was five months pregnant, she was sacked along with Mr
Green. She said 'they did everything ... to make me walk out of my own accord'.

> The company claimed that the couple were made redundant after a fall in orders, but later admitted to the tribunal that staff numbers had actually increased from 20 to 40 after the redundancies!
>
> The award of £24,233 covered injury to feelings and loss of earnings. The case was the first since the European Court of Justice had removed the limit of £11,000 on awards for injury to feelings. The tribunal chairman described the treatment received by Mr Green and Miss Jones from their former employers as 'grotesquely offensive' and said it had made them both feel disadvantaged.

Activity 1.12

In small groups, discuss and summarise the issues raised by the case study above.

Indirect discrimination is difficult to legislate against because it largely results from negative pre-judgements expressed through individual attitudes and language. Much of this is discussed in Chapter 3, as body language, tone of voice, and choice of words are all important. An important rule of thumb is never to describe an individual or a group by turning an adjective into a noun. For example, instead of 'the elderly', use 'elderly people'. Instead of being a 'schizophrenic', a person is 'having schizophrenic experiences'. The words we use to describe social disability in individuals and groups is explanatory, but does not diminish their essence as humans. All health and social care deals with people with problems – not just problems. Because indirect discrimination is such a problem, discriminated-against groups may still find attitudes and access to services less than even-handed in spite of legislation.

Activity 1.13

In small groups, determine five examples of both indirect and direct discrimination. Make sure you understand the differences.

The contexts in which discrimination may occur

As we have seen, discrimination may take the form of individual behaviour, which is the most obvious. This occurs when an individual or group members are treated differently because they look differently, speak differently, or have different beliefs to us. This often results from stereotyping another individual, resulting in unfavourable and distorted perceptions. We might unthinkingly avoid someone who is gay, or assume that older people are irritable and boring.

Societal discrimination occurs when the stereotyping is so widespread, that it is largely unquestioned. Discrimination may be reinforced unintentionally through the normal working of the system. The Swann Report (1985) described it as 'a range of long established systems, practices and procedures which have the effect, if not the intention, of depriving marginalised groups of equality of opportunity and access to society's resources'. Examples may be the design of buildings without access for people with disabilities, or unequal pay for equal work.

All organisations and systems provide evidence of structural discrimination. We have already reviewed some of the inequalities in care services. These inequalities often persist in spite of efforts to change them.

Activity 1.14

In groups, try to discover inequalities experienced by some students in your college or school. What attempts have been made to overcome them, and how successful have these attempts been?

The effects of discrimination on society and individuals

The effects of discrimination on society are profound. Instead of the enjoyment of a multi-cultural and egalitarian society, discrimination results in unrest and even violence. It creates great social and economic disadvantage, stretching the social security system because of the poverty it creates. The unavailability of adequate education and work for discriminated-against groups limits the available resources in society, creating further cultural and economic handicaps.

The effect of discrimination on the individual is serious. Victims feel dejected and powerless. They lose their self-esteem, motivation and confidence.

The vicious circle

Although discrimination begins with the attitudes of other people, negative social expectations cause individuals to devalue themselves and to act accordingly. Victims begin to behave in the negative ways expected of them. This reinforces initial prejudices, and makes them even stronger. This process is called a vicious circle, and is shown below:

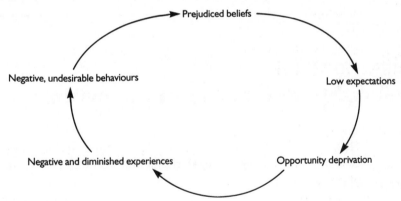

The vicious circle

Most vicious circles begin with statements that start with 'Everybody knows ...'. What 'everybody knows' is likely to be an unquestioned, limiting assumption about an individual's or group's potential, and their right to enjoy opportunities. If we can understand the vicious circle and how it works, we can work systematically to reverse its effects. Intervention into the vicious circle means changing our attitudes, and the policies in the places in which we work. We have here many targets for change. We can work to change expectations. We can expand opportunities for individuals and groups, and by doing these things, increase the status, power, self-esteem and confidence of those discriminated against. Turning vicious circles into virtuous circles is one of the essential tasks of health and social care. It is why the value base is so important (see page 24).

Activity 1.15

a Divide the class into pairs. Each pair should chose a group subject to discrimination in society. The list on pages 12–14 of the types of discrimination might prove useful.

Using the model of the vicious circle, explain how changing one or more of the elements of the circle can result in a virtuous circle. Express the 'prejudiced belief' as an 'everybody knows ...' statement.

b When each pair has satisfactorily completed the exercise, present it to the rest of the class for discussion and evaluation.

Review questions

1 Define direct and indirect discrimination, and give examples of each.
2 Describe how discrimination affects both individuals and access to services and opportunities.
3 Explain how, in certain circumstances, using legislation to prevent discrimination may be effective. When may it not be effective?
4 Identify sources of information and support in matters relating to discrimination and equal opportunities.
5 What forms of discrimination are prohibited by legislation? What forms are not?
6 Explain how the use of language is important in anti-discriminatory practice.
7 Provide several reasons for the differences in health between social classes in the UK, as reported by the Black Report.
8 **a** Do you believe that anti-discriminatory practice should be an issue for discipline and legislation, or education and training?
   b What are the positive and negative aspects of each approach?

Assignment 1.1
Legal rights to equality of opportunity

This assignment provides knowledge, understanding and portfolio evidence for element 1.1, **Investigate legal rights and responsibilities in relation to equality of opportunity.**

Your tasks

1 Equality of opportunity legislation has been effected in respect of gender, race, disability, pay, and employment. Choose *one* of these areas and identify the relevant legislation.
2 Prepare a report exploring the legislation you have chosen, and identify and explain the principles (e.g. equality of care, individual rights, and individual choice) which you believe underlies the legislation.
3 Each of the principles you have identified has major roles to play in providing health and social care services. Describe in detail how each principle applies to health and social care practice.

Both organisations and individuals have responsibilities to ensure equality of opportunity, and to respond to situations in which equality is denied.

4 Describe the role of both individuals and organisations in ensuring equality of opportunity. Do not limit your discussion to rules and regulations only, but also to raising awareness and training.

5 Explain how, within care organisations, a situation may be addressed where someone's rights have been denied. Describe the sources of redress, both within the organisation and outside, which the individual may make use of.

Equality of opportunity legislation is often the result of:

- changes in the values of society
- decisions by the European Court of Human Rights
- the availability or scarcity of resources
- the influence of key groups such as political parties, pressure groups, parliament, the European Union, or publicly funded bodies.

6 Choose three of the four factors above, and explain the ways in which each may influence equality of opportunity legislation, giving examples for each.

Assignment 1.2
The effects of discrimination on individuals

This assignment provides knowledge, understanding and portfolio evidence for element 1.2, **Explore how individuals can be affected by discrimination.**

It has been argued that discriminatory practices are endemic in UK society. An effective first step in dealing with discrimination is recognising it. We have supplied several examples in the text of evidence for discrimination from newspapers. This assignment asks you to organise and construct a scrapbook of further examples, and to comment on them.

Your tasks

1 Organise yourself to scan a range of newspapers over several weeks. You may have access to a newspaper at home. The library usually has most daily newspapers, and you may plan to look through them there. Collect anything which you perceive to provide evidence for discrimination. If using library newspapers, you will have to photocopy your examples.

2 Sort your collection of clippings into groups according to the type of discrimination. Refer to the list on pages 12–14, for example, gender, age, race, religion, etc.

3 For each type of discrimination, separate examples of direct discrimination (such as might be found in a jobs advertisements) from indirect discrimination (such as might appear through the use of language in news stories). In addition, you may have found news items whose subject is discrimination, and may wish to keep these separate from the other examples.

4 For each group of clippings you have collected, write a report. This should address the types of discrimination and the objects of discrimination. Refer specifically to clippings you have collected by reference numbers, when discussing them. Your report should specifically address discrimination by individuals, and discrimination in society as a whole, showing that you understand the difference.

Discrimination has both long-term and short-term effects on individuals. We have explained in this chapter how this occurs, and described the 'vicious circle'.

5 With reference to your newspaper clippings and report, describe how your examples of discrimination may affect the individuals concerned. Provide examples.

2 Ethical issues in health and social care practice

What is covered in this chapter

- Ethical responsibilities of care workers
- Ways of handling ethical issues and dilemmas
- Ethical issues and care organisations

These are the resources you will need for your portfolio for element 1.3:
- A report which:
  - describes the nature of the different ethical issues faced by health and care workers, considering all the range items
  - analyses examples of the handling of two ethical issues faced by health and social care workers
  - explains the responsibilities placed on health and social care workers
  - describes ways in which organisations and individuals handle ethical issues.
- Your written answers to the activities, review questions and assignment in this chapter.

Ethical responsibilities of care workers

What are ethical issues?

An ethical issue is one which has views which can be expressed in terms of right or wrong, desirable or undesirable. It implies definite points of view. The ethical issues in health and social care involve some of the most substantive issues in our society today. They include issues such as the welfare state, the role of older people, abortion, AIDS and euthanasia. Are the values reflected in professional care practice worked out arbitrarily, or do they result from rational reflection?

Is the use of care services a right? Is it a privilege? Is it a form of charity? What are the aims and roles of care workers, and what place has practical judgement in care provision? Do care services, through their implementation, support or undermine citizen's rights? Do they promote or hinder self-determination?

How do we balance our responsibility for social control with our concern for the individual? After all, there are times when the interests of society and the interests of the individual are *not* identical. There is great difficulty in treating the users of care services as equals in a society which emphasises their being unequal.

All of these very important questions have no clear answers. The problematic area of ethical issues and values may, however, become less problematic through rational discussion, the development of professional values and standards, and the training and development of care workers in the complexity of these issues.

It is generally agreed that care workers should act in the best interests of their clients, and indeed, some of the legislation referred to in Chapter 1 defines care workers' responsibilities. However, deciding what is in the best interests of the client is not always easy. For example, compulsory admission to a psychiatric unit, moving an older person into a residential home, or switching off a life-support machine are never easy or straight-forward decisions. Balancing the needs of society in general with the needs of individuals is also extremely problematic, particularly when an individual poses a danger to others, or cannot be managed other than in restrictive care.

Even in allocating resources, ethical decisions are being made every day. A recent case of a child with leukaemia who was refused treatment because her chances of recovery were so low, provoked a highly emotive response from the public.

There is some guidance on making ethical decisions in some of the legislation and charters. The Criminal Justice Act, the Mental Health Act, the Data Protection Act, the Access to Personal Files Act, and the Patients' Charter, all refer to and raise ethical issues. Professional bodies such as the British Medical Association, the Royal College of Nursing, and the British Association of Social Workers, all take an active interest in ethical issues and have published material on many of the various aspects. Nevertheless, the sorts of situation that raise serious ethical issues tend to be rather unique, and the care worker is often left to make the difficult decisions.

While being aware of how difficult and complex these issues may be, care workers may nevertheless develop the skill of exercising reasoned and informed judgement in their daily work. They will need to handle conflicting values and beliefs, and to demonstrate sensitivity in their work. This often begins by the care workers examining and understanding their own attitudes and values.

The development of attitudes

An attitude is an organised and consistent manner of feeling, thinking and reacting towards people, social issues, groups, or any event in one's environment.

Attitudes consist of thoughts, beliefs, and feelings. We develop our attitudes through the process of socialisation. The process of coping and adjusting to our social environment creates attitudes which regulate our reactions or behaviour.

Attitudes can become inflexible and **stereotyped**. If a person's attitudes become firmly set, he or she is then too ready to categorise people and events. Individuality is not recognised or examined. Fixed or stereotyped attitudes reduce the potential richness of a person's environment.

The large social system that surrounds us, with its many races, religions and classes, has shaped who we are. We live in a multi-cultural society that is constantly changing, and health and social care services must reflect this fact. All groups make contributions to the overall values of society, and every individual is affected by these values and attitudes.

Activity 2.1

In small groups, identify the contributions of various cultures to your school or college environment. Discuss how these contributions have helped widen your experiences.

In health and social care, understanding the attitudes of potential service users is important, because it helps those who provide services to provide them in a more acceptable manner. Some Asian families, for example, will not find residential care acceptable for elderly people, as they believe care of the elderly is a family responsibility. Many families will not accept help from social workers, as they do not accept the view of themselves as a 'problem' family. Such a label may be incompatible with their reference group. In order for all people in society to have equal access to care services, the attitudes and perceptions of service users should be given the highest regard.

Our own attitudes as carers must also be constantly re-evaluated. It takes conscious effort not to allow attitudes to develop into **prejudices** (see page 00). We are not fully conscious of most of our attitudes, and how they affect other people.

Our attitudes may change as we become exposed to more social situations. We incorporate attitudes that seem appropriate for belonging to groups (*reference groups*) that we consider important. Attitudes are particularly resistant to change if:

- they have been learned early in life
- they help to satisfy needs
- they are integral to one's personality and style of behaving.

Behaviour

Much of our behaviour is influenced by the attitudes we hold. They affect our judgements and perceptions, our reactions to others, and our basic philosophy of life. Attitudes organise themselves into patterns of activity which define our personalities. This activity is called behaviour. *Behaviour* is the observable responses that an individual makes according to his or her attitudes. The term 'observable' is important because although the attitudes and values themselves cannot be observed, our responses to them can.

The development of values

Values are principles, standards or qualities considered worthwhile or desirable. As with attitudes, an individual's values can be observed in his or her behaviour.

Although it is difficult to change attitudes, and hence values, some vocations, such as health and social care, require much attention to be paid to them. The caring professions support a single value base, and in fact there is a Value Base unit (Unit 0) for the National Vocational Qualifications (NVQ) in Care. It is hoped that by stimulating thought and discussion, and exposing carers to a wide variety of situations, attitudes may be developed that are consistent with the value base.

The Care Value Base
The Value Base of Care Practice was devised by the Care Sector Consortium in 1992 in order to provide a common set of values and principles for care workers. For the first time the Health and Social Care industry had basic premises from which ethical decisions may be made.

The Care Value Base addresses five elements:
- Anti-discriminatory practice
- Confidentiality
- Individual rights
- Personal beliefs and identity
- Effective communication.

Activity 2.2

Divide the class into five groups, each group taking one of the five elements that make up the Value Base Unit. Discuss the contents of the element assigned with reference to professional practice in care settings. Make notes of your discussion and report back to the whole class.

Power and empowerment

An intention of the Value Base Unit is to create equality for all individuals. This idea challenges the historical notion of power that has previously existed in professional caring relationships. Most professional carers are employed by agencies that have considerable power. Social service departments, health services and independent providers all have responsibilities in law to others besides service users. While we emphasise the therapeutic, supportive and counselling roles of care workers, these workers are also responsible to their agency of employment, and often to the general public, whose interests they also serve. The allocation of resources, and the soft 'policing' duty involved with many care jobs, backed up by legislation, require care workers to combine their caring roles with that of bureaucrat and controller. The compatibility of these roles is very difficult to manage. The care worker may be economically advantaged compared to his or her client. The worker may be better educated and, by definition, possess more power through position, than the client.

The social or health problems of some service users may create real dependency. To be perceived as anything other than fit, able, and making a valuable contribution to society is to be stripped of power. Some care services inadvertently reinforce this problem in the way they provide their services. Those who provide care services are not immune from the attitudes of the society into which they themselves have been socialised. They may have attitudes which reinforce many of the prejudices that society has about people who are different, for whatever reason. Care settings may mirror the effects of power on vulnerable individuals in both public and private settings.

There is often compliance in making the exercise of power legitimate. Those who are perceived to be in power must make very conscious efforts to encourage (i.e. enable or **empower**) the user of care services to take an interest, and to participate. The provision of care for those who need it is now perceived to be based on partnership. This means that the client is no longer regarded as a passive recipient of services, but has an integral part to play in decisions regarding his or her welfare.

The power of assessment

Activity 2.3

In a care setting (which may be a work placement), observe the behaviour of other care workers. Make a list of some of these behaviours, which may include things like assisting with bathing, eating or bedtimes. Decide for each of the behaviours that you listed whether the client is being empowered, or whether the care worker is exercising power over the client, and why.

Ways of handling ethical issues and dilemmas

The importance of individual rights and choices

Real power results from knowledge and choice. Historically, care organisations met the requirements of groups in society other than clients themselves. The needs of those perceived to be more able, including families, neighbours, professionals and politicians, dictated policies in respect of those perceived to be less able. Care professionals often made decisions with reference to significant others first, and the client second. The problem had been compounded by the lack of choice in service provision, with particular services being offered by only one local provider, almost exclusively in the public sector. Clients had to accept what was offered, or have no service at all. Financial constraints on available provision has also been a major factor in limiting the choice of clients. All of these factors, over many years, developed into an institutionalised belief that care providers know better than clients what is needed, or wanted.

It is now apparent that such attitudes significantly contribute to the problems of those disadvantaged through health or social difficulties. The very process of health or social disadvantage results in a loss of power in society.

A prime aim of health and social care is **empowerment** in respect of a client's rights and choice. Not only is such an aim morally correct, but it is also highly effective in terms of meeting the needs of those who require care services. By promoting and supporting individual rights and choice within service delivery, we may ultimately reduce a major source of difficulties that care workers themselves impose on clients.

Activity 2.4

In groups of three or four, each choose a particular client group and a particular public or private health care setting.

a List all of the ways you believe that the rights and choices of the clients may not be supported in the setting of your choice.

b Are there reasons that rights and choices are being denied?

c To what extent does the exercise of power in the care setting reflect the exercise of power generally in our society toward those with health or social difficulties?

Threats to individual rights and choice

The protection of an individual's rights and choice is established both in law, and in the Care Value Base (see page 24), and they should be preserved and encouraged. However, rights and choice may sometimes need to be limited for legal reasons. For example, children in care may have certain rights removed for their own protection (the Children Act 1989), and those requiring admission to a mental hospital may be detained against their will and given treatment, where it is necessary (Mental Health Act 1983).

Need versus choice

Where budgetary restrictions severely restrict provision, which is now commonly the case, decisions need to be made about priority in the allocation of resources. The National Health Service and Community Care Act 1990, for example, has established that elderly persons seeking residential care, and who would need to rely on state support for this care, will be assessed by the local authority. The local authority hold restricted budgets to be allocated annually. The consequences of restricted budgets may be:

- Resources will be determined by professional assessment of need, as opposed to user demands for choice.

- Choice will be removed from economically devalued elderly people. Those fortunate enough to be financially better-off will retain their right to choice.
- The closure of many NHS and local authority resources, such as elderly persons' homes or small community hospitals, limit the options realistically available to those who need services.

It is understandable that restricted budgets and limited resources require health and social care workers to be discriminatory in their allocation of services. This poses significant risks to a client's rights, without any easy solutions.

Maintenance of individual rights and choice

Essentially, clients should have the same choices and rights as afforded to all of us in everyday life. That means that the client's perception of his or her problems and preferred responses to those problems should be encouraged, listened to, acknowledged and recorded. This is very dependent on the effective communication skills of the care worker, which will be discussed in Chapter 3. Options, rather than solutions, should be presented to the client, and the differences among the options should be fully explained. Options should always be considered in respect of risk, but only in exceptional circumstances should the right to take risks be removed from the client. Most commonly, such a situation may arise when it is deemed that the client cannot make a reasonable assessment of the risk, such as in a case of mental illness or severe learning disabilities. In such a case, the client's rights would be legally protected by the Mental Health Act 1983.

We often talk of independence, but perhaps **interdependence** better describes the relationship that most clients would wish from a care service. For many, the care service becomes an important part of their lives, and the support offered should be emotional as well as practical. Care workers are often not allowed sufficient time to meet other than urgent practical needs. Therefore, it is important that clients are encouraged to develop relationships with their carers, and that these relationships are based on a mutual respect. Such relationships will be dependent on the carer's ability to promote

and acknowledge the individual's rights and choices. This may entail sensitive areas, such as the right to have sexual feelings and to be able to express these in activities and relationships. Particular attention is drawn to this area, because in the past, many clients of care services have been denied such rights.

Activity 2.5

a In groups, discuss the ways in which you would support a client in making choices in an institutional setting, such as a hospital or a residential home.

b How might your activities create conflict within the work setting?

A client may not choose to be as independent as the professionals involved believe him or her to be capable. Moving individuals toward independence can only be done by encouragement, but the rights of individuals to choose their preferred level of independence is what is important. For example, elderly people may wish more to be done for them because they choose not to push themselves. This process of disengagement is not unusual. Coercive pressure in this situation may be a consequence of the care worker's own feelings about the process of ageing.

Carers must not only develop tolerance towards different types of individual, but they must also actively promote and support individual rights and choice. This requires good interpersonal skills.

Effective interpersonal skills are particularly important in dealing with challenging behaviour. Service users may be angry or aggressive, and the care worker will need good rapport and listening skills to calm the situation down. However, care workers need to be careful not to expose themselves to dangerous situations, and may need to call on the support of others, including the police, where necessary.

What if a client is not capable of exercising choice?

If a client is not capable of exercising choice, for example because of a mental disability, his or her rights to choice are not diminished. First, communication may be other than verbal. Choice may be determined by observing the client's behaviour toward different options. An individual's delight or dissatisfaction is often clearly observable. The techniques of checking for understanding are described later (pages 45–8). Undoubtedly, an understanding of the options available should always be thoroughly attempted, using a variety of methods, if required. It may be necessary for the client to actually experience different options before making a choice. For example, a trial period in a residential home may be allowed before a decision about admission is reached.

When it is believed to be impossible for the client to comprehend, it is necessary to use a **client representative** or **advocate**. It is not accepted practice for the care worker, manager, or care agency to make decisions alone for such a client, because there may be a conflict of interests. The client's needs may be in conflict with the agency's or worker's needs. A suitable representative for the client in such a case may be a relative or a friend. Such an arrangement should be formal and recorded. Where a friend or relative is not available or willing, it may be necessary to use an advocate to represent the client.

Advocates are non-professional volunteers, preferably trained, who will get to know the client very well, and advocate (advise) the opinions that they believe the client would express if he or she was capable of understanding the available options. Advocacy schemes are formal, and advocates should be trained and supported. Hence, there are cost implications to the care organisation. Advocacy schemes have not generally been adopted by care organisations as widely as they should be, or would be expected to be by the Care NVQs Value Base.

Confidentiality

What is confidential, and what is not?

Clients have the right to expect that information about them will be kept confidential. The Data Protection Act 1984, the Access to Health Records Act 1990, and the Access to Personal Files Act 1987, all set out the legal rights of health and social care service users. Both the legislation and local procedures establish the requirement of care workers to breach confidentiality where risk to the client or others exists.

It should be apparent that the essence of the Value Base Unit is the importance of the client as a person in every conceivable situation. The choices, wishes and needs of clients are the main determinants of service provision. However, in ascertaining the client's views and needs, much information needs to be obtained, and much of that information, recorded and shared with others. The privileged position of care workers in determining and maintaining information about the individuals who use services has often been taken for granted. At its worst, breaches of confidentiality involve careless talk about the client with others, sometimes where it can be overheard. Chat on buses, in the staff lounge, or even with the care worker's own family about information disclosed in confidence is not uncommon. One of the most important of all clients' rights is the right to have control over the disclosure of information pertaining to them.

Clients and patients have many rights in respect of confidential information. Some of these rights are enshrined in law. The Access to Health Records Act 1990, the Medical Records Act and the Access to Personal Files Act 1987, all set out procedures for dealing with confidential information. Information kept on service users must meet with statutory requirements. The Patient's Charter (see pages 273–4) guarantees confidentiality of health records, and access for patients. Relatives and friends may be given information about the patient only subject to the patient's wishes.

The Access to Health Records Act 1990 allows patients to see all National Health Service (NHS) notes made after November 1991. However, access to your notes can be refused if a doctor considers that such access could be damaging to your physical or mental health. It is also permitted for a doctor to withhold certain information without your knowledge. Although the intention of the Act is good, it is not an entirely satisfactory piece of legislation and is open to professional abuse.

The Value Base of health and social care goes even further. It requires that **access to personal information be limited and agreed by the service user**. The service user must understand any limits placed on the confidential information. Sometimes, where there is a perceived risk to the service user or others, information may need to be passed to others without permission. In such circumstances, the service user must be told what is being done with the information and why. Examples of this might be in relation to a child at risk or a suicide threat. A care worker can never be certain what it is that is going to be told to him or her. If asked by a client, 'If I tell you something, will you keep it to yourself?', the only acceptable response is 'That depends on what you are going to tell me.' Care workers are never fully at liberty to keep secrets between themselves and clients, as the worker is representing his or her organisation, and may need to let specific individuals know any critical information, particularly where the client or others might be at risk.

Good practice

Sometimes, information may be transmitted by telephone. The identity of interested parties must be made clear beforehand. In fact, proof of identity should be obtained where there is any doubt. Proof may consist of personal knowledge of the person to whom the information is being communicated. In addition, identity cards may need to be used in face-to-face situations. Obviously, the use of fax machines is not recommended, as no control exists over who will receive the information.

Entries into case files should contain only factual information, and not personal opinions or hearsay. Entries should be checked by the service user for accuracy, and amended accordingly. It should always be explained to the service user exactly who has access to files.

What a care worker learns about an individual should always remain confidential. The temptation to discuss such things in a social context is often great, but must be resisted.

The maintenance of confidentiality is not only an important interpersonal skill, but also intrinsic to organisational procedures. The good practices specified by care organisations in respect of confidentiality will help care workers to develop their skills in this important area.

Activity 2.6

A domiciliary care manager is assessing a potential client for home help. The organiser needs to collect a great deal of information from this individual in order to make a decision about the sort of help the client needs, if any. Describe how this assessment would proceed with regard to confidentiality.

For Activity 2.6, your answer should have included the following points:
- The reasons why information needs to be collected should be explained to the client first, and agreement obtained.
- The client should be told that written notes will be made of the discussion, and that these notes will be written up and checked with them for accuracy before being entered into any official files.
- It should be explained to the client how decisions are reached in relation to the information recorded, and who will have access to the case file.

All of the above would need to be agreed with the client in advance of the assessment actually taking place.

It is important in all matters of confidentiality that the client has a full understanding of how personal information will be dealt with, and that all file entries are checked with the client for accuracy. The care worker should be convinced that the client understands this. Therefore, as with all other values, the skills of good interpersonal interaction are essential (see Chapter 3).

Personal beliefs and preferences

All users of health and social care services have a right to privacy, and a right to maintain their own beliefs and preferences in relation to self, religion, culture, ethics and sexual preference. Facilitating the client's right to choice and personal beliefs is essential to good care practice. It is believed to be reasonable, however, to restrict the choices of clients in situations where the exercising of the choice may infringe on the rights of others. The skill in promoting choice and beliefs is largely interpersonal. Clients are at risk of having their rights directly infringed by unskilled care workers. The interpersonal aspects of ensuring rights to choice and personal beliefs is dealt with in Chapter 3.

Activity 2.7

Consider the following situations:
a An elderly person is highly confused, at risk and perceived to be a danger to herself. Should her rights be restricted? If so, in what ways?
b A teenage boy is proving to be very difficult to relate to. He has been joy-riding with cars, putting both his own life and the lives of others at risk. Should his rights be restricted? If so, in what ways?

Personal beliefs include views that the client holds in relation to areas of self, religion, culture, politics, ethics and sexual preference. The right to some personal beliefs are protected in law. The Race Relations Act 1976 and the Sex Discrimination Act 1975 are examples. The right to hold one's own views on virtually anything is a highly regarded aspect of a free society, as long as those views do not infringe or restrict the liberty of others.

Those who receive services from a care worker have the right to be addressed in their preferred manner. That means the choice of whether they are referred to by first name or more formally is theirs alone, and it is the responsibility of the care worker to find this out. Even the use of the term 'Christian name' may prove offensive to those not of the Christian faith, and should therefore be avoided.

We live in an age of political correctness, where the labelling of client groups has come under much scrutiny. Ultimately, an individual client should be referred to as he or she wishes. For example, whether a client is referred to as 'deaf', 'hearing impaired' or 'hard of hearing' is solely a matter of the client's personal preference. Similarly, assumptions should not be made about the diet of a client from an ethnic minority. The client may, or may not, observe religious dietary laws. Every individual should be asked about his or her preferences at every opportunity.

If the care worker disagrees with particular views being expressed by a client, the worker must still respond in a way that is supportive of the client as an individual. The Value Base goes further than suggesting just tolerance of personal beliefs, it requires that **the personal beliefs of others should be positively encouraged, expressed, and listened to**. This would be the case even if the client was experiencing mental health problems, and his or her expressed beliefs appeared unusual to the care worker.

Activity 2.8

Identify situations in which you might find a client's beliefs in conflict with your own. How would you respond, and why?

Personal beliefs are important because they are an expression of the identity and uniqueness of the individual.

It is all too easy in a task-orientated care service to lose sight of the individual. When this occurs, institutionalisation can develop. It used to be believed that institutionalisation was a problem associated with care settings. We now know this to be untrue. Institutionalisation is a problem associated with bad care management, where interpersonal skills are poor and where the client's own personal beliefs and identity are discouraged from being expressed.

Responding to individual beliefs and identity

All elements of the Value Base require good interpersonal skills. The techniques of **listening** are the most important skills in responding to individual beliefs (see pages 45–8).

When a care worker is unsure about how to respond to a client expressing his or her beliefs, it may be appropriate to seek advice direct from the client. Alternatively, support and guidance may be obtained from another care worker or manager. It would be unacceptable not to respond to a client's expression of belief through lack of understanding. This might occur, for example, if the client comes from an ethnic background, or is experiencing a health or social problem, with which the care worker is not familiar.

Sometimes, a client may not share the same views as the care worker or other clients. This should always be thoroughly explored in a supportive way. If possible, when it pertains to differing perceptions of the nature of a client's problems or treatment, the client should be encouraged to express his or her views in the case file. Certainly, the client's opinion is as important as that of the professional's who would normally write in such records.

The acknowledgement of an individual's personal beliefs and identity is an important part of the Value Base. The expressed preferences of clients supersede almost all else, where possible.

Activity 2.9

1 In a residential home for elderly people, a couple are having an intimate relationship. Some of the other residents, and some staff, object to this. How do you believe this issue ought to be handled, and why?

2 You are a care worker in a residential home. Mrs Phillips is 82 years old and diabetic. This lunch time, she is insistent on having some sponge pudding. This is not recommended as part of her diet. What responses might you make to Mrs Phillips's request?

Activity 2.10

In Activity 2.9, Mrs Phillips should have her request acknowledged. The dangers of having sponge pudding would need to be explained to her, and perhaps she might be convinced to have something else. Provided that Mrs Phillips is mentally capable of understanding the risk to herself, this is ultimately a decision that *she* must make. However, the care worker should certainly make her manager aware of Mrs Phillips's request, and the incident should be recorded. To express disagreement with Mrs Phillips's choice is to express genuine concern for her, and this is what care is about. However, to permit her to make such decisions is a recognition of her identity, and respect for her as a person. This, too, is what caring is about.

Unacceptable risks for the client

Many of the criteria for the restriction of choice and rights are established in law. Two notable examples are the Children Act 1989 – which establishes statutory obligations to remove and protect children in certain circumstances – and the Mental Health Act 1983 – which provides for compulsory treatment and detention. Common law also allows for certain decisions to be made in situations of risk to life or property.

The removal of an individual's rights and choice is a legal and formal decision, often taken only by professionals issued with the legal authority to do so. When such decisions are made, they will be incorporated into the care plan for the client, and all care workers will be made aware of their responsibilities. When an client's rights or wishes are denied for whatever reason, this should be explained appropriately to the client, and recorded in a file, or reported to the appropriate worker. Such action can never be casual or informal.

Sometimes, a client's wishes may be denied, because of the impact they may have on others. All of us are sometimes restricted in our activities in relation to others. We may not be racist, obscene or physically belligerent. The same applies to users of health and

Steel worker

Civil servant

Long distance lorry driver

Catering manager

In the busy working day, it is easy to forget a client's individual identity

social care services, and this becomes particularly important in communal situations, such as residential homes and hospitals.

Anti-discriminatory practice

We have already discussed discrimination in Chapter 1. In this chapter we shall review why anti-discriminatory practice is part of the Value Base.

Discrimination can take many forms and may not be immediately obvious. It can be rather subtle, being communicated through body language, tone of voice or humour. Organisational or personal practices in care may reflect assumptions which are discriminatory, for example, a doctor who tells an elderly patient, 'What do you expect at your age?' or the manager of a residential home who disapproves of sex among residents. Perhaps there may be anxiety about employing gay men in children's homes or women with children as nurses.

Such discriminatory practices conspire to make us believe that those with such problems can make little contribution to an assessment of their own requirements. Similarly, discriminatory practice has made some believe that those disadvantaged by health or social problems should not be accorded the same freedom in society as the rest of us. Much discrimination has its roots in history and, while people today do generally have more understanding of others, discrimination still exists in our society, albeit perhaps in a more subtle form.

There are, of course, policies and laws regarding discrimination, such as the Sex Discrimination Act 1975, the Race Relations Act 1976 and the Disabled Persons Act 1986. However, legislation and organisational disciplinary procedures can never be wholly effective, especially against the more subtle forms of discrimination. To overcome discriminatory practice, efforts must be made to increase awareness. Many organisations now have publicised policies of anti-discriminatory practice, and some offer training courses to increase awareness among staff. Such training should target the fears that underpin intolerance, and involve modelling appropriate behaviours. These courses should be in an emotionally supportive environment, so that the fears of individuals may be safely expressed and dealt with. It should be emphasised that discrimination is not restricted to particular groups in society. Intolerance toward others may be demonstrated in every group.

Anti-discriminatory practice is not just about written policies. It is about positive, demonstrable behaviour. A thorough understanding of the needs and feelings of people who differ from ourselves is the foundation of good care practice. This understanding is communicated through interpersonal interaction (see Chapter 3).

Ethical issues and care organisations

Conflicting values – ethical issues in practice

Although it is possible to express values in care in fairly clear terms, putting values into practice is highly problematic. Real-life situations rarely present themselves in such clear-cut ways. Who should determine the best interests of clients? In care, we talk about 'needs', whereas in more commercially orientated industries, people talk about 'wants'. What clients need and what they want are not always the same.

When working with families and other interested parties, it may be unclear how to balance the needs of all in an attempt to define the best interests of the client. In fact, it is often difficult to clearly define who the client is. Care workers have many masters. One method used to analyse this situation is the stakeholder concept.

The stakeholder concept

The stakeholder concept is based on the idea that care workers are employed in organisations that represent a coalition of individuals with differing perspectives. A stakeholder is anyone who depends on the care organisation for the realisation of some of his or her goals. This would include not just direct service users, but often families, local communities, care agency employees, local councils and health authorities, and the public in general. In turn, the care organisation depends on all of these stakeholders in order to fully realise its own goals. The process of managing relationships with stakeholders is often a powerful determinant of the ethics of the care organisation and its employees.

In analysing the relative power of different stakeholders on the care worker's practice, several criteria should be considered:

- Who supplies, allocates and controls resources? In the care industry, this would be primarily central and local government. There may also be involvement of regulatory agencies.
- Who and what influences the supply and control of resources? These influences may include consumer groups, political parties, the electorate at large, and political lobbies.
- From where do these influences derive their power? This may be from the individuals and families who directly receive services, who may have agendas and value systems of their own.

It is important to understand that stakeholders in the care industry are numerous. They include the owners of independent services, service users, managers, care workers, councils, government, political parties, and society in general.

It is important to understand the perspectives and values of each of these groups, and be able to make an assessment of their relative power and influence.

Activity 2.11

Select a care service with which you are acquainted. Determine who the stakeholders are.

a What expectations does each stakeholder have?
b Identify possible conflicts between the expectations of the different stakeholders.
c How are these conflicts presently managed?
d How might they be managed better?

Case study

Mrs Jones is a 92-year-old disabled woman. She has been assessed by the home care service as being in need of considerable support at home. A home help has been allocated. Her name is Miss Beecham.

On the first day the home help appears, Mrs Jones is thrown into an hysterical panic. She was unaware that Miss Beecham is black. Mrs Jones has never actually met a black woman before, and she is very frightened and unsure about her new home help.

The home care organiser visits Mrs Jones, and Mrs Jones asks the organiser if she could have a different home help. Mrs Jones explains that it is nothing personal, but she cannot help her reaction to having a black woman in her home.

A conflict is established between the values of anti-discriminatory practice, and the client's right of personal beliefs and choices. The home care organiser informs Mrs Jones that the council could not possibly support her racist request, and that she should either accept Miss Beecham, or have no service at all.

What are the essential issues here, and which value assumes priority over the other? Is it right to use the council's position of power (a monopoly service provider) as a weapon against the racism of Mrs Jones. What should the council's home care services' responsibilities be in this matter?

The case study above demonstrates how complicated the resolution of ethical issues are in practice. The experienced care worker must take many views into consideration. How can it be ensured that the care worker will provide a balanced, considered and fair judgement?

Ways of handling ethical issues

In recognition of the fact that the management of values and ethical issues in care is highly problematic, and requires insight and skill, what methods of dealing with such complex issues exist?

First, an understanding of the stakeholder model, and its relevance to care is essential. Care workers should understand who the interested parties are, and what differing beliefs and needs are being expressed. Professional training is of primary importance here. There is an urgent and increasing need to train and develop the analytical and ethical skills of care workers. This requirement of the care industry will be reflected throughout your GNVQ education, and should be continued in higher education and employment. The emphasis put on care values in the Care NVQs, and a profound understanding of them, is an important recognition of the importance and complexity of ethical issues.

Professional supervision is also of great importance, as it supports and enables the ethical development of the care worker. In recognition of the ethical complexity of most care decisions, case conferences are an effective means of exploring the values of different interested paries. Even where decisions may go against a certain individual's values, the case conference provides an opportunity for people to be listened to, and their views recorded.

It is important to keep ethical considerations at the top of the agenda in care practice. It is only through such open recognition, discussion and resolution of competing values that the care industry can reflect in practice the real complexity of the issues it faces. There are no rules.

Review questions

1 Describe the relationship between ethical issues, and attitudes and values.
2 Define the concept of empowerment and what role it has in care services.
3 What are the threats to individual rights and choice in care services?
4 What is the role of the client advocate?
5 What are the five elements of the Value Base Unit?
6 What rights exist for clients in regard to confidentiality, in law?

7 In what ways does the stakeholder model explain ways in which to balance the needs of conflicting groups?

8 How does the level of resourcing affect (or even create) ethical dilemmas?

9 How is training and education for care workers ultimately important in making ethical decisions?

10 How should 'the best interests' of the client be decided upon?

Assignment 2.1
Managing ethical issues

This assignment provides knowledge, understanding and portfolio evidence for element 1.3, **Examine ethical issues in health and social care practice.**

Your tasks

1 Working in small groups, look through newspapers and professional care journals. Try to identify any issues in care which are ethical in nature. Sort out the references into the following headings:

 a Agreeing the best interests of clients

 b Balancing the differing needs of individuals

 c Allocating resources

 d Sharing information about clients

 e Handling conflicting values and beliefs.

2 Within your group, discuss each example of ethical issues you have found, attempting to analyse each type of issue and dilemma in detail. Each individual should make his or her own detailed notes of the discussions.

3 Using the notes from the previous discussions prepare your own report on ethical issues in care, and ways to handle them:

 • Prepare an introduction which explains the importance of ethical issues and dilemmas in care services.

 • Discuss, in turn, each of the types of issues above (a to e), emphasising how a range of different views needs to be taken into account for each.

 • For each type of issue or dilemma, describe the different ways in which organisations and individuals might handle it.

4 Select two types of issues or dilemmas. Analyse these in more detail in terms of:

 a how the issues might be handled

 b identifying the interested parties

 c the responsibilities of the care workers involved.

3 Interpersonal skills in health and social care

What is covered in this chapter

- Forms of effective interpersonal interaction
- The influence of interpersonal interaction on well-being
- Enhancing the factors affecting interpersonal interaction using skills
- Evaluating the effectiveness of interpersonal interaction
- The support needed for effective interaction

These are the resources you will need for your portfolio for element 2.1:

- A report which:
  - explains the different forms of interpersonal interaction
  - explains how interaction can be enhanced and inhibited
  - provides two examples of positive and negative influences of interaction on individuals' health and social well being
  - describes the sources of data used for an evaluation of interaction.
- A brief summary explaining the effect (as stated in the range) that gender, age and culture may have on interpersonal interaction.

These are the resources you will need for your portfolio for element 2.2:

- A record of a demonstration of:
  - one-to-one interaction
  - interaction with a small group
  - interaction with a large group.
  (At lease one of the group interactions should be with people of a different status to the student.)
  (At least one of the interactions should be through an activity.)
- Records of self-evaluation on the interactions and feedback from participants.

Finally:
Your written answers to the activities, review questions and assignments in this chapter.

Forms of effective interpersonal interaction

Effective interpersonal interaction consists of a variety of forms. These include:

- **Language** The use of words in making statements and asking questions, also known as verbal behaviour. The use of language includes how we emphasise words, and our tone of voice.
- **Sensory contact** This includes non-verbal behaviour such as body language, facial expressions, distance from the other person, and touching.
- **Activity** Interaction may consist of activities such as music, arts and crafts, drama, and movement. Sometimes, it is more effective to allow individuals to communicate through activity, and opportunities for this may be provided by, among others, occupational therapists.

All forms of effective interpersonal interaction require skill and training. This chapter identifies the basic skills required, and how they may be used to enhance interaction.

In addition, for interpersonal interaction to be effective, it must consider issues such as *gender, age* and *culture*. Some of these issues have been raised in Chapters 1 and 2. In this chapter we have integrated these issues in our discussions of using specific skills, as to have done otherwise would have made little sense.

What is effective interpersonal interaction?

The choice of interpersonal skills depends on outcomes. An *outcome* is a specific, desired result of an interaction. The care worker should be clear what outcome is desired in interacting with a client. Outcomes should incorporate the Value Base – the client should experience the worker's positive regard for choice, confidentiality, personal beliefs and identity.

There are three distinct phases of acquiring effective interpersonal skills:

- **Thinking** Intellectual awareness is developed. An understanding of the reasons behind the skills is acquired.
- **Doing** New behavioural skills are learned through practical exercises and analysis. The nuts and bolts of interpersonal skills are practised.
- **Feeling** To develop feeling, the skills are used in real-life situations, with real feedback. The worker gains an emotional insight into his or her effect on others, and how others affect him or her. In this stage, the values associated with the new behaviours are internalised, and the new behaviours become more natural.

When the learning of interpersonal skills is limited to just thinking and doing, the values of the worker may not change. For example, a care worker may learn how to express him or herself in a politically correct, anti-discriminatory way, but may still possess discriminatory beliefs. In such a situation, the worker will display *incongruence* – the subtle, non-verbal cues betraying the worker's discomfort with his or her own behaviour. The worker's posture, eye movements and other body language will communicate a message different from his or her words. To develop feeling requires considerable determination. The Value Base of Care cannot be communicated to clients simply because one has read it, or practised a few exercises. However, reading about the values of care and practising exercises are the essential first steps.

Effective interpersonal interaction is:

- gaining an understanding of the Value Base on the feeling level
- being able to communicate that to service users, both verbally and non-verbally.

A desirable outcome of interpersonal interaction in health and social care is the development of understanding. The care worker will need to be understood on both emotional and intellectual levels. He or she will also need to understand others, and be able to communicate his or her understanding to the client on both the emotional and intellectual levels.

Successful communication is about the results we achieve from being understood and expressing understanding. In health and social care it is always the client who determines whether the worker's communication is effective. If a client does not understand, the worker must find a different way of achieving the outcome of understanding. The responsibility for achieving understanding in health and social care always lies with the care worker. This is the nature of the professional relationship. Therefore, the care worker needs to have a repertoire of varied interpersonal skills to call upon.

Each of us is unique and different. Good communication skills:
• acknowledge the uniqueness of individuals, and bridge the differences
• increase understanding, by focusing on outcomes and not problems.
Ideally, the care worker and the client can share outcomes, such as a sense of belonging, increased independence, more support where needed, or accessing appropriate resources. All goals should be set *with* clients, in line with the Value Base.

Usually, words just come and talk just happens – the process is automatic. However, the demands on care workers to communicate competently and effectively make them suspect that they could do better. So, where do we start?

Effective communication

To promote anti-discriminatory practice, support individual rights and choice, acknowledge personal beliefs and identity, and maintain confidentiality, the most important skill is to **communicate effectively.**

Effective communication is essentially mutual understanding between the client and the care worker. The responsibility for mutual understanding clearly lies with the care worker. If the care worker is not being understood, he or she must find another way of expressing him or herself. If the client is not being understood, the care worker must use a different technique of communication.

Effective communication begins with the recognition that each of us is different and unique. Good interpersonal skills bridge these differences.

Why might the client not understand?

The problem may simply be one of language. The client may not speak English very well. In such a situation, the care worker would need to find an interpreter. The client may be hearing-impaired, in which case the worker may have to use an alternative method, such as signing or writing. The client's preferred method of communication should always be used.

A common problem is the use of technical jargon, particularly in medical settings. This should always be avoided, and the worker should attempt to communicate with the client in ways which are consistent with the client's level of understanding and perceived abilities.

Commonly, the client may not understand what the care worker is trying to communicate because the care worker lacks good interpersonal skills, both verbal and non-verbal.

The clients' preferred method of communication should always be used

Activity 3.1

Find out how care agencies in your area assist individuals for whom English is a second language.

The influence of interpersonal interaction on well-being

The ways in which we interact with others can have either positive or negative effects. By making individuals feel as if they are part of a community, the care worker can increase the client's sense of well-being. Emphasising the worth of others, and giving others the time that they need is important. In order to optimise the sense of well-being in others, care workers needs to systematically develop their skills. In order to achieve this, the worker must be committed to becoming more effective, and the care organisation must be committed to providing the appropriate support and training. Failure to do so may result in the negative consequences of clients becoming disempowered, feeling oppressed, and losing their sense of self-worth. Care workers must be vigilant and attentive in their interactions with others, recognising that the interactions may have both positive and negative effects.

The importance of interpersonal interaction in health and social care

Care is a service industry, where workers have an unusually high degree of contact with service users. Cowell, writing in 1984, said 'People are as much a part of the product in the consumer's mind as any other attribute of the service.' He explains that in service industries, such as health and social care, the 'product' of the service is created by the interpersonal interaction of its workers. Bateson (1977) argues that because the behaviour of the people who deliver the service is so important, the determinant of that behaviour should always be 'What benefits the service user?' He calls this the *consumer benefit concept*. The consumer's view should always be central to the service being offered. This is critical to the success of the service in meeting needs.

Gronross (1982) states that quality in a service is determined by:

- the attitudes of employees
- the behaviour of employees (interpersonal interaction)
- the general service-mindedness of personnel
- the elevated status of employees within the organisation who have direct contact with service users.

Activity 3.2

In small groups, decide what attitudes care workers should have in order to provide a quality service. Make a list of these, and discuss why each is important. Consider both social care and health care settings.

The values and attitudes of care workers can only be expressed through interpersonal interaction. The values and the behaviours appropriate to care have been established in the Value Base Unit for the NVQs in Care.

The Value Base and interpersonal skills

Health and social care is a service that not only requires a great deal of technical skill in physical care, but also considerable skill in emotional and psychological care. The style of help is of equal importance to any physical support offered. Indeed, some care services, such as mental health, are wholly dependent on proficiency in emotional care. All users of care services have emotional needs, so the ways in which care workers respond to them are crucial.

Surveys carried out in the United States on user satisfaction in care show that satisfaction with a care service is always measured in relation to the interpersonal skills of the staff. Recent publications from the Royal College of Nursing also recognise this, drawing attention to the differences between:

- **technical quality** (purely practical skills like taking blood pressure, or applying dressings) and
- **functional quality** (how the carer interacts with the patient in meeting his or her emotional needs).

In some businesses, functional quality is taught through 'customer care training'. However, this can be 'parrot-fashion', and can sound false if the **attitudes** of the staff are not also fundamentally changed. Attitudes result from values, and these are very difficult to learn or change.

Activity 3.3

Why do you think that attitudes are difficult to change? Give examples from your own experience.

Enhancing the factors affecting interpersonal interaction using skills

The first steps toward effective interpersonal interaction
- Observe what is going on around you, and make conscious decisions about how to respond.
- Acquaint yourself with the values of care (see page 24).

- Avoid generalisations about people. Regard every person as a unique individual, with his or her own views and feelings. Show an interest in the ways in which people are different.
- Work only with goals, not problems. It is easy to see what individuals cannot do. It takes skill and vision to see what they may aspire to.

The skills of interpersonal interaction

There are five basic skills in enhancing an interaction with a service user:

- questioning
- self-disclosure and prompting
- active listening
- giving information
- rapport.

Each of these involves both verbal and non-verbal skills.

Questioning

Questioning is the seeking of information, clarification, views, feelings, and thoughts. There are two basic types of questions: **closed** and **open**.

Closed questions

Closed questions are questions that can be answered in one or two words, often 'Yes' or 'No'. 'What is your name?', 'How old are you?', 'Do you eat chips?' and 'What is your nationality?' are examples of closed questions. They are essential for ascertaining facts. They should, however, be minimised in a conversation, as long strings of them make people feel interrogated and uncomfortable. Closed questions may inhibit conversation.

Open questions

Open questions are questions that require a more extended answer. For example, instead of asking a client, 'Do you eat pork?', the care worker might ask, 'What sorts of foods do you like or dislike?' Such an open question feels more comfortable, and allows the client to answer in his or her own way.

The use of open questions communicates to the client that the care worker is interested in the whole range of responses that the client might make. Open questions typically begin with words like:

- How ...?
- Why ...
- In what ways ...
- What sorts ...?

By using open questions, the care worker will find that much of the information which needs to be ascertained is freely given, without the need for interrogating the client endlessly with lists of closed questions.

It appears that the use of closed questions comes more naturally in our culture. In order to develop skill in open questioning, practice is required.

Activity 3.4

In pairs, ask each other questions about anything of your choice.

- If you are asked a closed question, give a one word response. Do not give any more information than you are asked for.
- If asked an open question, give as full an answer as you believe appropriate.

This activity will make you pay attention both to the sorts of questions you ask, and the sorts of questions asked of you. It is important to do this activity by the rules, as if you just have a chat with your partner, you will learn very little about open and closed questions.

Self-disclosure and prompting

Self-disclosure is another means of enhancing a conversation when seeking information. It is often used in conjunction with questioning. The purpose of self-disclosure is to make the client more comfortable and forthcoming, by telling him or her something about yourself. This helps to establish areas of common interest. Self-disclosure is necessary for making the client feel that he or she is not under scrutiny. It turns an interview into a conversation. Some examples of self-disclosure, used with an open question may be:

- 'I don't like hot desserts. What sorts of desserts do you like?'
- 'I broke my leg once, and found using crutches very difficult. How are *you* managing with them?'

Activity 3.5

a In pairs, repeat the exercise on open and closed questions, but this time add self-disclosure to the conversation. Keep to the same rules.

b At the conclusion of your conversation, spend a few moments discussing how different this exercise made you feel compared to the one where you asked only questions.

Self-disclosure is a type of prompt. Prompting is a means of getting the client to talk when he or she is finding it difficult. Most of us prompt quite naturally, by nodding our heads, or by saying 'Yeah' or 'I see'. These sorts of phrases combined with an attentive gaze and a raise of the eyebrows, are effective prompts. They tell the client that we are expecting him or her to say something.

In seeking information, the care worker may find that he or she needs to focus the client's responses. An information-seeking interview can easily evolve into a social conversation, with little being disclosed. The care worker may need to bring the conversation back to the topic being discussed. This can also be done with the use of prompts. A simple reminder will often work, such as 'Does any of that affect your relationship with your son, Mrs Jones? I'd like to discuss that if it's OK?'

Active listening

Questioning, prompting, and self-disclosure are the ways in which we obtain information, and enhance interaction. However, it is important that the care worker shows the client that he or she has been listened to and understood. This is called *active listening*. Active listening is a powerful way of optimising interactions. There are two types of active listening:

- **paraphrasing**
- **reflective listening**.

Some of the ground rules are:
- Avoid saying that you understand when you don't.
- Avoid jumping in with your own points of view.
- Use open questions.
- Pay attention to body language.

Good communication skills acknowledge the uniqueness of individuals

Paraphrasing

Paraphrasing is a simple and effective way to test understanding. A paraphrase is a repetition or a summary of what the client has said. It might begin with a phrase such as 'What you have been saying, if I've got it right, is ...', and then repeating what the client has said. Paraphrasing checks for accuracy of understanding, and provides the client with an opportunity to correct any misunderstanding. Importantly, it communicates to the client that the care worker has been listening and trying to understand.

Activity 3.6

Work in groups of three. Two of the three will initially take an active part in the activity, while the third is an observer.

a Choose a subject for discussion (preferably one which can produce some heated debate or disagreement).

b One participant starts off with an opening statement.

c When the first participant concludes, the second has to respond. However, before doing so, he or she must summarise what the first person has said.

d The third person assesses whether the summary was correct.

e The second can then continue.

This process continues for as long as has been agreed.

The third person then takes the place of one of the first two, and the process repeats with a different subject, and then again, until each pair in the trio has had a discussion, and has practised paraphrasing.

A variation of this activity can be played with a larger group. The individual who initiates the discussion passes a stick on to a person of his or her choice. This second person must then paraphrase the first person's contribution before proceeding with their own. On concluding, the second contributor passes the stick on to another and so on until the agreed time for the activity has elapsed.

Reflective listening

Reflective listening is less concerned with the summarising of facts, and more involved with understanding the emotions and feelings that are being communicated. All interactions between people communicate only three basic things:

- emotions and feelings
- needs and wants
- facts or opinions.

In reflective listening, the listener sorts out the information received from the other person into these categories, and responds only in the order above. Emotions and feelings are the first and most important to respond to, using emotion and feeling words. Some examples of *feeling words* are:

- happy • worried • sad • excited • concerned • angry
- frustrated • frightened • depressed • disappointed.

How many more can you think of? Feeling words are important for identifying the emotions of those with whom we converse.

Example 1

Mrs Johnson: Mike usually helps me with my bath. He will be here in an hour. Can you help me now instead?
Care worker: You seem worried about Mike giving you your bath.

Mrs Johnson might feel inclined to discuss what is worrying her because the care worker was able to label her emotion for her. If the care worker was mistaken, and Mrs Johnson was not worried, she had an opportunity to correct the care worker's mistaken perception.

Example 2

Bob (aged 8): The teacher caught me messing around, and kept me in during playtime.
Care worker: You must have felt embarrassed in front of your friends.

The care worker invites Bob to talk about what happened at school by suggesting he might have felt embarrassed. To have been condemning of Bob would have shut him up.

Essentially, in reflective listening we are saying that how people feel is often more important than the facts or details of the situation. The care worker will use both verbal and non-verbal cues to determine how he or she believes the client is feeling. This is then checked with the client. It does not matter if the care worker is mistaken. A feeling misread can give rise to many more incorrect responses.

Reflective listening is one of the major skills of childcare. Children need to have their feelings acknowledged. Much of our interaction with children is directive, prescriptive and factually based. Many of the problems we have with children are due to these forms of interaction. Telling a child that you can see when he or she is upset, happy or worried works wonders. By acknowledging the child's feelings, the child is likely to talk more. Perhaps it is because we often do not use reflective listening with children, that children grow up without learning this important skill themselves. All forms of interaction are learned by modelling. Those care workers who work with children will need to demonstrate desirable forms of behaviour.

Activity 3.7

Working in threes, start off with two participants and one observer. The two have a discussion about a topic of their choice, while the third scores them both for reflective listening. The observer will be watching each participant for the use of feeling words in checking out the other's emotions. This is repeated until all three have been observers.

Note: All of the activities in this section are for you to experience the interaction techniques being described. Considerably more work would be required to master these techniques. At this stage it is important that you develop an understanding of what the techniques are.

Giving information

The skill of giving information has been covered in the discussion of the Value Base (see Chapter 2). Information has to be provided to clients in ways of their own choosing and subject to their capabilities. Barriers might include language, hearing, visual impairment or mental state. It is important that clients always have as much information as possible in order to exercise their right to choice.

Rapport

All of the interpersonal skills described above will be ineffective unless rapport (sometimes called 'meshing') is established. Rapport is a powerful way of optimising the effectiveness of interactions.

It has already been stated that care workers are most effective when they can match their outcomes with those of their clients.

Your outcomes, or goals, will not be achieved unless the other person also achieves theirs. The purpose of information seeking is to determine what outcomes the client desires. The care worker will then dovetail, or mesh, his or her own outcomes with the client's, so both achieve satisfaction. When a client's outcomes are not realised, the care worker's outcomes are not either, and the care worker experiences dissatisfaction with his or her work. An aim of all care workers is to finish the day's work knowing that something has been achieved, and feeling good about the part they have played in it.

So much of the care worker's effectiveness depends on the skill of rapport. Rapport is composed of a number of basic skills which take much knowledge and practice to master. For example, the following skills can be used:

- **Mirroring and matching** Both the verbal and non-verbal behaviour of the client can be mirrored by the care worker, including body movements and tone of voice. To mirror effectively, the care worker just hints at the client's movements or tone, but is careful not to mimic them. This skill is only used very subtly. For example, if the client is moving his or her head from side to side when talking, the care worker may only very slightly use the same movement. The care worker may adopt the same body posture as the client, such as crossing a leg or leaning forwards.
- **Pacing** The pace of speech or the breathing pattern of the client can also be mirrored, and then changed if necessary by the care worker. For example, if the client is anxious, he or she is likely to be breathing quickly. The care worker can pace his or her own breathing to match the client's, and can then begin a process of slowing down, taking the client with him or her. The care worker can establish rapport with the client by matching the pace of speech. If the client speaks slowly, the care worker should adjust his or her tempo accordingly. Pacing can be particularly effective when faced with challenging behaviour.

Rapport is the process of developing a shared understanding with the client, and is therefore one of the core essential skills of health and social care. It is a process that we all engage in naturally up to a point. When brought into conscious control as a caring skill, its effect is powerful.

Activity 3.8

1 Work in groups of three. One person will be the observer. One of the other two engages in ordinary conversation about a topic of his or her choice. The other practises mirroring body movement.

The observer's job is to ensure that the other two do not get carried away by the conversation. He or she will describe how effective the mirroring has been. The first student will also describe how it felt to be mirrored.

The exercise is repeated until all three students have been the observer.

> **Remember not to mimic. Mirroring is a minimised reflection of the other person's behaviour.**

This exercise can be repeated with pacing.

2 Repeat 1 above, but this time mismatch as many verbal and non-verbal cues as possible. For example, if one person is speaking slowly and low, the other speaks quickly and loudly.

Neuro-linguistic programming

The understanding of how we both give out and interpret even the minutest of physical cues has been enhanced through the on-going development of neuro-linguistic programming (NLP).

In spite of its unfortunate name, NLP is highly practical in its models, skills and techniques. NLP has studied what makes outstanding individuals so successful and presents the patterns and skills of success in a way that is learnable. The process is called modelling. For an excellent introduction to this developing and influential area of psychology, the book *Introducing Neuro-Linguistic Programming* by J. O'Connor and J. Seymour is recommended.

NLP was developed by Richard Bandler and John Grinder in the United States in the 1970s. The 'neuro' part of NLP refers to the fact that all behaviour results from the neurological processes of sight, hearing, smell, touch, taste and feeling. Our neurology is also responsible for the visible, physiological reactions we make to feelings and events. The 'linguistic' part of NLP emphasise the importance of language in ordering our thoughts and behaviour and in communicating with others.

NLP is based on three essential ideas:
- Know what you want – have a clear idea of your desired outcome.
- Rely on alert and sharp senses to notice what you are getting.
- Be flexible in changing your own behaviour until you get what you want.

Heightened sensory activity needs to be developed to be successful. You need to see, hear, and feel all that is happening around you, and have a sufficient number of responses to what you are experiencing. The more choices open to you, the more chances of success.

Communication is so much more than the words we say. It has been estimated that body language comprises 55 per cent of communication, tone of voice 38 per cent, and words only 7 per cent. NLP develops the ability to respond effectively to others, and to understand and respect their model of the world. There are many techniques for doing this, some even based on intricate observation of eye movements (Figure 3.1).

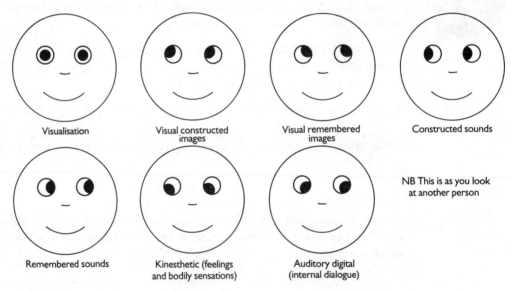

Figure 3.1 Eye movements

Eye movements can indicate the 'representational system' used by a person. Some individuals rely mostly on visual, auditory or kinaesthetic (feelings) senses in processing information. It is important to know which, so that we can present information to them that will be compatible with their information-processing system. For example, we might refer to 'seeing what you mean' (visual), 'hearing what you are saying' (auditory), or 'being moved or touched by what you have said' (kinaesthetic). Achieving rapport is helped by matching an individual's representational system.

Non-verbal behaviour and body language

Interpersonal skills depend not only on verbal skills, but also on non-verbal skills and body language. We converse with our whole body, including facial expressions, eyes, gestures, physical distance and skin tone. Although we read body signals all of the time, it takes considerable practice and skill to do this consciously. The non-verbal aspects of communication provide valuable clues about how an interaction is progressing and about the feelings of the other person.

- It is the *patterns* of body language that are important, rather than single incidents.
- Body language is easy to misread, and making false assumptions can create strong barriers to understanding.

Facial expressions

Our faces communicate complex and subtle messages. A smiling and alert face strongly attracts. A forlorn and helpless face arouses sympathy and concern. A tense and grumpy face sends out messages to stay away. While it is possible to smile and feel sad, the eyes and eyebrows are less amenable to control and are therefore valuable indicators of feeling. A long silent gaze with raised eyebrows evokes speech in the other person. We use our eyes to continue speech and to obtain feedback. We end conversations by looking away. People look more at the person they talk to when they like them, and also look more at the other person when listening than when talking.

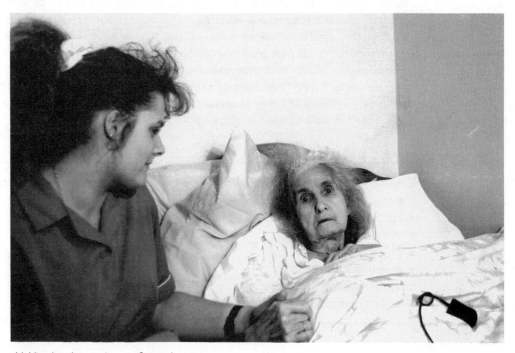

Holding hands can give comfort and reassurance

Personal space

All of us require personal space. The amount that we require is partly determined by cultural differences. Arabs, for example, interact more closely with each other than British people do. The amount of personal space used in an interaction is important in relation to intimacy and dominance. The closer the person gets, the more intimate or dominant he or she wishes to be. We all like to be in control of our personal space and the situations in which we wish to be close (intimate) with someone. For example, in a doctor's waiting room, people maintain distance from each other, unless numbers force them next to one another. To sit down right next to another person in an otherwise empty waiting room would make that person extremely uncomfortable.

Body contact

Body contact is another area of intimacy. Here, as well, the British use less physical contact than many other cultures. Touching is an area of great importance in care; some clients will welcome physical contact while others will not. It is a good idea to be guided by the way the client uses touch. If the client is physically expressive, he or she may not mind you mirroring his or her use of touch. However, if the client appears not to use touch, it is better to interact with him or her in the same way.

Gestures and body postures

These are popular topics of study. Here again, cultural differences will need to be taken into account. Gestures can reveal a great deal about an individual's emotional state. For example, fiddling with things and tapping can indicate stress, and so can embracing oneself, or placing the hands on the back of one's neck. In social situations, grooming, nibbling and tidying can indicate social anxiety.

Preparatory movements provide strong messages about the desires of individuals. Packing one's case to end a meeting, opening a door or rising from a chair to say goodbye to someone, or looking at one's watch to communicate an end to a conversation, are all powerful non-verbal signals.

Holding one's chin up communicates a desire to dominate. Nodding when listening communicates interest and support, and prompts the other person to continue to speak.

The skill of reading body language is important to be an effective care worker, and the student is well advised to develop such skills.

Activity 3.9

On your own, watch individuals and groups – on the bus, in restaurants, in family groups, etc. Watch for:
- facial expressions
- eye contact
- physical proximity
- gestures and postures.

Consider what you believe is being communicated. Repeat the exercise, watching your own body language in different situations.

The first steps in acquiring skills in non-verbal behaviour is to observe.

Assertive behaviour

Assertive behaviour is a way of behaving with other people, when a situation demands it, with a view to expressing honestly how we feel, and encouraging others to express their needs effectively. This way of behaving was popularised in the 1970s, as an off-shoot of behavioural therapy. Today, it is sometimes called 'personal effectiveness', and training in these skills is widely available, particularly for women.

The theory behind assertiveness assumes that there are three ways in which individuals may interact:

- **Aggressive behaviour** The overall goal is to win and demolish the other person's resistance. The rights of the other person are often violated, and the interaction is characterised by raised voices and angry personal attacks. It is virtually impossible, when being aggressive, for an individual to perceive another person's point of view. Aggressive individuals will often attempt to dominate the conversation.
- **Passive behaviour** The overall goal is to placate everyone and avoid conflict at all costs. To achieve this, the individual may refuse to respond appropriately, thus blocking further communication. Passive behaviour may be used to arouse guilt in another person. Passive individuals attempt to manipulate others.
- **Assertive behaviour** This is a way of behaving that fulfils six major requirements:
  - Assertive behaviour is **direct**.
  - Assertive behaviour is **honest**.
  - Assertive behaviour is **appropriate**.
  - Assertive behaviour is **informational**.
  - Assertive behaviour is **open** to further discussion.
  - Assertive behaviour is **responsible**.

If you have expressed what was important to you and allowed the other person to respond in his or her own way, you have been assertive, regardless of the outcome. Assertive behaviour is not about winning battles. It is about offering a choice in how to respond in a given situation, where, perhaps, none existed before. Assertion is an effective way to convey warmth and sincerity, through responding emotionally with reflective listening. Although assertive behaviour is primarily a verbal technique, it is supported by non-verbal techniques such a touching and posture. Putting an arm around someone in distress, or mimicking posture and movement, make assertive behaviour more effective.

We learn very early in life not to express our own needs in certain situations, where we allow ourselves to be dominated by other people. This is particularly true when dealing with people we perceive to be more powerful than ourselves. Assertive behaviour, however, assumes equal rights of expression for all people. For example, we all have the right to:

- change our minds and break commitments
- make mistakes
- make decisions or statements without justification
- not to know something or not to understand
- feel and express emotions, both positive and negative, without feeling that it is weak or undesirable to do so
- not to get involved in someone else's problems
- refuse demands made on us
- be the judge of ourselves and our own actions and the right to cope with the consequences
- do all of these things without giving any reasons for our actions.

The important thing about understanding interpersonal rights is they are just that – rights! You need not behave in these ways if you choose not to. However, it is your right to do so if you choose. Assertive behaviour is about alternatives and choices. There are times when it may be best not to be assertive, perhaps because you would not be pleased with the consequences. It is, however, important that you can be assertive where you feel you need to be, and that by doing so, you will achieve outcomes and goals that you set. Assertive behaviour is ineffective unless rapport is established at the same time.

Assertive behaviour is an important skill in negotiating, or working out differences between people. In reaching agreement or compromise, you begin by foregoing those demands on you which are relatively unimportant to you, but may provide difficulty for the other person. The other person should do the same for you. An effective compromise should take into account just a few items which really mean a lot to both of you, and can be dealt with without much resentment. It is very difficult to work out an effective compromise if assertive skills are not being used. Some of these skills, such as reflective listening and self-disclosure, have already been discussed.

Effective communication within groups

Much work in health and social care involves working in groups. Workers may be organised into groups, as may service users. Some of these groups will be natural and informal, while others may be structured and organised formally for specific purposes.

Groups are composed of individuals, so much of what we have already discussed in relation to individual interaction is also highly relevant for groups. Listening skills are very important, as are assertive skills. Individuals in groups possess the same rights, choices and freedom from discrimination we have already discussed in relation to individuals.

Groups are natural, and wherever people have contact with each other, groups will form. Individual members of a group will have their own personal expectations of what the group needs to provide them. For many, this will be a sense of belonging, safety and identity. On the other hand, the group itself will develop its own expectations. A group may exist to deal with specific tasks, share experiences or provide support. Once group goals are defined, there will be certain expectations which members may need to fulfil. Groups develop their own 'rules', and adaptation to these rules is part of the process of socialisation.

Groups can be very useful and productive in a number of areas:
- problem solving and decision making
- processing and sharing both information and feelings
- gathering ideas and suggestions
- gaining feedback on previous decisions
- increasing commitment and involvement
- negotiation and resolving conflicts.

Compatibility among group members helps the group to stabilise and survive. Developing cohesion is a primary objective of all groups. Cohesion is helped when:
- goals are clear
- all members listen
- all members contribute
- disagreements are comfortably dealt with
- hidden agendas are dealt with through assertive behaviour.

Hidden agendas are individual goals which oppose the outcomes desired by the group, and threaten group cohesion. Just as in interpersonal communication, groups should possess the ability to turn goals into outcomes. Outcomes should be clearly determined by the group early on, and rapport established among the members.

Individuals in groups should be aware of the interactive processes going on. Behaviour that demonstrates warmth, understanding and sincerity is a vital element in a successful group. Sensitivity is important. Tension must be detected early, and dealt with, as well as any bad feelings which are created. Negative acts produce negative responses in other people, so individual group members should remain positive, and not personally critical of others. Negative escalation will destroy group cohesion. Where there is potential for disagreement and negativity, the secret is not to challenge the person, only his or her information. This is where assertive behaviour can be really valuable. Just as negotiation was discussed with reference to assertive behaviour, it is also an essential group skill.

Tips on negotiating
- Establish rapport.
- Validate any proposal the other side makes as legitimate.
- Summarise what you understand to be their point of view or position.
- Do not become defensive.
- Do not attack.
- Do not personally insult.
- Remain flexible.
- Do not blame or accuse.
- Provide reasons before making proposals – only a few important ones, or the point might be lost.
- Express feelings as well as facts.
- Emphasise areas of agreement.
- Recognise and respect the value system of others.
- Question positions, but do not ignore them.

Groups are opportunities for close interpersonal contact, and work best when the goals of the group and the expectations of individual members are simultaneously met.

Behaviours helpful in group work

- **Questioning** – seeking information, opinions and ideas.
- **Listening** – showing verbally and non-verbally that you are paying attention, and understand what others are saying.
- **Informing** – giving helpful information, opinions and ideas.
- **Clarifying** – clearing up confusion, defining terms, and pointing out alternatives.
- **Sharing** – inviting comments using listening skills; keeping the communication channels open, and making people feel involved.
- **Supporting** – recognising the individual rights, choices and identity of group members.
- **Encouraging** – helping those who are shy, nervous, or reluctant to contribute. This involves being friendly, warm and responsive, both verbally and non-verbally.
- **Harmonising** – reconciling disagreements, reducing tension, and getting people to explore their differences constructively.
- **Assertion** – using the rules of assertion, particularly in negotiation, and to promote clarity and accuracy.
- **Constructive disagreement** – not upsetting people when there are disagreements. Other people's viewpoints may be incorporated into your own, so that the discussion becomes constructive. Focus first on what is agreed before disagreements are dealt with.
- **Humour** reduces tension.
- **Relaxation** – creating an atmosphere of calmness and confidence.
- **Cohesion** – referring to the group as a team, rather than as a collection of individuals.

Evaluating the effectiveness of interpersonal interaction

It is important that we have some measure by which we can evaluate how effective interpersonal interactions are. Listening is an important way of finding out how effective you are. Developing a style of interaction that effectively, but unobtrusively, checks out whether your understanding of the other person is correct, and whether what you have said has been understood, is of vital importance. We shall be examining in this chapter some techniques that you may wish to consider.

Specific training in interpersonal skills is essential for work in care. This will provide the opportunity, in relatively safe situations, of experimenting and practising. Your own improvement may be thereby systematically monitored for:

- quality of your contribution
- improvements from previous occasions
- knowledge and understanding.

This monitoring should be done with a variety of methods:

- Verbal feedback may be obtained from the individual with which you are interacting, or an observer, or both.
- Written feedback is best obtained from an independent observer, who may rate you against specific criteria (e.g. how many open questions were used).
- Video observation is useful, because you can observe your own behaviour, and may observe things you missed when in the process of interacting. An advantage of video observation is that you can watch it again and again.

- Self-reflection is useful in addition to the above three observational techniques. It is worth recording your own experience of the interview in some detail. The process of writing it down often makes things clearer. A traditional training method in social work is called 'process recording', which is a very detailed self-reflection on client interviews.

Observation of interaction is vital to understanding. Not just observing and reflecting on your own skills but observing others is also extremely valuable, and video-based learning programmes, such as *Caring for Mary*, allow the student to evaluate the interpersonal effectiveness of other care workers. Taking a step back to evaluate, enhances the care worker's sensitivity to the interpersonal world around him or her.

Ultimately, the care worker assumes a primary professional responsibility for the success of the interaction. Any misunderstanding on the part of the client, must be addressed by the care worker.

The meaning of communication is the response that you get. If you are not getting the response you want, change what you are doing.

The care worker must address any misundersanding on the part of the client

The support needed for effective interaction

In order for interaction to be effective, the situation within which the interaction takes place must be as supportive as possible. This means essentially having to remove as many sources of stress from the situation as possible. This may be achieved by the following:

- clearly introduce yourself
- clearly introduce any others present
- provide information about the background to the interaction
- ensure the physical environment is suitable, in that it is confidential and private, not noisy and uncomfortable
- the arrangement of seating should not reflect perceptions of power (e.g. one chair higher than another, or one participant behind a desk)
- all participants should have a clear view of each other
- establish rapport, making full use of non-verbal behaviour
- use open questions and self-disclosure where appropriate
- use reflective listening
- ensure all of the participants' uncertainties are resolved before concluding.

All of the skills explained in this chapter, whether in relation to individuals or groups, share the common objective of optimising the support of the interaction, and reducing the anxieties of participants.

In addition, the Value Base should always be applied. This means that the individuality of the participants is to be respected and positively responded to. Examples include arranging for translation where appropriate, respecting opinions which differ from your own, and exhibiting patience with those who have communication difficulties.

Chapter 4 discusses how care settings may be designed to support effective interaction.

Review questions

1 Give examples of how interpersonal skills can help to:
   a encourage personal preference
   b encourage choice
   c convey respect for others
   d convey warmth and sincerity.
2 Provide examples of how interpersonal skills can assist in anti-discriminatory practice.
3 How would the physical or intellectual abilities of clients affect the ways in which you communicate with them?
4 What is the relationship between the client's understanding of a quality service and the interpersonal skills of the care worker?
5 Explain the difference between technical quality in care and functional quality in care, and provide examples.
6 Define both verbal and non-verbal communication, and give examples of each.
7 Explain how effective listening can help understanding.
8 Define group cohesion, and give examples of obstacles to it.
9 Explain the differences between aggressive, passive, and assertive behaviours.
10 Explain the process of successful negotiation and compromise.
11 Identify and describe the different types of effective listening.

12 Discuss how our interpersonal skills can convey warmth, sincerity, and understanding, with particular reference to:
   a choice of words
   b tone of voice
   c body language.
13 What sources of data are used to evaluate effective interaction?
14 What are the different forms that interpersonal interaction may take?
15 What types of support may be provided in order to make interaction more effective?

Assignment 3.1
Understanding effective interpersonal interaction

This assignment provides knowledge, understanding and portfolio evidence for element 2.1, **Explore interpersonal interaction.**

In this chapter, we have described various ways to make interaction more effective. You will need to demonstrate that you have an understanding of these.

Your tasks

1 Write a report which explains each of the following in detail, and provide two examples of each:
   a communicating through language
   b communicating through sensory contact
   c communicating through activity.
2 **a** For each of your examples, explain how the interaction can be enhanced.
   b For each of your examples, explain also how the interaction can be inhibited.
Be sure that you include environmental, interpersonal and cultural factors for both **a** and **b**.
3 For each of the above forms of interaction (a to c), explain the effects that gender, age and culture may have. Be sure to address:
   ● use of sensory contact
   ● distance between individuals
   ● body language
   ● accepted forms of respect
   ● preferred forms of interaction
   ● personal strengths
   ● items of interest.
Evaluation of interpersonal interaction is an important way of improving skills.
4 Identify and describe as many ways as you can of evaluating interaction.
5 For each way you have identified, design a means of recording all relevant information for evaluation. This may include forms, feedback sheets, and ways of comparing your own perceptions to those of others. You should be able to use these sheets in Assignment 3.2.

Assignment 3.2
Demonstrating effective interpersonal skills

This assignment provides knowledge, understanding and portfolio evidence for element 2.2, **Demonstrate skills of interpersonal interaction.**

This assignment requires you to demonstrate basic effective interpersonal skills. You may find it useful to video-tape or audio-tape the interactions.

Your tasks

1 As a class, decide on at least three topics which can be discussed for each of the following situations:
   a one-to-one interactions
   b interaction with a small group
   c interaction with a large group.

Your topics should include some suitable for interaction with people of a different status to yourself (an adult, a child, a professional person). The people of different status may be genuine or role-played.

Your topics should also include an example of interaction through activity. You will need to produce evidence that one of the above interactions has been with individuals of a different status, and that one of the interactions has been an activity.

- *One-to-one interactions* These are best done in groups of three, where you can record a self-evaluation, a participant evaluation, and an observer evaluation. Choose one of the agreed topics, and take turns interacting one-to-one, with one observer. Use the forms developed in the previous assignment to record the evaluations.
- *Interaction with a small group* Organise the class into groups of five. Each group should select one of the agreed topics. The group should then engage in interaction, with each participant recording an evaluation on the forms developed in the previous assignment.
- *Interaction with a large group* The whole class may be used for this exercise, having selected a topic. Each participant should produce a self-evaluation, and an evaluation of at least one other person.

2 You will need to organise your evidence for your portfolio. For each of the above situations in which you participated, produce the following:
   a Someone else's evaluation of your performance.
   b Your own evaluation of your performance.
   c A report reflecting on the situation, comparing the evaluations, and making recommendations for improvement.

4 Methods of interacting with clients in health and social care

What is covered in this chapter

- The effects of different care settings on clients
- The optimisation of interaction in different care settings
- The effects of the caring relationship on clients
- Improving interactions in the caring relationship

These are the resources you will need for your portfolio for element 2.3:

- A report which:
  - explains four methods used to improve interaction in a caring relationship
  - recommends how interaction in a caring relationship with which you are familiar might be improved.
- A summary based on two care settings, one domestic, one institutional, which:
  - explains and contrasts the possible effects of the care settings on clients
  - explains two positive and two negative effects of the caring relationship for one client group
  - explains four ways of optimising interpersonal interaction.
- Your written answers to the activities, review questions and assignment in this chapter.

The effects of different care settings on clients

In the previous chapter we examined the role of the individual care worker in optimising interactions with clients. However, even the most skilled care worker may not succeed in settings where either the physical aspects of the service or the management regime inhibit both effective communication and implementation of the Value Base.

All people are influenced by the messages they receive from the settings they are in. These messages affect their expectations about their own abilities. In the care industry, these messages communicate what the care organisation, and society in general, think about the clients who use the services. The care setting and the atmosphere created in it, influence the receptivity of the client, and send out strong messages about the kind of behaviours expected.

The design of the care setting and the way in which it is managed indicate how important the individual is perceived to be. Successful care settings value the centrality of the individual by their location, physical design and management. Some assumptions, based on years of social psychological research, are that:

- people make conscious choices about their behaviours
- the information people use to make choices comes from their environment

- their choices are based on:
  - the things that are important to them
  - the views they have about their own abilities
  - the consequences they perceive resulting from the behaviours they choose.

The individual's environment is the most powerful source of information about behaviours and their consequences. We all learn from each new environment we are in, and possess complicated behaviours for many different settings. The ways in which we behave sitting in a college classroom will be different from the ways in which we behave in a pub in the evening. The different environments of the classroom and the pub send messages to us about what is deemed appropriate for each situation.

Activity 4.1

Compare the environment in your own home to a care setting with which you are acquainted. What do you feel as you enter each setting? What sorts of things can you do in one setting that you cannot do in the other?

The consumer benefit concept

Bateson (1977) argues that any service should be based on the *consumer benefit concept*. This concept proposes that the decisions taken by service organisations should be soundly based on how those decisions will affect the consumer. In care, that means that the ways in which the organisation provides its services (management), and the location and physical aspects of its settings should be wholly explained by how the client benefits. This concept is central to evaluating the effect of care settings.

Activity 4.2

Select a care setting, and describe a number of physical aspects of that setting (eating arrangements, sleeping arrangements, visiting, decor, etc.). List these aspects and for each one describe how the client benefits. If you cannot find any benefit for the client, you may need to ask some questions as to why the setting has been organised in that particular way.

Draw conclusions from this activity as to whether the setting is person orientated or institutionally based.

Location of the care service

One factor to consider is the location of the care service. Some clients will have services provided in their own homes. For the most part, this is an ideal situation, as the care provider must do the most adjusting. The client maintains control over the setting's appearance and demeanour. The care worker will probably be more conscious of respecting the client's space, and appreciating that the setting may be part of the client's emotional history.

It is important to note that not all clients will want to remain in their family homes. There may be unpleasant memories or social isolation. For a long time it was believed that institutionalisation was a function of physical settings. This is far from the whole story. Institutionalisation is a consequence of the style of caring. Where the service is not person-orientated, but rather constructed to fulfil the need and expediences of the organisation, institutionalisation will inevitably occur.

The impersonal regimentation of service delivery is not confined to institutions. The Care in the Community legislation has created many isolated individuals, totally institutionalised into their own homes and care plans. The mistake made here is to assume that care in the community is always a better option when available. The Value Base implies that the best option available is the one desired by the client, provided that meeting the client's requests is practicable.

Some clients will always need and prefer more institutional settings, such as day centres, clinics, residential or nursing homes, or hospitals. How can these settings be made more comfortable, and be made to contribute positively to the encouragement of interaction? While still on the topic of location, accessibility remains an important issue for care establishments.

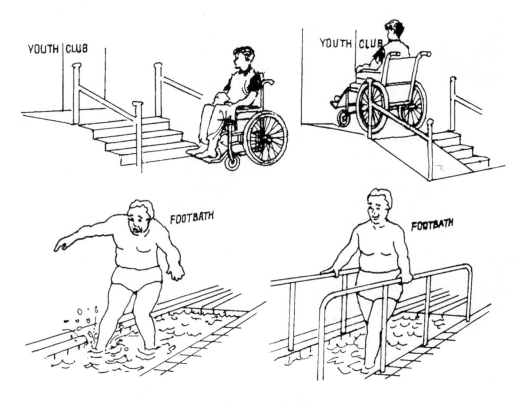

Some thought and simple changes can remove barriers to physical access

Where clients are not too disabled, they should use facilities that are close to local amenities and public transport. This will encourage the client to feel part of a community, and reflect the high regard with which client independence is valued by the care organisation. Accessibility also encourages visits from the client's friends and family. Safety and security are also important location issues, as badly lit or dangerous neighbourhoods will threaten client independence.

The optimisation of interaction in different care settings

Methods of analysing care settings

There are a couple of useful models from which we may analyse particular care settings. One model allows us to make judgements about the organisational style in delivering services. The second focuses on the more physical aspects of the care setting itself. It is important to have the means by which we can make objective evaluations of care settings, so that care workers may make recommendations for change which are:

- realistic in that they can be achieved
- valid in that they clearly satisfy the consumer benefit concept
- constructive in that the recommendations do not rely on criticism and negativity.

Care workers must possess a knowledge of the effects of the care setting on clients, and become aware of their own abilities to structure or make changes in the setting so as to encourage social interaction. An analysis of the care setting should be in relation to any constraints the setting imposes on clients, and on what opportunities exist to encourage interaction.

The style of the care service

A system of analysing the style of care services was devised by King and Morgan in 1976. Although their research was on the prison service, the model is more widely applicable. They identified five inter-related variables, describing the style of service offered:

1 Block treatment This is where the care is highly regimented. The administrative requirements of the organisation take precedence over all other considerations. Everything is run to a schedule, which must not be deviated from.

2 Rigidity This is a variable measure of to what degree clients are allowed to make some of their own choices. Unlike strict block treatment, the care service will have some degree of flexibility to permit this to happen.

3 Restrictiveness This is a measure of the amount of freedom allowed the client to go where he or she wishes to go. This may range from being locked into one room, to coming and going as the client pleases. Restrictiveness also considers the 'off-limits' area for clients. Some care establishments have separate dining facilities for staff and clients. Many establishments (particularly hospitals and colleges) even have quite separate toilets for staff and clients. The more 'no-go' areas for clients, the more the service is seen to be restrictive.

4 Supervision Part of the task of any care service is to observe. Observation is an important means of acquiring information. Nevertheless, there are numerous ways in which this may be achieved, ranging from observing in the course of interacting, to using two-way mirrors, which is infinitely more invasive. The extent of privacy allowed is important to evaluate. In some circumstances, where there is considerable risk, privacy may have to be forsaken in what is perceived to be the best interests of the client. However, in some care services, privacy is restricted for little reason. In deciding on a reasonable level of client supervision, the consumer benefit concept should be used.

5 Autonomy This is a measure of the extent of choice and control allowed the client over his or her own personal activities. Obviously, there may be good reasons to impose restrictions on autonomy, particularly where the risk to the client or others is too great. However, in King and Morgan's model, we are not looking at individual cases, but rather the accepted structures in the day-to-day running of a care service. Again, some services may severely restrict autonomy for no justifiable reason. In such circumstances, advocacy schemes should be organised and used.

A further aspect of autonomy is in respect of groups of clients. The concept of collective response refers to the amount of power the client group has over the running of the service. All care services must give considerable thought to involving client groups in planning and policy making.

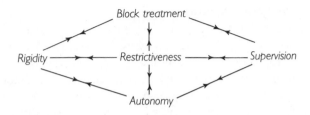

King and Morgan's model describing style of care service

The general ways in which service is provided is a function of the values of the organisation, and the effectiveness of the management in communicating these values. This is commonly referred to as the organisation's culture. Culture is the accepted, and often unquestioned, way of both thinking and doing within the organisation. Where care staff are not valued or rewarded for good work, we expect to see apathy, and poor service to the client. This is a very significant problem in care services.

It is generally agreed that senior managers establish the values they wish to see in the organisation. Management is the process through which these values are communicated and reinforced. Managers cannot be evaluated on what they say, or against 'mission statements'. They can only be evaluated by their behaviour. Management behaviour is an important part of the care setting. It establishes the culture of the service, and easily differentiates good service from bad.

The physical setting of the care service

Porras (1987) describes four aspects of the physical setting which have been shown to significantly affect behaviour. These are space configuration, physical ambience, interior design, and overall architectural design.

Space configuration

The ways in which space in the care setting is actually laid out affect clients' and care workers' behaviour in two ways. Physical restrictions may limit or direct the behaviour of people in the care setting as well as having psychological effects. Issues such as noisiness and privacy are important. Walls are good in that they may provide some privacy, but they may also create isolation. Both privacy and the opportunity for interaction are necessary, and creating the right balance in the physical environment is not easy. The location of lounges, eating areas, administrative facilities, bedrooms, activity areas and so on, determine what relationships are formed, who people approach for help and advice, and who they trust.

Physical ambience

This aspect of the physical setting includes lighting, heating, levels and types of noise, odours, and general cleanliness. These rather subtle variables can have a significant influence on the degree of comfort the client experiences.

An often debated issue in health and social care is the wearing of staff uniforms. This issue involves many complex variables, and it should not be assumed that there is one simple answer.

One variable is the requirement of protective clothing where needed. Some jobs in health and social care require the worker to wear suitable protective clothing. This will certainly be evident in hospitals, nursing homes and some residential homes.

Another variable is the specific role of the care worker. For example, in working with young people or some individuals with learning disabilities, particularly in the community, the care worker may need to dress casually and inconspicuously.

In important meetings or case conferences, the care worker may need to be dressed more smartly and formally.

Psychiatric nurses are an important example where uniforms have been largely abandoned in the last decade. This resulted from a shifting view of the mentally ill as sick to a view of the mentally ill as individuals with problems, who need to be befriended, supported and helped.

There are advantages and disadvantages associated with uniformed staff

Once again, the consumer benefit concept is important here, as the views of clients need to be valued. Many clients in hospitals and residential homes for elderly persons consistently express a desire for the staff to be uniformed. In fact, research from other service industries generally supports the view that where service personnel are in uniform, the 'feel-good' factor in using the service is enhanced. Hence, we now are seeing the staff in many service industries in uniform: in banks, shops, hotels, etc. The use of uniform in the personal service industries is said to create a stronger corporate image, and to reinforce the image of trustworthiness and professionalism of the staff.

There remains, however, a deep unease in the care industry about uniforms. It has long been felt that uniforms put barriers in the way of truly caring relationships. It may be possible that uniforms may, in some instances, enhance the caring relationship. Our concerns about a home help in uniform, may reflect our own prejudices and uncomfortableness about our clients. There may be an argument to create strong corporate identity in caring services, to reflect pride in the work that care workers do, and to develop a higher profile in the community. Should care workers be embarrassed about their vocation?

Activity 4.3

1 Divide the class into a number of small working groups. Each group will be assigned one client group. The group will then explore the range of care workers involved in providing services to that group, and discuss the pros and cons of staff uniforms.
2 Each group should then present its arguments to the whole class, with whom further discussion will take place. It may be interesting to put some of the suggestions about when uniforms may be appropriate to a vote.

Interior design

Many individuals use both social and physical cues from their environment to figure out what others think about them. Their perceptions of this often affect how they perceive themselves. Where clients are allowed an influence on the design of their immediate surroundings, they typically feel more a part of the care system, and feel more valued. Personalising the care setting results in more positive attitudes in clients. This may be achieved by using more personal effects – from plants and pictures to items of furniture. While this may be obvious in the client's personal space, much may also be achieved by allowing clients to personalise communal areas as well.

Generally, people feel more comfortable in 'warm' environments, where there are soft seats, subdued lighting, carpets, curtains, and pot plants. By involving clients, and avoiding harsh furnishings and lighting, the care setting can be optimised for supporting interpersonal interaction.

Architectural design

This refers to the overall structural design of the building in which the care service is provided. Many of the same comments about the architectural design can be made as with the interior design. The overall design of the building has a massive influence on how both clients and care workers perceive how others feel about them, and how individuals function in the care setting.

Activity 4.4

Choose a care setting with which you are familiar and, using the headings above, describe the physical aspects. For each physical aspect you described, explain the effect on clients. Make recommendations for improvement.

It is true to say that a day centre is not a service; an elderly persons' home is not a service; a hospital is not a service; and nor are clinics. These are all physical settings within which services are provided. The nature of care services is interpersonal – from person to person. However, it should be understood that the physical setting itself has a great effect on how and when clients and care workers interact.

Constraints on optimising interactions in the care setting

There are numerous reasons why many of the methods of optimising the care setting's effectiveness in supporting interaction are not used. Foremost is probably the cost.

Cost constraints

Cost should be borne in mind in relation to all possible improvements. Low staffing levels and old and dingy buildings are real problems in care services. Optimising the care setting would require these factors to be addressed and improved upon.

Case study

Myra Adams is an 83-year-old widow suffering from angina, impaired hearing and general fragility. She was assessed as needing home care assistance but this was withdrawn. Sally Hale, a home care worker, can no longer help Mrs Hale with heavy housework or personal laundry.

Source: UNISON

Health and safety concerns

Health and safety concerns are frequently used as reasons for limiting the freedom of clients. For example, an elderly persons' home may restrict clients to the lounge during the days, because they may be better supervised, and would not come into contact with potentially dangerous equipment, such as might be present in the kitchen. Naturally, the protection of clients is an important consideration, but must always be balanced with the need for autonomy. Unreasonable physical restrictions create feelings of negativity in clients, reinforcing the view that they are merely passive recipients of care, and are not valued as human beings.

Lack of training

Another problem is the relative lack of training of both care workers and their managers. While NVQs are making slow progress in the care industry, it is basic level care workers who are being targeted. Managers are still heard to say 'What Value Base?' Care workers are being asked to implement a value system which is not entrenched in their organisations. There is an urgent need to educate managers in the management of care services. The BTEC Higher National Certificate in the Management of Care Services is an example of one of the educative programmes on offer. However, at present, not enough managers have achieved this sort of qualification. These kinds of courses focus, among other things, on developing the care setting, and using the setting to further the aims of the service.

The manager of care should also be skilled in counselling and developing the care workers he or she manages, so that their skills and perceptions will continue to develop. Care workers enter into complex relationships with clients, which need a great deal of skill. The on-going development of interpersonal skills permits the worker to use his or her relationships with clients to promote positive feelings. However, the caring relationship is perhaps the most challenging feature of care work which the worker will ever encounter.

Activity 4.5

Describe any problems as you see them occurring over the course of a working day in a care setting. Explain how these problems might relate to:

a the physical aspects of the care setting
b the 'culture' of the care organisation
c poor management of the service.

This activity may also be done using the *Caring for Mary* video, either individually or in groups. By using such a video, all class members will be observing the same events, which can result in much interesting discussion.

The effects of the caring relationship on clients

The nature of the professional caring relationship

No aspect of being a worker in health and social care is more rewarding, or more problematic, than the relationship between the professional care worker and the client. The importance of that relationship cannot be overstated. It is absolutely essential to successful care provision, and respects the values of care, particularly the respect of individual dignity and the appreciation that each human being is special. It is difficult

The care worker needs to understand and communicate understanding on both emotional and intellectual levels

to reflect the nature of this relationship in words, as words possess a certain analytical coldness. The caring relationship is characterised by warmth and genuineness. The caring relationship is the soul – the very core – of professional care work.

The professional caring relationship is quite different from normal personal relationships. It differs in three major ways:

- **Purpose** The caring relationship is a *controlled* involvement with the client. Its purpose is to provide an atmosphere or milieu through which the caring service may be offered and accepted. This is developed quite clearly from the Care Value Base. The Value Base is a statement which summarises the basic terms upon which a client will accept the relationship. The caring relationship is the avenue through which the service is delivered. No matter how well resourced the service may be, it will be of little use unless it is delivered through the caring relationship.

- **Orientation** The caring relationship is solely devoted to meeting the needs of the client. The worker's own personal interests are not imposed on it. The worker uses his or her knowledge and skills to provide a service that the client needs and wants. The professional care worker is motivated by the ideal of service to others, rather than personal profit or gain. The relationship recognises the potential of the client, and seeks to develop that potential.

- **Objectivity** The caring relationship is based on objectivity. The care worker does not respond to the client from his or her own feelings. The care worker uses that information to assess the effects the client has on others, and to offer help and support. This requires care workers to be creative and responsive, and very much aware of personal hang-ups which might interfere in their work. Accurate self-awareness is very important for the care worker. A thorough knowledge of human growth and development, psychology and social behaviour is necessary as a

framework in which the individual client may be understood. In fact, one may view all the other chapters in this book – representing all the other units of the GNVQ – as providing the necessary underpinning of the knowledge you will require to make the caring relationship work.

Types of caring relationships

There are essentially two types of relationships in which the care worker will be involved: collaboration and bargaining.

Collaboration

Using the Value Base as a starting point, the care worker must establish a working agreement with the client. Regardless of what the worker's personal beliefs may be, he or she must instil trust and confidence into the relationship. This is achieved by being sensitive to the client's perceptions. The collaborative relationship is based on a model of participation and partnership. The process of caring is 'owned' by both the client and the worker. There is always some form of 'contract', either explicit or implicit. In all cases the 'contract' is the result of discussion and negotiation, and will provide clarity to the purpose and nature of the caring relationship. The actual working relationship with the client is enhanced by actively attending to the client, using many of the skills described in Chapter 3. Of particular importance are the skills of rapport and reflective listening.

Bargaining

Caring relationships often begin with a gross imbalance of power between the care worker and the client. The initial aim of the caring relationship is to rebalance the power between care worker and client. This will allow both the care worker and the client to achieve goals through the relationship. The client is often weakened by being dependent on the care worker, and may be reluctant to confide, or even interact. In some cases the client may be positively hostile and aggressive toward others. In such situations, it may be necessary to 'bargain' with the client. This may be particularly important where the care of the client imposes certain restrictions on choice or movement. Often, poor interpersonal relations are a principal source of unhappiness for individuals. The care worker needs to convince the client of the benefits of the caring relationship. The skills of negotiation in Chapter 3 are particularly useful here.

Improving interactions in the caring relationship

Implementation of the caring relationship

In the process of care planning (see Chapter 11), a key worker is often identified. The key worker is the individual care worker who will be expected to develop a primary caring relationship with the client. The client should be able to select a key worker, or request a change. Where the client is incapable of this, an advocate should be used.

The caring relationship will never be static. It will change over time, and will be quite different from client to client. While it is important that the relationship be focused on agreed issues of care, it should not be clinical in nature. The relationship will be as human as the care worker is capable of. Rigid responses should be avoided, and flexibility is an important attribute of the relationship. In order to make the caring relationship comfortable and more natural, it should reflect all of what is involved in life. It should not just be task based, but include subjects such as poetry, music, books, fun, politics, and hobbies. Almost all caring relationships are temporary in nature, and sight of this fact should never be lost. Clients should not be led to believe that you, personally, will always be there for them. However, the relationship can still be something quite special, and this may be best achieved by thoughtfulness in attending to details.

Controlled involvement

The professional caring relationship is composed of a controlled involvement. Biestek (1957) provides a useful model of how the involvement may be controlled.

> **Biestek's model**
>
> **Sensitivity** The care worker must demonstrate sensitivity to the client's feelings at all times. This is not just understanding on the part of the care worker, but effective demonstration, using the skills describes in Chapter 3.
>
> **Understanding** The special kind of understanding that is typical of the caring relationship is understanding that is wholly in relation to the client – who they are and what difficulties they may be facing.
>
> **Response** While there may be many practical tasks involved in caring for the client, response must always incorporate feelings. These feelings may be communicated

either verbally or non-verbally. The response the care worker makes to the client should communicate an acceptance of that client. Acceptance is communicated through warmth, courtesy, respect, concern, and interest. Clients may posses beliefs that we do not share, and behave in ways of which we do not approve. Clients usually both fear and expect disapproval, because they sometimes lack self-esteem. It is important to note that acceptance does not mean approval.

Activity 4.6

Using the three headings above (sensitivity, understanding, and response) discuss each one with reference to the skills described in Chapter 3. It is important that the concepts which underpin the nature of the caring relationship are clearly linked to the skills required.

Activity 4.7

Using observations made in a care service of your choice, or using a video such as *Caring for Mary*, discuss the relationships you observe with reference to the concepts developed in this chapter. If you are in a class situation, using the video will be useful because you will all be observing the same relationships.

Guidelines for caring relationships

Establishing and maintaining effective caring relationships is not easy. Aside from the skills involved, the relationship must be continually monitored. It may be useful to use a list of questions to ask yourself.

1 What are the values upon which I am establishing this relationship?
2 How do I personally feel about this client?
3 Are there any conflicts between my values and how I feel?
4 What am I communicating to this client both verbally and non-verbally?
5 Am I and the client considered equal partners in the relationship?
6 Am I clear about what the outcomes of this relationship is to be?
7 To what extent does this relationship require an emotional component, and how will I manage it?
8 How long is this relationship likely to last?

It is clear from the above list of questions that there is much to think about in any professional caring relationship. The individual care worker needs support on the job in order to be effective in such relationships.

Activity 4.8

In a care service of your choice, how are the eight questions listed above dealt with? Describe the methods used on the job to support the worker in his or her caring relationships. If you cannot find much evidence of support, discuss how the effectiveness of the service might be improved if such support was available.

A conceptual understanding of the nature of the caring relationship does not provide the skills required for either establishing it or maintaining it. These skills are developed through repeated intelligent practice, enhanced by skilled supervision on the job. The concept of coaching or supervision in care services in built around developing skills in professional caring relationships. Undoubtedly, this is the most challenging aspect of caring and, as such, there are many problems associated with it.

Problems in caring relationships

The use of professional caring relationships between client and care worker is at the heart of caring. It is vital to the success of the service that these relationships are optimised. Lack of attention to the caring relationships means not just failure to provide an effective service, but causing considerable damage and distress to clients.

There are many common problems that arise in caring relationships, and it is useful to recognise them when they occur.

Common problems

Lack of self-awareness Not all relationships will work or go smoothly. Invariably, this is due to the care worker's lack of self-awareness in some areas. This is the sort of issue where regular supervision is useful, and perhaps continued training. Care workers have a professional obligation to strive continuously to develop their awareness and skills, and there is a responsibility on the part of the agency which employs them to ensure this happens through the provision of supervision and training.

Loss of respect for the client We have stressed the importance of acceptance of the client in the caring relationship. This is based on the philosophical conviction that every person has innate dignity and worth. However, sometimes the client may behave in ways, or express beliefs or feelings, which may be reprehensible to us. Only a skilled care worker can successfully manage such a dilemma. When the care worker experiences difficulty with this, supervision should be urgently sought.

Over-identification Sometimes, the care worker feels very strongly about the difficulties a client is experiencing. Perhaps the care worker has had personal experience of similar problems. Commonly, this may involve attitudes toward authority. The worker soon starts to respond to his or her own needs, rather than the client's. Here too, diligence is required, and supervision should be urgently sought.

The feeling of power Sometimes, the care worker will assume that because he or she has the responsibility of care, this is somehow a statement of competence, which is interpreted as a hallmark of personal adequacy. The powerlessness of the client can provide a real sense of control on the part of the care worker. When things go well, the care worker takes the credit. However, when things go badly, the client is often blamed. Clients do not often share the freedoms which the care worker may have. The care worker may withdraw from the relationship, while the client is dependent on it. Examples of withdrawal include changing jobs or gaining promotion. These problems are quite serious, and often not just the fault of the individual care worker, but of the whole culture of the care setting. In order to avoid this problem developing, active vigilance is required by both care workers and managers.

Insincerity This is often the problem of the more seasoned care worker, who has given so much emotionally, with little reward.

Most care workers seek moral, rather than financial, rewards and the feedback they require to continue to motivate them is often lacking. Care workers are in danger of not just ceasing to care, but of actually despising their clients. A teenager in care once accused a care worker of being an 'emotional prostitute'. The care worker, she claimed, established caring relationships for money. Is this not immoral? While this is a serious allegation which must be addressed, it is hoped that it is not the money which is the initial attraction for the care worker. After all, the care industry is notoriously underpaid. Nevertheless, the sources of satisfaction for the worker are fragile. The process of supervision, and the ways in which the service are managed must be orientated to preventing the care worker from losing his or her sincerity.

Ruthlessness and expediency Care workers often face emotional bombardment, and develop high levels of stress. In this condition, the care worker cannot thoughtfully monitor his or her relationship with the client. Remember, the professional caring relationship is controlled: it has boundaries. Under stress, however, these boundaries may be overstepped. Workers respond by doing what is most expedient – the easiest course. This results in inappropriate ruthlessness, where clients' feelings are not considered. The recognition of stress in care work is important.

Methods of stress reduction at work should be used, and care workers should be taught the techniques of stress management. Caring and concerned employers also establish staff counselling services. The care organisation must address this most problematic, and inevitable outcome of ruthlessness and expediency caused by understaffed resources, overworked care workers, and unskilled managers.

The feeling of power: one of the common problems a care worker must recognise

The six problems for caring relationships described above are serious and commonplace. They are issues which must be focused on by every care organisation. If they are not addressed and resolved, it will be the professional caring relationships that will be damaged, and along with them the individuals who use care services.

Activity 4.9

Analyse a care setting of your choice for problems in care relationships. Interview staff about their feelings with regard to the six problem areas above. Draw conclusions and make realistic, valid, and constructive recommendations for improvements.

The enhancement of interaction with clients in health and social care depends upon a variety of factors involving both the care setting and the caring relationship. It is important to understand how problems arise. Some problems result from care workers not being very good at their job. However, even more problems are organisationally-based. To maximise the effectiveness of both care settings and caring relationships in achieving the aims of health and social care, the potential problems must be addressed by care organisations. First, they must be recognised. Second, they must be solved. The solutions will require commitment and creativity on the part of all care workers and managers.

Review questions

1 What is the relationship between the care environment and the behaviour of individuals?
2 Should clients be cared for in institutional settings, or in their own homes?
3 What is the difference between the style of the care service and the setting of the care service?
4 What are the four aspects of the physical setting that can be analysed?
5 What issues need to be considered in describing the appropriate dress for care workers?
6 What are the three ways the professional caring relationship differs from normal relationships?
7 In what ways is involvement in the caring relationship controlled?
8 What are the six major problems of caring relationships?
9 What does the 'culture' of a care organisation mean?
10 What support do care workers need in monitoring their caring relationships?

Assignment 4.1
Optimising caring interactions

This assignment provides knowledge, understanding and portfolio evidence for element 2.3, **Analyse methods of interacting with clients in health and social care.**

Your tasks

1 This task is based on your experiences in a work placement. You will need to select a client from your placement, with whom you have a relationship.

   a Write a report which explains in detail, at least four methods which may be used to improve interaction in a caring relationship. These may include, the personal appearance of care workers, supplying appropriate information, empowerment of clients, education and training for care workers, and support for care workers.

   b You have selected one client in placement, with whom you have a relationship. With reference to the issues covered in this chapter, evaluate that relationship, and make recommendations as to how interaction in that relationship might be improved.

2 Select two different care settings: one must be institutional, and the other domestic (i.e. in the client's own home).

   a Provide a description of the two settings.

   b Using the two settings, explain the effects that each setting has on the clients who use them.

   c Within those two settings, explain at least four ways in which interaction might be optimised.

3 Select one client group. For that group, explain at least two positive and two negative effects that the caring relationship might result in.

5   The structure and function of human body systems and organs

What is covered in this chapter

- The function and roles of major cell components
- Tissue types
- The interpretation of micrographs
- Cellular respiration
- Systems and functions of the human body
- Homeostatic mechanisms and factors regulated by homeostasis
- The effects of aging

These are the resources you will need for your portfolio for element 3.1:
- A report explaining:
  - the role of types of major cell components in human body cells
  - the processes involved in cellular respiration.
- A summary of an investigation which:
  - describes the key features of the four main tissue types in relation to their respective functions
  - identifies each of the different types of tissue from micrographs.

These are the resources you will need for your portfolio for element 3.2:
- A short report describing, in broad terms, how body systems carry out the functions of communication, support and locomotion, reproduction, energy supply, excretion and defence.
- Notes on homeostasis which:
  - explain homeostatic mechanisms
  - identify the normal ranges for temperature, blood sugar and respiratory rate.
- A short report describing changes in support/locomotor and reproductive systems throughout life.

Finally:
- Your written answers to the activities, review questions and assignments in this chapter.

The function and roles of major cell components

The human body is made up of an enormous amount of tiny units of living material called cells. Groups of cells form tissues and these tissues make up the organs that are concerned with the functions of our bodies. The organs, in turn, are grouped into systems which function interdependently. The study of the form and arrangement of organs is called *anatomy*, sometimes referred to as *structure*. *Physiology* relates to the working of the organs, and may be referred to as *function*.

As creatures evolved with more cells it became necessary for different cells to adopt certain functions. This process of specialisation is called *differentiation*; it is vital to the functioning of the human body.

Examples of differentiated cells

Type of cell	Function
A nerve cell	Conduction of impulses
A red blood cell	Transport of oxygen
An egg cell	Reproduction
A muscle cell	Contraction
A gland cell	Secretion

Despite cells being highly differentiated all animal cells have certain common features:
- They are enclosed by a membrane (plasma membrane), which is semi-permeable. Water and nutrients can pass into the cell, but not all substances.
- They have a nucleus; the control centre of the cell. Genetic material is contained within the nucleus; this acts as a 'blueprint' for the replication of the cell. The genetic material is carried on a highly specialised substance called DNA (deoxyribonucleic acid).
- They are filled with cytoplasm; a jelly-like substance in which the chemical reactions of the cell can take place.
- Within the cytoplasm are organelles; tiny bodies of which there are several types, each with its own function. Ribosomes and endoplasmic reticulum play a part in protein synthesis; mitochondria extract energy from glucose.

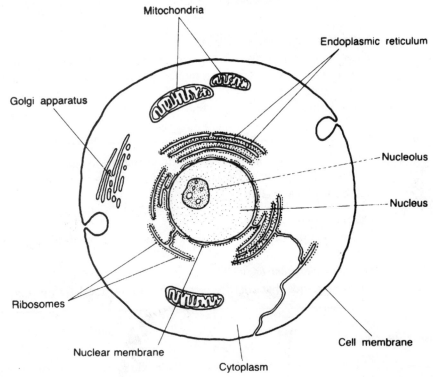

A typical animal cell

Tissue types

The different tissues of the body are made up of groups of cells of the same type. There are four main tissue types
- epithelial (protective, secretory)
- connective (support)
- nervous (communication)
- muscle (movement).

Epithelial tissue

Epithelial tissue is made up of cells that form a continuous layer and cover external and internal surfaces. They protect, repair and regulate the passage of substances that cross them, and may be absorptive or secretory.

There are two categories of epithelial tissue:
- covering and lining
- glandular.

Covering and lining epithelial tissue
These are further subdivided into:
- **Squamous epithelium** Flattened, thin, irregularly-shaped cells that line the body cavities, blood and lymphatic vessels. Stratified and keratinized squamous epithelium form the outer layer of the skin.
- **Cuboidal epithelium** Cube-shaped cells that line the kidney tubules and cover the ovaries.
- **Columnar epithelium** Elongated, pillar-shaped cells with the nucleus usually located near their base. They are often ciliated (covered with tiny hairs) at the outer surface. They are widely distributed throughout the body, for example, lining the digestive system.

Glandular epithelial tissue
These comprise cells which are specialised to secrete substances such as milk, perspiration, sex cells and hormones. There are two categories of glandular tissue:
- exocrine
- endocrine.

Activity 5.1

From the following information, identify the meanings of the prefixes 'exo' and 'endo'. Try to find other words, relating to the structure and function of the human body, that also have these prefixes.

Exocrine glandular tissue
This makes up glands with a duct to the outside surface (e.g. sweat and mammary glands).
Endocrine glandular tissue
Ductless glands that secrete directly into the bloodstream (e.g. thyroid, pituitary).

Connective tissue

These are made up of cells whose intercellular secretions support and hold together the other cells of the body, forming an intercellular matrix. There are two categories of

connective tissue:
- fibrous
- supporting.

Fibrous connective tissue

This is made up of widely distributed cells with supportive carbohydrate and flexible protein secretions. They form tendons and ligaments and wrap many organs, muscles and nerves.

Supporting connective tissue

These can be further subdivided into:
- **Cartilage** Its cells secrete a firm, rubbery matrix. They support the embryonic skeleton and parts of the adult skeleton.
- **Bone** Calcium salts are secreted into cartilage, imparting great strength. Bone supports the skeleton and protects the nervous system.
- **Areolar tissue** This may be described as the general packing and supporting tissue of the body. The basement membrane is a thin layer of modified connective tissue supporting layers of cells to be found at the base of the epidermis (see *Skin*, pages 101–2).

Nervous tissue

This is made up of elongated cells or neurons specialised for the expression of irritability or conductivity. Irritability is the capacity of cytoplasm to respond to a stimulus. Irritability is an expression of life itself and disappears with cell death. Conductivity indicates that cytoplasm can transmit a wave of excitation (an electrical impulse) throughout the cell from the point of stimulus. This is also known as excitability and is a property that is highly developed in the cell membrane of nerve cells.

There are two categories of nervous tissue:
- that which forms the central nervous system; the brain and spinal cord
- that which forms the peripheral nervous system, ganglia, autonomic nervous system and sense-organ nerve endings (see *The nervous system*, pages 95–9).

Muscle tissue

This comprises elongated, cylindrical or spindle-shaped cells containing contractile fibres. They perform mechanical work by contracting. *Contractility* is the property of changing shape, usually in the sense of shortening, and is highly developed in muscle cells.

There are three categories of muscle tissue:
- **Cardiac muscle tissue** This consists of branching fibres with many nuclei and striations. Cardiac muscle is under involuntary control, and is located only in the walls of the heart.
- **Skeletal muscle tissue** This consist of elongated cylindrical fibres with many nuclei and striations. It is under voluntary control. In general it is attached in bundles to the bones of the skeleton.
- **Smooth muscle tissue** This is made up of spindle shaped uninucleate cells with no visible striations. It works under involuntary control and generally occurs, for example, in sheets in the walls of the digestive tract.

Case study

Abnormal cell physiology – epithelial cells

Kirsty, a five-year old girl, contracted what appeared to be the flu. Her mother kept her away from school. Kirsty became weak; she had a raised temperature; her body ached and she suffered from diarrhoea and vomiting immediately after attempting to eat anything.

The family GP diagnosed *viral enteritis*. He instructed Kirsty's mother to give her fluids only for the following two days, after which she should gradually be able to resume eating solid food. A special fluid, containing glucose and electrolytes was prescribed.

Kirsty's condition was caused by a virus that invades the intestine via the epithelial cells in its lining, thereby disrupting normal cellular function. As the virus replicates inside cells, it decreases the cells' ability to use cell energy for cell processes. The virus often destroys many of the intestinal epithelial cells it invades. Because of this, normal digestion of food is interfered with.

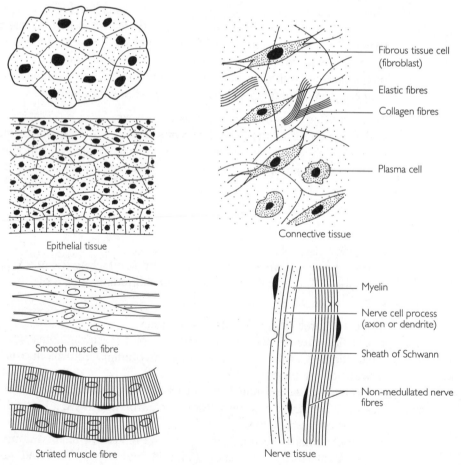

Epithelial tissue

Connective tissue

Fibrous tissue cell (fibroblast)

Elastic fibres

Collagen fibres

Plasma cell

Smooth muscle fibre

Striated muscle fibre

Nerve tissue

Myelin

Nerve cell process (axon or dendrite)

Sheath of Schwann

Non-medullated nerve fibres

Tissue types

The interpretation of micrographs

A *micrograph* is a photograph of a minute object or specimen as seen through a microscope. An electron micrograph is a graphic reproduction of an object as viewed with an electron microscope.

In order that cells and tissues can be studied, they have to be suitably prepared for microscopic examination. Generally, fixed and stained preparations of specimens are used, which then become permanent. Fixing fluids preserve the specimen. Staining enhances natural contrasts, to make more obvious various cell and tissue components.

Simple and stratified squamous epithelial tissue

The section on tissue types refers to squamous epithelium and its physical characteristics. Simple squamous epithelium is composed of very thin, flat cells of irregular outline fitted closely together to form a continuous sheet. From the surface, this epithelium has the appearance of a tiled floor, but with grossly irregular outlines. Stratified squamous epithelium is a thick membrane: its deeper cells varying from cuboidal to columnar; its basal layer showing considerable irregularity.

Activity 5.2

From the slides of micrographs, identify which is of simple squamous epithelium, and which is of stratified squamous epithelium, referring to the descriptions just given of each.

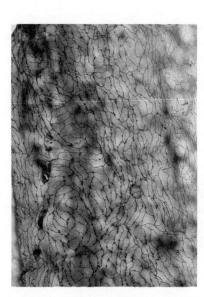 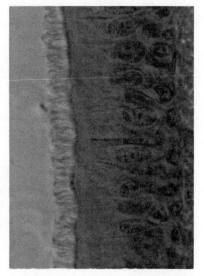

Skeletal muscle tissue

This was also described in the section on tissue types. Fibres are skeletal muscle that is striped (striated) in appearance.

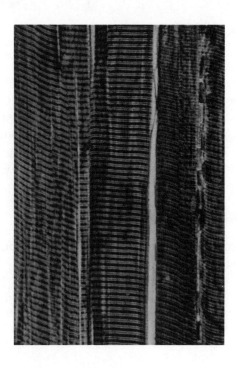

Micrograph of a section of striated skeletal muscle

Connective tissue

Blood

Blood is composed of plasma, red cells (erythrocytes), white cells (leucocytes) and platelets. In this instance, leucocytes will be used for illustrative purposes.

There are two main types of leucocytes
- agranular
- granular.

Although there are different types of leucocyte, they are all concerned with fighting disease.

Agranular leucocytes

- **Lymphocytes** The most striking feature of the lymphocyte is that it has a relatively large nucleus surrounded by a narrow rim of cytoplasm. The nucleus appears spherical and generally shows a small indentation to one side.
- **Monocytes** Large cells with a nucleus that is kidney shaped, sometimes with a deep indentation.

Granular leucocytes

- **Neutrophils** These show specific granules. The nucleus can show a variety of forms, but usually shows three to five irregular lobes.
- **Eosinophils** These are larger than neutrophils; the nucleus is usually bi-lobed. The cytoplasm is filled with coarse granules of uniform size.
- **Basophils** About the same size as neutrophils. Their nucleus is often irregular in outline. The cytoplasmic granules are spherical. Some characteristically overlie the nucleus and tend to obscure its outline.

Activity 5.3

From the five types of leucocyte described try to identify the three cells shown on the following micrograph.

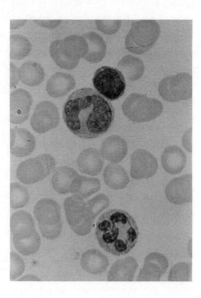

Compact bone

To the naked eye, compact bone appears to be solid. It is actually made up of lamellae (layers) regularly arranged in a manner determined by the distribution of blood vessels which nourish the bone. Between the layers are small cavities, or lacunae, which contain the bone cells. The bone is crossed by longitudinal channels (haversian canals), which cross over each other at different angles. The following shows a micrograph of compact bone.

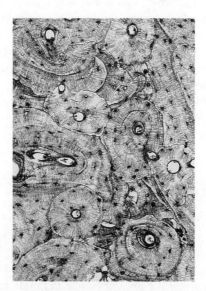

A micrograph of compact bone

Cellular respiration

There are two definitions that are important:
- **Metabolism:** The flow of materials through the living system.
- **Catabolism:** The breakdown of food compounds or cytoplasmic constituents into simpler compounds (see *The functions and roles of major cell components*, pages 78–9).

Cell metabolism involves one of two biochemical pathways; one that requires oxygen, and one that does not. If oxygen is available, glucose and fatty acids can be catabolised to acetic acid and then further catabolised to water and carbon dioxide. This is known as the Krebs Cycle.

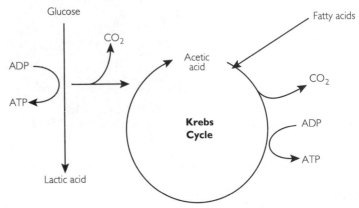

The Krebs Cycle

If oxygen is in short supply, glucose can be catabolised into lactic acid. The build-up of lactic acid in the muscle can be painful. To avoid the muscle over-using the anaerobic system of energy production, it is important to warm up gradually before strenuous exercise, so that muscle cells produce energy in the presence of oxygen.

The catabolism of glucose to acetic acid and ultimately to water and CO_2, is termed *aerobic* cellular respiration, because oxygen is needed. Aerobic cellular respiration produces a great amount of ATP energy for the cell.

ATP (Adenosine triphosphate) is the immediate source of energy in the muscle. ATP is broken down to ADP (Adenosine diphosphate) when energy is required. For the continuing production of energy, a cyclical process involving the resynthesis of ATP is necessary.

The aerobic metabolism process occurs within the mitochondria; specialised structures within the cell (see *The functions and roles of major cell components*, pages 78–9).

Case study

The heart attack

James Anderson is a 56-year-old management executive. One day at work, he felt a crushing pain in his chest and experienced shortness of breath. His worried colleagues called an ambulance immediately. At the Accident and Emergency department, a myocardial infarction or (heart attack) was diagnosed. The results of blood tests showed that he had raised levels of lactic acid in his blood, as a result of his heart attack.

The catabolism of glucose to lactic acid is called glycolysis. Oxygen is neither used or needed. Cells will use glycolysis in greater proportion to aerobic respiration in such conditions as when there is inadequate blood flow to the cell, for example in heart failure, as in the case of Mr Anderson. Although glycolysis is useful in that it produces energy in times of oxygen scarcity, it can be detrimental if the process continues for too long. Lactic acid will lower the blood pH, which should be kept in a state of constant slight alkalinity. The respiratory centre in the medulla of the brain is particularly sensitive to any change in the pH of the blood.

Activity 5.4

Read the section on *Homeostasis*, further on in this chapter. Which part of the last paragraph describes a state of homeostasis, and refers to homeostasis being disturbed?

The prefix 'myo' refers to muscle. Infarction means 'death'. The term 'myocardial infarction', therefore refers to death of heart muscle, which has been starved of its oxygen supply, due to a blocked coronary artery.

Systems and functions of the human body

An awareness of the structure of the body, the inter-relationship of its parts, and the way in which these parts function enhances the skills of the individual who cares for others. An insight into systems and functions of the human body underpins the carer's ability to recognise disorder. Furthermore, carers would benefit from a degree of understanding of the rationale for treatment of disease, including any procedures they may be required to participate in, such as urine testing. Such a rationale has its basis in an understanding of the body's systems and functions.

An awareness of these systems and functions also helps the individual to be more in tune with the functioning of his or her own body and therefore to understand, for example, the benefits of adopting a healthy lifestyle.

Case study

Teaching self-care

Mrs Williams, aged 75 years, lives alone. She was admitted to hospital for stabilisation of her diabetes mellitus. The Ward Doctor ordered investigations of her blood to detect the levels of her blood glucose. On receipt of the results of the blood test, the Doctor ordered a special diet for Mrs Williams, in conjunction with medication that would stimulate cells in her body to produce more insulin, in order to promote utilisation of the glucose. The nurses taught Mrs Williams to test her urine on a daily basis for the presence of glucose, so that her stabilised condition could be monitored.

The above case study demonstrates that a basic knowledge of a particular system (i.e. the endocrine system) of the body, along with its functions, will enable carers not only to understand more about the condition of diabetes mellitus, but also to be able to carry out procedures related to this condition armed with knowledge and understanding that gives meaning to this aspect of their work. The carers in this case were also able to pass on their knowledge so a self-testing regime could be established.

The systems of the body

For communication:
- Circulatory
- Nervous
- Endocrine
- Sense organs

For support and locomotion:
- Musculo-skeletal
- Nervous

For reproduction:
- Reproductive organs
- Endocrine
- Circulatory

For energy supply:
- Digestive
- Respiratory
- Circulatory

For excretion:
- Renal
- Respiratory
- Skin
- Liver

For defence:
- Skin
- Immune
- Circulatory
- Lymphatic

The skeletal system

Functions: support and locomotion

The skeleton is the framework which gives the body its shape. The skeleton is composed of two types of tissue; cartilage and bone (see *Tissue types*, pages 80–2).

Cartilage is softer than bone. It forms the temporary skeleton of the developing foetus, but is gradually replaced almost entirely by bone. It is, however, retained throughout life on the joint surfaces of many bones, and as the costal (pertaining to the ribs), nasal, laryngeal ('voice-box') tracheal ('wind-pipe') and bronchial cartilages. (The bronchi are the tubes leading from the trachea into the lungs – see *The respiratory system*, pages 105–7.)

Bone is rigid and non-elastic. It is formed by a process called ossification, which is not complete until an individual reaches the early twenties. Most bones are formed originally by replacement of cartilage. Osteoclasts destroy unwanted cartilage while osteoblasts build bone around themselves by removing calcium from the bloodstream and becoming osteocytes. The process commences in the middle of the shaft of a long bone, from whose centre calcium is laid down in both directions, forming the diaphysis.

This occurs when the baby is *in utero;* after the birth secondary centres develop at the ends of the bone. These ossified extremities are called the epiphyses. The rudimentary cartilage (perichondrium) becomes the periosteum (outside layer of bone). Spongy, or cancellate bone is found inside.

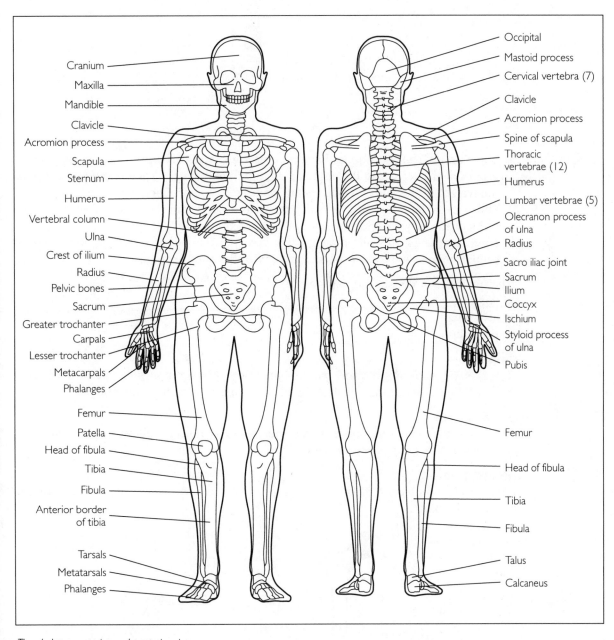

The skeleton: anterior and posterior view

There are four categories of bone:
- **Long bones** These provide the framework of the limbs and allow movement. Each long bone has a tubular shaft with a central cavity called the medullary canal, and two rounded extremities. The tibia is an example of a long bone.

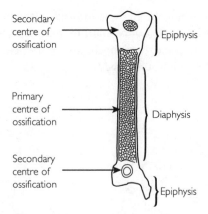

The formation of bone

- **Short bones** The short bones have no uniform shape. They are collected together in groups at the wrist and the ankles, forming units that are strong enough to support the weight of the body. A talus is an example of a short bone.
- **Flat bones** The bones of the skull, thorax and pelvis are flat bones. They form the walls of the major cavities of the body, protecting their contents.
- **Irregular bones** The vertebrae and the bones of the face are irregular in form and cannot, therefore, be categorised with any of the above groups.

The functions of the skeleton are to provide:
- support
- attachment
- protection.

Support
The skeleton supports the soft parts of the body. All the tissues except cartilage and bone are soft. The arrangement of the bones also gives shape to the body.

Attachment
The skeleton gives attachment to the muscles. The muscles allow movement made possible by the joints of the skeleton.

Protection
The skeleton protects the more delicate parts of the body, for example, the cranium protects the brain.

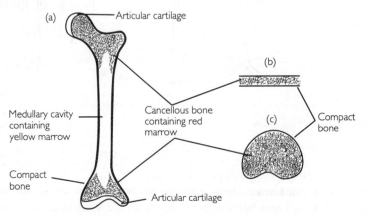

The structure of (a) a long bone, (b) a flat bone and (c) an irregular bone

Joints

Wherever one bone meets another, there is a joint. Joints are classified by the amount of movement that is possible between the articulating surfaces. The classifications are as follows:

- **Synarthroses** Fixed joints at which there is no movement, for example between the bones of the skull; also referred to as fibrous joints.
- **Amphiarthroses** Joints at which slight movement is possible, for example, between the vertebrae; also referred to as cartilaginous joints.
- **Diarthroses** Also known as synovial joints, these are freely movable although their actual movement is restricted by the ligaments that hold the bones together. Synovial joints have a fluid-filled cavity between their surfaces. The fluid acts as a lubricant.

Synovial joints are classified as follows:

- **Gliding joints** Small flat surfaces which glide on each other. The joints between the neural arches of the vertebrae are examples of gliding joints.
- **Hinge joints** Movement is only possible in one plane, for example the elbow joint.
- **Condyloid** Movement is angular in two planes with slight circumduction, for example the wrist joint. (*Circumduction* refers to a movement of the extremity of a part around in a circle.)
- **Saddle joints** Angular movements and circumduction can be performed freely, but rotation is impossible, for example, the thumb.
- **Ball and socket** This joint is shaped as a rounded head fitted into a cup-shaped cavity. Angular movements, circumduction and rotation can be performed freely, for example the hip joint.

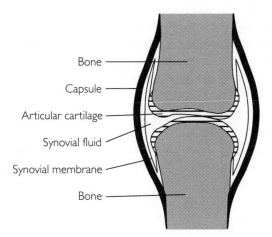

Bone
Capsule
Articular cartilage
Synovial fluid
Synovial membrane
Bone

Section through a synovial joint

The muscular system

Functions: support and locomotion

The main framework of the skeleton of the body is covered by muscles. Their function is to permit movement. Muscle tissue consists of cells which are capable of contraction (see *Tissue types*, pages 80–2).

Skeletal muscle

Skeletal muscle works in conjunction with the skeleton, while smooth and cardiac muscle produces movement of the internal organs. Skeletal muscle is composed of striated (striped) cells bound together by connective tissue. These cells form muscle fibres.

Activity 5.5

Examine a piece of lean meat. If you tease it apart, it will reveal the existence of bundles of threadlike structures. These are muscle fibres.

Muscle fibres

Bundles of muscle fibres are called fasciculi. An individual muscle consists of many fasciculi enveloped in a sheet of areolar tissue, which is continuous with the tendon. The tendon attaches the muscle to the bone.

Each muscle fibre is served with at least one nerve fibre. In normal use a few muscle fibres are stimulated in turn, which maintains muscle tone, even when the muscle as a whole is at rest.

The muscle requires an adequate blood supply for glucose and oxygen to be received. Chemical changes involving these substances release the energy that is necessary for the muscle to contract.

Muscular movement will be inhibited or prevented altogether if, for whatever reason, the blood or nerve supply is reduced or completely cut off. Damage to the brain, spinal cord or nerves may result in paralysis. The type of paralysis depends on the site of the damage. If injury or disease occurs in the brain or spinal cord, the muscles become spastic. In this instance, the muscles cannot relax. They are *hypertonic* (higher than normal muscle tone) which makes them susceptible to becoming permanently contracted. This can be prevented by physiotherapy, and continued passive exercise administered by carers (see the case study of Anna, page 95).

If the nerves are diseased or damaged, the muscles conversely lose their tone and become flaccid. The muscle is soft and cannot contract. Deformities can occur and should be minimised with correct positioning by carers.

Smooth muscle

Smooth muscle, also known as *unstriated muscle*, is associated with the internal organs and the blood vessels. The muscle cells are bound together into sheets by connective tissue. Contraction of smooth muscle is controlled by involuntary nerves of the autonomic system.

Cardiac muscle

Found only in the heart, cardiac muscle is composed of polygonal cells with very little connective tissue. Cardiac muscle contracts rhythmically even without nervous stimulation. It is stimulated by nervous impulses received by the sinoatrial node.

The muscular-skeletal system

Functions: support and locomotion

As highlighted at the start of this chapter, the functioning of the systems of the body is interdependent. This is particularly appropriate in relation to the muscular system and the skeletal system – collectively referred to as the *muscular-skeletal system*.

An example of this interdependence is the fulcrum and lever mechanism employed in the process of lifting. The bones act as levers; the joint is the fulcrum (the balance point of the lever). The skeletal muscle is the effort; the part supported or moved is the load. The contracted muscle pulls one bone towards another, thus producing movement of the joint.

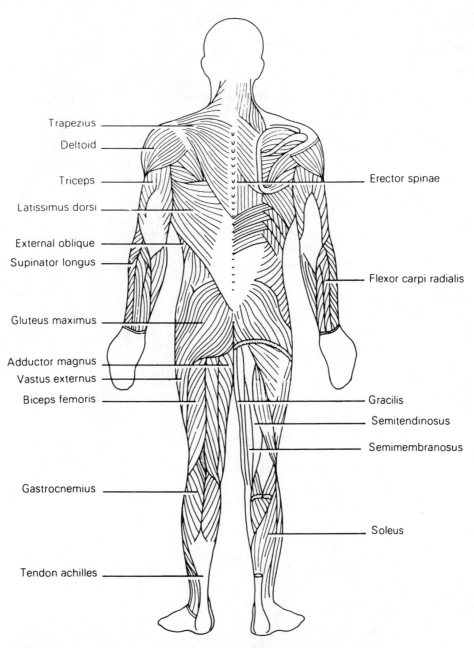

The major skeletal muscles (posterior view)

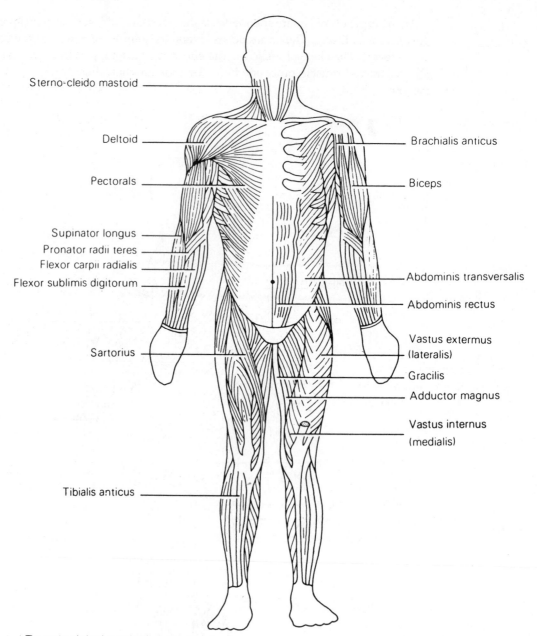

Sterno-cleido mastoid

Deltoid

Pectorals

Supinator longus
Pronator radii teres
Flexor carpii radialis
Flexor sublimis digitorum

Sartorius

Tibialis anticus

Brachialis anticus

Biceps

Abdominis transversalis

Abdominis rectus

Vastus extermus
(lateralis)

Gracilis

Adductor magnus

Vastus internus
(medialis)

The major skeletal muscles (anterior view)

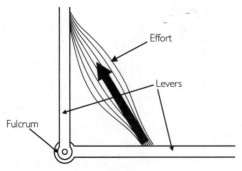

Effort

Levers

Fulcrum

Lever and fulcrum principle

Case study

Problems with mobility – the muscular-skeletal system

Anna is 12 years old, and has mobility problems associated with cerebral palsy. She had fixed flexion of the knees and limited extension of the hips, which was corrected by surgery. She still experiences difficulty in walking without help. Her muscular development and control are very poor. She also has a learning disability. A vital part of the caring team's role is to prevent further deformity by ensuring correct positioning of Anna's limbs. Physiotherapy is essential to develop muscle control, and carers can continue to encourage passive and active exercise.

Because of the lack of normal voluntary muscular control, Anna needs to be taught to use an appropriate aid to mobility. Anna's learning disability may mean that additional encouragement, with gentle teaching, will be needed.

The effects of cerebral palsy vary according to the nature and degree of the damage caused to the brain and nerve pathways. In Anna's case, such damage has resulted in spasticity of the muscles, leading to the fixed flexion and limited extension of knees and hips respectively because of increased muscle tone. Although these have been surgically corrected, it is the continuing responsibility of the caring team to prevent further damage occurring.

The nervous system

Functions: communication, support and locomotion

Consider the following situations:
- You are driving home late at night and a fox runs out in front of you. You swerve to avoid it.
- You are busy studying with radio music on in the background, which you are not really hearing. A favourite song of yours is played; you suddenly 'listen in'.
- You are sitting doing a crossword, and puzzle hard over a difficult clue until at last you have the answer.

What do these activities have in common? They are all examples of how your nervous system deals with everyday life. It is constantly buzzing with activity, and even when you are asleep, it will be alert to unusual activity or noise.

The nervous system is the major controlling and communication system of the body. Although it works alongside the endocrine system in the maintenance of homeostasis, it is far more sensitive, fast-acting and complex. There are three main functions of nervous tissue:
- The sensory nerves monitor changes in the environment; these changes are called *stimuli*.
- These changes are interpreted and decisions made as to what action needs to be taken; this is called *integration*.
- A response occurs – the contraction of muscles or the stimulation of glands. This is a *motor response*.

The central nervous system

The brain and spinal cord make up the central nervous system and are the control centres of the body. The brain has been compared to a telephone exchange – messages from all over the body being transported to and relayed from it. It has also been compared to a computer: when the messages arrive the brain interprets them and decides on what action to take.

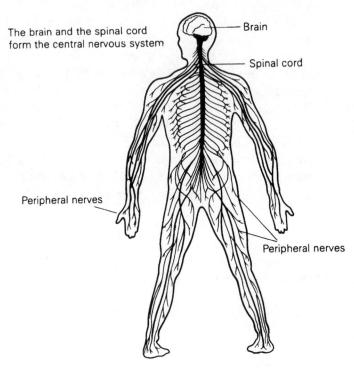

The brain and the spinal cord form the central nervous system

Brain

Spinal cord

Peripheral nerves

Peripheral nerves

The central nervous system

The peripheral nervous system

Sensory nerves

Sensory nerve fibres travel to the brain bringing information from all over the body. Some fibres are sensitive to temperature, some are sensitive to touch, others are sensitive to pain. The sensory fibres in the eye are sensitive to light and those in the ear respond to vibrations.

Motor nerves

Travelling away from the brain to our muscles are motor fibres. These carry messages away from the brain to the muscles and control body movement. This control is conscious; we are aware of what we are doing.

The autonomic nervous system

Another part of the peripheral nervous system is automatic and based on reflex action. We are not usually conscious of its effects and have very little, if any, control over it. This is called the *autonomic nervous system*. Nerve fibres of the autonomic system go to and from the gut and control its movement. They control the rate of secretion of many glands as well as the acid secretion in the stomach. They also regulate our heart rate and control our blood pressure.

The autonomic nervous system is very important in the maintenance of homeostasis. It keeps our internal environment constant while our external environment is always changing.

The autonomic nervous system has two opposing parts – the sympathetic nervous system and parasympathetic nervous system. Normally, there is a balance between the two systems. In an emergency, or when the body is preparing for action, the sympathetic nervous system takes over.

The sympathetic nervous system

The effects of the sympathetic nervous system are:
- increased heart rate and force
- increased breathing rate and depth
- dilated bronchioles on the lungs
- increased sweating
- dry mouth.

Even without any more effects being listed you may realise where you may have seen these effects before: they are those given by the hormone adrenaline. Its action is immediate, however, and does not last as long. The sympathetic nervous system stimulates the adrenal glands to produce adrenaline which then prolongs the above actions. This may happen in an emergency, such as an accident, when a person is very frightened, or is in a lot of pain. If blood has been lost, the action of the sympathetic nervous system raises the blood pressure and helps to combat shock. If someone is in a state of shock or in a lot of pain they feel cold and clammy; a sure sign that the sympathetic nervous system is dominant. Their pulse rate will be increased, and their breathing faster than normal.

The parasympathetic nervous system

This part of the autonomic nervous system is in control when the body is relaxing; for example, sitting in an armchair following dinner. The effects of the parasympathetic nervous system are:
- to slow down the heart rate
- to steady the breathing
- to increase peristalsis and secretion of enzymes in the gastro-intestinal tract
- to increase secretion of acid by the stomach
- to allow the body to get on with its everyday activities, such as digesting the food just eaten.

The autonomic nervous system works with the endocrine system to maintain our internal environment in a steady state. It does this without us being aware of all the changes it is constantly making. People may only become aware of its actions when they are anxious, for example, and feel their hearts thumping away in their chests.

Reflex action

- A reflex is a rapid automatic response to a stimulus.
- It does not have to be learned, is not premeditated and is involuntary.
- The same stimulus always causes the same motor response.
- Reflexes are usually protective.

Activity 5.6

Make a list of situations when you reacted rapidly and automatically to a particular stimulus. Divide your list into three columns: stimulus, response and reason for the type of response. An example could be:

● Stimulus: ● Response: ● Reason:
  A very hot plate   Dropping the plate   Pain.

The sort of reflexes that you may have identified are triggered by the spinal cord without any help from the brain, so we do not have to think about them. Some reflexes can be overridden. For example, if the hot plate that you picked up was a very expensive one you may think twice about dropping it!

Doctors test some reflexes to see if the nervous system is functioning adequately. An example is the 'knee jerk' where a tendon hammer is used to tap the area just below the knee and the lower half of the leg then automatically kicks forwards.

Nerve cells

Nerve cells are called neurones and are very specialised for the transmission of electrical messages. They use up a lot of energy and need a constant supply of oxygen and glucose from the blood. They cannot survive for more than a few minutes without oxygen.

In a resuscitation attempt, if the circulation is not re-established within three minutes, neurones will die and permanent brain damage will result

Neurones are not replaceable if destroyed, but with good nutrition can live and function well for at least 100 years. However, the brain reaches its maximum weight in

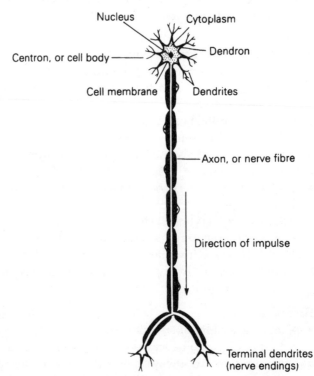

The nerve cell or neurone

the young adult and for the rest of our lives neurones are damaged and die, and the brain weight decreases. Fortunately, the lost neurones are only a very small percentage of the total and there should be very little change in thinking powers in the healthy adult until the age of 70 or well beyond.

The cerebral hemispheres

The part of the brain that is responsible for our conscious thought is called the cerebrum. It is divided into two halves: the cerebral hemispheres. Each half has several lobes all with their own functions. This part of the brain is awesome in its complexity and staggering in its flexibility of thought. Some functions of the cerebrum are:

- maintaining consciousness
- integration of information
- memory and learning
- speech
- language processing
- personality
- perception, that is interpretation of vision, hearing and situations
- movement
- interpretation of feelings
- control of emotions.

The sense organs

Function: communication

The eye

Our sense of sight is the response of the brain to light stimuli which are received through the eye. The eyeball is a hollow, spherical structure, its walls consisting of three principal layers:

- the *sclera*, a tough, fibrous opaque coat which is modified in front to form the clear, transparent cornea
- the *choroid*, or middle coat consists of interlacing blood vessels and pigment granules supported by loose connective tissue. (The iris is a pigmented muscular curtain suspended behind the cornea. In the centre of the iris is an aperture known as the pupil through which light reaches the interior of the eye.)
- the *retina* forms the delicate inner layer of the eyeball. (In this layer are found the receptor and sensory optic nerve endings sometimes referred to as rods and cones.)

The eyeball has a number of appendages – the various muscles which directionally rotate it and the lachrymal or tear glands which moisten and clean the outer surface of the eye. Excess secretion of the lachrymal glands overflows onto the cheeks as tears. From the inner corners of the eyes the tears drain into a channel which opens into the nose, which is why weeping is accompanied by sniffing!

If you have ever met a person who has Down's Syndrome, he or she may have had reddened eyelids and conjunctiva (the mucous membrane lining the eyelids). This is because a feature of the syndrome is that those with Down's do not have the enzyme lysozyme, which has antiseptic qualities, present in their tear fluid (see *The immune system*, pages 116–18).

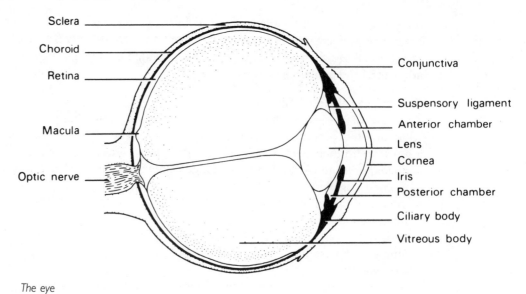

Sclera

Choroid

Retina

Macula

Optic nerve

Conjunctiva

Suspensory ligament

Anterior chamber

Lens

Cornea

Iris

Posterior chamber

Ciliary body

Vitreous body

The eye

The pupil controls the light image by contracting in bright light and dilating in dim light. These light images strike the retina as an upside-down image which is then conveyed to the brain through the optic nerve. The brain then reinverts the impulse so that it becomes a right way up image.

The ear

The ear is made up of three parts; the external ear, the middle ear and the internal ear.

The external ear consists of the auricle attached to the side of the head and the external auditory meatus leading from the auricle (or pinna) to the tympanic membrane or ear-drum. The function of the auricle is to collect sound waves and conduct them to the external auditory canal and tympanic membrane. The external auditory meatus or canal contains ceruminous glands which secrete cerumen or wax.

The middle ear or tympanic cavity is a small air-filled cavity containing a chain of small bones – the auditory ossicles. Sound waves are transmitted from the tympanic membrane by the auditory bones (malleus, incus and stapes, popularly known as hammer anvil and stirrup) to the oval window (fenestra ovalis), a membrane connecting with the internal ear. The Eustachian (auditory) tube links the ear with the nasopharynx to ensure that air pressure in the middle ear is the same as atmospheric pressure. The middle ear also communicates with the mastoid antrum and mastoid air cells in the mastoid process of the temporal bone.

The internal ear or labyrinth consists of bony cavities (osseous labyrinth) enclosing a membranous structure (membranous labyrinth) which approximately follows the shape of the bony labyrinth. Between the bony walls and the membranous part of the labyrinth is a clear fluid; perilymph. This transmits the vibrations from the oval windows to the cochlea (the essential organ of hearing) which connects to the brain via the auditory nerve. The three semi-circular canals (membranous canals or ducts) are situated in the bony labyrinth and control balance.

The skin

Functions: excretion and defence

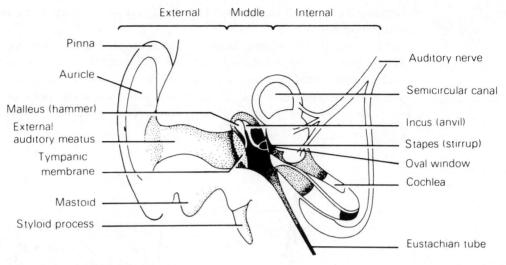

A section through the ear

The skin has three primary functions:
- it serves as a protective cover
- it regulates body temperature
- it provides a sensory covering over the entire body.

The skin has two principal divisions, the *epidermis* or outer skin, and the *dermis* or true skin.

Skin is a large organ. The average human adult is covered by about 1.7 m^2 of skin, varying in thickness from thin over the eyelids to thick on the soles of the feet. It weighs about 3.2 kg and provides an excellent protection against germs as very few can penetrate unbroken skin. Normal body processes produce heat and most of this is eliminated from the skin by radiation to the surrounding air or by evaporation of perspiration.

As an indication of the complexity of the skin it has been estimated that 1 cm^2 of skin contains approximately 3 million cells, 13 oil glands, 9 hairs, 100 sweat glands, 2.75 m of nerves, 1 m of blood vessels and thousands of sensory cells. It is, therefore, easy to see how skin could be indicative of one's state of health.

The epidermis is the outer layer of the skin which contains nerve endings but no blood vessels. It is nourished by tissue fluid derived from the dermis. The dermis is a thicker layer of connective tissue which supports the hairs, each hair growing from a hair follicle. The erector pili muscles, which are attached to the hair follicles, contract in response to cold and fear.
- The sebaceous glands secrete sebum; sweat glands extract water, salts, urea and other waste products and discharge them on to the skin surface as sweat.
- Sensory nerve endings give sensations of touch, pain and temperature; superficial blood vessels play a part in regulating body temperature.
- Nails are really appendages of the skin, being outgrowths from the epidermis.
- Adipose tissue beneath the skin is one of the principal fat deposits of the body.

The sweat glands of the skin are of two types. The first produce apocrine sweat which has more social than physiological significance. The apocrine sweat glands are limited to a few regions of the body, primarily the axillary and genital areas. They are inactive in infants, develop with puberty and enlarge premenstrually. Freshly produced sweat is normally sterile and inoffensive but its decomposition by bacteria gives rise to perspiration odour.

The second kind of sweat is called eccrine; there are millions of these sweat glands all over the body and the sweat they give out is little more than diluted salt water. They are involved in the vital heat regulating system that enables the body to keep its constant internal temperature of 36.8 C. These eccrine sweat glands disperse large quantities of water which, in extreme circumstances, can reach as much as 2.3 litres a day.

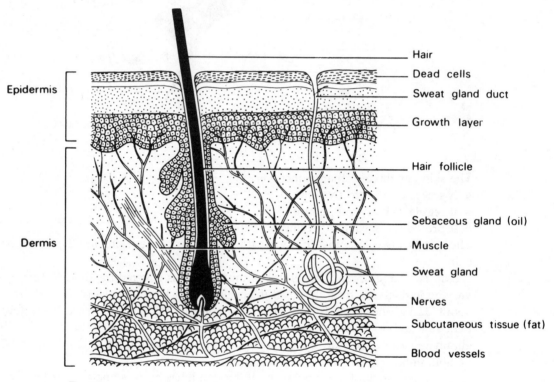

The skin

The digestive system

Function: energy supply

The food that we eat is not in a suitable form for use as an immediate source of energy. It has to be broken down in order to be used. This work is carried out by the digestive system.

A healthy digestive system is essential to maintaining life. It converts the food into the raw materials that build and fuel our bodies' cells. The digestive system takes in food, breaks it down into nutrient molecules, absorbs these molecules into the bloodstream and then excretes the indigestible remains not required by the body.

The organs of the digestive system can be divided into two main groups:

- the alimentary canal
- the accessory organs of digestion.

The alimentary canal

The alimentary canal, also called the *gastrointestinal tract*, is a continuous, coiled, hollow muscular tube that winds its way through the ventral body cavity and is open to the external environment at both ends.

The organs of the alimentary canal are:
- the mouth
- the pharynx
- the oesophagus
- the stomach
- the small intestine
- the large intestine.

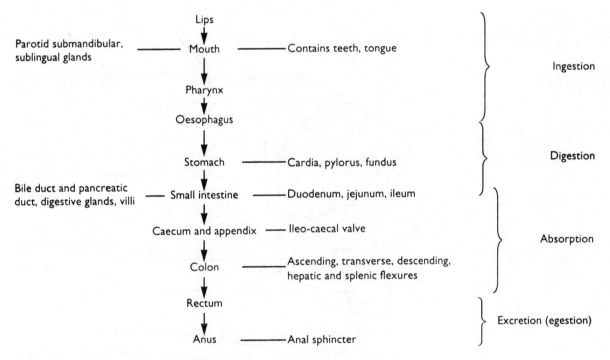

Diagrammatic representation of the alimentary canal

The accessory organs of digestion

The accessory organs are:
- the teeth
- the tongue
- the gallbladder.

The digestive glands are:
- the salivary glands
- the liver
- the pancreas.

These glands produce saliva, bile and enzymes, which contribute to the breakdown of the food.

Digestive processes

Food is prepared for consumption by the digestive processes of ingestion, mastication and swallowing.

Ingestion (the taking in of food) and mastication are functions performed by the mouth and teeth, aided by the tongue. In the mouth the food is chewed and mixed with saliva. Chewing reduces the food to suitable sizes for swallowing and increases the available surface area for enzymes to act upon.

Movement of food along the alimentary canal

Food moves along the alimentary canal by the process of peristalsis. The walls of the alimentary canal contain circular and longitudinal muscle fibres. The circular muscles,

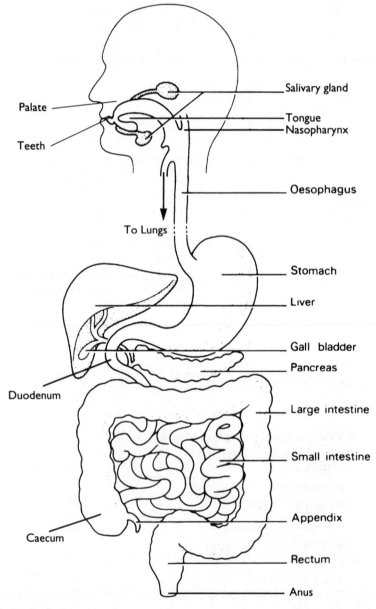

The digestive system and accessory organs

by alternately contracting and relaxing, squeeze the food steadily forward along the alimentary canal in a wave-like movement from one organ to the next.

The breakdown of food by mechanical and chemical processes

Mechanical digestion prepares food for chemical digestion by enzymes. Mechanical processes include chewing, mixing of food with saliva by the tongue, churning food in the stomach and mixing it with digestive juices. Chemical digestion is accomplished by enzymes secreted by various glands into the alimentary canal. It is a catabolic process (see *Cellular respiration*, pages 86–7) where large food molecules are broken down into chemical building blocks which are small enough to be absorbed into the bloodstream.

Absorption The transport of the digested food from the alimentary canal into the cardiovascular and lymphatic systems for distribution to cells.

Excretion The elimination of indigestible substances from the body via the anus in the form of faeces

The liver

Function: excretion

The liver is one of the supporting organs of digestion. It is situated on the right-hand side of the body just below the diaphragm. It is the largest organ in the body measuring about 25–30 cm across and 15–18 cm from back to front. It is divided into two lobes; the large right lobe and the smaller left lobe. The liver has many functions, one of which is the formation and storage of bile, of which it produces up to one litre per day. This passes to the gall bladder, which stores and concentrates bile. Bile has a part to play in the breakdown of food substances. The liver also detoxifies certain substances, such as alcohol.

The respiratory system

Functions: energy supply and excretion

Respiration is the process whereby oxygen is obtained and used for the oxidation of food materials to liberate energy and to produce carbon dioxide and water as waste materials.

Internal respiration

Internal respiration is the chain of chemical processes which take place in every living cell to free energy for its vital activities.

External respiration

External respiration is the means by which oxygen is obtained from the environment and carbon dioxide is released into it. This process is referred to as *gaseous exchange* and takes place in the lungs. The bloodstream carries oxygen away from, and carbon dioxide to, the lungs. Air reaches the lungs through the respiratory passages. The

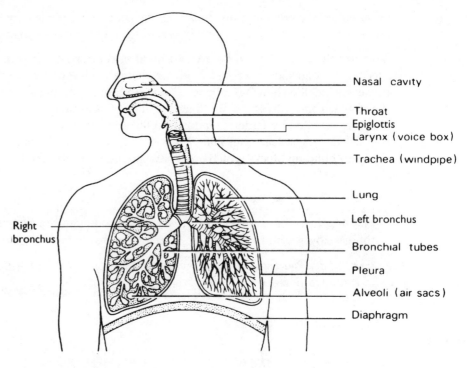

Nasal cavity

Throat
Epiglottis
Larynx (voice box)

Trachea (windpipe)

Lung

Left bronchus

Bronchial tubes

Pleura

Alveoli (air sacs)

Diaphragm

Right bronchus

The respiratory system

system dealing with external respiration involves nasal passages, pharynx, larynx, trachea, bronchi and lungs, in addition to the muscles involved in making the breathing movements.

The alveoli
Oxygen from the air in the lungs dissolves in the thin film of moisture on the cells lining the alveoli. The alveoli are small pouches situated at the ends of the bronchioles, which in turn are attached to the bronchi. They are close to a dense network of very fine blood capillaries which link the pulmonary arteries to the pulmonary veins.

Gaseous exchange
Oxygen diffuses through the cells lining the alveoli and through the walls of the capillaries into the plasma of the blood. From the plasma it diffuses into the red blood cells, combining with haemoglobin to form oxyhaemoglobin. In other parts of the body, the oxyhaemoglobin breaks down and oxygen diffuses out of the blood, while carbonic acid from dissolved carbon dioxide diffuses in. Carbonic acid combines with haemoglobin to form carbaminohaemoglobin.

When blood returns to the lungs, the carbaminohaemoglobin breaks down to liberate carbonic acid, which in turn liberates carbon dioxide.

Inspiration and expiration
Although breathing can be controlled voluntarily, it is normally a reflex action (see *The nervous system*, pages 95–9) with the rate varying with body activity, that is with carbon dioxide production. *Inspiration,* or breathing in, is brought about by contraction of the diaphragm and the intercostal muscles (between the ribs); *expiration* is brought about by elastic recoil when the muscles relax.

Activity 5.7

It is difficult to measure your own respiratory rate, as awareness of the intended activity will cause you to involuntarily alter the rate. Try to measure the respiratory rate of another person, at rest, preferably when he or she is unaware! Count the rise and fall of the chest as one. Expect the rate to be between 16–22 movements per minute for a healthy adult.

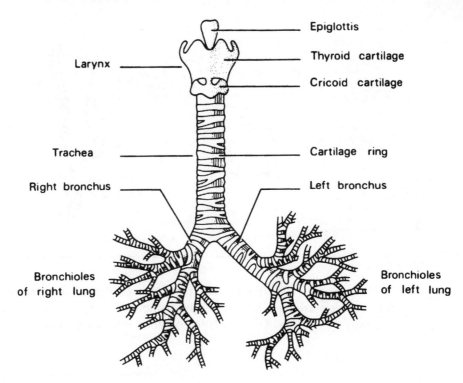

The respiratory passages

The circulatory system

Functions: communication, reproduction, energy supply and defence

The heart and circulation

The heart is completely divided in order to keep oxygenated and deoxygenated blood separate. As a general rule, arteries transport oxygenated blood and veins carry deoxygenated blood, the only exceptions being the pulmonary arteries and veins.

Arteries have strong muscular walls, whereas veins have comparatively little elasticity or muscle. The pressure of blood in the arteries is therefore higher than in the veins. The force exerted against the walls of the arteries is referred to as *blood pressure*.

Arterioles are the smallest arteries which break up into a number of minute vessels called capillaries. These consist of a single-cell layer through which small-molecule substances can pass.

Blood in the arteries flows in spurts which are synchronous with the heart beat. The wave of contraction which passes along an artery wall is called a *pulse,* which can be felt in many places where the vessels are sufficiently superficial.

Activity 5.8

Pulse rate is usually counted in the radial artery. Using three fingers (not your thumb) find your radial pulse, which you should be able to locate on your arm near the base of the thumb of the other hand. Try timing your pulse by counting it for one minute.

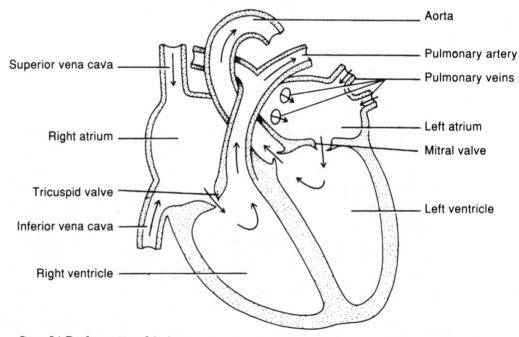

Taking the radial pulse

The heart is divided into four chambers; two ventricles and two atria (see Figure 5.1). Blood vessels are connected to each chamber. The direction of the flow of blood is maintained by valves. The circulation of blood through the body is shown in Figure 5.2.

Figure 5.1 The four cavities of the heart

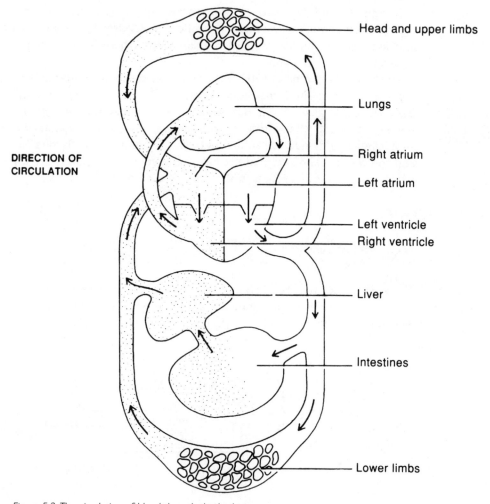

Figure 5.2 *The circulation of blood through the body*

The lymphatic system

Function: defence

The lymphatic system is a secondary circulation intertwined with the blood circulation. The basic material of the lymphatic system is the lymph, which is plasma after it has been exuded from the capillaries. It gives nourishment to the tissue cells and takes away their waste products. The liquid is drained off by tiny lymphatic vessels which join together to form larger lymph vessels. As these lymph vessels convey lymph towards the heart, they are supplied with valves in much the same way as veins. Along their course towards the heart there are receiving or reservoir areas known as lymph nodes.

Lymph nodes
The purpose of lymph nodes is to filter the lymph as it passes through, thereby preventing infection passing into the bloodstream.

Eventually, all lymph passes into two principal lymph vessels, the thoracic duct and the right lymphatic duct, which open into the bloodstream at the junctions of the right and left internal, jugular and subclavian veins where it becomes part of the general systemic circulation again.

There are approximately 100 of these lymphatic nodes scattered throughout the body along the line of the lymphatic vessels. The most common superficial ones are the inguinals in the groin, the nodes in the depression behind the knee (the popliteal fossa) the inside of the elbow (the supratrochlea), the axillary glands in the armpit, the supraclavicular glands, the submandibular glands underneath the mandible (jaw-bone), and the cervical and occipital glands. These superficial glands are the ones that swell when an infection is present in that part of the body.

The renal system

Function: excretion

The kidneys are two bean-shaped organs, approximately 10 cm long, 5 cm wide and 2.5 cm thick. They are positioned against the posterior abdominal wall at the normal waistline, with the right kidney slightly lower than the left.

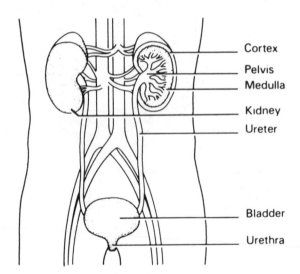

Cortex
Pelvis
Medulla
Kidney
Ureter
Bladder
Urethra

The excretory system

The kidneys consist of three principal parts:
- the cortex, or outer layer
- the medulla
- the pelvis – the hollow inner part from which the ureters open.

Activity 5.9

Obtain a raw animal kidney (from the butcher or from somebody about to make a steak and kidney pie!); the larger the better. Slice it in half along its length. You should easily be able to identify at least some of the various structures referred to within this section and on Figure 5.3.

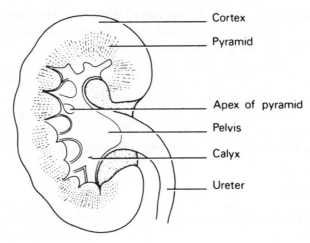

Figure 5.3 Section of kidney

The function of the kidneys is to separate certain waste products from the blood and this renal function helps maintain the blood at a constant level of composition despite the great variation in diet and fluid intake. As blood circulates in the kidneys, a large quantity of water, salts, urea and glucose is filtered into the capsules of Bowman and from there into the convoluted tubules. From here all the glucose, most of the water and salts and some of the urea are returned to the blood vessels; the remainder passes via the calyces into the kidney pelvis as urine.

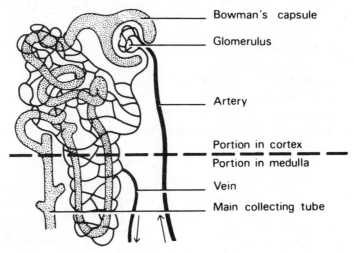

The internal kidney structure

It is estimated that 150–180 litres of fluid are processed by the kidneys each day but only about 1.5 litres of this leaves the body as urine.

Activity 5.10

Given this last fact, regarding the difference in amounts of fluid processed by the kidney and that expelled from the body in the form of urine, suggest what happens to the remaining fluid. Check your answer by studying the other systems of the body written about in this chapter.

The ureters are two fine muscular tubes, 26–30 cm long, which carry the urine from the kidney pelvis to the bladder. This is a very elastic muscular sac lying immediately beneath the symphysis pubis.

The urethra is a narrow muscular tube passing from the bladder to the exterior of the body. The urethra in women is 4 cm long, and in men 20 cm long.

In the male, the urethra is the common passage for both urine and semen. In men, it passes through a gland known as the prostate gland, which is the size and shape of a chestnut. It surrounds the neck of the bladder and tends to enlarge after middle life when it may, by projecting into the bladder, produce urine retention.

The endocrine system

Functions: communication and reproduction

The endocrine system is a system of ductless glands whose secretions are called hormones. Hormones are released directly into the bloodstream from an endocrine gland and have their effect upon distant target sites. This differs from the other type of gland in the body, the exocrine gland, which do have ducts (see *Tissue types*, pages 80–2). A salivary gland is an example of an exocrine gland; it releases its secretion which travels to the mouth via a duct. The saliva then has an effect within the mouth itself, by lubricating food and commencing the digestion of starches.

The secretion of an endocrine gland does not act near the gland itself but travels in the bloodstream to its target cells. For example, the adrenal gland, which releases adrenaline, is situated on top of the kidney, but the adrenaline works upon distant sites such as the heart and the lungs.

There are six main endocrine glands in the body:
- the pituitary gland
- the thyroid gland
- the parathyroid glands
- the adrenal glands
- the pancreas
- the gonads, i.e. ovaries and testes.

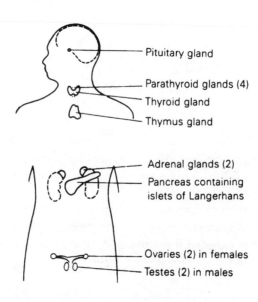

The endocrine glands

Certain diseases are caused by under- or over-secretion from one of these glands; some of which will be referred to later in this chapter.

The endocrine system and the nervous system are not entirely separate entities; there is a small area of the brain, called the hypothalamus, that helps to control homeostasis (see *Homeostatic mechanisms and factors regulated by homeostasis*, pages 119–22) and provides the link between the nervous system and the endocrine system. The hypothalamus exerts control over the master gland of the body; the pituitary gland.

The pituitary gland

The pituitary is a small gland the size of a pea. It is situated at the base of the brain, attached to the hypothalamus by a short stalk. It exerts control over many of the other endocrine glands. Therefore, a disease of the pituitary gland affects other endocrine glands. The pituitary gland produces more hormones than any other endocrine gland, and is divided into the anterior and posterior lobes.

The anterior lobe

Three hormones are produced by this part of the pituitary:

- **Growth hormone** This is produced mainly in childhood. Excess of this hormone leads to gigantism; a deficiency leads to dwarfism, which can now be treated by injection of growth hormone.
- **Melanocyte-stimulating hormone** This affects the melanocytes, which produce melanin, a pigment which colours the skin.
- **Prolactin** This is produced after the birth of a baby and stimulates milk production.

These hormones are called *stimulating hormones* because they stimulate other glands; the adrenals, the thyroid and the gonads, to produce their own secretion.

The posterior lobe

This part of the pituitary produces only two hormones:

- **Antidiuretic hormone** This concentrates the urine. More is produced when the body needs to conserve water, for example on a very hot day if insufficient fluids are taken.
- **Oxytocin** This hormone causes contraction of the uterus in labour, and also controls the release of milk during suckling.

Activity 5.11

Alcohol prevents the release of the antidiuretic hormone. Think through the implications of this fact, and the physical symptoms that result from drinking more than a moderate quantity of alcohol.

The thyroid gland

This gland is situated in the neck, spanning the trachea. It produces thyroxin and controls the body's *metabolic rate* – the rate at which the body releases energy – which in turn controls the body's level of activity.

Activity 5.12

Outline a brief profile of the type of person who has a high metabolic rate. Aim for three characteristics.

To produce thyroxine, the thyroid needs an adequate supply of iodine in the body.

Activity 5.13

Find out which foodstuffs contain iodine. This information should be easily found from a nutrition textbook, or one of the GNVQ texts that include sections on diet and nutrition.

If the thyroid is overactive the symptoms include:
- loss of weight
- increased appetite
- always feeling hot, even in cool weather
- fast pulse, even when sleeping
- hyperactivity; difficulty in relaxing
- an alert mind
- insomnia
- tremor.

If the gland is underactive, the opposite of these symptoms will occur. Underactivity of the gland is sometimes called myxoedema, and is more common in the older person (see *The effects of ageing*, pages 122–4).

The parathyroid glands
There are four of these small glands embedded in the four poles of the thyroid gland. They produce parathormone, which maintains the blood calcium at the correct level.

The adrenal glands
There are two of these glands, one on top of each kidney. They are divided into an outer part, called the cortex, and an inner part called the medulla, both of which produce their own hormones.

The adrenal cortex
This produces:
- **Steroid hormones** The most important being cortisol, which is essential to life. Among other functions, it has anti-inflammatory properties and suppresses the immune system.
- **Aldosterone** This helps to regulate the sodium and potassium balance of the body.

The adrenal medulla
Adrenaline is produced by the adrenal medulla to prepare the body for activity. It is important in the 'fight, fright and flight' response. In other words, it prepares the body for any of these three responses to a crisis; being released at times of acute fear or anger.

Activity 5.14

Think of a situation when you were very frightened, received a sudden shock, or had cause to be very angry. Your bodily responses to all three scenarios would be similar. List the physical changes that occurred, for example, increased heart rate. There could be several others. Your list of effects are the result of adrenaline production.

The pancreas
The pancreas is situated in the abdomen and is both an exocrine and an endocrine gland. Its exocrine secretions are enzymes released into the duodenum that help to digest food. Its endocrine function is to produce insulin and glucagon.

Insulin

The release of insulin is dependent upon the levels of glucose in the blood. Insulin is released when these levels are raised, commonly after a meal. The insulin enables the glucose in the blood to pass into the body cells and to be used for energy. If there is too much glucose, insulin allows the body to store the excess as fat. Without insulin, the body cannot utilise glucose, which accumulates unused in the blood. As the glucose level gets higher, some of it is excreted by the kidneys in the urine. This is the condition of diabetes mellitus. It can be treated by the administration of insulin by injection throughout life.

Whichever client group you care for, you are very likely to encounter people who have diabetes mellitus. If a person develops diabetes when they are young, it is likely that they will need insulin therapy. Some people who develop diabetes in later life do still produce some insulin, and control their diabetes by changing their diet and/or by taking tablets which stimulate insulin production by the pancreas (see the case study of Mrs Williams, page 87).

Regular injections of insulin are necessary for many diabetics

Gonads

Gonads are the ovaries in the female and testes in the male. They produce sex hormones necessary for the normal development of the body at puberty.

Female hormones

The most important hormone is oestrogen, but progesterone is also produced. Oestrogen gives the woman a different bodily shape. Following menopause, reduced levels of oestrogen can lead to various problems, most notably osteoporosis (see *The effects of aging*, pages 122–4), and can be replaced via hormone replacement therapy (HRT). Oestrogen and progesterone regulate the menstrual cycle.

Male hormones

The male hormones are called androgens and include testosterone. Androgens are responsible for the muscular development of a young man as well as body hair distribution and the deepening of his voice. Male hormones are also needed for the production of sperm.

The control of endocrine secretion
The secretions of some of the endocrine organs are regulated directly by feedback mechanisms, for example insulin is secreted in response to a high blood glucose. Others, such as cortisol, are regulated by the pituitary, which is in turn influenced by the hypothalamus.

The hypothalamus
The hypothalamus is situated in the brain and is the link between the endocrine system and the nervous system. The hypothalamus:
- is vitally important in the control of homeostasis (see *Homeostatic mechanisms and factors regulated by homeostasis*, pages 119–22)
- controls the output of some hormones
- is the centre for control of body temperature
- regulates eating behaviour according to levels of nutrients and hormones
- regulates thirst, and if body fluids are too concentrated the person will feel thirsty.

The immune system

Function: defence

The immune system is the body's defence system against disease; helping to protect us from everything from the common cold to cancer. Some parts of the immune system are present from birth; the *innate immune system*. This responds to any infection in the same way. Others are *adaptive* and make special antibodies to each disease that is met.

The innate immune system
The protection provided by this system can be divided into two categories:
- physical and chemical barriers to infection
- white blood cells that engulf bacteria.

Physical and chemical barriers
The skin This is the body's first line of defence. Most pathogens (disease-causing micro-organisms) cannot penetrate unbroken skin. When this barrier becomes broken, there is a real risk of infection.
- **Mucous membranes** These line the body tracts, for example, the gut.
- **Acid in the stomach** This destroys many of the micro-organisms present in food.
- **Lysozyme** An enzyme present in tears, milk, saliva and other secretions. It digests bacterial cell walls.
- **Cilia** Tiny hairs that line the respiratory tract in order to trap bacteria, and waft it to the outside of the body.
- **Coughing/sneezing** Effectively expels micro-organisms trapped in the mucus.
- **White blood cells** The process by which white blood cells engulf bacteria is called phagocytosis (see Figure 5.4).

The adaptive immune system
The adaptive immune system is specific in that it responds differently to different infections. It involves the white cell called the lymphocyte.

T cells and B cells
There are two type of small lymphocyte, both originating in the bone marrow; T cells and B cells. The B cells make antibodies (see below). The T cells regulate the immune response by releasing chemicals to stimulate or suppress antibody production. They

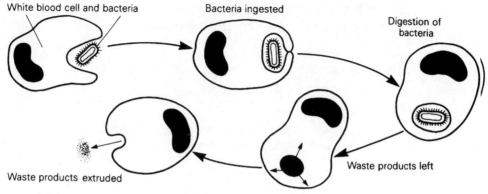

White blood cell and bacteria   Bacteria ingested   Digestion of bacteria

Waste products extruded   Waste products left

Figure 5.4 Phagocytosis of a bacteria by a white blood cell

take part in inflammation and in cytoxicity (cell killing). In cases of AIDS, the virus attacks the T cells and the victim cannot then make antibodies effectively. The person with AIDS can no longer fight infections which a person without AIDS would be able to.

Antibodies

Anything which stimulates antibody production by the lymphocytes is called an *antigen*. Bacteria, viruses, fungi and all foreign cells (e.g. on transplanted organs) have antigens on their surface. These antigens stimulate the body to make antigens against them.

Specificity of antibodies

An antibody will only combine with one type of antigen. This means that if you have had measles and have made antibodies to this virus, these will only protect you from this particular infection.

When an antibody has attached itself to an antigen it is called an *immune complex* and is more easily attacked by the phagocytes in the body. This means that if the body makes antibodies to bacteria, these will attach themselves to the antigens on the bacterial cell surface and the phagocytes will be able to engulf and kill them.

Auto-immune disease

It is essential that the body does not make antibodies to itself, or it would destroy its own tissues. Normally this does not happen as the body can distinguish between self and non-self. When the system does go wrong, an auto-immune disease such as rheumatoid arthritis may occur. The body makes antibodies to, and starts to destroy its own joints, causing inflammation and pain.

Lymphocyte memory

Once certain infections have been contracted, the risk of contracting them a second time becomes reduced. This is because the immune system 'remembers' the causative micro-organism and responds rapidly to fight it. This is the principle underlying vaccination.

Vaccination

An injection of dead or weakened micro-organisms is given which is sufficient to stimulate the immune response, but insufficient to produce the actual disease. When the person comes into contact with the disease at a later date, the immune system remembers and quickly produces enough antibodies to prevent illness. Vaccination may supply either active or passive immunity

Active immunity
The body has to make its own antibodies to the disease. Protection will be long-lasting.

Passive immunity
This a more temporary measure, involving the administration of the actual antibodies to the disease in the form of gamma globulin.

The reproductive organs

Function: reproduction

The female reproductive system
This is composed of the ovaries, the fallopian tubes, the uterus and the vagina.

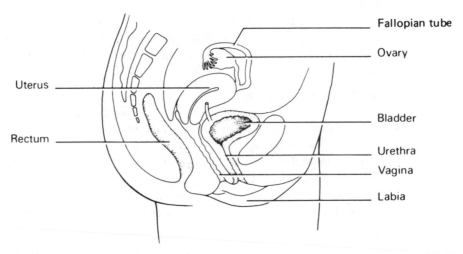

Section of the female pelvic cavity showing the reproductive organs

The ovaries
There are two ovaries, each about the size of an almond. They comprise masses of tiny sacs called ovarian follicles. Each follicle contains an egg, or ovum. The ovaries have two principal functions:
- To develop the ova and expel one at approximately 28-day intervals during the reproductive life of the female. It is estimated that, at birth, there are approximately 30,000 ova in a female child. No fresh ova are formed after birth. During the female reproductive life the ova develop within the follicles in which they are embedded. They travel progressively nearer to the surface of the ovary where they mature and increase in size. About every 28 days, one of the follicles bursts and the ovum it contains is expelled into the fallopian tubes and thence into the uterus where it may or may not be fertilised. If the ovum is fertilised by a male reproductive cell or

spermatozoon it then attaches itself to the uterine wall and develops there. If the ovum does not become fertilised, within a few days it is cast off and the process of menstruation is initiated. If it is fertilised, it quickly becomes many cells which develop in a bag of membranes and soon fill the uterine cavity.

● To produce hormones – oestrogen and progesterone (see *The endocrine system*, pages 112–16).

The fallopian tubes

Sometimes referred to as uterine tubes, these are about 10 cm long and their function is to transport the ova from the ovaries to the uterus.

The uterus

This is a pear-shaped muscular organ approximately 7.5 cm long, 5 cm wide and 2.5 cm thick. It is positioned in the centre of the pelvis with the bladder in front and the rectum behind. It is divided onto three parts; the fundus, body and cervix. The cervix projects into the vagina.

The vagina

This is the muscular canal connecting the reproductive organs to the external body.

Male reproductive system

The principal organs are the testes which are the essential male reproductive glands, the scrotum which is a pouch-like organ containing the testes and the penis which is suspended in front of the scrotum. (See *The renal system*, pages 110–12, regarding the function of the urethra, which is a narrow muscular tube passing from the bladder to the exterior of the body and is the common passage for urine and semen.)

The spermatozoa which are responsible for fertilisation are contained in a substance called seminal fluid. An average ejaculation of seminal fluid contains several hundred million of these mobile sperm.

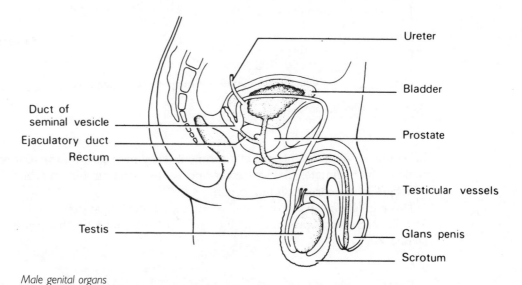

Male genital organs

Homeostatic mechanisms and factors regulated by homeostasis

The essential chemical processes in the body cells are controlled by enzymes which are biological catalysts made of protein. Enzymes can only operate within narrow temperature and acidity ranges. This means that the internal environment of the cell must be kept relatively constant to maintain normal body function.

Maintaining a stable internal body temperature of about 37°C when the external environment is constantly changing, for example, is called *homeostasis*.

To maintain this stability of environment in each cell, there has to be a good system of communication throughout the body.

This 'communication' involves the nervous system and the hormones (see *Systems and functions of the human body* earlier in this chapter). In simple terms, an example of this is if cells do not have enough glucose for energy, they have to ask for more. The glucose required may come from the liver.

Maintaining homeostasis

The balancing process required to maintain homeostasis involves three functional parts:
- receptors
- a control centre
- a responding organ.

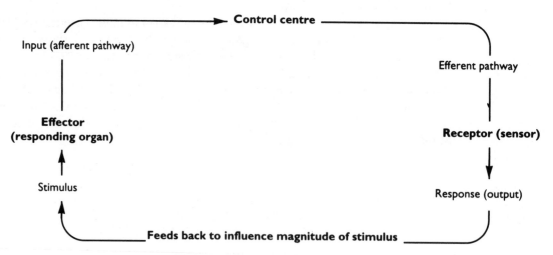

An example of homeostatic feedback

Receptors monitor the internal environment. They pass their information to the control centre which initiates the correct response by sending out nervous or hormonal messages to the corresponding organ.

This regulation can be compared to the central heating system in a house (see Figure 5.5). Most chemical processes in the body are controlled by this process of negative feedback.

Maintaining body temperature

The nerve endings in the skin are the receptors that monitor temperature. If the temperature rises they send a nervous impulse to the brain; the control centre. The brain then sends a message to the sweat glands and stimulates them to function. Evaporation of sweat causes cooling, and homeostasis is restored.

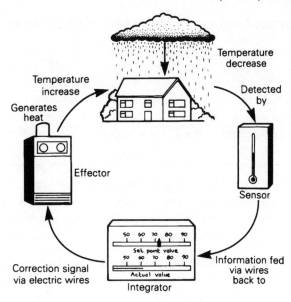

Figure 5.5 A domestic heating system is an example of negative feedback

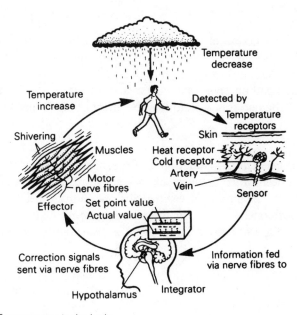

The feedback control of temperature in the body

Feedback mechanisms in the human body

When the body is in homeostasis the needs of its cells are being met and all is functioning smoothly. If homeostasis is disturbed this results in an imbalance which may have serious consequences for the cells. Every body system has some part to play in the maintenance of internal consistency.

Communication and control systems in the human body

The nervous system is the body's main communication network and is a system of control as well as communication. It works closely with the endocrine system which produces chemical messengers called hormones. The vital role of the hypothalamus in the control of homeostasis, as a link between the nervous and endocrine systems, is described in *Systems and functions of the human body* earlier in this chapter. These two systems regulate the body's responses to the internal and external environment.

Activity 5.15

Parallels are often drawn between the function of the hypothalamus and that of the thermostat in a car. How would you use the example of the thermostat to explain to someone the similar function of the hypothalamus?

The messages relayed by the nervous system are very fast, whereas those sent via the chemical messengers take longer to produce a change in the body.

Blood glucose

Homeostasis in relation to blood glucose is referred to in *The endocrine system*, in the *Insulin* section earlier in this chapter.

Respiration

The function of the autonomic nervous system in the maintenance of homeostasis is mentioned in *The nervous system* earlier in this chapter, and has a part to play in the regulation of respiration, which alters according to the demands of the situation. The sympathetic nervous system can increase breathing depth and rate; the parasympathetic nervous system has the effect of steadying breathing.

Fluid balance

Homeostasis in relation to fluid balance is essential because constancy of electrolyte concentration is necessary for the transfer of water between blood, tissue fluids and cells. (Examples of electrolytes are sodium, calcium and potassium.) The antidiuretic hormone secreted by the posterior lobe of the pituitary gland has a part to play in relation to fluid balance (see *The endocrine system* earlier in this chapter).

The effects of aging

This section will cover:
- reproduction
- support and locomotion
- homeostasis.

But first we have to consider our growth patterns.

From birth, there is significant rapid physical development for the first three years of a human's life. A growth spurt occurs in girls from about 11 or 12 years, and in boys from about two years later. Look at the growth charts (see Figure 7.2 on page 153) showing average heights for boys and girls at different ages.

Reproduction

Puberty

During puberty the sex hormones (gonadotrophins) are secreted and bring about the characteristic changes (see *The endocrine system*, pages 112–16).

Activity 5.16 ─────────────────────────────

Without reading ahead, list the physical changes that occur during puberty in both males and females.

> Your list should have included the following:
>
> *Puberty in males*
> Enlargement of the testes
> Growth of the penis
> Facial, underarm and pubic hair growth
> Voice deepening
>
> *Puberty in females*
> Development of breasts
> Onset of menstruation
> Underarm and pubic hair growth

The onset of menstruation signals that the female's ovaries are beginning to release ova; commonly one ovum during each monthly cycle (see *The female reproductive system*, pages 118–19).

The menopause

There is a clear stage of development in women (at anytime between their mid-thirties and late fifties, although it is more likely to occur between their late forties and early fifties) at which their natural ability to reproduce ends. The ovaries reduce production of the sex hormones. As a result, egg release is reduced and menstruation becomes irregular. These changes may have effects upon the skeleton.

Body function changes with the passage of years without there being any disease process involved. However, many disease processes profoundly affecting function show an increasing incidence with increasing age.

Support and locomotion

Osteoporosis

After the menopause, a woman's bones may become brittle due to lack of calcium (see *The endocrine system – Female hormones secreted by the gonads*, page 115). This is due to a decreased amount of oestrogen being produced. This condition is called *osteoporosis*, and is responsible for the much higher percentage of older women than men who break their hips. Osteoporosis can also result in loss of height. The risk of this occurring can be reduced with Hormone Replacement Therapy (HRT).

Osteoarthritis (reduced joint mobility)

Osteoarthritis is a degenerative joint disease, which involves degeneration of articular cartilage, reduction of joint space, sclerosis of bone and formation of bone spurs (see *The skeletal system – Joints*, page 91). These degenerative changes, mainly occurring in the hands and leg joints, cause pain, stiffness, swelling and deformity. A large number of older people, however, show radiological evidence of osteoarthritic joint degeneration which is mainly asymptomatic (without symptoms).

Case study

Mrs Abbot

Mrs Abbot is 82, and suffers from osteoarthritis. She weighs 12 stone. She is now unable to climb stairs, and has her own room on the ground floor of her married daughter's house. She needs help with washing and dressing. She is very inactive, spending much of her time sleeping or watching TV. She often eats cakes and biscuits between meals.

Caring for her mother is placing a lot of strain on Mrs Abbot's daughter, and indeed on her marriage. This factor, together with some additional physical problems experienced by Mrs Abbot has led to her being admitted to an hospital ward for older people that also functions as an assessment unit. Once in the unit, Mrs Abbot's dietary intake is reviewed, with a view to her losing some weight. She is also taken to the physiotherapy and occupational departments where it becomes evident that she has the ability, with some encouragement and motivation, to become more independent.

Away from her daughter, Mrs Abbot begins to realise that she had perhaps come to allow her to do too much for her. The pain associated with osteoarthritis has been brought under control with appropriate medication. The occupational therapist has suggested some aids to independence, such as velcro fastenings on her clothes. Although joint replacement is a possibility in some cases of osteoarthritis, this has not been deemed to be appropriate for Mrs Abbot. She is now ready to return to her daughter's home, hopefully now able to function more independently. Various support agencies have also been identified such as weekly day care, and voluntary groups.

Homeostasis

In some older people, the thyroid gland becomes less efficient (see *The endocrine system*, pages 113–14). This may lead to hypothermia, to which the older person would be particularly prone during a cold winter. The body temperature of anyone suffering from hypothermia has to be increased gradually, and thyroxin tablets should subsequently restore the body's ability to regulate its temperature. Reduced circulation may also increase the risk of developing pressure sores.

Review questions

1 Despite cells being highly differentiated, all animal cells have certain common features. Name three of these.
2 Which tissue type lines the intestine?
3 If you saw a micrograph of a blood cell that has a large, spherical nucleus surrounded by a narrow rim of cytoplasm what sort of cell would you be looking at?

4 Outline the sequence of events that occurs within the Krebs Cycle.

5 Explain why a knowledge and understanding of the systems and functions of the human body should enhance the work of the carer.

6 Name the four types of bone in the human body.

7 Why do some people who have cerebral palsy develop contractures of their limbs?

8 What are the two subsystems of the autonomic nervous system?

9 What are the accessory organs of digestion?

10 Which are the two systems of the body that are particularly significant in the maintenance of homeostasis?

Assignment 5.1
The structure and functions of different cell types

This assignment provides knowledge, understanding and portfolio evidence for element 3.1, **Investigate the organisation of structures within human body systems.**

Your tasks

Prepare a report for your class colleagues that will enable them to have a greater understanding of the following:

● the role of the major cell components in human body cells

● the processes involved in cellular respiration (use diagrams)

● the structures and functions of the four main tissue types

● the identification of tissue types from micrographs or representations of micrographs (either from slides, photographs or drawings, according to availability).

Include a summary of the methods used in preparing and examining micrographs.

Assignment 5.2
The inter-relating functions of the main body systems

This assignment provides knowledge, understanding and portfolio evidence for element 3.2, **Investigate the functions of the main organ systems.**

Your tasks

1 Prepare a presentation for your class colleagues that explains, in broad terms, how body systems carry out the functions of:

● communication

- support and locomotion
- reproduction
- energy supply
- excretion
- defence.

Use models, posters and examples from everyday life that illustrate the principles involved.

Ensure your presentation includes a poster highlighting how the support, locomotion and reproductive systems of the body change throughout life.

2 Summarise your work in a short report.

3 Produce a poster explaining homeostatic mechanisms and identifying the normal ranges for temperature, blood sugar, water and respiratory rate.

6 The healthy functioning of the human body: monitoring and maintenance

What is covered in this chapter

- Monitoring the cardio-respiratory system
- The analysis of cardio-respiratory observations
- The analysis of secondary source data
- Imaging techniques and further interpretation of secondary source data

These are the resources you will need for your portfolio for element 3.3:

- An analytical report based on your own monitoring of one individual's cardio-respiratory system, that reaches valid conclusions about the physiological status of that individual.
- An analysis of secondary source data and an explanation of how this provides additional information for monitoring the cardio-respiratory system.
- An explanation of the role of imaging techniques in displaying anatomical features.
- Your written answers to the activities, review questions and assignment in this chapter.

Introduction

It is not always possible to tell if the body is healthy just by looking at a person. Likewise, a doctor may not be able to diagnose ill-health by examining a patient. To help diagnosis and to attempt to detect disease at an early stage there are ways of monitoring body processes.

Some investigations are very simple and non-invasive – they do not cause the client any distress, yet they may detect and allow treatment of potentially lethal diseases. One example is the measurement of blood pressure, described in more detail later.

There are many ways of monitoring body processes, including physiological measurements such as recording the electrical activity of the heart and tests of respiratory function. There are also imaging techniques, such as radiology and ultrasound, that give a picture of the internal organs of the body. All these tests are inter-related and good communication between the services concerned is essential for early diagnosis and the sharing of information to benefit the patient.

Prevention is better than cure. The emphasis within the health service is now placed upon remaining healthy rather than treating disease. The government white paper *The Health of the Nation* emphasises the importance of the early detection of possible causes of ill-health.

Monitoring the cardio-respiratory system

Safe practice

The following procedures described within this section are non-invasive. It is still important, however, to observe safe practice when carrying them out. The level of knowledge and skill acquisition required prior to practising on another person differs according to the activity in question. With all procedures, however, correct and safe techniques must be used. If at any time during the implementation of a monitoring activity, pain, discomfort, breathlessness or any other difficulty is experienced by the subject, then the procedure must be stopped immediately and medical advice sought if further problems arise. More detailed safety aspects are referred to in relation to specific procedures.

Pulse rate

As described in Chapter 5, blood in the arteries flows in spurts which are synchronous with the heart beat. The wave of contraction which passes along an artery wall is called a *pulse*.

The average resting pulse rate of a person varies throughout his or her life span. At birth, the heart beats about 130 times per minute, at six years about 100 times per minute, and in an adult between 65–80 times per minute.

Activity 6.1

Refer back to *The circulatory system* in Chapter 5. Revise how to take a radial pulse and practise, either on yourself, or with a friend.

Although the radial pulse is the most common one to record, there are several other sites in the body where a pulse can be found, i.e. where an artery is sufficiently superficial. Examples are:
- the temporal artery (at either side of your forehead)
- the carotid artery (at either side of your neck)
- the brachial artery (can be felt on the inner arm, between the forearm and upper arm).

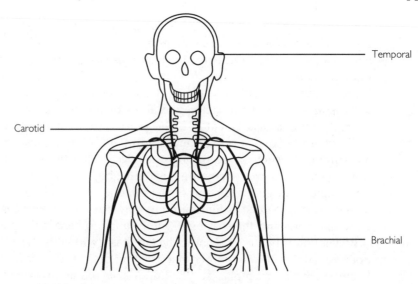

The location in the body of the temporal, carotid and brachial arteries

Activity 6.2

Try to find the three pulse sites mentioned above. Always remember not to use your thumb, which has a small pulse in it. This may distort a reading if you are taking someone else's pulse rate.

Safety point: Take care not to press too hard.

Factors affecting pulse rate

Activity 6.3

Once again, refer back to *The nervous system* in Chapter 5. There the body's 'fight, fright and flight' responses were described. These are enabled by the production of the hormone adrenaline by the adrenal medulla. Why, in response to such a situation, would one of the physiological effects be an increased pulse rate?

In contrast to a response to being frightened or angry, you may actually choose to create a situation where you deliberately increase your heart rate, and therefore the rate of your pulse, for example, if you take planned exercise. During exercise, the skeletal muscles require more oxygen and glucose, which is transported to them via the blood. Cardiac output and, therefore, the pulse rate and blood pressure rise and there is redeployment in the capillary circulation (from other parts of the body) to ensure adequate supplies of oxygen and glucose.

Exercise increases the heart rate

Activity 6.4

1 Record your pulse rate for one minute, when you are at rest. Then using an aerobic step, a suitable stair or a gymnastics bench, step up and down for three minutes. Record your pulse for one minute immediately afterwards. How long does it take for you to regain your resting pulse rate?

> **Safety point:** Stop this activity immediately if you experience pain or breathing discomfort.

2 For the resting pulse and after exercise, calculate the volume of blood pumped by each ventricle (of the heart) in one minute. (Each ventricle pumps about $70\,\text{cm}^3$/beat.)
(Refer back again to Chapter 5 in relation to the structure of the heart.)
3 Does the volume change? Why should this be?

A longer-term effect of exercise is that your resting pulse rate will drop, which is an indication of a more efficient functioning of the circulatory system.

Activity 6.5

Calculate your target training zone – the level of increase in your pulse rate during exercise which depends upon how fit you are. To calculate it, subtract your age from 220. Your target training zone is between 60 and 90 per cent of the result. However, if you are not very fit, you should restrict the raising of your pulse rate to between 60 and 80 per cent of the figure reached.

> **Safety point:** Do not over-exert yourself. Raise your fitness level gradually.

Activity 6.6

If a person's heart beats 70 times a minute for 24 hours a day and for 365 days a year, how often has your heart beaten in your lifetime? How often has it beaten for a person who is 70?

Blood pressure

Blood pressure is the amount of pressure that the blood exerts on the walls of the arteries as it flows through them. It is an important measurement because it can give significant clues as to the state of a person's arteries and is often an early sign of cardiovascular disease. The pressure is measured in millimetres of mercury using a sphygmomanometer.

The most common way to record blood pressure is as follows:
- The bell of the stethoscope is placed over the brachial artery (see *Pulse rate*, page 128).
- The sphygmomanometer cuff is applied to the arm above the elbow.
- The cuff is inflated and mercury rises up the manometer, from which the pressure is read. The cuff is inflated to approximately 20–30 mm Hg (mercury) above the last

> **Safety point:** Being able to record a blood pressure reading is a fairly complex skill, involving plenty of instruction and practice. Student nurses, for example, receive theoretical input, demonstrations and then practise on one another long before taking patients' blood pressure, by which time they would be competent at this skill.

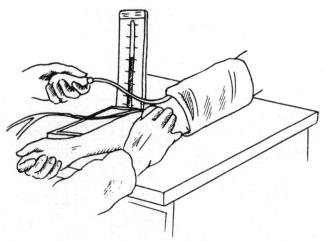

Measuring blood pressure

recorded reading, or until the pulse can no longer be heard or *palpated* (felt with the fingers).
- There is a control valve to deflate the system. The pressure valve on the cuff should be released slowly. The first sound to be heard through the stethoscope is the *systolic* (see later). The point at which the pulse that can be heard fades is the *diastolic reading*.

Blood pressure varies with age, sex, weight, race, socio-economic status, mood changes, posture, physical activity and general health status.

Activity 6.7

Given these variables, what do you think would be an important factor to bear in mind when monitoring a client's blood pressure?

Other factors that affect blood pressure are shock, myocardial infarction (see Chapter 5) and haemorrhage. These would all cause blood pressure to drop below the normal level.

Blood pressure is recorded as two figures. The upper figure, the *systolic*, is the pressure in the blood vessels as the heart contracts. The lower figure, the *diastolic*, is the pressure in the vessels when the heart is relaxing between beats. In healthy adults at rest, systolic blood pressure varies between 110 and 140 mm Hg (mercury) and diastolic pressure between 75 and 80 mm Hg. This would be written down as, for example, $\frac{110}{75}$.

Alternatively, on a chart that can be seen in a hospital ward, blood pressure may be recorded as shown in Figure 6.1 (overleaf).

Activity 6.8

If a patient or client's blood pressure is recorded, for example, twice daily in the way demonstrated in Figure 6.1 (overleaf), what would be the benefit of using such a method?

When a person is in hospital, the doctor usually decides how often his or her blood pressure should be taken and recorded. The frequency depends upon the person's condition. When a patient returns from the operating theatre, his or her blood pressure

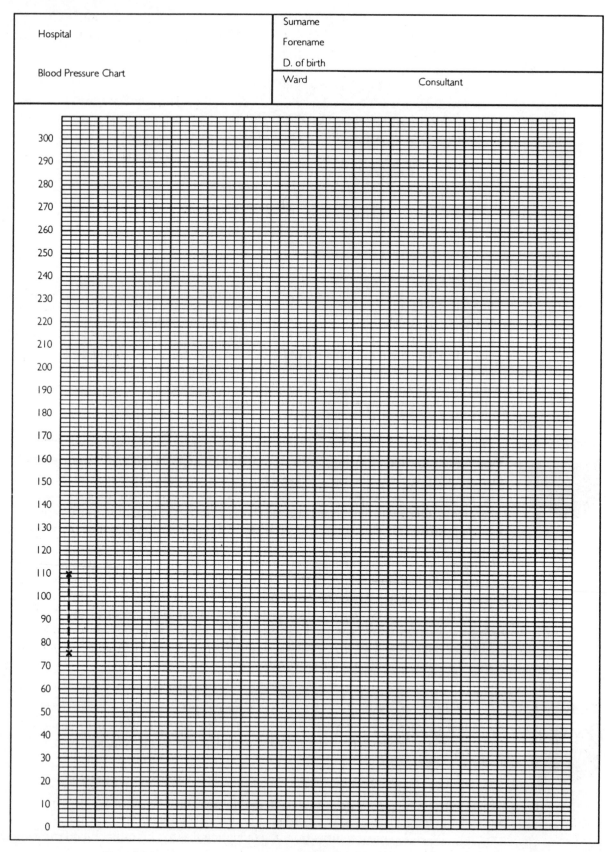

Figure 6.1 A representation of a section of a blood pressure chart, indicating one way in which blood pressure may be recorded

is monitored very frequently for a while, perhaps once every 15–30 minutes. This again depends on the seriousness of the operation. Lowered blood pressure could indicate internal blood loss, for example.

Activity 6.9

Given the information already provided, explain why blood pressure that is becoming lower than is normal for the individual, may be an indication of blood loss in certain circumstances.

Activity 6.10

If somebody is available who has been trained to record blood pressure accurately and with minimal discomfort to the client, repeat Activity 6.4 but this time measure blood pressure as well.

> **Safety point:** Do not attempt this activity unless you are confident that the person taking the blood pressure readings is adequately trained to do so.

About one-third of people aged over 50 have raised blood pressure. It is believed that if these people were detected and their blood pressure returned to normal limits, the incidence of strokes would be reduced by about 30 per cent.

Activity 6.11

Find out the meanings of the prefixes 'hypo' and 'hyper', so that you are able to define the terms *hypotension* and *hypertension* in relation to blood pressure. Find some other medical terms that are prefixed by these stems.

In some instances, the monitoring of blood pressure is essential for the detection of potentially life-threatening conditions, such as pre-eclampsia, the term that describes the symptoms that precede eclampsia in pregnancy. *Eclampsia* refers to fits that occur as the result of toxaemia. Good antenatal care, which includes regular blood pressure checks, should ensure that this condition is diagnosed early and can, therefore, be treated.

Atherosclerosis is a condition involving the narrowing and hardening of the arteries. This occurs because they become 'clogged up' due to plaques of a substance called atheroma building up inside the arteries. This process is associated with raised cholesterol levels, and is made worse by factors such as smoking, stress and obesity. Eventually the lumen (the internal passage) of the artery becomes narrowed. Because the space through which the blood has to pass has been reduced, the pressure that it exerts on the walls of the arteries increases.

Activity 6.12

Illustrate the process described above in relation to increased blood pressure next time you wash the car with a garden hose. If you compress the hose, water gushes out in a more diffuse and faster stream.

If increased blood pressure is thought by the doctor to be an early indication of atherosclerosis, certain lifestyle modifications can be taken by the individual in order to help slow down the process, and to increase the quality of his or her health generally.

Activity 6.13

Suggest lifestyle modifications that could be taken by a person who shows early signs of developing atherosclerosis.

The last example demonstrates the importance to us all of having regular blood pressure checks as any changes from our individual norm may be an indication of a *preventable* health problem.

Breathing rate

Chapter 5 outlined the respiratory system and guided you through measuring respiratory rate.

The control of breathing is normally undertaken by the respiratory centre in the medulla oblongata of the brain. There is a rhythmical inspiration and expiration without conscious thought. Tidal volume refers to the air which passes in and out of the lungs in normal respiratory action. It is possible, however, to voluntarily control the rate of one's breathing. Hence the caution to be taken when observing respiratory rate, referred to in Activity 5.7.

The rate and depth of breathing alters with exercise. This is controlled by the level of carbon dioxide in the blood. As energy use increases, so carbon dioxide levels increase, and the demand for oxygen also increases. Small rises in the level of carbon dioxide in the blood cause a large increase in the rate and depth of breathing.

Activity 6.14

Once again, repeat Activity 6.4 but this time monitor respiratory rate throughout.

Lung volume

The measurement of air taken into and expelled from the lungs is spirometry. Changes in lung volumes provide the best measurement of obstruction to air flow in the respiratory passages.

A spirometer (Figure 6.2) consists of a hollow drum floating over a chamber of water and counterbalanced by weights so that it can move freely up and down. Inside the drum is a mixture of gases, usually oxygen and air. Leading from the hollow space in the drum to the outside is a tube that has a mouthpiece through which the patient breathes. As he or she inhales and exhales through the tube, the drum rises and falls, causing a needle to move on a nearby rotating chart. The tracing recorded is called a *spirogram*.

Various measurements are taken of lung capacity. Vital capacity refers to the volume of air breathed out after a person has breathed in as fully as possible. The normal capacity is approximately 2500–3000 millilitres. It is higher in males than females. Forced vital capacity measurements are taken in the form of peak flow measurement.

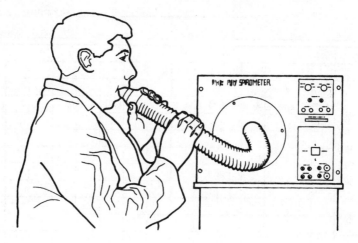

Figure 6.2 A spirometer in use

Vital capacity is reduced in obstructive lung diseases, such as bronchitis which is inflammation of the bronchi (see *The respiratory system* in Chapter 5). A person suffering from asthma would also have a reduced vital capacity, due to difficulty in expiration because of the muscular spasm of the bronchi.

Activity 6.15

If possible, obtain a mini peak flow meter (see Figure 6.3). This is a small tube-shaped structure with a calibrated measuring scale and disposable cardboard mouthpieces for the purpose of preventing cross-infection. The more basic versions are fairly inexpensive (under £20), and can be obtained from sports equipment suppliers. They are frequently used as part of fitness assessment testing. Alternatively, you may be able to borrow one from a hospital or clinic, or your college or school may have one. Mini peak flow meters are simple to use. You should inhale and then forcibly and rapidly exhale into the mouthpiece. Normally, the 'best of three' readings is recorded. Compare readings with your friends.

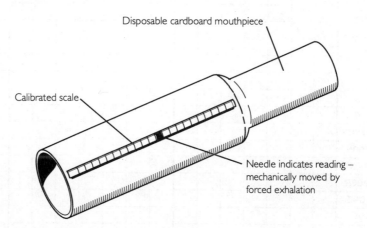

Disposable cardboard mouthpiece

Calibrated scale

Needle indicates reading – mechanically moved by forced exhalation

Figure 6.3 Mini peak flow meter

_____ HOSPITAL

NAME _____ AGE _____ REG. No _____ WARD _____

		MONTH																																								
		DATE																																										
			M	E	M	E	M	E	M	E	M	E	M	E	M	E	M	E	M	E	M	E	M	E	M	E	M	E	M	E	M	E	M	E	M	E	M	E	M	E	M	E
T E M P E R A T U R E		**C.** 40.5 40.0 39.5 39.0 38.5 38.0 37.5 37.0 36.5 36.0 35.5																																									
P U L S E **R E S P I R A T I O N S**		150 140 130 120 110 1100 190 80 70 60 50 40 30 20 25 20 15																																									
BLOOD PRESSURE																																											
STOOLS																																											
VOMIT																																											
FLUID INTAKE																																											
FLUID OUTPUT																																											
U R I N E	**SP. GRAVITY**																																										
	REACTION																																										
	PROTIEN																																										
	SP. SUGER																																										
	ACETONE																																										
	BLOOD																																										
	BILE																																										

An example of a temperature, pulse and respiration chart

Safety point: Ensure safe practice. If you or any of your friends experience any pain or discomfort as a result of this activity, stop immediately and seek medical advice. Ensure that you use a new disposable mouthpiece for each person, in order to avoid the risk of cross-infection.

The analysis of cardio-respiratory observations

Activity 6.16

1 Try to obtain an empty chart that could be used to record the monitoring of a patient's temperature, pulse and respiration during a stay in hospital. There may be space on this chart to record blood pressure also, or a separate chart may be used. You may be able to obtain a chart from a hospital, a college of nursing, or from your work placement. Otherwise, you can photocopy the example opposite. Study the chart to see how the observations would be recorded. Why do you think it is important to keep such a record?

2 Keep a record for a few days of your own, or a friend's, resting pulse rate. Use the chart to record your findings. Of course, you may well not see any variations. If there are, what may have caused them?

3 There may well be obvious variations in the temperature, pulse, respiration and blood pressure recordings of a patient who is ill in hospital. What factors may have caused these variations?

One of the purposes of Activity 6.16 is to illustrate the importance of recording the results of various observations made during the monitoring of an individual's cardio-respiratory system. This constitutes data which is necessary for analysis of an individual's physiological status. Analysis of data involves the use of statistics. There are various methods of statistical analysis which could be applied to a set of data in order to make sense of it. However, in relation to analysis for clinical relevance, it is common practice to compare findings with a set of existing norms, for example, comparing a child's height to normal growth charts.

Activity 6.17

How were the readings on the charts in Figures 7.1 and 7.2 (on pages 152–3) arrived at? Why do they constitute 'norms'?

Activity 6.18

When patients enter hospital one of the first things that happens to them is that they have their temperatures, pulse rates, respiration and blood pressure taken and recorded. These recordings are known as *baseline observations*. Why do you think that these are important?

In a sense, these baseline observations are the patient's own 'norms', against which any subsequent changes can be compared.

Activity 6.19

The way that information is presented may affect one's ability to make sense of it. Consider once more the growth charts. Why is the information presented in such a way? Why not instead just list the facts and figures in tabular form?

Graphs assist in the comparison of information, both with the same person over time, and between people. In the case of the temperature chart, changes can be seen at a glance. Graphical representations may even suggest complex associations between variables that may otherwise not have been picked up.

The use of formulae

A formula is a rule or fact expressed by symbols or figures. In physiology, formulae have been devised in order to enable the calculation of certain values.

Spirometry is described in *Monitoring the cardio-respiratory system* (earlier in this chapter) and *The analysis of secondary source data* (later in this chapter). Before proceeding, read the relevant parts of these two sections.

Activity 6.20

Explain what is meant by the *functional residual capacity*, having read the relevant sections.

The functional residual capacity in a young adult male is 2400 ml. Approximately 150 ml of this volume is dead space. Dead space constitutes the air in the smallest, terminal bronchioles, which does not exchange gases with the blood. If the next inspiration were to admit 450 ml of fresh air, then 150 ml of stale air would be displaced into the alveolar region (see *The respiratory system* in Chapter 5) from the dead space, followed by 300 ml of fresh air, leaving the remaining 150 ml of inspired air in the dead space. Thus the percentage of air inspired which actually reaches the alveoli is:

$$\frac{300}{450} \times 100 = 66\%$$

In terms of a formula:

$$\frac{\text{Inspired fresh air} - 150}{\text{Total amount of inspired fresh air}} \times 100 = \text{Percentage of air reaching alveoli}$$

This example represents a typical resting value. However, if the inspired volume is increased by physical effort, the percentage of fresh air reaching the alveoli would be greater.

Activity 6.21

1 Calculate the percentage of air reaching the alveoli, given an inspired volume of 1500 ml, using the above formula.
2 How does this indicate the benefit of exercise?

The analysis of secondary source data

What is secondary source data?

As a result of carrying out some of the previous activities, for example by counting and recording a pulse rate, you would have collected some *primary source data*. This constitutes information that you have collected yourself. *Secondary source data*, on the other hand, refers to data that has not been collected directly by you. It could, however, be used by you as a source of information from which certain conclusions could be drawn.

As with a knowledge and understanding of the systems and functions of the body (Chapter 5), an ability to recognise the significance of certain health-related monitoring activities enhances the knowledge and skills that underpin the activity of caring for others.

The electrocardiogram (ECG)

Heart tissue is highly specialised and is capable of automatic, rhythmic contraction. The heart beat starts as an electrical impulse at a specific point in the heart, the sino-atrial node. From this point, the impulse travels through the conducting system of the heart (the Bundle of His) causing first the atria (upper chambers) then the ventricles (lower chambers) to beat. The atrioventricular node is situated between the atria and ventricles, and transmits impulses. The phase of activating the muscle membranes within a section of the heart is called *depolarisation*. The process of returning the muscle membranes in that area of the heart to it's resting phase is referred to as *repolarisation*.

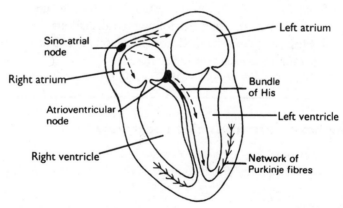

The conduction system of the heart

Electrodes applied to the skin can increase the currents produced by the electrical activity in the heart. The electrocardiogram records these electrical impulses in the form of waves on the graph.

An electrocardiogram can help to diagnose heart attacks and is a valuable tool for the observation of people with heart disease. In many disorders of the heart the electrocardiograph changes in a certain way and this can help the doctor in a diagnosis. If a patient suffers a heart attack or lowered blood supply to the heart, the shape of some of the waves changes. Other abnormalities may occur in an infection of the heart or in heart failure, when the heart can no longer pump efficiently.

139

The electrical activity of the heart may be continuously monitored using a cardiac monitor. Electrodes are placed on the client's chest and attached to a monitor. The monitor displays the ECG so that any changes can be noted. This is necessary if the client has an irregular beat or disorders of rhythm following a heart attack. These rhythm disturbances could be the first indications of possible problems which may lead to a cardiac arrest.

On Figure 6.4, the vertical axis is used to represent the amount of electrical activity in the myocardium. 10 mm (10 small boxes) is equivalent to 1 millivolt. Therefore, if a wave is 10 mm high this is the result of 1 millivolt of electrical activity.

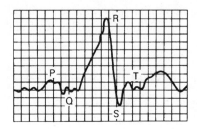

Key
P = Atria contract
QRS = Ventricles contract
T = Heart relaxes

Figure 6.4 A normal electrocardiogram

Activity 6.22

Study Figure 6.4. Given that each small square represents 0.04 seconds (on the horizontal axis), make the following calculations.
1 How long does the QRS complex last? (The QRS complex signifies contraction of the larger ventricular muscular mass.)
2 How long does one PQRST cycle last?

Determining heart rate from electrocardiographs

Electrocardiographs are printed out on graph paper with large boxes divided into smaller squares (5 x 5 squares in each large box). An example is shown in Figure 6.5.

Activity 6.23

1 Activity 6.22 provided the information that each small square on the electrocardiograph represents 0.04 seconds. How much time does each large square represent?
2 What length of time is represented by 300 large boxes?
The method for determining heart rate from an electrocardiograph is to count the number of large boxes between consecutive beats and divide this number into 300. So, if there are two large boxes between consecutive beats (as in **A** of Figure 6.5) then 300/6 gives 150 beats per minute.
3 Calculate the heart rates from **B**, **C** and **D** in Figure 6.5, using the formula given above.

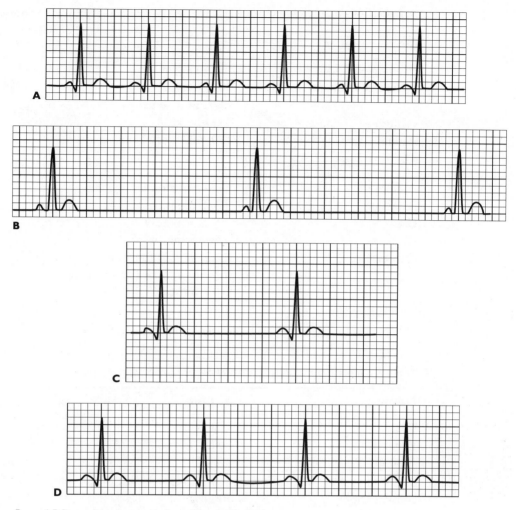

Figure 6.5 Determining heart rate from electrocardiographs

Blood cell counts

Investigations of blood are used as a method of screening to ascertain an individual's health status. Blood is the only fluid that comes into contact with all areas of the body and samples are relatively easy to obtain. The composition of blood reflects the function of many bodily activities and the results obtained from blood tests are always compared to a normal body range. The normal ranges are given in the Table 6.1. Table 6.2 explains the metric readings.

Activity 6.24

1 Study Table 6.1; it provides normal blood ranges. Haemoglobin (see *The respiratory system* in Chapter 5) is measured in g/dl. From Table 6.2, deduce what is meant by this measurement.
2 Given the information in Chapter 5 about the function of haemoglobin, what would be the implications for an individual who has a reduced haemoglobin level?

Table 6.1 Normal blood ranges, including cell counts and electrolyte concentrations

Blood count	Men	Women
Haemoglobin	13.5–18 g/dl	11.5–16.5 g/dl
Packed cell volume	40–54%	36–47%
	Men and women	
White cell count	4–11 × 10^9/l	
Platelet count	150–400 × 10^9/l	
Biochemistry		
Sodium	135–147 mmol/l	
Potassium	3.8–5.0 mmol/l	
Urea	2.5–6.5 mmol/l	
Glucose	3.4–6.5 mmol/l	
Cholesterol	<5.2 mmol/l (desirable)	
	5.2–6.2 mmol/l (borderline)	
	>6.2 mmol/l (high)	
Serum albumin	35–55 g/l	

NB 'Normal ranges' may vary slightly in different texts.

Table 6.2 Metric measures, units and SI symbols

Name	SI unit	Symbol
Mass	gram	g
Volume	litre	l
Amount of substance	mole	mol

Standard prefixes are used for decimal submultiples of the units.

Submultiple	Prefix	Symbol
10^{-1}	deci-	d
10^{-2}	centi-	c
10^{-3}	milli-	m
10^{-6}	micro-	
10^{-9}	nano-	n
10^{-12}	pico-	p

Haemoglobin is carried on the red blood cells, the erythrocytes. There are five million erythrocytes in every cubic millimetre of blood. Average blood volume is 5 to 6 litres, depending on the gender and size of an individual.

Activity 6.25

Calculate how many blood cells there are in a person with a blood volume of 5.3 litres. If 1 per cent of this person's red blood cells are replaced every day, how many red blood cells will need to be replaced, and therefore made, in one week?

An erythrocyte count of 3 million per mm³ would be an indication of anaemia in an individual.

Electrolyte concentrations in body fluids

Electrolytes were referred to in *Homeostatic mechanisms and factors regulated by homeostasis* in Chapter 5. An electrolyte is a substance that produces ions when it is dissolved in water. Electrolytes are associated with blood plasma, gastrointestinal fluids and saliva, as well as other body fluids. In these situations single ions, such as the sodium ion, chloride ion, or calcium ion, are usually referred to. The amounts of such ions present in body fluids can provide important clues about a person's state of health and they are very commonly determined in the clinical situation.

The main fluid analyses in the biochemistry laboratory is blood. The most frequent investigation is the measurement of the levels of the different electrolytes in the blood. These include sodium, potassium and chlorine. The levels of these substances change rapidly in cases of dehydration or in any imbalance of the body. The importance of maintaining constancy of electrolyte concentration was highlighted in *Maintaining homeostasis* in Chapter 5. Table 6.1 provides information about normal ranges of electrolyte concentrations.

Case study

Correcting potassium levels

Mrs Clarke, aged 74 was admitted to a coronary care unit for treatment of severe heart failure. As part of her treatment she was given lasix, which is a powerful diuretic. (A *diuretic* is an agent that increases the flow of urine. It usually works by preventing reabsorption in the renal tubule – see *The renal system* in Chapter 5.) The reason for giving lasix was to lower her blood volume, in order to decrease the workload of her heart.

On the third day, Mrs Clarke began to develop observable muscle weakness and complained of a strange feeling in her chest. Blood tests revealed that her serum potassium level was reduced. The doctors knew that if they did not correct her potassium level, she would possibly develop cardiac arrhythmias (lack of rhythm in the action of the heart) and perhaps even suffer a fatal heart attack.

Lasix has the effect of reducing the level of potassium in the blood. A potassium supplement is often given in conjunction with lasix. The reason for the physical effects experienced by Mrs Clarke was that potassium is a determinant of cellular excitability (see *Nervous tissue* in Chapter 5) and reduced amounts of serum potassium therefore affect the normal functioning of cells and tissues.

Spirometer tracings

Spirometry was referred to earlier in this chapter (see *Monitoring the cardio-respiratory system*). The tidal volume (normal breathing), so called because the air flows in and out like the tide, is the first measurement made with a spirometer. Next, the person recording takes a maximal inspiration followed by a maximal expiration, and the vital capacity is recorded. The air still remaining in the lung (despite the maximal expiration) is the residual volume. The volume of air in the lung after a normal expiration is the functional residual capacity. Neither the functional residual volume or the residual volume can be measured with a simple spirometer.

Measurements from the spirometry reading are expressed as cm^3, or in litres. For example, $1000\,cm^3$ is equivalent to 1 litre.

Activity 6.26

Given that 1000 cm³ is equivalent to 1 litre; how many litres would be equivalent to 2300 cm³?

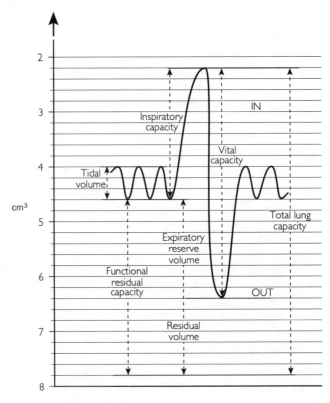

Figure 6.6 A spirometer reading

Activity 6.27

1 From Figure 6.6, estimate the following :
   a tidal volume
   b inspiratory capacity
   c expiratory reserve volume
   d vital capacity.
2 If a man's respiratory rate is 20 per minute and his tidal volume is 300 cm³, how much air does he breathe in one minute?

Imaging techniques and further interpretation of secondary source data

There have been many different methods of imaging developed since the late nineteenth century when x-ray examinations were first used. Imaging techniques are tests which provide a picture of some kind that can be interpreted. Particularly rapid advances have been made in the technology associated with them during the last 20 years. Examples of imaging techniques are:

- x-rays (plain, and with contrast media, body scanning)
- ultrasound
- magnetic resonance imaging.

X-rays

X-rays take their place within the electromagnetic spectrum, which is the continuous range of frequencies from radio waves to gamma rays (see Figure 6.7).

X-rays use high-energy electromagnetic radiation of very short wavelength. They are produced by the collision of a beam of electrons with a metal target in an x-ray tube.

X-rays have great penetrating power in matter that is opaque to light. This means that solid matter shows up very well on x-rays. Bones are easily seen and fractures can be detected. On a chest x-ray, the ribs are white and the lungs are almost black.

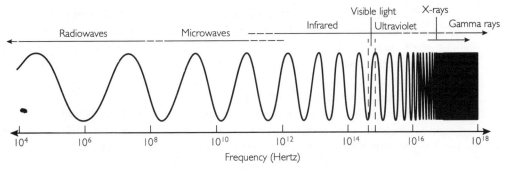

Figure 6.7 The electromagnetic spectrum

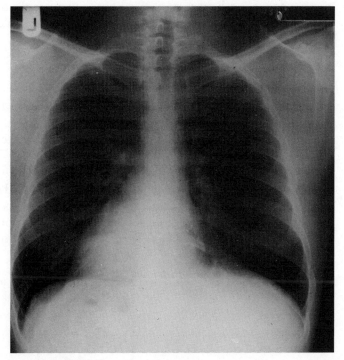

An x-ray of the chest of a healthy adult

The chest x-ray is probably one of the most frequently performed. Lung diseases, such as bronchitis, can be detected by this method and sometimes lung cancer can be seen. Fluid accumulation in the pleura (the covering of the lungs) can also be seen. X-rays are best performed in the radiography department, although portable x-ray machines can be used at the bed-side of a very ill patient in hospital.

Activity 6.28

1 Try to organise a visit to a radiography department, to see first hand the equipment used. Ask specifically about the safety procedures that have to be observed in relation to radiation.
2 Find out the cost to the health service of taking a chest x-ray.
3 Ask if you can taste some barium meal, to see for yourself what it is like! (You will come across barium later in this chapter.)

Great care is needed to avoid unnecessary exposure to x-rays as radiation is harmful in large quantities. It can cause cell damage and may increase the risk of some types of leukaemia. The x-ray room is a 'controlled area'. This is a legal requirement in order to restrict entry to authorised staff only. There are warning lights outside the rooms containing x-ray machines, which are on while the machines are producing radiation (there is no residual radiation).

Radiographers and others working in the x-ray department have to wear a badge that registers the accumulative amount of radiation to which they have been exposed. The badge contains special photographic film that is sensitive to radiation. The level is checked monthly to ensure that safe levels are maintained. These detectors record the radiation received measured in milliSieverts (mSv). People who are occupationally exposed to radiation should receive no more than 50 mSv per year. In practice, most receive only a small fraction of this limit – on average about 2 mSv.

In order to minimise exposure, there are three principles that staff must adhere to:
- minimise the time of exposure
- keep a maximum possible distance (by doubling the distance from the source the dose is reduced by three quarters)
- use shielding.

Lead is a material used for shielding devices. The walls of diagnostic x-ray rooms are lined with lead. Radiographers and other personnel necessarily involved wear lead aprons. Fixed lead screens allow operators to be protected while the x-ray is being taken.

Females of childbearing age who present for x-ray are always asked if there is any chance that they could be pregnant, as radiation could damage the developing foetus.

Overall, although it is essential to observe safety procedures carefully it is important to realise that the benefits of x-rays far outweigh any potential risks.

The symbol adopted to denote the actual or potential presence of radiation looks like this:

The use of contrast media

Sometimes radiographs can reveal more if the organ under investigation is first made opaque. For example, if a person is to have a stomach x-ray, a barium meal is given. Barium is a harmless contrast medium which is taken orally. The barium is radio-opaque and makes the outline of the stomach show up clearly on the x-ray. Stomach ulcers as well as cancer of the stomach can often be identified by this method. Sometimes radio-opaque dyes are used to show up certain areas or organs. In the investigation of kidney disease, for example, a dye is injected into the vein of the arm. When the dye reaches the kidneys it outlines them on the x-ray and the doctor can tell if one of the kidneys is not working well or if there is a stone in the kidney. This procedure is called intravenous urogram (IVU) and is the most frequently used radiological technique in urological disorders.

Activity 6.29

For 4–6 hours prior to an IVU, the patient is asked not to take any fluids. Why do you think this may be?

Body scanning

In computed tomography (CT scanning), an x-ray beam is rotated around the body and its absorption at different angles is measured by multiple detectors. From the differences in tissue density, a computer then reconstructs cross-sectional images ('slices') of the body with a remarkable degree of anatomical detail. In some cases, contrast medium may be used during CT scanning, for example, to display part of the urinary tract. The advantage of CT scanning over conventional radiography is that cross-sectional display demonstrates structures in a third dimension unobscured by overlying tissue. Soft tissue, fat, air and bone are more easily distinguishable from each other than in conventional x-rays.

The use of ultrasound

Ultrasound uses high frequency sound inaudible to the human ear to produce pictures of body structures, in a non-invasive way. Diagnostic uses of ultrasound employ echo techniques similar to the SONAR echo-location of underwater objects by submarines

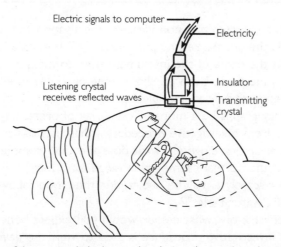

Representation of the way in which ultrasound works in order to gain an image of a foetus

and fishing vessels. Structures inside the body that are not opaque to x-rays can be seen. Unlike x-rays, the procedure does not subject the client to harmful radiation. Ultrasound is used, for example:

● to see the foetus in the womb and to monitor its development
● to locate tumours and gallstones
● to break up kidney stones by using the vibratory effects of the sound waves.

Ultrasound is more expensive than x-rays.

Activity 6.30

Obtain an ultrasound scan showing a normal ten-week pregnancy. The limbs, head and placenta should all be visible. Can you identify these?

Magnetic resonance imaging

Magnetic resonance imaging (MRI) is a non-invasive tool, which does not present a potential hazard to the patient, as there are no x-rays involved. It has been developed to the extent that its image quality and diagnostic abilities surpass other imaging procedures. It is an imaging technique based on the nuclear magnetic resonance properties of the hydrogen nucleus. Cross-sectional images in any plane may be obtained and it provides excellent pictures of soft tissue. MRI signals are displayed on an oscilloscope screen. MRI is sometimes used to produce images of foetal anatomy in obstetrics.

MRI is a valuable technique in assessing diseases of the nervous system and is increasingly being used in disorders of the urinary tract.

Review questions

1 Give one example of a non-invasive investigation to monitor body processes.
2 What is the normal resting pulse rate for a healthy adult?
3 What is the name of the instrument used to measure blood pressure?
4 What is the name given to 'the volume of air breathed out after a person has breathed in as fully as possible'?
5 Why may graphs be a more efficient way of presenting information about findings derived from investigative procedures, than lists of figures?
6 On an electrocardiograph, what does the QRS complex represent?
7 What is the normal haemoglobin range for a man?
8 Which electrolyte may be depleted in the blood following the administration of a diuretic ('water tablet')?
9 On a chest x-ray, what colour would you expect bone to be represented as?
10 Which investigative procedure is used to view the developing foetus?

Assignment 6.1
Focusing on an individual's cardio-respiratory system

This assignment provides knowledge, understanding and portfolio evidence for element 3.3, **Investigate methods for monitoring and maintaining the healthy functioning of the human body.**

Your tasks

Design and write an illustrated report in booklet form which focuses on one individual's cardio-respiratory system.

1 Your report should include:
- A brief outline of the structure and function of the system.
- An explanation of the procedure for monitoring pulse, respiration, peak flow and blood pressure as appropriate. Include reference to safe practice.
- An explanation of the most appropriate way to record the observations made.
- Your clearly reasoned conclusion as to the physiological status of your chosen individual.
2 Attach an appendix analysing secondary source data, explaining how this provides additional information for monitoring the cardio-respiratory system.

7   The development of individual identity

What is covered in this chapter

- Key stages of human development
- Ways in which individuals develop personality
- Influences of inherited and environmental factors on human growth and development
- How individuals cope with transition and change in their lives
- Methods used by individuals, families, groups and communities to support each other.

These are the resources you will need for your portfolio for element 4.1:
- a summary of your findings which:
  - explains the key stages of human development
  - explains how individuals are thought to develop personality
  - describes the importance of inherited and environmental factors in determining human growth and development and offers a reasoned conclusion on their respective importance
- a report which in broad terms:
  - explains how individuals cope with both expected and unexpected transition and change in their lives, with examples of both for two individuals
  - explains three different methods of support used by individuals during times of transition and change
- your written answers to the activities, review questions and assignment in this chapter.

Key stages of human development

Introduction

Life is a process of change, some stability and more change. How a person changes will be determined by the significance his or her culture attributes to key events in that person's life, the person's view of his or herself at any one time, in the past and in the anticipated future. Biological ageing will have an ultimate effect on a person, but the variation will be wide amongst individuals. The changing social norms and values will all influence how and if individuals develop.

The key life stages approach to human development illustrates the fact that as individuals age they go through periods that are separate and distinct from other periods with respect to rights, roles, responsibilities, capabilities and characteristics. As individuals grow older they move into and out of life periods as a result of physical changes, social changes and psychological changes. The *life period approach* illustrates that people in society develop and lose certain roles, responsibilities and privileges at certain points in their lives.

Life stages break down into four stages:

- childhood
- adolescence
- adulthood
- old age.

What is human development?

Human development means more than change – for a change to be developmental a movement towards a greater realisation of a person's potential to acquire new skills, increase self-awareness and clarify his or her values is needed. Development should involve a person being 'empowered', being less dependent on others and valuing the integrity of others as well as him or herself. Change does not involve a progression from one theme in the life cycle to the next; development does. At critical points in a person's life he or she may regress, 'ossify' or grow. Growth involves effort and risks which can lead to greater creativity, awareness and openness to one's own potential and that of others.

Developing one's potential can be seen as moving towards greater maturity. It is not merely moving from one stage to another, it also involves awareness and decision making, asking oneself where one is going and why, having control over one's direction and building on what one has experienced as one achieves more of what one is truly capable of.

Whilst growth and development are often tied together, it is useful to consider the two separately. Growth, being related to size, can easily be represented graphically. Figure 7.1 (overleaf) shows a typical chart, known as a *centile chart*. This is used by health visitors and paediatricians to monitor children's growth. The chart shows typical growth curves for a new-born boy from 12 weeks premature to two years old.

The central line of the graph represents the 50th centile, or average for a child of that age, whilst the upper and lower lines show the boundaries within which 80 per cent of children lie. A child's growth is plotted on such charts against the 'typical' growth curve. More detailed charts are used to assess growth against norms and identify children not following a normal pattern, particularly those in the top or bottom 3 per cent of 'normality'. This does not mean that a child identified in this way is developing inappropriately, but it does mean that he or she may merit further investigation.

Similar graphs for height showing typical growth from birth to adulthood (16 years) are given in Figure 7.2 (overleaf). These graphs show a slight break at around two years because we are all slightly shorter standing up than lying down. There is a second feature occurring in girls between 11 and 12 and in boys about two years later. This is the growth spurt associated with puberty. Adult height is usually reached in late teens.

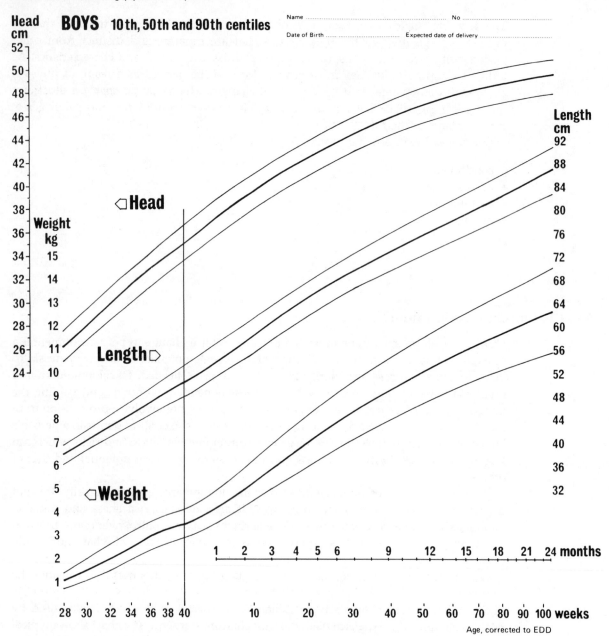

Figure 7.1 Centile charts showing typical growth curves for a new-born boy from 12 weeks premature to 24 months (EDD = estimated date of delivery)

Ways in which individuals develop personality

Every individual is different, yet we all have many things in common. No model is able to explain how these differences occur; there is no single answer. Different theories of personality adopt different explanations of how human beings develop their individual personality. Because of the diversity of theories it is impossible to find a definition that all would accept but the following is a definition which makes clear that personality is

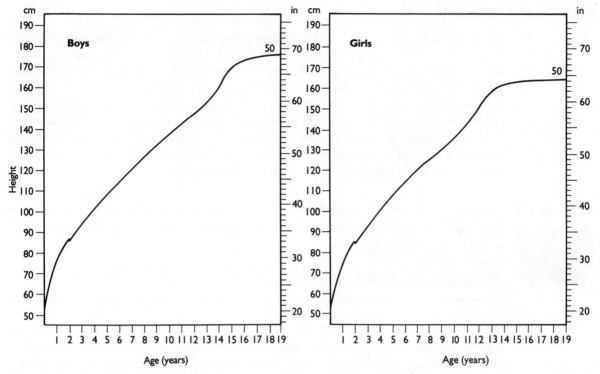

Note: The 50th centile for length is given from birth to 2 years, and for height from 2 years of age onwards.

Figure 7.2 Growth chart for boys and girls

not something a person 'has' but rather is something related to how individuals interact with each other. These individual differences (*personality*) have been defined as:

> 'the enduring characteristics of the person that are significant for interpersonal behaviour'.

Personality development in childhood

Children are no longer viewed as small adults but as human beings that operate at qualitatively different intellectual, emotional and social levels to that of adults. Many theorists have proposed that personality develops through a series of stages and that this development is a life-long process. There is much agreement that the early two years of life (critical period) are of vital importance to understanding an individual's personality, identity and ability to form relationships.

Human beings may be born into any of a number of different societies, all of which have different expectations of the way people should behave. In nearly all societies men and women are expected to behave differently. They perform various roles, which have a great effect on behaviour. These roles differ from society to society, so it is unlikely that the human baby is born with this knowledge. How are new-born babies expected to learn the subtleties of these roles and develop their personalities in the process?

Four theories of personality are examined in this section:

- social learning theory
- psychoanalytic theory
- cognitive development theory and its relationship to personality development
- temperament and self-concept.

Social learning theory

Observational learning, the basis of social learning theory, is where behaviour is learned not by direct reward or punishment for particular behaviour, but by watching others behave and observing the consequences of that behaviour for the individuals concerned. With children, as well as adults, the other person is a model whom the child identifies with and whose behaviour he or she imitates. The behaviour of the model provides crucially important information about the consequences of behaving in that way. Social learning theorists accept that people learn a great deal from reinforcement and punishment, but the theory also leaves room for the belief that children also learn by observation and by imitating others.

Activity 7.1

In a small group, discuss which is the most relevant to how children develop:
- observational learning, or
- punishment?

Give examples to illustrate your argument.

Social learning theory emphasises the effects of the consequences of our actions on our later behaviour and applies the rules of reinforcement and conditioning discussed above. It takes into account the expectations of reward and punishment in modelling a person's behaviour. The person is not, however, a passive recipient of reinforcement and punishment but will modify his or her environment and choose to do particular things that will have a greater expectation of pleasant rather than unpleasant outcomes.

It is important for children, for example, that the right or correct behaviour is reinforced if a child's performance is to improve. Learning is an active process and is done by the child. You cannot make a child learn; you can only provide the best situation possible for learning to occur. For example, if a child's behaviour results in a kiss, hug or other form of pleasant behaviour, then the child has good reason to carry on doing whatever he or she was doing. On the other hand, if good behaviour does not result in a reward then the child may have no incentive to improve his or her behaviour.

In addition to reinforcement, the social learning theorists also stress the role of observation learning or imitation to guide behaviour. The child will not simply copy some actions, the relationship of the person to the child is also important – the child is more likely to copy someone who is important to him or her. The child will model his or her behaviour on these important people. Learning by watching someone else is much more effective than learning by trial and error or waiting until some reinforcement is given.

As all families are not identical and behave in different ways towards children (eg some will be more strict than others), each child's personality will inevitably be quite different. This process does not produce an individual with set characteristics that will be displayed in all situations. Rather, the individual's personality is controlled by the situation he or she finds him or herself in. One classic example of this aspect of social learning theory was demonstrated by Hartshorne and May in 1930.

Eleven thousand children were given the opportunity to cheat, lie or be dishonest in different situations. In one situation children were given a multiple choice test and requested to circle the right answer. Later they were given the correct answers and asked to mark their own work. As a copy of the original paper had been taken without the children's knowledge, it was possible to see if a child cheated in the second test. The children took part in a number of tests varying in type, in the rewards for being honest and in the likelihood of being caught. There was no consistency of honesty in the results – the honesty of the children seemed to be governed by the situation, rather than characteristics of honesty or lack of it. The work of other psychologists supports the view of Hartshorne and May.

> **Summary of social learning theory**
> Social learning theory proposes that moral behaviour is learned from observation of others – mere exposure may be sufficient. The consequences of the behaviour for the other person determine whether the child is likely to imitate that behaviour or not. Parents or other significant persons serve as models for children. However, television as a socialiser is also increasingly considered to be an important influence.

Activity 7.2

Think about your own upbringing and list the events or relationships that you feel have shaped your personality.

Psychoanalytic theory

Freud (1914), working in Vienna in the latter half of the last century, was one of the first writers to emphasise the importance of the first years of a child's life in determining the personality for the whole of life. Freud's theory is one of the most influential and is normally regarded as an *instinct theory*. How children develop emotionally will have some influence on how their identities will develop. Freud claimed that children's personalities are to some extent formed through identifying with their parents and that deep instinctive urges direct much of human behaviour. Social learning theorists do not emphasis the early years as much because they believe that the effects of these years may be changed by experiences in later years.

Freud argued, however, that development through the first few years, which he considered very important, followed a particular pattern with each phase overlapping one another. The phases are:

- the oral phase
- the anal phase
- the phallic phase.

The oral phase

During the first year or so, children gain satisfaction from putting things in their mouths. At this age, pleasure is gained through the mouth, the 'feeding instinct' that must be satisfied. The child at this stage is only interested in his or her own needs and will only do things that will give him or her pleasure – the 'pleasure principle'. Too little or too much satisfaction at this stage will result in the child becoming arrested or fixated. For example, some see smoking or nail-biting in adult life as evidence of frustration or over-indulgence during these very early years. A child who is frustrated by too little stimulation at this stage may become aggressive, depressed and often unable to develop personal relationships. Too much stimulation may lead to people having a high opinion of themselves and being dependent on others.

The anal phase

During the second and third years of life, the child becomes more capable of control over his or her bowels and is said to obtain pleasure from the retention and expulsion of faeces. Potty training starts during this period and if parents approach this training in too strict a manner, Freud argued, it could result in the formation of what he called the 'anal personality' in adulthood. People with an 'anal personality' may become excessively concerned with order and cleanliness and be unable to bear unpredictability or untidiness. They become over-possessive, obsessive, sadistic and generally miserable.

The phallic phase

This is the last of the important phases in child development in Freudian theory. During this phase, between three and five years, the genitals become the area of the body from which the child gets most pleasure. Freud saw this stage as the most important one in personality development. During it, children will be socialised into learning what is right or wrong and learning sex roles. Girls unconsciously want their fathers (what Freud called the 'Electra complex') and boys their mothers (what Freud called the 'Oedipus complex'). It is at this stage that the sex role develops – masculine behaviour in boys and feminine behaviour in girls – through the process of identification that involves the adoption of the father's or mother's whole range of attitudes, values and beliefs. After this stage, a child may act as he or she thinks the mother or father would in a given situation.

Freud's theories have been criticised because he worked as a therapist and gained most of his experience and insights from the behaviour of his patients. It is argued that his experience was limited and his sample biased because it was middle-aged, middle-class and mostly women. His theory is said to be unscientific, cannot be repeated and has too many hypothetical notions that are not directly observable.

Summary of psychoanalytic theory
- **Oral stage 0–2 years** According to Freud this is the first stage of personality development. The baby has the instinct to take pleasure from feeding. Fixation at this stage can occur because of too little or too much stimuli.
- **Anal stage 1–3 years** The stages may overlap and at this stage the child continues to derives pleasure from his or her mouth. During the anal phase the child starts to learn to control his or her body, arms, trunk and anus. Fixation at this stage may be caused by lax or too strict potty training.
- **Phallic stage 3–6 years** Freud argued that at about three years of age the child begins to experience sexual feelings about his or her parents. Boys develop such feelings for their mothers and girls towards their fathers. Children begin to develop feelings of guilt because of these sexual feelings and so begin to 'identify' with the respective parent to solve the feelings. Boys begin to act like their fathers and girls like their mothers. If this stage is not successfully negotiated then problems may develop later with sexual relationships.

Cognitive development theory and it relationship to personality development

This theory focuses on the cognitive aspect of morality and, hence, on moral development. The approach offers a progressive view of morality. It differs from Freud's approach because it views morality as developing gradually throughout childhood and adolescence into adulthood. During the 1930s and 1940s Piaget developed a theory of how children learn about things. His theory is concerned with how the child's knowledge and understanding change with age. He did not believe that intelligence was fixed at birth. His theory is concerned with how our senses take in information from our environments that we store in our brains and as we process this information our behaviour changes as a result. His theory emphasises the importance of imitation, imaging and symbolic representation during the period two to seven years.

Piaget claimed that human thinking develops in a fixed sequence of stages and it is not possible to skip a stage. He stressed that children think in a different way to adults. Over a number of years and numerous experiments, he came to the conclusion that the morality of the five to nine-year-old is subject to another's laws or rules, and that the child of ten years or over is subject to his or her own law or rules.

Piaget was particularly interested in how children understand the world. The child's development takes place through the development of what he calls 'schemata' – mental representations or ideas about what things are and how we deal with them – that can be likened to a set of rules about how to interact with the environment. The first schematas are for reflexes: thinking in the young child is only concerned with the information he or she picks through the senses that are mostly concerned with the child's needs and wants. These 'reflexes' allow a young child to survive during the first few months of life. The reflexes are stimulated by any stimuli. For example, if a child touches a hot object he or she will pull his or her hand away. It is not until about the age of seven that the child begins to think about his or her own actions and their effect upon other people.

As the child reaches 10–15 years, he or she starts to develop logic and reasoning and starts to thing about what things 'ought' to be like. Piaget stresses self-motivation and emphasises self-regulation, which he calls the 'process of equilibration'. This process has two aspects:

- **assimilation** – children absorb experiences into structures that they already possess through the process of 'assimilation'.
- **accommodation** – structures within the child have to be modified and adjusted to take in experiences that do not fit into the structures already in existence. For example, John a two-year-old has established that wheels are round. When he was given a wooden truck with squared wheels that moved when pulled by a string, he had to adjust his thinking to take in this new fact.

Essentially, Piaget shows that the child's thinking moves from a stage of egocentricity in early childhood to that of reversible reaction in early adolescence. Although he was primarily concerned with intellectual development, his theory has important implications for personality development.

A child in the egocentric stage is intellectually only able to see the world from his or her own point of view. For example, a mother told her six-year-old daughter off for wandering away while playing on the swings and getting 'lost'. The child was quite unable to understand her mother's anxiety and said, 'But I knew where I was'. In other words, the child could not see or appreciate that the situation could look different from the mother's point of view.

One could argue that the primary consequence of personality development is to be able see a situation from another person's point of view. According to Piaget, this is quite a late development and in many cases it is not until adolescence that the logical ability to 'go back to the beginning' (i.e. reversible reactions) develop, enabling a child to look at the same situation from different viewpoints.

Piaget devised many simple but elegant experiments to illustrate this progression. For example, he had a piece of cardboard that was blue on one side and red on the other. He sat opposite the child and showed both sides of the cardboard to the child so the child could see each side was a different colour. He then placed the cardboard vertically between himself and the child, asking the child, 'What colour can you see?' The child would answer, 'Red'. He then asked, 'What colour can I see?' and the younger children would answer, 'Red'. They were unable to see that the piece of cardboard looked different from his point of view, even though they had been shown both coloured sides beforehand.

In this way Piaget shows that the process of development is inextricably linked with the developing brain and intellect of the child. Furthermore, at different ages the thinking of the child operates according to different rules to those of the adult. Piaget claimed that children tend to spend their first ten years not able to use the rules of logic that most adults would use. He argued that logical thought develops from about puberty.

One criticism of Piaget's work was that he was always looking for what the average child could do at various stages. By doing this, he ignored the great variations in the ways individuals think. Others argue that Piaget under-estimated the ability of younger children.

Summary of the cognitive development theory

- **Adaptive stage 0–1 year** This is often referred to as the 'sensory motor stage'. Piaget believed that children were born with reflexes that helped babies to survive and adapt to their environments. As the child adapts to the environment he or she has different kinds of experience and cognition. This cognition, in Piaget's terms, is not something that can be measured as it is individual to each child.

  Piaget calls this process of organisation and adapting 'invariant' functions. These functions are individual to each child, as are the 'schematas' (mental representations about how to deal with things, for example, cross the road, or eat bread), and 'operations' that allow the child to order 'schematas' in a logical way. This allows children to imagine what might happen if they take a particular course of action.

- **Pre-operations stage 2–7 years** During this stage the child sees the world only from his or her own point of view (egocentric), and also believes that everyone else holds the same view. The child also believes that everyone holds the same way of thinking about right or wrong (moral realism). Seeing things from other people's point of view can begin when the child develops the ability to imagine this – known as 'decentring'. During this stage the child also believes that all objects have consciousness and feel emotions (animism).

- **The concrete operational stage 7–12 years** During this period the child begins to think logically. He or she can think about objects without the object being present. The egocentric stage declines as does the belief in animism. Children begin to see situations from other people's points of view.

- **The formal operations stage 12–16 years** The teenager begins to think in an abstract manner, to work things out in his or her head. Young people begin also to consider moral and philosophical matters.

Activity 7.3

What explanation would you give to a parent to explain why his or her child always seems to get lost if not watched every moment.

Language

Language is an organised system of symbols which humans use to communicate with one another. Every known human society has a language. This ability to use language is one of the main characteristics that separates humans from the animal kingdom. Humans are the only species that have the ability to use language. However, not every human brain is adequate for the acquisition of language.

There is no society in the world where the new-born baby immediately begins to imitate speech he or she hears. It is argued that in the first year the baby is maturing and developing some of the ideas that it may want to communicate using language in later years. Before a child can produce recognisable words, he or she will produce sounds that will become steadily more varied and deliberate. Many children, before speaking recognisable words, pass through a stage of jargon. This is the stage at which an adult may feel sure that a child has said words but cannot make out what the words could be.

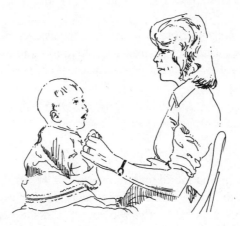

Activity 7.4

Talk to a mother with a very young child. Find out what sounds the child produces and discuss with the mother how she knows what the child is trying to communicate.

By the time a baby is about three months old, if his or her attempts at communication are positively reinforced by adults, he or she will be producing a variety of sounds. The baby will vocalise – make sounds in response to others. The sounds that are reinforced are likely to continue to be used by the child, while those that are not are less likely to be repeated. By the time a baby is six months old, he or she has begun to listen and can distinguish familiar and unfamiliar voices. He or she also begins to understand some of the emotional tones in the speech heard. By nine months, there are usually clear signs that the baby has grasped that making sounds results in action from others and by the time the baby is 12 months old, he or she will often show, by behaviour, that he or she understands a few familiar words in context. From around the first birthday, the words used are likely to be for people or things the child is most familiar with such as 'mama', 'dada', 'cat' or 'teddy'.

Early in the second year, the child begins to produce words and by the middle of the second year he or she starts to make two-word sentences. By the end of the third year, the child is able to use a large part of the basic grammatical apparatus of the local language.

Some psychologists argue that the first ten to 11 years are a critical period for language development. However, some studies indicate that the first ten years may not be so important, as illustrated by the following case study.

Case study

Genie was confined to a small bedroom, harnessed to a potty seat and left, unable to move. She heard no sounds, saw no daylight, was force-fed and deprived of all stimulation until she was discovered when she was 13 years old. Essentially, she then had to learn her first language, which was constrained and lacked the spontaneity of normal speech. She had to be taught the rules of language long after a normal child would have picked them up, although it was more difficult for her than a younger child.

However, the fact was that she did learn a language which tends to contradict the argument of those who say that the first ten years are critical in language development.

Biology is critical for language acquisition, but a number of situations have made it quite clear that learning opportunities and environment are also important. There are a number of sad cases of children being deprived of stimulation that illustrate this.

Case study

Isabelle was found in America in the 1930s, hidden away, with no contact with anyone but her mother who could neither hear nor speak. Isabelle was just over six years old when she was found, and she could not talk. After care and training she began to vocalise and two years later her speech could not easily be distinguished from the speech of other children of the same age.

Certain groups of children lag behind others in their speech development. Middle-class children have been shown to talk more and produce a greater variety of vowels and consonants than children from working-class backgrounds. Children also seem to have a tendency to develop language in some form or other. This is illustrated by the case of four children, all deaf from birth, who developed sign language, including grammar, even though their parents had no knowledge of sign language.

Activity 7.5

How important do you think contact with other humans is for the development of language? (Look back at the case study of Genie.)

Table 7.1 Development: birth to three years

Age	Physical development	Intellectual development	Emotional development	Social development
1 month	Holds head erect for a few seconds. Eyes follows a moving light.	Interested in sounds.	Cries in response to pain, hunger and thirst.	May sleep up to 20 hours in a 24-hour period. Stops crying when picked up and spoken to.
3 months	Eyes follow a person moving. Kicks vigorously.	Recognises carer's face. Shows excitement. Listens, smiles, holds rattle.	Enjoys being cuddled and played with. Misses carer and cries for him/her to return.	Responds happily to carer. Becomes excited at prospect of a feed or bath.
6 months	Able to lift head and chest up supported by wrists. Turns to a person who is speaking.	Responds to speech. Vocalises. Uses eyes a lot. Explores using hands.	Can be anxious in presence of strangers. Can show anger and frustration. Shows a clear preference for mother's company.	Puts everything in mouth. Plays with hands and feet. Tries to hold bottle when feeding.
9 months	Stands when supported. May crawl. Gazes at self in mirror. Tries to hold drinking cup. Sits without support.	Tries to talk, babbling. May say 'Mama' and 'Dada'. Shouts for attention. Understands 'No'.	Can recognise individuals – mother, father, siblings. Still anxious about strangers. Sometimes irritable if routine is altered.	Plays 'Peek a boo'. Imitates hand clapping. Puts hands round cup when feeding.
12 months	Pulls self up to standing position. Uses pincer grip. Feeds self using fingers. May walk without assistance.	Knows own name. Obeys simple instructions. Says about three words.	Shows affection. Gives kisses and cuddles. Likes to see familiar faces but less worried by strangers.	Drinks from a cup without assistance. Holds a spoon but cannot feed him/herself. Plays 'Pat-a-Cake'. Quickly finds hidden toys.
1.5 years	Walks well, feet apart. Runs carefully. Pushes and pulls large toys. Walks upstairs. Creeps backwards downstairs.	Uses 6–20 recognisable words. Repeats last word of short sentences. Enjoys and tries to join in with nursery rhymes. Picks up named toys. Enjoying looking at simple picture books. Builds a tower of 3–4 bricks. Scribbles and makes dots. Preference for right or left hand shown.	Affectionate, but may still be reserved with strangers. Likes to see familiar faces.	Able to hold spoon and to get food into mouth. Holds drinking cup and hands it back when finished. Can take off shoes and socks. Bowel control may have been achieved. Remembers where objects belong.

continued

Table 7.1 *continued*

Age	Physical development	Intellectual development	Emotional development	Social development
2 years	Runs on whole foot. Squats steadily. Climbs on furniture. Throws a small ball. Sits on a small tricycle and moves vehicle with feet.	Uses 50 or more recognisable words; understands many more words; put two or three words together to form simple sentences. Refers to self by name. Asks names of objects and people. Scribbles in circles. Can build a tower of six or seven cubes. Hand preference is obvious.	Can display negative behaviour and resistance. May have temper tantrums if thwarted. Plays contentedly beside other children but not with them. Constantly demands mother's attention.	Asks for food and drink. Spoon feeds without spilling. Puts on shoes.
2.5 years	All locomotive skills now improving. Runs and climbs. Able to jump from a low step with feet together. Kicks a large ball.	May use 200 or more words. Knows full name. Continually asking questions, likes stories and recognises details in picture books. Recognises self in photographs. Builds a tower of seven or more cubes.	Usually active and restless. Emotionally still very dependent on adults. Tends not to want to share playthings	Eats skilfully with a spoon and may use a fork. Active and restless. Often dry through the day.
3 years	Sits with feet crossed at ankles. Walks upstairs using alternating feet.	Able to state full name, sex and sometimes age. Carries on simple conversations and constantly questioning. Demands favourite story over and over again. Can thread wooden beads on string. Can copy a circle and a cross. Names colours. Cuts with scissors. Paints with a large brush.	Becomes less prone to temper tantrums. Affectionate and confiding, showing affection for younger siblings. Begins to understand sharing.	Eats with a fork and spoon. May be dry through the night.

Temperament and self-concept in the development of personality

As a community, we negotiate the meaning of words. This makes 'self' a difficult term to define. Much of its meaning will derive from personal experiences that are difficult to communicate and agree upon. The term 'self' refers to the way a person would like to describe him or herself, i.e. the kind of person he or she thinks he or she is.

One way of finding out how people see themselves is to ask, 'Who am I?' This question usually produces two main categories of response:

- social roles
- personality traits.

We are continually measuring these traits and social roles against our own self-concept, and seeing how they 'fit' with it. Each of us entertains a notion of our own separateness from others and relies on the essential privacy of our own consciousness. This idea of self-concept is wide-ranging. We know roughly how we would behave in a particular situation, what music we like, what clothes we wear, what food we like, what people we like – all these add up to what we call our 'self'. This self develops over the years. We change our likes and dislikes, and all our experiences contribute to our self-concept. As we grow during childhood, we develop a clearer sense of self, which includes the ways that we can influence the environment.

Gradually, the self-concept develops, and forms a basis for our interaction with the rest of our environment. We extend the notion of 'me' into the notion of 'my world'. We think of events as more or less relevant to us. We distinguish between what concerns us and what does not concern us. In this way we can use the phrase 'my situation' to indicate the boundaries of our important experiences and the ways in which the various parts of it relate to make up our personal worlds.

Activity 7.6

Think about the changes in your personality that you have experienced over the years. Have these experiences contributed to the way you behave today?

Argyle (1967) argued that four main factors affect the way an individual's self-concept develops:

- other people's reactions to us
- comparisons which we make with other people
- the roles we play
- the identifications we make.

Getting to know ourselves is a developmental process; it is something we learn in the same way that we learn to walk or to relate to others. Underlying our notions about ourselves are theories called 'trait theory'. *Trait theory* argues that there are, in each of us, characteristics that differentiate us from others – the notion that we are 'bad tempered', for instance, or that other people are 'anxious' or 'excitable'.

To try to understand ourselves is not simply an interesting pastime, it is a necessity of life. To plan for the future, we have to make choices and be able to anticipate our behaviour. This makes self-knowledge a necessity. In some situations, it is simple to anticipate what we would do, but others are far more difficult. How could you deal with a difficult manager? Could you live with another person in marriage? Could you live by yourself after living with a family for many years? The stranger the situation, the more threatening the prospect becomes and the more we realise that some degree of self-change is necessary. The more self-change that is necessary, the more we must rely upon our understanding of ourselves, our character and our potential.

At times of change we are acutely aware of the dangers of that change and may take a rigid approach to ward off any change in ourselves. We do not lightly abandon our theory of what we are, since doing so might threaten our identity. We may destroy a close relationship in order to 'prove' that we are independent, or we may see some teachers 'proving' that students are stupid in order to show that they themselves are clever.

Activity 7.7

Have you had any experience in the past that might now help you to deal with a client exhibiting challenging behaviour? Discuss it with your class colleagues and explain why you find it helpful.

Personality development in adolescence

Adolescence describes the period of time during which a person passes into adulthood. It encompasses physiological, emotional and social development, a stage where the experiences of childhood will be re-evaluated and re-formulated in preparation for the new status of adolescence. In western culture adolescence normally coincides with the growth spurt and physiological changes of puberty. In other cultures this rite of passage is determined by age and is not necessarily related to an individual's physical development.

During puberty the sex hormones (*gonadotropins*) are secreted and bring about the characteristic changes. Early signs in boys are axillary sweating in the armpits and groin, enlargement of the testes and growth of the penis. Later, facial, under-arm and pubic hair develops and the voice deepens. In girls, breasts develop and axillary sweating commences. Later, there is the onset of menstruation (menarche) although few if any eggs are released in the first year. As with boys, underarm and pubic hair grows, although the distribution pattern of pubic hair differs between the sexes.

Changes in the composition of sweat, together with changes in hormones can lead adolescent boys and girls to develop spots. While this is common and can develop into acne, it should not be seen as acceptable and is treatable. Acne has a second effect in that it often affects behaviour at a time when there is rapid psychological development.

Some of the issues related to adolescence are psycho-social in nature. It is a time when an individual's identity becomes established and moral, social and personal responsibilities are developed. Adolescent people often challenge accepted norms in order to test and establish their own mores. This is occurring at the same time as sexual awareness is developing and so establishment of intimate relationships, sometimes involving sexual experimentation, occurs. Unfortunately, this can lead to unwanted pregnancy, the prevention of which may well reflect the quality of learning and support given to the adolescent in the rite of passage to adulthood.

The 'classic' theory of adolescence sees the adolescent as a rebellious person, rejecting parental authority. The adolescent is seen as substituting the authority of the peer group for that of parents. Some argue that the development of the adolescent passes through unstable periods which is an inevitable part of development. Others argue that this emotional instability is due to physical bodily changes which occur during adolescence.

Sorenson (1973) puts forward the view that boys, in particular, experience stress as a result of biological changes and developing sexual awareness which produces tension, anxiety and a likelihood of confrontation with authority.

The 'classic' theory has three main components:

- storm and stress
- identity crisis
- the generation gap.

Activity 7.8

Discuss with your colleagues the feelings that you experienced during your adolescence. Did you all experience the same feelings or experiences? It is true that adolescence is a period of rebellion?

Psychoanalysts also view adolescence as a period of emotional upheaval which stems from the sudden eruption of genital needs during puberty and the need to work through many of the sexual conflicts which have been encountered during childhood. Freud (1968) argued that this re-working of old conflicts results in mood swings from elation to suicidal depression. The balance within the personality of the individual becomes disturbed.

Erikson (1968) states that puberty and adolescence is a period of identity versus role confusion in which the individual has to develop a consistent sense of identity. Erikson believes that rapid body growth disturbs the previous trust in the body and mastery of its functions that were enjoyed in childhood. The individual has to grow into his or her new body. Erikson argues that adolescence was one period in a series of developmental stages which span the individual's life. The unsuccessful resolution of conflicts in earlier stages could produce lasting consequences by leaving unsettled conflicts to interfere with current psychosocial development. Healthy resolution of conflicts means that the individual is able to adjust to the demands of adolescence while still retaining a strong sense of personal identity.

Any conflict with parents during adolescence tends to centre around such things as clothes and hairstyle, homework and time of getting home at night. The majority of parents and adolescents report harmonious family relationships. Coleman (1990) sees adolescence as a time when individuals are active agents of their own development, managing the transitions of adolescence, choosing whether or not to confront parents, seeking or not seeking the acceptance of peers, or resisting the persuasion of others. As adolescents exercise choice they are not overwhelmed by the stresses of everything happening at once.

Adult development

During adulthood most people reach a peak of performance. Skeletal growth ends in the late teens or early twenties and physiologically a person is also then at a peak. Intellectually, this peak may occur later and social development may also take longer.

From the age of about 30 signs of ageing begin to show and physiological changes indicate a slowing down of many processes. This is often associated with increase in the bulk of adipose tissue and a loss of elasticity in connective tissues resulting in the development of a 'middle-age spread' and wrinkles. Skeletal changes mean that joint strength and flexibility are diminished; cartilage becomes less resilient.

There is a clear stage of development in women (at any time from their mid-thirties to late fifties) at which their natural ability to reproduce ends. During this period, called the *menopause*, the ovaries reduce production of the sex hormones. As a result, egg release is reduced and menstruation becomes irregular. Eventually, ovulation and menstruation cease. As we have already seen, these changes have significant effects on the skeleton. The reduction of oestrogen production also means that the balance between oestrogen and adrenal testosterone alters. An effect of this is often observed as increased facial hair. Changes at the cellular level are also noticeable. Some cells, such as nerve cells, die and are not renewable. Others function less well and accumulate toxic metabolites and other substances. Environmental effects can lead to damage to chromosomes giving rise to gene mutations which occasionally lead to abnormal cell growth and cancers.

The range of individual differences is enormous and no physical change during adulthood can be exactly predicted from chronological age – the one possible expectation being grey hair (Foazard, Nuttal & Waugh, 1972). Longevity and youthfulness run in families and are more class than age related. People from lower socio-economic groups tend to age faster and die sooner then those from middle and upper-socio economic groups; they also suffer from poorer health throughout their lives.

> **Physical development:**
> - maximum height is attained at the beginning of adulthood
> - strength peaks about 30 years, after which the muscles weaken somewhat unless maintained by exercise
> - manual dexterity is greatest at 33 years of age
> - sight diminishes throughout adulthood
> - there is a gradual hearing loss after 20, especially among men
> - sensitivity to smell and taste decreases and diminishes after 45
> - adults get fewer acute illness and more chronic ones than children
> - appearance alters at middle age – hair goes grey, skin coarsens and darkens, wrinkles appear
> - sexual potency reaches its peak in late adolescence for men and the mid-twenties for women
> - women cease menstruation at 40–50 years of age.

Personality development

As with other dimensions, although generalisations can be made, the range of individual variations is so great that it is dangerous to make assumptions about any

Maximum height is attained at the beginning of adulthood

individual on the basis of his or her age. Bearing this statement in mind, some generalisations are given below:

- people change 50 per cent of their interests (hobbies, vocational) between adulthood and middle age (Kelly, 1955)
- middle-aged people (45–55) are more sensitive to themselves and aware of their ability and responsibility to make things happen for themselves
- those in their middle age restructure time in terms of time-left-to-live rather than time-since-birth
- the middle-aged place more importance on reflection, introspection and the structuring and restructuring of experience (Neugarten, 1977)
- self-esteem generally seem to increase with years
- people who cope well with early life stresses seem to be able to cope well with later ones.

The analysis of adult development by Erikson (1951) reveals a richness and orderliness in the psychological stages and transitions of the adult life beginning between the ages of 20 to 65 years of age. Erikson proposes an eight-stage progression over the whole life span. Each stage being characterised by a different crucial issue that is either resolved successfully or not. Failure to so impedes all later development.

The first stages are infancy and childhood, the last four beginning with adolescence are:

- identity versus role definition
- intimacy versus isolation
- generativity versus stagnation
- ego integrity versus despair.

Some researchers (for example, Gruen 1964) have found some support for the sequential nature of these stages but found them unrelated to age, sex or social class.

Havighurst (1953), on the other hand, proposes a universal stage theory involving developmental tasks. The tasks for early adulthood are:

- selecting a mate
- learning to live with that mate

Selecting a mate

- starting a family
- rearing children
- managing a home
- getting started in an occupation
- taking on civic responsibilities
- finding a congenial social group.

In later adulthood the tasks are:
- achieving civic and social responsibility
- establishing and maintaining an economic standard of living
- assisting teenage children to become responsible and happy adults
- engaging in appropriate leisure activities
- relating to one's spouse as a person
- accepting the physiological changes of middle age
- adjusting to ageing parents.

Engaging in appropriate leisure activities

Some theorists, like Havighurst, maintain that certain attitudes, behaviour and problems are highly correlated with chronological age. Others, like Neugarten, believe that it is the nature of the individual's experience which determines behaviour, etc. For example, it is not being 40 years old that causes people problems, but the fact that reaching 40 has been emotionally charged by the culture – the person concerned has probably been married for 20 years, has children leaving home, his or her career has peaked and parents are dying.

Collin (1977) concludes that the mid-life crisis is not a developmental stage of life through which everyone must pass, rather that it results from:

'1. Ineffective adjustment to the normal stresses of growth and transition in middle age;
2. The reaction of a particularly vulnerable person to the normal stresses of growth and transition in middle age;
3. Attempted adjustment to the stresses of "abnormal" growth and transition in middle age.'
(Collin, 1977)

The mid-life crisis clearly manifests itself in extreme patterns of response to stress – denial, depression, anger, regression and acting out.

Old age

Ageing may be defined as all the regular changes that occur in biologically mature individuals as they advance in chronological age (Birren & Renner, 1977). This change involves structural changes in the body and also the adjustment and behaviour of the individual. There are several important theories of ageing, for example:
- the phenomenological theory
- the age stratification theory
- the labelling theory
- the disengagement theory
- the activity theory
- the personality theory

When people suffer physical decline in later life they also lose roles especially when they have to enter residential care

- the subculture theory
- the role theory.

Some of these will be examined below.

As a person ages his or her role changes and new roles are added. The major role losses that characterise old age come with retirement, widowhood and institutionalisation. As a rule the majority of retired people never return to the workforce as full-time workers and most widows do not remarry (Blau, 1981). When people suffer physical decline in later life they also lose roles especially when they have to enter residential care. The type of role losses experienced by the elderly underlies the basis for two important theories of ageing, the activity theory and disengagement theory.

The disengagement theory

This theory has been persistent and controversial, emerging in the early 1960s as the first formal theory to try and explain the ageing process. Since then it has gone through a number of refinements. The approach is basically functionalist, that is for society to function properly, the 'old' must be gradually phased out of important roles or replaced by the 'young', thus causing minimal disruption to society when they die. Cumming and Henry (1961), the originators of the theory, contend that the individual and society prepare for death through a gradual process during which the individual and society withdraw from each other.

This theory is based on the tenet that the process of disengagement is inevitable but will vary from individual to individual because of differences in personality, physical or mental health or opportunities. Life satisfaction for the elderly is connected with the reduction of the number and importance of roles, and this suits the society the old person lives in. So happiness in old age consists of the elderly recognising the fact that they are no longer young and that there are more competent young people to fill their roles.

Activity 7.9

You have been appointed the manager of a residential establishment for elderly people. You believe in the disengagement theory of ageing. How would you organise the regime in the establishment to put the theory into practice?

It is supposed that both society and the elderly person concerned contribute to the disengagement process although the level of 'voluntariness' may vary from individual to individual. The process is gradual and the theory supposes that disengagement is the norm, demonstrated by mandatory retirement laws.

The disengagement theory has been criticised because research findings have been contradictory. The theory is simplistic as not all the elderly experience ageing this way. It can also be seen as a self-fulfilling prophecy as many elderly people have a lack of opportunity to be active because of health or economic factors.

The activity theory

This theory originated as the antithesis of disengagement theory although the basic ideas had been postulated for some time. Activity theory is seen as the 'golden years' concept of ageing. The theory claims that to be happy in old age the individual must keep active. Although society withdraws from the individual this is against the

Mrs L has the typical 'stoop' of osteoporosis. She lost 6 inches in height and is now being successfully treated with HRT

individual's desire. To minimise the effects of this withdrawal the individual must keep active.

Those who believe this theory state that if roles and relationships are lost they must be replaced by suitable alternatives. If roles are not replaced the activity level will fall and as a result so will the quality of life. Activity theorists acknowledge that this is a simplistic theory and is unlikely to explain the behaviour of all elderly people.

Those who criticise activity theory point to findings that suggest that a few stable meaningful relationships are the key, not necessarily high levels of involvement.

To minimise the effects of society's withdrawal the individual must keep active

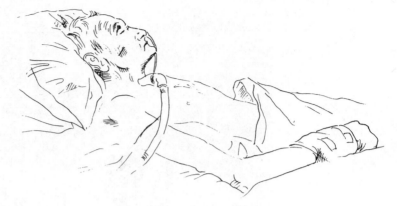

Health rather than wealth becomes more of a status factor as one gets older

The personality theory

This theory attempts to explain the inconsistencies between activity and disengagement theory. The proponent of this theory (Havighurst, 1968) argues that activity and disengagement theory are inadequate to explain the research findings on ageing. Havighurst suggests that it is not the amount of activity but rather the personality type of the individual that is crucial. Different personality types need different levels of activity and involvement to achieve satisfaction. Eight basic personality types have been identified which encompass at one end 'reorganisers' (activity theory) to 'disengagers' (disengagement theory).

The subculture theory

Rose (1965) put forward the theory that the elderly form a subculture which defines and gives direction to their behaviour. The subculture has developed as a result of:

- The growing numbers and percentage of the elderly population in society. This subculture has its own values, ideas and beliefs and now has an impact on society and the individual old person him or herself.
- The aged are 'excluded' by society, through retirement, ill health and the emphasis on youth. The elderly subculture has its own characteristics different from the young.
- This developing 'age consciousness' has united the elderly as a group which has led to the recognition of the elderly by society as a 'peer group'.
- There are subcultures within the subculture based upon wealth, ethnic background, environment and health. These affect status and self-image so that 'health' becomes more of a status factor in old age than wealth as one gets older.

The role theory

A number of writers believe that behaviour in old age can be explained through role theory. A role is behaviour expected from individuals who occupy certain positions, for example, father, mother, social worker or doctor. These roles call for certain types of behaviour that we should or should not be involved in. One major factor which determines how we view the different roles in society is the development of our personality and the process of socialisation. The role is also influenced by our expectations of self and society's expectations.

The implications of role theory for the elderly are that they will behave:

- generally within expected ranges (role prescription/expectation)
- individually different from others (individual interpretation)
- differently with individuals according to their roles (e.g. daughter, doctor, social worker, child, manager, etc.).

Goffman (1961) put forward the proposition that whenever we enter into a social interaction, we commonly seek information about those with whom we are interacting. We ask questions about what the other person looks like, observe his or her mannerisms and speech patterns, and form opinions about occupation, status and other variables. This information gathering is the process which allows us to make a judgement about the situation and the other person which in turn allows us to know how to behave in the interaction.

Goffman believes that we all have the ability to put forward any number of selves. The self is something that is malleable and can assume a number of different forms or roles. After analysing the situation we present the role (self) that we consider appropriate to the situation. Role theory can be used to explain the wide fluctuations in behaviour of the elderly.

Activity 7.10

Discuss Goffman's theory in relation to residents in homes for the elderly. List the reasons how and why seemingly independent people can become dependent after some time in care.

The labelling theory

This theory focuses on the processes by which some people label other members of society as deviant. According to labelling theorists, it is a person's label rather the his or her actions that is important. One of the basic tenets of labelling theory is that through the process individuals are forced into acting out specific behaviours.

When we are given a label such as 'old', 'senile' or 'confused' by others, this has a significant impact on how we are seen by others. This in turn affects our identity or behaviours. Sometimes a particular facet becomes dominant in how others see or relate to us. For example, if a person is labelled 'senile', this label will lead to their behaviour

Sometimes a particular facet becomes dominant in how others see or relate to us

being seen in those terms (senile) and interpreted as such. The 'senile' reinforcing behaviour will be noticed and enhanced. People will respond to the 'senile' person in terms of the label. As a consequence, the person accepts the label and begins to see him or herself as deviant (senile) and then behaves in accordance with the label.

To integrate and relate effectively to their environment the person has to behave in a way consistent with the label 'senile'. The label proves to be a self-fulfilling prophecy.

The age-stratification theory

Just as most societies are stratified by social class they are also stratified by age, race, sex and ethnicity. Riley (1972) argues that age, like social class, divides society into categories on the basis of wealth, prestige and power. This theory is still in its formative stages. It puts forward the tenet that age is the determinant of behaviour because:
- it may limit an individual's ability to perform certain roles (biological, legal, social or sexual)
- society allocates rights and responsibilities, roles and privileges on the basis of age.
In essence, society is seen as being divided into age strata, each of which has a defined set of rights, roles, obligations and opportunities. As individuals move from one age stratum to another they acquire the expectations and roles of that new stratum. Each age stratum contributes to society in different ways from the others. Different sanctions exist and one is continually being socialised into the appropriate behaviour of the new age stratum.

As people move through the different age strata so an individual's attitudes, values and aspirations change with time in a way that is appropriate to his or her age stratum. In each age stratum one has a different experience of life from that in the others.

Influences of inherited and environmental factors on human growth and development

Environmental influences/genetic factors

The nature–nurture debate has been going on for centuries. Psychologists have carried out a number of practical studies to test if it is nurture or nature that affects the development of the personality. Galton, a psychologist in the late 1800s, looked at a number of families and found that parents with high intelligence quotients (IQ) tended to have children with high IQs as did their children's offspring over a number of generations. Did the parents pass on 'intelligent' genes to their children or were the children of a high IQ because of the environment provided by the parents? Certain parents may have provided books and had more stimulating kinds of conversation with their children. A more scientific way to argue this debate is to look at studies involving twins.

The use of twins allows us to study and compare individuals with the same genetic make-up but different environmental experiences or those with different genetic make-ups but the same environmental experiences. This is possible because of the two types of twins. *Monozygotic* twins develop from the same fertilised egg, this means that they have the same genetic make-up. *Dizygotic* twins develop from two separate fertilised eggs and so are not genetically identical.

Monozygotic twins brought up together tend to have similar IQs. What happens when monozygotic twins are separated at birth? It would be reasonable to suppose that any differences would be environmental. Burt argues from studies of separated twins that IQ was 80 per cent inherited and 20 per cent due to environmental factors. However, Burt's studies must be treated with caution as they have been the subject of much criticism. The data used by Burt was used by other (McNemar, 1938 and Kamin, 1974) to provide evidence that environment factors played a big part in the development of IQ. This would point to the fact that any evidence for the existence of a heritable gene factor, must be taken as having a very limited value.

The so-called *nature–nurture debate* assumes that development is caused by either genetic or environmental factors. However, it may be that both together have an influence of personality development. Hebb (1949) tried to point this out by showing how both factors were essential for the development of an egg. He argued that if you take the gene (genetic factor) away you have no egg and if the environment is not warm (environment factor) then the egg dies. He states that it is not an either/or question – each factor is essential for growth.

At conception every person is provided with a mix of genetic material from his or her parents. This genetic make-up governs much of the person's later development. Many disorders of later life are as a result of these inherited genes.

Inherited gene disorders

Just as we inherit characteristics such as eye colour from our parents, and a tendency to diseases such as asthma and heart disease, so we can also inherit defective genes from our parents that give rise to ill-health. Included in this category are single gene disorders such as:

- phenylketonuria
- cystic fibrosis
- Huntington's chorea
- sickle cell anaemia
- colour blindness.

Other inherited disorders involve whole chromosomes and cannot always be traced in families. These include:

- Down's syndrome
- Turner's syndrome
- Kleinfelter's syndrome.

Single gene disorders

A person inherits two copies of most genes; one from the mother and one from the father. (In sex-linked disorders, such as red–green colour blindness, a male child inherits a copy from his mother only.) If one of the genes is defective, it is likely that the second is 'normal' and so normal function is achieved. However if two 'abnormal' genes are inherited, then the function of the 'normal' gene is lost. With phenylketonuria the lack of normal copy means the metabolism of the amino acid phenylalanine, controlled by the gene, does not occur and so the disorder develops. The 'abnormal' gene is masked by the 'normal' gene and so people can carry the defective gene and pass it on without showing any effects themselves. In this way so-called *recessive disorders* can skip generations in families.

With some disorders, the presence of the 'abnormal' gene always has an effect. If the gene is sufficiently dominant just one copy brings about the full abnormality. An example of this is in the relatively rare bone disorder, inherited multiple exostoses. This gene, if present, must express itself and so the disorder cannot skip generations.

Some genes do not exhibit full dominance and so the presence of one copy brings about a reduced effect compared with the full effect from two copies. A disorder in this category is sickle cell anaemia. A person with 'normal' and 'abnormal' copies of the gene exhibits sickle cell trait. The trait creates problems for the person during times of physiological stress because of the abnormal haemoglobin produced by the gene. A double dose of the gene is normally a lethal condition with children not surviving to adulthood. Again, this disorder does not skip generations.

Sickle cell disorder is interesting. In some cases, the disorder has a positive advantage. People with the sickle trait are less susceptible to some forms of malaria and so natural selection has favoured the gene in areas where malaria is endemic.

Chromosome abnormalities

Occasionally, the meiotic cell division to produce gametes goes wrong and a gamete receives too much or too little chromosome material.

Case study

Down's syndrome

In the case of Down's syndrome, a gamete from either the mother or the father contains an extra chromosome number 21 as a result of a genetic 'accident' either when the gamete was made or during the initial cell division following fertilisation. The child produced as a result has three copies of the chromosome 21, and therefore 47 in all, rather than 46. Ninety-five per cent of cases of Down's syndrome are a result of this 'accident'. The effect is to produce characteristic physical features and a level of mental incapacity. Most people with Down's syndrome have a reduced life expectancy and a reduced level of fertility.

It is not fully understood why the abnormal gametes are produced but it is known that the older a woman is the greater the chance that a pregnancy will result in a child with Down's syndrome. However, the majority of babies with Down's syndrome are still born to younger women, simply because the overall birth-rate is higher in that group.

Approximately one in 100 people with Down's syndrome have inherited the condition from the mother or father because of a genetic abnormality called *Translocation*. There is a third, equally rare, type of Down's syndrome known as Mosaic Down's syndrome.

Source: Information supplied by the Down's Syndrome Association

Control and cure for inherited disease

Should we say that people from families with genetic disorders should not have children? Should we test for genetic disorders in the womb and then abort the foetus?

It is easy to identify simple ways in which people with genetic disorders could ensure they do not pass on the genes. Some extreme regimes have even tried to cleanse the population of people they consider to be genetically inferior. Nazi Germany was an extreme example of this. It has not been, and never can be, a viable way of 'controlling' inherited disorders. Apart from the very clear moral issues, biology is also against any such programme. A simple example in the case study of phenylketonuria can identify the weakness.

People with Down's syndrome can enter the open job market and become reliable employees

Case study

Phenylketonuria

Phenylketonuria is controlled by a single gene, the defective one being recessive. A test is available for babies born in the UK, soon after birth, to identify if they have inherited two defective genes and have the disorder. About one in 25,000 babies have the disorder. Surely if people carrying the gene could be persuaded not to have children, then the disorder could be eliminated and the cost of 24,999 wasted tests could be saved? The question then arises, 'How many people would be asked not to have children?'

The Hardy–Weinberg equation can be used to calculate the number of people carrying the gene in the population. It relies on several issues but at its simplest it can be expressed thus:

Assume that there are two versions of a gene that occur with the frequency p and q, where $p + q = 1$. Any person can have a double dose of either gene or one of each. The frequencies of these is related by the formula:

$$p^2 + 2pq + q^2 = 1$$

So, for the gene controlling phenylketonuria we can say that the normal version K has a frequency of p, while the abnormal one k has a frequency of q. The frequencies of each combination of genes are expressed thus:

$KK = p^2$

$Kk = 2pq$

$kk = q^2$

We know that $q^2 = 1/25{,}000$

Thus $q = \sqrt{1/25{,}000}$

$\quad\quad = 0.0063$

As we know $p + q = 1$ and also that q is very small, we can say that for easier calculation $p = 1$.

By putting these figures into the Hardy–Weinberg equation we calculate the frequency of people carrying the abnormal gene:

$$2pq = 2 \times 1 \times 0.0063$$
$$= 0.0126$$

This means that the frequency of 'carriers' in the population is 0.0126 or 1 in 80.

So to get rid of phenylketonuria, 1 in 80 people would have to give up having children. This may seem almost possible but everyone carries at least five versions of genes that could give rise to inherited disorders. To follow this to its logical conclusion, i.e. to eliminate all genetic disorders, everybody should stop having children. There would then be no problem of inherited disorders in the next generation. But who would form the next generation?

Obviously from this case study it can be seen that eliminating defective versions of genes is not easy. However, the understanding of inherited disorders does mean that people can be counselled by trained counsellors about the risks and can make informed decisions about having or not having children.

How individuals cope with transition and change in their lives

Stress

One of the most common causes of illness and disease is stress. It is a major part of our everyday lives. Most of us realise that too much stress can be harmful; it can lead to acute or chronic ill-health. The term 'stress' is used in two distinct ways:

- **external stressors** – conditions in the world around us that induce feelings of discomfort, tension and pressure
- **internal stressors** – internally induced reactions.

A biological indication of stress is an increased level of the hormone adrenaline in the blood. This hormone is naturally released in preparation for fight or flight. It prepares the body by increasing the heart rate, breathing rate and increasing the production of muscle glycogen. The muscles are made ready for action. There is a heightened awareness as the senses are made more acute.

These reactions are natural and help in times of major emergency. However, many lifestyles now involve a constant background level of stress. There is a constant release of adrenaline at low levels which keeps the muscles in a state of readiness without allowing them to actually make use of the heightened levels. Over time this affects the heart muscles and also the psychological well-being. A second, less well understood effect is the weakening of the immune system. People suffering from stress have decreased resistance to infection and take longer to recover from infections and other traumas.

There are now many people teaching stress-management to employers, employees and the general public. They teach strategies for relaxation and reducing the current physiological stress, as well as techniques to prevent the stress levels developing. In supporting well-being promotion, it becomes important to identify the causes of stress and to develop strategies to deal with them.

It must be emphasised that some level of stress can be useful. It would be difficult to imagine an examination without the pre-exam nerves which can help performance. It is the long-term effects of a constant drip feed of adrenaline as a result prolonged stress that is physiologically and psychologically damaging.

Case study

Stress in the health service

In the latter half of the 1980s there was a dispute between two factions in a mental health unit in the Midlands. The dispute was over the setting up of community-based mental health care. One group was very strongly in favour of moving patients away from the hospital environment, whilst the other wished to establish mental health units within general hospitals. The former group was advocating the development of care in the community sometime before the ideas were put forward in the NHS and Community Care Act 1990.

There were two consultants on the anti-community-based care side, and one consultant, a head of psychology and the head of social work on the pro-community side. Acting as a neutral referee was the unit general manager. There then ensued a battle of wills that went on both in and outside meetings. The different factions were constantly pushing forward their own views and trying to 'sabotage' the other's position.

As a result of all of this, the participants were under a great deal of stress for over two years. The final decision was to set up a mental health team in the district general hospital and another in the community. Thus neither viewpoint had prevailed and the original mental health unit had been split into two.

The effects on the personnel were more marked. Of the three consultants, one had a heart attack and two had nervous breakdowns. The head of psychology had a heart attack and the head of social work developed myalgic encephalomyelitis (ME). The neutral unit general manager also suffered a stroke.

While none of these incidents can be proved to be a direct result of the conflict, all of them have been identified as linked to persistent, high stress levels. It is reasonable to assume that the constant stress of the conflict contributed to the ill-health described.

Activity 7.11

How might the participants have attempted to reduce their stress levels, given that their individual views were strongly held and, in their eyes, professionally justified?

Stress: a definition
'There is a potential for stress when an environmental situation is perceived as presenting a demand that threatens to exceed the person's capabilities and resources for meeting it.'

In the last century, the emphasis of research into the causes of disease was on 'science'. Causes were sought in agents such as germs and pathological processes. As a result, social or psychological explanations for the causes of disease (such as stress) were ignored because they were unscientific.

Freud was the first to argue that certain illnesses could be explained in terms of the individual's response to internal psychological conflict. This anxiety is an emotional state that involves feelings of uneasiness, fear or apprehension. According to Freud, we develop a number of defence mechanisms to counteract this anxiety.

Stress-related diseases such as ulcers, skin diseases and asthma began to be seen as the body's expression of unconscious tensions that the individual could not deal with in any other manner. We now know that psychological stress produces vulnerability to a wide range of diseases.

Measuring stress

Estimating stress is one approach to the examination of the impact of key life events and the extent to which stress may contribute to subsequent illness. In 1967, Holmes and Rahe published a table of stress factors (see Table 7.2). It attempted to express, in quantitative terms, the amount of stress involved in a range of specified key life events. Events near the top of the list are highly stressful and often seem to produce adverse effects upon health. Those events near the bottom of the list are only mildly stressful and have less impact upon personal health. A score of 300 points or more, accumulated over a 12-month period, is considered high and a strong indication of ill-health. Most people can cope with up to 150 points over a 12-month period.

Table 7.2 Stress scale

Key life events	Points	Key life events	Points
Death of husband or wife	100	Major change of work	39
Divorce	73	Large mortgage taken on	31
Marital separation	65	Starting a new school	26
Jail sentence	63	Leaving school	26
Illness or injury	53	Change in residence	20
Marriage	50	Change in sleeping habits	16
Loss of job	47	Major change in eating pattern	15
Retirement	45	Holiday	13
Pregnancy	40	Christmas	12
Sex problem	39	Minor violation of law	11

Job-related stress

Many jobs are more stressful than others. The most stressful occupations are:
- advertising
- journalism
- acting
- dentistry
- doctor
- social worker
- pilot
- police
- nursing
- mining
- construction.

The least stressful occupations include:
- banking
- nature conservancy
- nursery nurse

- beauty therapy
- biologist
- linguist.

Student nurses, for example, find certain aspects of their job more stressful than others – top of their list is care of the dying, conflict with other nurses, insecurity about competence and fear of failure. Engineers, on the other hand, put wasting time and interpersonal conflict as the top stressors.

Some jobs are more stressful than others

Reaction to stress

Events have different effects on different people. Certain changes in life, such as divorce, leaving school or change in residence may ultimately reduce stress, as those events may improve the quality of our lives. Why do some people readily succumb to the stress produced by traumatic life events? Why are some people quite resistant to this factor and continue to function effectively in the face of one personal disaster after another? What factors account for these differences in susceptibility? People who believe that they are in control of their lives and those with a sense of purpose and meaning seem not to let themselves be affected by stress factors. Those who perceive change as a challenge or an opportunity for development rather than a threatening burden are also less likely to suffer from stress.

Activity 7.12

a List as many situations or activities that cause you, as a student, stress.

b What factors in a person's lifestyle would lead you to believe that he or she is capable of dealing with intense levels of stress or pressure?

There are a number of times when we can go through overwhelming changes in our lives, such as:

● marriage
● giving birth
● unemployment
● a new job
● the loss of someone close
● the loss of a limb
● starting university or college.

These key life events can often cause us anxiety and stress. During these times of major life changes, the individual has to come to terms with a new status. Such changes force the individual to become aware of what they have lost – the old patterns and relationships. The anxiety that may be experienced can be influenced by a range of personal and social factors, but may be less where the change is expected and shared with others. Ceremonies, such as weddings and funerals, may serve to reduce anxiety by offering a formal, ritualistic set of responses.

Activity 7.13

List the reasons why you think that many societies have 'rites of passage' such as funerals and wedding ceremonies.

Bereavement and loss

A most devastating form of stress experienced by individuals is bereavement – a state characterised by loss. The most frequent, and obvious, example of loss is that occasioned by the death of a close relative or friend, but people may be bereaved by other losses, such as loss of job, loss of status, loss of a limb or loss of a home.

The bereaved person may need to learn new skills

Studies have shown that individuals who have lost a close relative have a much increased risk of sickness or mortality themselves as a result. In a study of widowers, Murrey Parkes (1975) observed an increased mortality, usually from heart disease, for six months following the individual's loss. Men seem more vulnerable than women to suffer ill-health or death following the loss of a close relative. It has been suggested that people become more vulnerable to stress following such loss because of the pathological effects of bereavement due to the loss of meaning in their lives and severe disruption to assumptions about the world created by the death. These effects combine to undermine basic coping abilities in the individual, including resistance to illness.

Coping with bereavement and loss

Grief is the individual's response to bereavement. It is a complex response which may include 'symptoms' such as:

- fatigue
- anxiety
- loss of appetite
- withdrawal
- depression
- guilt
- sleep disturbance.

Other symptoms include:

- searching behaviour
- suicidal thoughts
- panic
- heightened vulnerability to physical illness.

Stages of grief

The complexity and stress of grief is now appreciated by all professionals. Although everyone's experience of grief is unique, several studies suggest that most people experience a number of stages; these are also associated with people's reactions to serious illness. The most commonly observed stages are as follows.

Stage one: denial

Sometimes the bereaved person will behave as if nothing has happened, they may not believe that the dead person has died. Denial may be expressed by keeping all the dead person's belongings ready for use, or alternatively getting rid of everything that reminds them of the deceased.

Stage two: shock

The second stage begins when the bereaved person begins to feel the pain of loss. Some people may cry, but others may feel anger at the dead person for dying, or guilty for not having prevented the death. The bereaved may also feel a sense of rejection by the dead person.

Stage three: acceptance

The acceptance of the situation usually happens after a short period. Attending the funeral, for example, is part of accepting the loss and facing the pain of carrying on without the dead person. Once the bereaved person has accepted the reality of the situation, he or she can begin to live life again. Most people will not return to their former levels of functioning – they may move on to a new level where the pain and loss of grieving are incorporated. The bereaved may need to learn new skills: cooking, looking after themselves or living on their own.

The length of time that a person may spend in each stage of grief will depend upon the circumstances of the loss, the relationship that they had with the animal or person they have lost, and the cultural and religious background of the grieving person.

Most people agree that is desirable for the bereaved to give way to grief. Grief has to be worked through, if it is not, the bereaved person will continue to have troubles of some sort. The problems must be brought out into the open and confronted. The bereaved person should be helped and supported at his or her own pace until the loss begins to be accepted.

Activity 7.14

a How would you support someone who has lost a close relative?
b How would you try to alleviate the effects of stress on a bereaved person?

Loss can occur at any age, but we are only now beginning to appreciate the effect of loss in old age. Many people remain remarkably fit into extreme old age and stay strong and mentally agile. However, there are many losses that affect the elderly, including:
- loss of status and defined role, as a result of retirement
- loss of income, as a result of retirement
- loss of health and bodily function, leading to loss of mobility and independence
- loss of sexual function
- loss of company, for example, spouse, friends or pets
- loss of independence and home by admission to a residential home or hospital
- loss of life.

Changes in employment

Some groups are particularly vulnerable to becoming unemployed, such as those on low wages. A survey in 1980 of over 2,000 registered unemployed men found that as many as 50 per cent had been receiving the lowest earnings in the national earning distribution. There is clear evidence that there is a high rate of unemployment among young people, older workers, those in poor health and women.

Researchers suggest that the loss of a job is comparable to bereavement. Many unemployed men, for example, experience feelings of hopelessness, self-blame, sadness, lack of energy, loss of self-esteem and self-confidence, insomnia, suicidal thoughts and an increase use of tobacco and alcohol. People react to unemployment in different ways depending on:
- the availability of work in the future
- the individual's feelings about the circumstances surrounding his or her loss of job. (For example, does the unemployed person feel the victim of circumstances and not personally responsible?)
- the response of spouse, children and relatives
- the sense of 'loss of face' or respect in the community
- the financial implications
- the extent of supportive networks in the community.

Many unemployed people experience significantly fewer positive feelings, and more strain, anxiety and depression. Becoming employed again very quickly restores well-being.

Researchers suggest that loss of job is comparable to bereavement

The effects of unemployment upon health, however, are not at all clear. Some US studies have found little correlation between unemployment and ill-health but UK studies indicate that it may be a factor in poor health. The latter studies found high levels of stress among the unemployed. Unskilled people (social class V) and those who have been unemployed for long periods tend to have higher blood pressure and also tend to be fatter than those people in the professional class. They are also more likely to suffer from arthritis, angina, respiratory problems, alcohol-related disease and mental illness.

Activity 7.15

What do you think the effect of job loss could be upon an individual?

Coping with change and transition

Despite the possibility of positive outcomes, change is often resisted by individuals. Resistance to change, or the thought of the implications of change, appears to be a common phenomenon. People seem to be naturally wary of change.

Resistance to change

Resistance to change may take a number of forms:

- **Selective perception** An individual's own perception of stimuli presents a unique picture of the 'real' world and can result in selective perception. This can lead to a biased view of a particular situation, which fits comfortably into the individual's own perception of reality. For example, lecturers may have a view of students as irresponsible and therefore oppose any attempts to involve them in decision making about their own learning or course organisation.
- **Habit** Individuals tend to respond to situations in an established and accustomed manner. Habits may serve as a means of comfort and security. Proposed changes to habits may be resisted.
- **Inconvenience or loss of freedom** People will resist change if it is perceived as likely to directly or indirectly make life more difficult or reduce their freedom.

185

- **Security in the past** People tend to find a sense of security in the past. In times of frustration or difficulty, individuals may reflect on the past. They may wish to retain old and comfortable ways.
- **Fear of the unknown** Situations which confront people with the unknown tend to cause anxiety. People may resist a job change because of the uncertainties over changes in responsibilities.

People attempt to adapt to change by adopting what are commonly called defence mechanisms; these they are unaware of. People will react to change in individual ways. For example, some will become depressed, while others may see it as a challenge.

Defence mechanisms

It is always important to remember that *defence mechanisms* are defences against anxiety and are always unconscious, which means that the individual is not aware that they are using such mechanisms. If a person is aware of what he or she is doing, then it cannot be a defence mechanism.

Defence mechanisms are sometimes seen as protection against the pain of traumatic life experiences. Some of the most common forms of defence mechanisms are:

- **Identification** This occurs when an individual unconsciously copies the dress, behaviour or mannerisms of the person he or she admires or envies.
- **Repression** People may repress from their consciousness any thought of a situation which may cause anxiety. They may, therefore, refuse to come to terms with the change in their lives. For example, you may forget a dental appointment or some other unpleasant appointment.
- **Denial** People often deny that some change in their lifestyle has happened. For example, after bereavement a person may carry on as if the dead person is still around the home.
- **Regression** This involves a return to earlier modes of functioning. The most extreme form may manifest itself in the individual reacting to a traumatic shock by regression to childhood behaviour. For example, a previously toilet-trained child may revert to incontinence on the birth of a sibling.
- **Projection** A person uses this defence mechanism when he or she attributes his or her own feelings to another person. This is the most common form of defence mechanism. It may be as 'normal' as blaming someone else for some everyday incident, such as seeing all the problems on a ward or in a residential home as due to the shortcomings of the other shift, or it may be more serious as in the individual who is suffering from paranoid delusions.
- **Introjection** This is the global taking in of attitudes. The individual will tend to internalise the attitudes of those who may be creating a threat. For example, a child might pretend to be a ghost to cope with his or her fear of ghosts.
- **Reversal or reaction formation** This is the transformation of feelings into their opposite. For example, a person tempted by unacceptable feelings of love may instead hate the object of such love.
- **Sublimation** This is also one of the common forms of defence mechanism. To keep his or her mind off a situation, a person may become obsessed with work or single-mindedly take up some new sport or hobby.
- **Displacement** This is particularly applicable to people in institutions. Emotions stirred up by one situation are displaced and expressed in an inappropriate situation. For example, a senior member of staff shouts at a junior member who, instead of shouting back, shouts at a yet more junior member.

Activity 7.16

Mary, a residential care worker, has just experienced a serious telling off by her senior manager. On returning to the main day room she see a resident spill some tea on the carpet. Mary shouts at the resident who then goes into the garden and tries to take out her frustration on the establishment's cat.

What defence mechanisms have Mary and the resident exhibited?

Methods used by individuals, families, groups and communities to support each other

Case study

Women's refuges

The first attempt to provide support for women who suffered violence was in 1971 by Erin Pizzey who opened the first women's refuge in Chiswick, London. Since then the Women's Aid Federation, founded in 1975, has encouraged the setting up of refuges to help women who suffer from male violence. Most, if not all, of the refuges are run by volunteers with some funding from local authorities. The aims of the Women's Aid Federation refuges are:

- to provide temporary refuge for women and their children who have suffer harassment
- to recognise and care for the emotional needs of the children involved
- to offer encouragement to women to determine their own future
- to offer support and advice to any women who requests it
- to offer aftercare to women who have left the refuge
- to provide an educational service to inform the public, police, the media and other services of the position of women in society.

The addresses of the refuges are usually kept secret to avoid interference from men. This allows women to think about their future without the fear of attack or violence from men.

Support for women

Women who are made homeless must be provided with accommodation by the local authority housing department if they fall into one of the following priority areas:
- if they have dependent children, usually under 16 years of age
- if they are pregnant
- if they are at risk through disablement or old age.

Activity 7.17

In your locality identify those support services that exist to help women who have been subjected to violence.

Counselling

Care staff may be called upon to offer counselling advice to those in their care at critical periods in a person's life, such as retirement, bereavement, becoming unemployed, divorce, etc.

By exercising skills of observation and by careful listening to the problems expressed by people during these times of stress, the carer can begin to understand the anxieties and problems as other people see them and so can offer support and practical help.

Support for carers

Carers need support too – they can feel isolated when left to care for an elderly, ill or disabled person alone. Professionals now recognise that carers can be subjected to considerable stress and strain, and that this may sometimes lead to abuse by the carer.

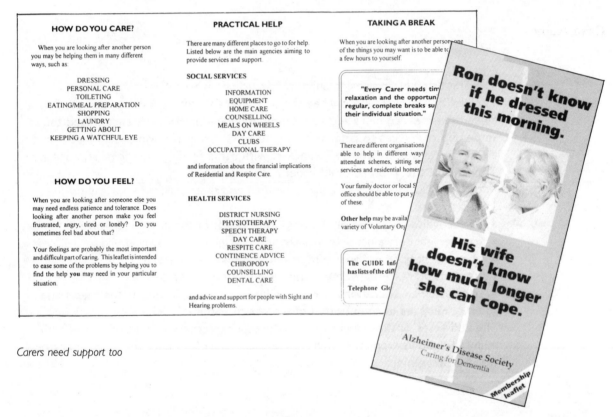

HOW DO YOU CARE?

When you are looking after another person you may be helping them in many different ways, such as:

DRESSING
PERSONAL CARE
TOILETING
EATING/MEAL PREPARATION
SHOPPING
LAUNDRY
GETTING ABOUT
KEEPING A WATCHFUL EYE

HOW DO YOU FEEL?

When you are looking after someone else you may need endless patience and tolerance. Does looking after another person make you feel frustrated, angry, tired or lonely? Do you sometimes feel bad about that?

Your feelings are probably the most important and difficult part of caring. This leaflet is intended to ease some of the problems by helping you to find the help **you** may need in your particular situation.

PRACTICAL HELP

There are many different places to go to for help. Listed below are the main agencies aiming to provide services and support.

SOCIAL SERVICES

INFORMATION
EQUIPMENT
HOME CARE
COUNSELLING
MEALS ON WHEELS
DAY CARE
CLUBS
OCCUPATIONAL THERAPY

and information about the financial implications of Residential and Respite Care.

HEALTH SERVICES

DISTRICT NURSING
PHYSIOTHERAPY
SPEECH THERAPY
DAY CARE
RESPITE CARE
CONTINENCE ADVICE
CHIROPODY
COUNSELLING
DENTAL CARE

and advice and support for people with Sight and Hearing problems.

TAKING A BREAK

When you are looking after another person one of the things you may want is to be able to a few hours to yourself.

"Every Carer needs tim relaxation and the opportun regular, complete breaks su their individual situation."

There are different organisations able to help in different ways attendant schemes, sitting se services and residential homes

Your family doctor or local S office should be able to put y of these.

Other help may be availa variety of Voluntary Org

The GUIDE Inf has lists of the diff

Telephone Glo

Ron doesn't know if he dressed this morning.

His wife doesn't know how much longer she can cope.

Alzheimer's Disease Society
Caring for Dementia

Membership leaflet

Carers need support too

Example

Carers and Alzheimer's disease

Carers of people with Alzheimer's disease, particularly close relatives, often feel a sense of bereavement and loss for the person 'they once knew'. As the disease develops, the sufferer will have increasing difficulty communicating and making him or herself understood. The sufferer loses the ability to remember, learn, think and reason. He or she may forget recent events (actions only just performed) but still remember things that happened years ago – he or she may even forget who the carer is. The symptoms of this disease can be particularly difficult and distressing for a carer to deal with alone – it can be likened to looking after a child, but a child who was once a 'normal' adult!

The family still pays an important role in the support of its independent members

Social support groups

One of the most important social support groups is the family. Recent changes in society have highlighted the role of the family. Recent policy has emphasised a diminishing role for the state and an increasing role for self-help and care by the family. Professional services are changing and a greater burden of responsibility for the sick has shifted back to the family from the state. Some families, however, do not have the resources (capital, financial or psychological) to provide support for the long-term sick. Unemployment, poverty, the increase in one-parent families and the necessity for women to work outside the home have rendered many families incapable of looking after their dependent members. Families with young children, the unemployed and the elderly living alone are less likely to have the necessary resources.

However, the family still plays a major role in the support of its dependent members. It provides for health by means of maintaining a home, provision of housing, proper diet, teaching standards of hygiene and health care, facilitating professional help and also caring for those who fall ill.

Activity 7.18

a How does the family provide support for its dependent members?
b What services exist in your area to help families to look after their members?

There is a body of knowledge that suggests that a lack of social support, such as practical assistance, financial help, information and advice, psychological support, and close social or emotional relationships can increase vulnerability to illness and disease. In one study, those who were classed as socially isolated were two to three times more likely to die than those who were part of an extensive social network. Other studies show that disabled people with few social contacts were more likely to deteriorate in physical functioning than people with high levels of contact with others. The main contribution of social support would seem to be that of a buffer, particularly when people are experiencing adverse life events.

Activity 7.19

a Make a list of reasons why the socially isolated are more likely to die than those with an extensive social network.
b Compare and discuss your list with those of your class colleagues.

Access to information and health maintenance services

Who uses the health services? Table 7.3 shows the uneven use of health services by children under seven from different social classes.

Table 7.3 Social class and use of health facilities (percentage of under sevens)

Social class	Visited dentist	Immunised against		
		Smallpox	Polio	Diphtheria
I	16	6	1	
II	20	14	3	3
III	21	21	3	5
IV	27	29	6	8
V	31	33	10	11

Source: Adapted from OPCS, 1978 and *Occupational Mortality Decennial Supplement 1970–2* (HMSO)

The Black Report (1980) strongly argues the need to improve the distribution of health service resources in order to match the greatest need with most effective care. It argues that there is unequal access to health services because there is less provision in some localities, such as inner cities, and the ways in which existing services are organised are not always appropriate for the nature of the population they serve. Class differentials in the use of various services derive from the interaction of social and ecological factors. In addition, the structure of the services is organised in accordance with the values and assumptions of the middle-class patient. Less attention has been paid to the less well-off and less able who are unable to express themselves in acceptable terms and who suffer from lack of command over resources in terms of time and money.

Activity 7.20

Visit your local social services department or your GP's surgery. Examine the information, publicity, leaflets, etc. produced by these organisations. Do they invite communication from users? Could they be improved?

People in different social classes seem to behave differently when confronted by a medical problem because of the different levels of knowledge they may have. Those who understand the nature of illness, the services available and the procedures for using them will get better support than those who lack such knowledge. Middle-class people are more likely to have access to this knowledge than working-class people. On the whole, middle-class people will question and be critical of any shortcomings in services more often than working-class people. It is suggested that different social classes perceive health services in the same way but the working class are more diffident about expressing their views. Because a particular group of people (a social class or ethnic group) does not make full use of a service as expected, attention is often focused on what is wrong with members of that group, rather than what may be wrong with the service or its delivery.

Activity 7.21

Why do you think that middle-class people are more likely to criticise shortcomings in services compared to working-class people?

Just as individuals react differently to available medical facilities, so the providers of these facilities react differently to differing groups in the community. Middle-class patients are given longer consultations by doctors and more problems are discussed during these consultations. Doctors are most frequently drawn from the middle classes so they may find it difficult to empathise with other groups.

Difficulties of access to health care may be compounded for black and Asian people by direct or indirect discrimination, and by lack of knowledge and awareness among health care staff of their ways of life and economic circumstances. Different ethnic groups are susceptible to different illnesses, for example:

- Cystic fibrosis is more likely to occur in white groups than in other ethnic groups.
- People of Afro-Caribbean origin are more susceptible to high blood pressure than any other ethnic group.
- Babies with dark skin may suffer from jaundice more than white children.
- Children from the Asian culture suffer from a higher incidence of rickets. (This was thought at first to be a problem for those of Asian culture because of the traditional vegetarian diet that may Asians follow. However, recent studies have now shown that this traditional diet is not in itself a significant factor.)

Review questions

1 What are the four life stages discussed in this chapter?
2 What is a centile chart used for?
3 What are the four theories of personality described in this chapter?
4 What is the basis of social learning theory?
5 Write a definition on language. Why do humans use language?
6 What does the term 'self-concept' refer to?
7 What has the writer Erikson have to say about the life stage of adolescence?
8 What are the physical and psychological manifestations of the menopause in women?
9 List four theories of ageing and write down brief details of each one.
10 What is the assumption underlying the nature–nurture debate?

Assignment 7.1
How individuals develop and cope with change

This assignment provides the knowledge, understanding and portfolio evidence for element 4.1, **Investigate human growth and development.**

Your tasks

1 You have been asked by your lecturer to explain to your class colleagues the differences in the stages of human development (physical, language, cognitive and emotional) between children, adolescents, adults and the elderly. Write down a brief outline of what you will say.

2 Give an explanation of how individuals develop personality.

3 List the environmental influences that might affect individual development.

4 What are the affects of genes and chromosomes on such development.

5 Describe the importance of inherited and environmental factors in determining human growth and development. What are the importance of the respective influences?

Gidion who has worked for the same company as a salesman for the past 35 years has been made redundant at the age of 49. He held a senior position in the accounts department but never found the time to gain formal qualifications.

6 Explain how Gidion might cope with this unexpected transition in his life.

Sandra has just experienced the death of her mother who was 95-years-old. She had lived with her mother all her life and was very close to her.

7 Explain how Sandra could cope with this unexpected change in her life.

8 Finally, give an explanation of three different methods of support available to Gidion and Sandra.

8 How individuals function in and are influenced by society and the effects of socio-economic factors on health and social well-being

What is covered in this chapter

- The process of socialisation
- How social constructs change over time
- Potential conflicts within a multi-cultural society
- How the values promoted by health and social care workers differ from those of clients
- Demographic characteristics used in assessing health and social well-being
- The inter-relationships between socio-economic factors, demographic character-istics and health and social well-being
- Socio-economic factors and lifestyle choices
- The impact of social policies on health and social well-being.

These are the resources that you will need for your portfolio for element 4.2:
- An analytical report which in broad terms:
  - explains the effects of socialisation on the development of an individual by contrasting three different influences in the range
  - explains how two social constructs have changed over time.
- A short report which:
  - explains the potential conflicts which exist between the norms and values of two different groups in a multi-cultural society
  - explains how values promoted by health and social care workers may differ from those of clients.

These are the resources you will need for your portfolio for element 4.3:
- An analytical report which:
  - describes the use of three demographic characteristics in assessing the health and social well-being of the population
- – considers the inter-relationships between health and social well-being and socio-economic factors
  - assesses the impact of one social policy on the health and social well-being of the population, using three demographic characteristics in the range
  - makes two reasoned recommendations for possible ways of improving the health and social well-being of the population.
- A summary of how the other demographic characteristics are used to assess the health and social well-being of the population.

Finally:
- Your written answers to the activities, review questions and assignment in this chapter.

The process of socialisation

The ways in which people assimilate values

Social attitudes are learned through a process of association. We are all driven by basic needs that need to be satisfied. When we behave in ways that satisfy needs, the behaviour or response, is rewarded or reinforced. We are then likely to use the same behaviour again and again to satisfy the need. In a social context, if we behave in ways that meet with the approval and praise of those around us, those behaviours will be reinforced.

Many of our attitudes are also shaped by the responses of those around us. Thus, the attitudes of the social class we belong to are likely to be adopted by us because we are socially rewarded by the approval of others. Similarly, our gender, race and religion will all play a role in shaping our attitudes, as all of these constitute social groups that will reward certain attitudes and disapprove of others. For example:

- social class may determine our views about education and work
- gender may influence beliefs about roles within the family or safety in the streets
- our race may influence the realistic expectations we may have about being treated fairly in employment, or our tastes in music and food.

Religion is a major shaper of attitudes, as it often constitutes an organised system of beliefs about right and wrong. Most of these attitudes will be learned within the context of the family.

Activity 8.1

a In small groups of three or four, define your own religious attitudes.
b How do you believe that these attitudes may help or hinder your activities in supporting a client?

Examples of issues which you may wish to consider are euthanasia or contraception.

The learning process described above is called *socialisation*. Our personalities are shaped and developed through social contacts with other people. The process starts when we are infants and progresses throughout our lives. We come to behave, to feel, to evaluate and to think similarly to those around us. Most societies tend to reproduce their social

Most societies tend to reproduce their social kind from generation to generation

kind from generation to generation. However, the process is complex and not fully understood. We all know of examples of lack of socialisation – for example, the child who rebels and adopts a lifestyle completely different from the parents!

Sources of socialisation

Socialisation is influenced by two groups in society:
- membership groups, such as a person's culture and social class, where socialisation occurs through one-to-one contact with family (the strongest socialising influence, and the most studied), friends and neighbours
- reference groups, which are perhaps the most personally significant influence of attitudes.

Membership groups

Family

The family is the best-known and strongest socialising influence. Parents essentially want to guide the child's acquisition of values, behaviour and personality characteristics into what the culture considers appropriate. Parents direct the child's learning toward what the culture defines as desirable characteristics and behaviour. At the same time, undesirable behaviours and values are inhibited.

The inhibition of undesirable behaviours in the child is referred to as *repressive socialisation*. Repressive socialisation usually begins during the child's second year. The child is asked to stop making so much noise at dinner, to stop jumping up and down on the bed, and to curb tantrums. Repressive socialisation emphasises obedience and respect for authority.

Some parents, however, soon begin to move away from this socialising technique towards *participatory socialisation*. This gives children freedom to try things out for themselves and explore the world on their own terms.

Participatory socialisation is child-centred, rather than parent-centred. Children are more likely to be motivated by their desire to be like someone they respect, love and admire. This is called the *process of identification*.

Children watch what you do. So watch what you do!

Early socialisation is probably most readily accomplished through a combination of both techniques. Rewards and punishments are both effectively used. However, as the child gets older, the acquisition of values and behaviours is more likely to be product of identification with a model.

Both types of socialisation are not quite randomly distributed in society, but are correlated with socio-economic level and education. The evidence indicates that repressive socialisation is more characteristic of the working class, while participatory socialisation is found more commonly in the middle class.

The socialisation that occurs within the family develops notions of what is right and wrong. It also determines the level of importance put on traditional roles. Importantly, the family have a powerful influence on the value of education. Religious beliefs are also largely socialised through the family.

Culture

Culture is the set of beliefs and values that people regard as natural and normal in a particular society. For example, the expectations of people in Britain are very different from those of people in China. The values of our society are taught to us in the family and in school, and are communicated to us through television and newspapers.

Sub-culture

There are variations within a national culture that are determined perhaps more locally, or related to special interests or lifestyle. The attitudes of people from Yorkshire, for example, may differ from those of Londoners. Examples of lifestyle sub-cultures are punks, hippies and travellers. Race and religion may also be sub-cultural influences. For example, African and Caribbean culture will influence the attitudes of that sub-culture in Britain and Chinese culture will influence the attitude of the British Chinese community. Religions such as Judaism and Islam rely on sub-cultural influence on an international level in order to remain intact.

Social class

Divisions in labour and education create other sub-cultures known as *social class*. Social class is characterised by values and attitudes acquired through contact with others in a particular class. Some young people, for example, go to special, privileged schools with the intention of socialising them into particular class attitudes and behaviours.

Peer groups

Peer groups have a strong influence on attitudes, as they may be simultaneously membership and reference groups (see below). Peer groups are formed by individuals with a common interest or identification. A good example is the friends you choose when you are young. They are likely to influence your attitudes toward school work, the music you like, the way you dress, and even the way you express yourself both verbally and non-verbally. Later in life peer groups may be identified more in relation to vocation or profession. Teachers, for example, may relate as a peer group, members often dressing alike and possessing similar views.

Activity 8.2

a In small groups, make a list of other peer groups that influence dress and appearance. Examples may be based on age, profession, or social groups.

b Do you think that the groups you identified are stereotyped by their dress and appearance?

Imposed membership groups

These include elderly people, disabled people, unemployed people and mentally ill people. Health and social care services have been largely ignorant of the importance of reference groups (see below) to people's own sense of identity. Hence, access to care services is often determined by establishing the client as a member of a group with a negative label (i.e. imposing a membership group upon the client) that stresses his or her 'abnormality'. These are not likely to be the membership or reference groups that the individuals would choose for themselves.

Putting individuals into groups creates a language for us to describe them. Language determines attitudes. This has been well-documented by sociologists such as Goffman (1961), psychiatrists such as Laing (1960), and neurologists such as Sacks (1985). Sacks describes how we use a language describing deficit, shortcomings and problems for users of health and social care services, and how our language does not describe the capabilities, potential or hopes of clients.

Reference groups

Aspirational reference groups

These are groups with whom the individual may have little or no contact, but whose standards and attitudes are aspired to. The individual will have internalised the values of the group to which he or she wishes to belong (i.e. to which he or she 'refers'), and wants to be perceived as a member of. Such aspirations are often associated with upward mobility through the class structure. For example, young medical students often will quickly internalise the conservative values of the medical profession to which they hope to belong. Some people may value flashy cars, and expensive clothes, because they want to be rich one day.

Imaginary reference group

This is where people adopt what they believe to be either the values of the future or the past. They might fancy themselves as 'ahead of their time' or 'longing for the good-old days'. The slow uptake of services and benefits by elderly people may reflect former cultural attitudes about self-reliance.

Dissociative reference groups

This is where the individual, in rejecting a group's values, makes choices that puts him or her at odds with the group. This phenomenon is seen in some people who offend, where the challenging of cultural values is rewarding, as it reinforces the image with which they wish to be perceived.

The importance of reference groups

Reference groups are important to understand, as more than any other influence, they direct our decisions and choices. Individuals are fiercely loyal to their reference group, and strongly influenced by particular people who represent its values. Such a particular person might be a teacher, an employer or a minister. It might be a politician, an actor, a sporting personality or a member of the royal family. We are socialised not just into who we are, but who we would like to be.

Activity 8.3

a Work in groups of three or four. Individually determine which social class you 'believe' you belong to, and how this has influenced your attitudes.

b Do the same for other membership groups, and then reference groups. Make sure that you understand the differences between these groups and how they affect you.

c Compare your answers with others in the group, and draw conclusions. Make a note of the conclusions to contribute to a summary session involving all of the class.

The development of attitudes and values

Attitudes and values were discussed in Chapter 2 (pages 22–4). Read those pages again and do Activity 2.1 and Activity 2.2, if you have not already done them.

How social constructs change over time

The family

The family is the smallest of the formal associations in society and as such it is one of the most influential and important in the development of the individual identity. Any account of how individuals develop should take account of the social context in which the person has been reared.

The family is, and has always been, the most important and most intimate of human groups. The human family is centred on the biological needs of mating, begetting, rearing of children and providing for the physical and emotional needs of its members. It is a natural grouping rooted in fundamental instincts such as emotions, serving biological functions and regulating sexual and parental behaviour. For the child, therefore, the family is a vehicle by which it comes gradually to experience wider, or secondary, social groupings that influence the development of the individual. Through this introduction, most families provide the child with values and modes of behaviour that are appropriate for life. The experience of family life and wider groupings are therefore the means by which the individual is 'converted into the person'.

Gender

Sociologists make a distinction between sex and gender:
- *sex* refers to the biological differences.
- *gender* refers to the social and cultural differences between men and women.

A person's sex is a fundamental part of his or her self-concept and interactions with others. How do children acquire gender roles? How do they learn what sex they are?

One of the first things that we may notice about someone is whether they are male of female. It seems that we need this information about a person if we are to be able to interact with them in a socially acceptable manner. It is argued that children pick up the appropriate sex role by imitating the same sex parent and being reinforced for behaving in a manner that the particular culture expects of a boy or a girl. By reinforcing masculine behaviour in a boy, either parent could ensure that he showed masculine behaviour; similarly for feminine behaviour in a girl.

So in the case of a single parent rearing children, provided the parent had an idea of normal male or female behaviour he or she would be able to reinforce any behaviour in children that corresponded to the sex of the child. Children tend to categorise certain behaviours as 'boy' or 'girl' behaviours and also learn that they should not cross the gender role lines if possible.

Activity 8.4

How might you use the theories outlined above to support a single male parent bring up his young daughter? What advice would you give him?

There are some myths about the behaviour of boys and girls. In the early 1970s, researchers spent three years examining the stereotypes about males and females and came to the conclusion that the following may not be true:

- Boys are more 'analytic' than girls.
- Girls are more affected by heredity and boys by environment.
- Girls lack achievement motivation relative to boys.
- Girls have lower self-esteem than boys.
- Girls are 'auditory' while boys are 'visual'.
- Girls are more suggestible than boys.
- Girls are more 'social' than boys.

However, they did find some evidence for the following differences:

- Males are more aggressive than females.
- Girls have greater verbal ability than boys.
- Boys excel in visual–spatial ability.
- Boys are better in mathematical ability.

Other workers since the 1970s have suggested that:

- Males take greater risks than females, or are conditioned into believing that they can.
- Boys are more active than girls.
- Girls tend to be more likely to comply with parental requests.
- Girls seem to be more interested in, and responsive to, babies than boys or men are.

Some research findings would tend to point to the fact that men and women, boys and girls are more alike than they are different.

How do we explain the differences that do occur between the sexes?

There are two approaches to this question:

- **The biological approach** – this would argue that sex differences are innate; males and females are programmed for certain types of activities that are comparable with male or female roles. Bowlby (1951), whose theories are examined later in this chapter, argued that some differences in the behaviour of children are genetically transmitted. He believed that mothers must have maternal instincts to form bonds with their babies and that these show themselves some time after puberty. This theory is not well accepted now: many women today choose not to have children or to have them later in life. These facts are put forward to argue that the maternal instinct is not as strong as Bowlby thought.
- **The biosocial approach** – this takes social factors into account in relation to biological ones. This theory emphasises how children of different temperaments or social conditioning contribute to their own development by influencing how others treat them. Parent or adults prefer to spend time with children who respond to them and the more demonstrative or demanding children tend to get most attention.

Activity 8.5

You are working in a playgroup as a helper. How would you use the information you have gathered to help you support a child in the playgroup who is unresponsive to adults?

Potential conflicts within a multi-cultural society

Role status

When considering the role of wife as a carer, we usually think of a wife as having childcare responsibilities. However, at any one time in Britain there are more women caring for elderly and handicapped dependants than for children (Briggs, 1981). Most carers do not have a choice regarding having to look after a dependent relative; spouses can be seen as having the least choice of all.

When a member of the family becomes ill or disabled there is universal expectation, from the health and social care services, that the wife will take on the role of carer. Professionals hardly ever ask or consider the wishes of the female carer. They assume that the ability to cope is bestowed by taking on the role of wife or mother. For the average wife there is conflict – she is under pressure from every side to care for the dependent members of society. She sometimes may feel that she exists only in her caring role and receives no support form doctors, social workers or other health or care services.

The state gives implicit support to the sexual division of care – men are not expected to look after themselves and are not able to look after dependent relatives. The fact that there is a conflict between men and women in the care of dependent relatives is demonstrated by the inequality between them. Men spend very little time carrying out care activities. A woman's identity is still organised around the home, domestic work, child-rearing and caring for dependent members. Women have been assigned a lower status than men in today's society and women are seen as having only a role within the home while the male is perceived as the bread winner.

There is still a substantial and unequal division of labour between men and women in western families which is a vehicle for conflict. Carers in minority ethnic communities may not get support because of the stereotyped attitude which says that families in those groups 'look after their own'.

Deviance

If you go against the rules of society you may be viewed as deviant. *Deviance* refers to forms of behaviour which are considered unacceptable in a particulate culture. Hagan (1984) put forward a framework identifying varieties of deviance. Deviance is seen simply as a variation from a social norm on a continuum of seriousness between two extremes. He argues that the more serious acts of deviance, such as murder, rape or robbery are likely to be seen by most people as wrong while at the other end of the scale such acts as using marijuana may not provoke such agreement. Janet Paraskeva, a magistrate and director of the National Youth Agency, in the *Times* newspaper (24th March 1995) put forward the view that many young people see smoking cannabis as no more harmful than drinking gin and tonic. Research, she states, 'shows that soft drugs have taken the place of alcohol as the social cement between young adults'.

Defined deviance changes over time. For example, soft drug taking or abortion is no longer seen as a crime; neither is homosexuality. However, not been classified as a crime does not mean that members of society accept these behaviours. Many Roman Catholics would not agree to abortion and many people still think it wrong to smoke cannabis. Whether an activity is seen a normal or as deviant does not depend upon there been legislation deeming it a crime. Deviance depends on how society and groups within it view the activity. Deviance is relative because it depends on the situation and the groups concerned.

Deviant behaviour is behaviour which, once it has become public knowledge, is usually subject to correction, treatment or punishment. Illness is seen by many as deviant behaviour (Freidson, 1970) as it represents a deviation from culturally established standards of 'good health'. Anyone who is ill, therefore, wants treatment to correct the illness; anyone who does not want treatment is often seen as deviant. This can be seen when elderly dependent people who refuse to leave their homes for treatment or support in residential establishments are often see as deviant by neighbours, relatives or friends. If a person neglects to accept treatment he or she is seen as irresponsible or misinformed; his or her behaviour deviates from what is expected, i.e. to accept treatment and get well. In particular, a number of illness are seen by our society as deviant, for example, sexually transmitted diseases and Acquired Immune Deficiency Syndrome (AIDS).

Concepts and identification of illness

How have changes in medicine unsettled assumptions about the nature of illness? Medicine in the eighteenth century was based on a number of schools of thought about disease. The eighteenth century doctor took a very person orientated approach to the patient, taking into account the temperament, social background and psychological characteristics of the patient which were modified by the illness. There was no scientific body of knowledge available to the whole medical profession. Jewson (1974) argues that the medical system could be described as 'person orientated' because doctors made their diagnoses fit the emotional and theoretical perspective of their powerful and rich clients.

The late eighteenth and nineteenth centuries saw a move from this 'person orientation' to a more 'hospital medicine' approach where the feeling of the patients were secondary to the signs and symptoms of internal pathology. This approach and the later development in 'laboratory medicine', where only specialists understood the illness process, reinforced the autonomy and power of doctors. Medicine today is sometimes criticised for its over-dependence on technology, which in some cases leads to the patient becoming of secondary importance to the illness.

Not all of the medical profession or lay people can agree on a definition of health or ill-health. There are many conflicting definitions of ill-health and for that matter health. There is considerable conflict between the lay person in the street and the professional within the health and social care field as to definitions of ill-health. Concepts of ill-health are complex social constructions. The functional model of health is concerned with the ability of the person to fulfil his or her roles and responsibilities in society. Disability, for example, is defined by functionalists as the extent to which an illness causes loss of normal function, particularly the ability to undertake daily living activities. Treatment within this model is not only concerned with curing the illness but also minimising the disability and making the person more independent.

The medical concept of health is based upon a *disease model*. This model is concerned with health as the absence of disease with the focus being upon the pathological processes affecting particular physiological functions of the person. Those who defer to this model identify the disease, prescribe treatment whose success is judged against whether the disease is cured or not. This model treats the person in isolation from their social, economic and environmental context.

Some doctors see the *holistic* concept of health as emphasising 'the biological and physiological aspects of the human condition', and relating them to social, psychological and cultural aspects. This concept is based on the notion of well-being, the absence of illness and the degree of satisfaction of the individual with their physical, mental, environmental and interpersonal state. This concept of health implies a recognition of the interdependence of all the above factors in the well-being of the individual. It importantly recognises that the individual is not a passive recipient of treatment but is an active participant in the activity.

Young (1983) argues that healing refers to practices which are 'efficacious from the point of view of patients in affecting illness or illness behaviour in a desirable way'. He see curing as referring to 'practices which are efficacious, from the point of biomedical science, in either reversing, limiting or preventing disease'. Thus those doctors who 'cure' but do not 'heal' are not addressing the patients' or their families' anxieties in relation to the illness.

A conflict may also arise between the doctor and patient because the expectations of both may not be shared. The differing interests, expectations and knowledge may come between the ability of both parties to develop a positive relationship. Friedson (1970) puts forward the view that the 'separate worlds of experience and reference of the layman and the professional worker are always in potential conflict with one another'. This conflict may arise because of the differing priorities of the doctor and patient – the individual patient is only interested in his or her health but the professional may also have to weigh up the competing needs of other patients. The patient may want a long discussion with the doctor about his or her condition but may only get a few minutes, and thus be left feeling dissatisfied.

Doctors may want to carry out tests with the aim of furthering knowledge of the disease. This process may provide little comfort or cure to the particular patient in question. Other sources of conflict may arise when the doctor's perception of the seriousness of the illness differs from that of the patient. Many doctors do not appreciate the effect of the illness or disability on the patient's daily living (Fitton & Acheson, 1979). However, changes are taking place as people are becoming more knowledgeable about health matters and consequently are questioning more openly the attitudes and diagnosis of their doctors.

Cultural conflict

It is important for the health and social care professions to understand how people from differing cultures perceive illness or disability. Zborowski (1952) found that in a study of Americans, people with an Old-American or Irish origin displayed a stoical attitude towards pain and if the pain was severe withdrew from the company of others. On the other hand, people with Jewish or Italian backgrounds were more demanding, dependent and looked for public sympathy. Others following Zborowski's research have found marked cultural differences in the interpretation of, and response to, symptoms between differing groups.

Most ill-health suffered by ethnic groups is common to the rest of the population. There is evidence, however, to suggest that certain diseases occur more frequently among such groups (DoH, 1992). People in the Asian community are more likely to suffer from coronary heart disease and diseases such as strokes. There is also a disproportionately high incidence of diabetes in West Indian and Asian communities. Little is know about why these health differences exist. However, when looking at the incidence of disease within ethnic groups we must be aware that most of the medical research has been carried out by white researchers. Some black researchers argue that health research has not 'kept in touch with the social realities of "multi-racial" Britain. It keeps its head buried in the sand of white health concerns, is made up almost exclusively of white researchers, works from white perspectives, and publishes in white journals with white editorial boards' (Amhad, 1993).

How the values promoted by health and social care workers differ from those of clients

The values that professionals hold about the family in western society may differ from that of the values held by many groups. Families in Britain with different cultural norms and values may find that because of the perception of health and social care workers, they are not able to make the best use of services. It is not only families from ethnic groups that are affected by professional perceptions of what is 'normal'. The differences in perceptions between professionals and clients from different classes in Britain has been acknowledged for some time. However, many workers still think that all families are 'good' and that, for example, children should stay with their families at all costs.

The myth of the normal family

A particular image of 'normal' family and family life prevails in the mind of many professionals. If the patient's or client's family does not conform to this 'norm' then conflict may appear. The process of socialisation involves a person forming ideas about family life. In adult life we are pressured into believing ideas and values by advertisements involving the 'typical family'. What is the typical view of the family held by professional groups today? It is still all to often the image of two parents and two children, with the husband working and the wife working part-time or looking after the children. This assumption about the 'typical' family is influenced by social policy and in turn influences social policy decision makers. In fact, many household in Britain now contain only one person. Changing social values have meant that many households are now composed of homosexual partners, unmarried partners and single parents. This diversity of family forms involves many professionals having to confront their perceptions of what is 'normal'.

Activity 8.6

How has the changing 'family' influenced child care policies in the past decade. (Did your answers include a discussion on such issues as the placement of foster children with single people or homosexual couples?)

Most professional groups see the family as a secure place where people, particularly children, can grow and develop their personalities. Many children and adults have been subject to much violence because of this perception held by social workers, doctors and other authority figures. There is much violence by men and women to children in families and also by men to women. It is now also recognised that there is a greater amount of violence by women towards men in the family.

Some professionals have the perception that people from ethnic communities should adapt to the services offered by the British health and care services. Each person has a set of beliefs about families – they have perceptions about size, relationships and the type of support that the family should give to its members and how much freedom each family member should have. When professionals come into contact with those who do not perceive family values as the same as theirs, there is a danger that such a family or individuals within it may be seen as deviant. The professional then wants to change the deviant or at least see him or her as a problem.

Activity 8.7

a At what age do you think people should be independent from their parents? For example, when are they able to make their own judgements about marriage and education?.

b Can you think of groups in your locality who have different values and perceptions about such matters?

To function as a professional carer you must be aware of your own perceptions about how people should behave. It is very important that social workers or doctors do not impose their deeply held beliefs on the people who turn to them for help and support. For example, social policy in Britain is founded upon the belief that the family will look after its dependants but it does not rest upon the belief that children should subordinate their rights to the wishes or demands of other members of the family. Some minority groups would find this very disturbing – individualism may be seen as undesirable and a sign of lack of respect, and obligations to family members may be expected to override all others. The effectiveness of the work of professionals may be lessened if they try to impose views which are alien to the client.

Mares *et al* (1985) identifies some possible conflicts between professionals and clients from ethnic groups brought about by their perceptions:

- The health and care workers' tendency to work in a one-to-one relationship may cause conflict with the family. Older women within the family may have to be consulted if the individual client is to be helped. If this is not done the older members of the family may oppose the worker or give conflicting advice.
- It is not part of the traditional role of women to make decisions in some societies. In Pakistan and Bangladesh, the consent of a male guardian is always required for an operation on a woman.
- The visiting restriction in many hospitals (to two visitors) may cause distress to relatives from an extended family.
- In a number of societies, men and women live separate lives. Pregnancy and childbirth are considered as a female matter and may not even be discussed in front of men. This contrasts with the trend in Britain to involve men more and more in the preparation for the birth of a child and in the actual delivery.
- In many ethnic groups family decision making may be more formal than in the traditional British family. The father of a sick child may wish to consult his father or older brother before making a decision.

Demographic characteristics used in assessing health and social well-being

You have a right to know as much as possible about the causes of ill-health and social problems, and to know what you as an individual may be able to do to reduce the risks. This basic human right was affirmed by the World Health Organisation in 1978. The provision of information on health care, health and safety, and social issues enables individuals both to influence political decision making on a broad scale and to make personal decisions about their own health and lifestyles. Knowledge is power; it is the basis on which people can make informed choices.

The process of promoting health and social well-being is a highly skilled activity which differs little from activities more commonly referred to as education, marketing and public relations. In the past, health and social care organisations have put little effort into promotion. Policies and budgets were targeted more directly at treatment and care rather than at prevention. More recently, however, the arguments in favour of applying marketing and public relations skills to health and social care have become more apparent. This can be seen in the present government's policies relating to community care, the purchaser–provider split, and the mixed economy of care.

Risks to health

Most accidents occur in the home. About 6,000 people a year die on roads in Britain. Many others are injured and die because of accidents at work. We all take risks: we smoke, drive cars, drink alcohol and work in situations which cause ill-health. All these activities present health risks of varying degrees; all have been the subject of media attention; all have been related to health promotional activities. Modern health and social well-being promotion is not just about saying what is good for people, it is also about assessing risk.

Activity 8.8

  I a List as many risks to health and social well-being as you can.
   b From this list select and rank in order of importance the five risks that concern you most and the five risks that you feel are most worrying in society in general. Keep these lists – you will need to refer to them again.
  2 Use your personal list to begin to develop an individual action plan for your own health and well-being. Discuss this action plan with your class colleagues.
Continue to develop your action plan as you work through this chapter.

It is likely that your list from the last activity will have included concerns about specific diseases, accidents, assault, drug abuse, cancers, heart disease and poverty. The precise nature of your five main concerns will vary according to your current circumstances and issues currently being highlighted by the media. They will reflect some of your perceptions of risk. Other people will have different priorities. For example, with many elderly people the fear of assault ranks high because of stories in newspapers and on television about elderly people being mugged, while people from some parts of the world would have more pressing concerns about obtaining sufficient water and food.

It is clear that promotion of health and social well-being is not an absolute, but is based on the perceived needs of the individual within the wider contexts of the needs of society. We all see risks in different ways. There is a massive industry gathering information to support decision making; to provide the facts which contribute to the assessment of risk. In this chapter we will help you to identify the factors that affect health and social well-being and give you the opportunity to assess risks using as much evidence as possible.

Children at risk: accidents in the home

As children develop they become more capable of injuring themselves. The changes are rapid and need to be planned for in order to avoid putting the child at risk. What seemed impossible one day becomes easy the next. As the child's skills develop, the risks increase.

Table 8.1 Developmental stages and potential risks

Developmental age and abilities	Risk
3 months: wriggles and waves limbs	Can move sufficiently to fall from raised surfaces Head can be trapped in badly-designed cot
5 months: puts objects in mouth	Choking from small objects, e.g. buttons and pins
8 months: crawling	Falling down steps Cuts from contact with and grasping sharp objects Climbing/falling out of buggies and high chairs
12 months: opens lids	Choking and poisoning from things put in boxes and tins
18 months: imitates, climbs and explores	Climbing onto window sills May be able to open medicines without child resistant containers May be able to undo child restraint in cars
2 years: turns on taps	Risk of scalding from hot water system

Why look at risks?

To talk of risk is to talk of the chance that something will happen. When flipping a coin, probability theory tells us that half the time a coin will land showing tails and half the time it will show heads. To gamble £5 on heads, yet have to pay £10 if the coin turns up tails, incurs a high financial risk.

Assessing risk

There is a massive industry based on taking risks related to health – life insurance. The insurance industry makes use of statistics to judge the chance of almost any occurrence

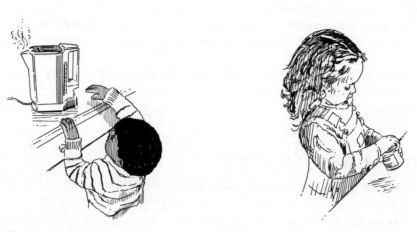

There are many areas of potential risk to young children in the home

and uses this to determine the premiums to be paid. Data gathered from millions of individuals is used to predict the potential risks associated with insuring the life of, for example, a 30-year-old, non-smoking man with those of a 30-year-old woman who smokes.

Activity 8.9

The figures in Table 8.2 show, for example, that the premium per £10,000 of insurance for a man wanting insurance for a 25-year term varies from £0.73 to £3.64 according to his age, if he is a non-smoker, and £0.96 to £5.73 if he is a smoker.
What would be the figures for a woman wanting a ten-year term?

Table 8.2 Life insurance premiums, monthly contributions (in £s) per £10,000 insurance

		Age next birthday					
	Term	19		30		40	
Women	(yr)	Non-S	Smoker	Non-S	Smoker	Non-S	Smoker
	5	0.28	0.46	0.36	0.46	0.65	0.98
	10	0.28	0.46	0.44	0.56	0.86	1.36
	15	0.34	0.53	0.44	0.67	1.17	1.89
	25	0.55	0.65	0.75	1.09	1.97	3.08
Men							
	5	0.51	0.77	0.66	0.88	1.26	1.82
	10	0.63	0.87	1.32	1.36	2.74	3.92
	20	0.65	0.88	1.50	2.03	3.17	4.76
	25	0.73	0.96	1.57	2.26	3.64	5.73

Source: Figures adapted from Allied Dunbar tables

Government involvement in health statistics

The study of patterns of ill-health, mortality and the causes of disease is not a new science. You may think that the link between tobacco and cancer has only recently been established. In fact, the link between snuff-taking (inhaled powdered tobacco) and cancer of the nasal lining was described in the early 1900s. Another chemically induced cancer known in the nineteenth century was cancer of the scrotum. This was common in child chimney sweeps and was caused by soot. Links between sunlight and skin cancer have also been known since the last century.

When John Snow identified the source of a cholera outbreak as the water from a pump in Broad Street, London in 1844, the organism that caused it, *Vibrio cholera*, was not known. His later work, using data gathered by William Farr about the source of water supplies to houses of cholera victims relative to a sewage outflow, led to the identification of sewage pollution as the source of cholera infections.

It is easy, with hindsight, to say that the link is logical and that pathogens (disease-causing organisms) and drinking water should not be allowed to mix. What in many ways is more important is to recognise that the results were an almost immediate success for the new science of epidemiology.

Gathering statistics

Both Snow and Farr had a powerful friend in Edwin Chadwick, the Secretary of the Poor Law Board. In the mid-nineteenth century, Chadwick instigated the legislation that required the gathering of statistics relating to birth and death which helped in Snow's analysis. This work still continues and much of the data used today has its origins in statistics gathered by the Office of Population Censuses and Surveys.

Table 8.3 Live births in the UK

(All figures in thousands with earlier ones representing an annual average from a three-year period)

Year	Total	Male	Female
1900	1,095	558	537
1920	1,018	522	496
1940	723	372	351
1950	803	413	390
1960	946	487	459
1970	880	453	427
1978	687	353	334
1979	735	378	356
1980	754	386	368
1981	731	375	356
1982	719	369	350
1983	721	371	357
1984	730	371	351
1985	751	385	366
1986	755	387	368
1987	776	398	378
1988	788	403	384
1989	777	398	379
1990	799	409	390

Source: OPCS

Activity 8.10

a Using Table 8.3, plot a graph with the birth rate on the y-axis and the year on the x-axis.

b What trends do you notice?

c Try to predict how many births there will be in the next decade. Remember that the number of births will relate in some way to the birth figures of 25 years previously.

Save the graph to help you in Activity 8.11 related to life expectancy.

From such data, health risks can be analysed and health promotion developed. There is an increasing knowledge and understanding of people not only from sociological but also biological and psychological points of view. Putting all of these data together it is possible to assess risk and propose actions taking into account the broader context within which the risk is based.

What are life tables?

Life tables provide information about statistical life expectancy and are produced and used by insurance companies when they determine the risks for life insurance. In this crude form (see Table 8.4) they give no indication of cause of death and so cannot be used to show increased risk factors.

Table 8.4 Life expectancy

Age	Males		Females		Key
	I	ex	I	ex	I = the number of people out of 100,000 who would survive to the exact age stated if the death rates do not change over their lifetime.
0	100,000	72.4	100,000	78.0	
10	98,710	63.4	99,086	68.8	
20	98,238	53.6	98,786	58.9	ex = the average future lifetime of a person of the age stated if the death rates do not change over their lifetime.
30	97,396	44.1	98,442	49.1	
40	96,240	34.5	97,723	39.4	
50	93,451	25.4	95,858	30.1	
60	85,361	17.2	90,828	21.4	Source: OPCS. Figures based on the interim life tables for 1987–9 produced by the Government Actuaries Department
65	77,087	13.8	85,705	17.6	
70	65,369	10.8	78,242	14.0	
75	50,075	8.3	67,536	10.8	
80	32,993	6.3	53,154	8.0	
85	17,410	4.7	35,317	5.8	

Example
- Of every 100,000 men born in the years 1987–89, 96,240 will live to their 40th birthday at least.
- A woman at birth has an average future lifetime of 76.4 years. However, if she were already 75, she would have an average life expectancy of 10.4 years.

Activity 8.11

It is important in planning provision for health and social care to be able to predict the demand for services. In this activity you will have to use the data from the birth tables and the life tables to predict some of the market need for care.

a Using data from Tables 8.3 and 8.4, plot graphs of the number of people born in the years 1978 to 1990 who will live to be 20. (To do this you will need to assume that the life table data in column I can be applied throughout the range of years 1978–90.) This graph represents the potential number of people entering the workforce.

b What use do you think these data might have in terms of planning care services?

c Using the birth data from Table 8.3 for 1980, 1985 and 1990, together with the life table data in Table 8.4, predict the number of 75, 80 and 85-year-old men and women that will be alive in 2065. (Assume the life table data apply to all of these birth years.)

d If it is assumed that these people will be in need of some level of social care use the figures you have calculated to make predictions about possible demand.

The inter-relationships between socio-economic factors, demographic characteristics and health and social well-being

Personal situations and ill-health

There are many facets of ill-health that have no causative organism or that are made worse by the situations in which people find themselves. In this brief section we will try to identify some of the factors related to ill-health where the environment contributes to the nature of the health.

Mental and physical disabilities

This broad group contains:
- people with identifiable inherited disorders, such as Down's syndrome
- people damaged at birth, such as those with cerebral palsy
- people who have become ability-impaired during their lifetime, such as accident victims and those with Alzheimer's disease.

The common feature of all these is that the ill-health (with current knowledge) is permanent – there is no cure. However, for many people it is the disability that is recognised by society and not the ability. This is often expressed by communicating with a carer rather than the person. A failure to recognise the abilities can have a very powerful demotivating effect. The stigmata characteristic of many of these 'handicaps' prove a handicap themselves.

Down's syndrome is most easily recognised externally by characteristic facial features. Some children with Down's syndrome have been offered surgery to alter these facial features. This in no way changes the biological nature of the syndrome but it does affect society's attitudes. The children are not automatically seen as disabled and so their abilities come to the fore.

This stereotyping of ability by identifying an infirmity is true across a wide range of people. Those with cerebral palsy may be classified as unintelligent because of their spastic movements. The effect of this can be to reduce the level of educational input to young children so that they do not reach their full potential.

At the other end of the scale, it is all too easy to accept that a person with Alzheimer's disease is in need of physical care only. However, when the person is presented with appropriate stimuli through such things as reminiscence therapy and reality orientation, the progress of the disease can be slowed and so the person remains more able for longer. These examples show how the disability brings about a double jeopardy situation. Not only do the sufferers have to work against the problem but they also have to fight the handicap imposed by society's stereotypes.

Psychiatric ill-health

This area of ill-health includes disorders of mood, perception and thinking. These can be classed as mental illnesses, but as Clare (1980) suggests 'the concept of mental illness, appears to permit a bewildering number of interpretations'. The complex interrelationship between mind and body makes it often difficult to differentiate between mental and physical ill-health.

Mood

Illness related to mood, such as depression, may well have a biochemical origin. There can be obvious physical changes, such as childbirth, that are linked to depression. Depression can also follow physical illnesses such as glandular fever. However, it is not known whether one is the cause of the other. In some people there has been evidence that depression may be linked to low levels of serotonin, a brain neurotransmitter.

A hormone linked to mental illness is adrenalin. This hormone is released at times of stress, but in situations where there is constant raised level of stress then the level of the hormone is constantly higher than would be normal. This can lead to physical illnesses or mental illness – one cause with many effects.

Perception

Disorders of perception occur when one or more of the senses misinterpret stimuli. Most of us, especially as young children, have interpreted shadows as monsters. We may also have interpreted random sounds as speech, especially if we were expecting to hear something. These are cases of the brain trying to interpret stimuli by matching them to an already known pattern. When the stimuli are totally internally generated they are called *hallucinations*. Some drugs have the effect of causing these internal stimuli and their use has been linked to cases of mental illness. In controlled doses, some of these drugs have been used therapeutically to support treatment of other illnesses. In particular some hallucinogens are used to ease the effects of chemotherapy for some cancer patients.

Two illnesses in which changes in perception are symptomatic are chronic alcoholism and schizophrenia. In the former, the cause is chronic drug abuse (alcohol), while in the latter the cause, or more likely causes, are not well understood.

Socio-economic and environmental factors

A child brought up in a block of damp, draughty, high-rise flats with no other children to play with may have damaged emotional and physical development. A lack of contact with other children would clearly affect social development and may give rise to behavioural difficulties relating to interacting with peers when starting school. The lack of peer group stimulus could lead to depression which tends to reduce the efficiency of the immune system. This in turn would make the child more prone to infection.

Poverty and ill-health go together. A study of ill-health related to family or personal finance would show increased episodes of ill-health in low-income families. This closely matches the relationship between social class and ill-health. The Black Report of 1980 highlighted the inequalities in care, relating them to social class. Included in the Report was epidemiological evidence that some diseases are more common further down the social class scale. It also highlighted the fact that access to health care and ill-health prevention was also related to class.

A variety of explanations has been put forward relating to such factors as education, access to health care, nutrition, family size and housing – you will be able to add other examples. Clearly, the example of the young child, given above, indicates how the immune system can be compromised by the way a person is feeling. It is also easy to identify how poor nutrition has a direct relationship to ill-health. It should also be possible to see how health levels alter in relation to more indirect causes such as the development of the welfare state, and more recently with the increased number of unemployed and homeless people.

Cancers

Cancer is a layman's term to describe a variety of specific diseases. The common feature of all of them is that they involve inappropriate growth of cells which is often rapid and uncontrolled. The causes of this growth vary and, while it is possible to link some cancers with specific causes, there are normally other factors involved.

Table 8.5 gives some examples of different cancers and major factors in their development. Clearly prevention, where possible, is easier with some of these and so individuals should reduce their exposure to the risk. However some factors, such as an inherited tendency, cannot be removed and so it is not possible to remove all risk.

Table 8.5 Examples of causes of cancer

Type of cancer	Possible causative link
Lung cancer	Tobacco smoke Radon gas (radioactive) from certain building materials
Cancer of the cervix	Infection with herpes virus causing genital warts
Bowel cancer	Lack of dietary fibre
Skin cancer (Melanoma)	Exposure to ultra-violet light, in particular from the sun
Scrotal cancer	Exposure to soot and tar products of burning. This was particularly common in nineteenth-century boy chimney sweeps

The list is not exhaustive but gives examples from a range of types of cause.

Health improvement without an obvious medical reason

A feature of many of the indirect causes of ill-health is that not all people in similar situations develop the same levels of ill-health. The 'feel good factor' is often used to describe an unquantifiable state that can lead to reduced ill-health. If a person, whilst in an 'at risk' situation, has a level of confidence and happiness, then the level of illness is reduced. This may be related simply to an improved immune system, but it may also be related to maintaining the body systems in a natural biochemical balance. It is an interesting thought that feeling good about yourself may help improve your health.

Case study

Using the 'feel good factor' to promote recovery

The Starlight Foundation is an organisation founded in the USA but which is active in the UK. This organisation makes the dream of critically, chronically or terminally ill children come true by granting them wishes, such as organising trips to Disney World, swimming with dolphins and appearing in the *Beano*. The original concept was to provide a special, memorable experience for the child and family.

However, there has been a second, more surprising effect in that granting the wish appears to enhance not only psychological but also physical well-being. This has resulted in a need to use fewer pain-killers or for shorter treatment periods. There is also anecdotal evidence, although not scientific proof yet, that some children, having been granted a wish, receive a boost to their compromised immune system. In the light of these positive effects the Foundation is trying to open children's rooms in hospitals which will contain computer games, toys and TV, but which will be off-limits to medical and nursing staff.

The case study of the Starlight Foundation is just one example of a whole series of stories that could be described as mind over matter. Other examples that appear to work but have limited scientific support in western medicine include homeopathy and acupuncture. The latter has been shown to increase levels of brain endorphins and encephalins which act, as do artificial opiates, in reducing pain and increasing the person's 'happiness'. It may be that many of the alternative therapies work in similar ways to promote health.

Peter, who has leukaemia, portrayed in the Beano, *in August 1992*

Socio-economic factors and lifestyle choices

The association between social class and health shows that death and disease are not randomly distributed throughout the population – there are indeed inequalities in standards of living. The conventional wisdom that the introduction of the National Health Service would prevent disease has received a sudden jolt with the discovery of the existence of the systematic and widespread social inequalities in health. In particular, in 1980 the Black Report drew together evidence that demonstrated:

- that members of the 'lower' social classes suffered increased rates of nearly every category of disease
- that such differences affected them over the whole of their life span, and
- that particularly since the 1940s these differences appeared to be on the increase (see Table 8.6).

A considerable percentage of the population moves from one social class to another at some time and it is possible that health influences this mobility. Those with good health move up the ladder and those in poor health are likely to move down the hierarchy.

Another explanation for inequalities in health is the different rate of access to medical

Table 8.6 Mortality rates by occupation

Occupation	Direct age-standardised death rate per 100,000	SMR*
University teachers	287	49
Local authority senior officers	342	57
Office managers	377	64
School teachers	396	66
Postmen	484	81
Machine-tool operators	934	156
Steel erectors, riggers	992	164
Fishermen	1,028	171
Policeman	1,270	109
Bricklayers, labourers	1,644	274

*SMR The Standardised Mortality Ratio – figures below 100 indicate a below-average mortality rate and figures above 100 an above-average rate.

Source: Adapted from Townsend, P. and Davidson, N., *Inequalities in Health* (Penguin, 1982)

care. This results from the relatively poor state of medical facilities in working-class areas. Certain preventative services are used by those in the higher social classes. It is difficult to unravel cause and effect. Does poverty breed chronic illness? Or do those who become chronically ill inevitably become poor?

Activity 8.12

Why do you think inequalities in health are associated with standards of living?

Mortality statistics show an inverse relationship with social class. For example, the (age standardised) mortality rates from 1959–63 of social class V were double those of social class I. There is a similar pattern for chronic sickness amongst the broad socio-economic groups. Unskilled men of working age were three times more likely to suffer from chronic illness as professional men of the same age. Unskilled workers are also more likely to lose more days through sickness than any other group (see Table 8.7).

These variations between social classes in term of their relative mortality and morbidity is the subject of debate. However, it is widely accepted that poor housing and unemployment are associated with ill health. Differences in income and wealth result in differences in such things as housing, possessions, diet and lifestyle.

Table 8.7 Illness by socio-economic group (rates per 1,000)

Condition	Professional workers	Skilled workers	Semi-skilled workers
Mental disorders	6.5	10.4	19.3
Heart disease	20.3	20.8	34.5
Bronchitis	8.0	17.9	28.2
Arthritis/rheumatism	20.1	21.8	44.2

Source: *General Household Survey* (HMSO, 1973)

Housing

Housing conditions are in a number of ways associated with health status. An obvious indicator is inadequate heating which can give rise to hypothermia in the old and very young. Overcrowding may cause respiratory diseases and may also contribute to mental illness. The homes of managers and professionals are likely to possess more amenities than unskilled workers (see Table 8.8).

Table 8.8 Possession of amenities in the home

	Professional/managerial	Unskilled manual
Central heating	87%	44%
Refrigerator	99%	90%
Telephone	96%	50%
Car	93%	33%

Source: OPCS, *General Household Survey* (HMSO, 1982)

As many as two million dwellings in England are considered unfit for human habitation because they lack basic amenities such as showers or bath, or require repairs to them. These dwellings are likely to be inhabited by unskilled workers. They are also likely to be in areas where the air is polluted with industrial waste. One survey of pre-school children carried out in 1977 found one in ten inhabited dwellings where at least one of the following criteria applied: overcrowding, no separate unshared bathroom, shared WC, and no sole use of fixed water supply.

Social improvements have cleared the air of the more visible pollutants such as smoke, removed the most serious contaminates from food and the water supply, and provided for the hygienic disposal of waste. As a result, the diseases that affect people in the past, such as tuberculosis and cholera, have now been replaced by heart disease and cancer.

Diet

Diet is an important lifestyle factor affecting health (WHO, 1988). Some argue that social class differences in health may result from differences in exposure to factors such as poor diet, which may contribute to illness and disease:
- Studies have shown a clear decline in vitamin intake with rising family size and declining income.
- Protein consumption rises with income, but calcium intake showed no such trend.
- Poor families tend to consume more sugar in the form of sweets, biscuits and soft drinks.
- The quality of a child's diet tends to be class related, falling with declining occupational class.

However, it should be borne in mind that people who eat certain types of food may make up for the disadvantage this might cause in some other way. For example, by obtaining food, such as sugar, from drinks or sweets.

Inadequate diet has been implicated as a factor in poor health and infant mortality. The theory of 'transmitted nutritional deprivation' suggests the existence of a cycle of nutritional deprivation that leads to low birth weight and congenital malformation. It is

215

difficult to break this cycle because it originates in the nutritional deprivation of the mother, not at the time of the birth of the child, but at the time of her own birth. However, the chances of becoming ill and surviving as a child are at their greatest during the post neonatal phase of life. It is during this period the class differences play a large part. Factors that have been found to increase the child's chances of survival are the level of material resources in the family, household income, warmth and hygiene, and such things as a car or telephone, which are a means of rapid communication with services.

Activity 8.13

Why do you think that a middle- or upper-class child's chances of survival are greater than a working-class child's?

Diet can be crucial in both preventive and curative health. All countries, including the UK, have regions that have developed their own local diet based on the availability of foods, and on such social factors as religion, culture, class and lifestyle. Each usually contains a balance of essential nutrients. Problems arise when people move area or migrate and take their diet with them. The climate, agricultural patterns, economics and food technology may be different and so traditional foods may not be available.

One of the most important factors affecting diet is obviously the amount of money the family has available to spend on food. Families with children ate less food during January to March 1982 compared to the same period in 1981. The food intake of families with three children was only just over 80 per cent of the recommended levels for energy and iron consumption. As unemployment rises there is a danger that food levels will fall.

Activity 8.14

List as many reasons as you can why income or capital might affect a family's or a person's ability to cope with ill-health.

Accidents to children

Unskilled workers' homes are likely to be lacking gardens which means that their children are more likely to have to play in the streets or an already overcrowded house or flat – conditions which are likely to contribute to the number of accidents that children from this group in society experience. The increased risk of death faced by children in the 'lower' classes in ordinary everyday activities such as play and travelling to school by foot or bicycle, has to be seen against a background of the differences in the environment to which children from different levels of society are exposed. The risk of death from accidents with motor cars is seven times greater for children from social class V compared to social class I. Children from the lowest social class are nearly five times more likely to die before reaching school-leaving age.

The Black Report (1980) commented on the sex differential in each social class (apart from professional households). Boys were more likely to suffer a higher risk of accidents than girls – a fact that might reflect the greater range of careless risk-taking behaviour among boys and also, in part, reflects cultural practices in socialisation. Class differences between children regarding the risk of accidental death appear to be in part a manifestation of distinctive patterns of child-rearing. However, the Report does point out that such patterns must be seen in the light the differences in the material resources of parents, which places constraints on the level of care they are able to provide for their children.

Activity 8.15

a Write down as many reasons as you can think of why children from middle-class families are less likely to have accidents.

b What part does socialisation play in this?

Health of children

One of the most important causes of death amongst children aged 1–14 is as the result of infections. This does not seem to vary as much between social classes as do accidents, poisoning, violence, respiratory disease and congenital abnormalities. The principal cause of respiratory symptoms is the extent of air pollution in the child's area of residence. For example, younger children in families where the parents had respiratory problems or smoked were most likely to have respiratory problems. For older children, the social class difference is larger. As the child gets older, the difference between the social classes becomes more pronounced for death from accidents, poisoning and violence.

Activity 8.16

Discuss with your class colleagues why the difference in social class affects a child's chance of suffering from accidents or violence.

Smoking and health

Smoking-related diseases kill about 100,000 people every year. Smoking's role in heart disease and its role in causing respiratory illness is well documented. If smoking is so bad for people why does the government not ban it? This would seem to be a legitimate question to consider in a discussion of health promotion.

As stated earlier, the links between tobacco and ill-health were known in the nineteenth century. Further links with lung cancer and circulatory disorders have been established this century. There has been more recent evidence that the pollution of the air by tobacco smoke can induce cancers in non-smokers by so-called 'passive smoking'.

Activity 8.17

- Do smokers have the right to smoke – after all it's their health they are damaging?
- Do non-smokers have the right to breath smoke-free air?
- What is the real risk of smoking? (Look back at the life insurance data in Table 8.2.) It is possible to find out the mortality figures for cigarette smokers, but an easy exercise is to look at some of the 'junk mail' that is delivered to your home. Insurance companies often send out details of insurance policies and quote premiums for both smokers and non-smokers.

It is interesting to note that life insurance companies do not usually 'load' premiums for those who drink alcohol or who are overweight in relation to height. (On the other hand, car insurance companies will give reductions for non-drinkers.) The figures indicate that insurance companies rate a non-smoker as having a significantly better chance of living for longer than a smoker. Between 13 and 24 per cent of all deaths are smoking-related.

Are children at risk from smoking?

The Health Education Authority has identified evidence of the risks of passive smoking in children. The effects start with the unborn child and it has been estimated that there are four million children under ten years old at risk in the UK.

The simple statistic is that 48 per cent of pregnant women are either smokers themselves or live in a house with a smoker. The possible effects of parental smoking include:

- an increased risk of spontaneous abortion (4,000 per year)
- an increased risk of lower birth weight
- an increased risk that babies are born earlier and suffer more infections
- an increased risk of death in the first week of life (one in ten infant intensive care beds are filled by babies affected by smoking)
- an increased risk of cot death – 25 per cent of such deaths could be related to parental smoking
- a 30 per cent chance of the child developing glue ear (a normally temporary hearing impairment)
- an increased risk of the child developing asthma – those from smoking households are twice as likely to develop asthma compared with those from non-smoking households
- an increased tendency for children to be shorter than average and to have a lower intelligence.

The risks associated with passive smoking are such that many fostering and adoption agencies will not place children in families where there are smokers.

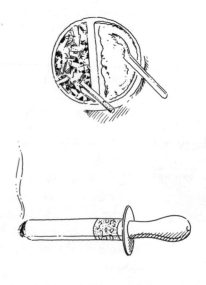

The anti-smoking campaigns use effective images such as these to put over the effects of passive smoking on unborn babies and young children

Other forms of drug abuse

Alcohol

Alcohol is implicated in a wide range of health and social problems, and physical and mental disorders. Approximately 40,000 people die from alcohol abuse each year. We have considered one drug that if it were discovered today would almost certainly have been banned because of the health risks – tobacco. We will now consider alcohol, a drug that is widely accepted in society and that is readily available. The effects of alcohol have been acknowledged in the licensing laws, the minimum age for its purchase and areas relating to driving.

Health education reflects society's general views on drinking alcohol. The message is clearly one of moderation with guidance on what constitutes 'safe' doses (see Table 8.9). The effects of the drug are normally short-term and it is not strongly addictive. However, for those who do develop an addiction there is no cure. Abstinence is seen as the only way to deal with the addiction.

Table 8.9 Recommended alcohol consumption, in units, per week

	Maximum recommended	Increased risk	Harmful	Recommended number of alcohol-free days
Men	21	50	50+	2–3
Women	14	35	35+	2–3
Pregnant women	Ideally no alcohol, at most 4 units			5–6

Typical values in units:
a pint of beer or lager = 2 units
a pint of extra strong beer or lager = 5 units
a small glass of wine = 1 unit
a small glass of sherry = 1 unit
a measure of vermouth or aperitif = 1 unit
a standard measure of spirits (in the UK) = 1 unit

Source: Health Education Authority

Activity 8.18

While alcohol is socially acceptable and contributes to the economic status of the country it is also linked to many deaths. It may not be the drug itself that kills but it has a contributory effect.

1 Make a list of the positive and negative ways in which alcohol contributes to the economy. Try to quantify these contributions.

2 Using nationally published statistics or those for your region, find out how many deaths are alcohol-related.

Illegal drugs

These include marijuana, heroin, cocaine, d-lysergic acid diethylamide (LSD), and amphetamines in various forms. They are often broken down into the categories of soft

Health education reflects society's views on alcohol – sensible drinking

and hard drugs with heroin and cocaine (including the smokeable form, crack) in the latter category.

The use of all of these drugs is illegal (with some exceptions for medical use and research). However, there is a level of ambivalence over the use of soft drugs as it is difficult to justify their ban when drugs with similar effects are legal. The risks put forward are often that the use of soft drugs leads to people moving on to hard drugs and that people under the influence of the drugs may endanger themselves and others. There is also evidence that some of the illegally obtained drugs are contaminated with potentially lethal materials.

A recent survey in the north-west of England has shown that over 40 per cent of a sample of 16-year-olds had tried cannabis in some form. Health promotion in such situations is difficult as it is difficult to get the message across without inviting the response that the drugs are no worse than tobacco and alcohol.

Activity 8.19

Carry out a survey to determine people's views on the soft drugs. Try to identify the sort of message that a health promotion campaign could use with respect to these drugs.

Solvent abuse

One area of abuse that is very difficult to control or legislate for is solvent abuse. This abuse involves people inhaling the fumes from organic solvents. The hallucinatory effects are related to the reduced oxygen uptake and from the interference with brain biochemistry by the solvents.

The solvents are commonly used in glues and aerosols. They almost invariably are capable of dissolving in fats and can damage tissues with high fat content such as the brain. They also damage the liver and kidneys as they carry out their functions of detoxification and excretion.

The difficulty with these drugs is that they are commonly available and serve a very useful purpose in a variety of applications. To ban their sale would require replacement of many glues and also a return to paraffin (rather than butane) cookers for camping. Health promotion therefore has to target abusers and potential abusers without inadvertently promoting the abuse.

Activity 8.20

Discuss with your colleagues ways of identifying the number of solvent abusers in the population. How could you target the abusers without encouraging others to start? (For example, a health warning on tins of glue might help people identify glues for experimentation.)

HIV and AIDS

It is a current concern of government and the medical profession that there is a pandemic (global epidemic) of HIV-1 (Human Immunodeficiency Virus) and AIDS (Acquired Immune Deficiency Syndrome). There has been a determined effort to raise public awareness of the issues and provide a health education message. This is a useful area to look at because, like smoking, the message to be passed on relates to lifestyle changes and risks. It differs because in the case of HIV there is no obvious campaign against the health promotion message.

Background

AIDS was identified when studies of medical statistics showed an increase in the number of cases of rare forms of cancer as well as an increase in the number of unusual presentations of common diseases. Further investigation showed that these increases were almost totally confined to homosexual or bisexual men. This information provided the first barrier to the investigation of the problem. It was perceived as a 'gay' disease and therefore of limited importance to the 'normal' population. As a result, little funding was available for research.

Any research that was carried out initially focused on two areas:

● trying to find a causative organism
● looking for an environmental link.

Transmission through contaminated blood products and whole blood concentrated the search for a micro-organism as the cause. The current state of knowledge indicates that the syndrome manifests itself in people infected by HIV and this group of viruses is now thought to cause the disease.

The reported cases of HIV infection in the UK by March 1991 was 15,337. It is clear from the numbers that they form a very small percentage of the total population of the UK and that at least 87 per cent of cases come from people in high-risk categories, which include:

● homosexual men

- intravenous drug users
- those infected with contaminated blood or tissue
- people who have had sexual intercourse with a partner from countries where HIV is almost endemic and the sexual partners of these people.

Acceptability of risk

The acceptability of a risk can be determined by:
- an individual – for example, climbing stairs, for most people, presents an acceptable risk
- legislation – for example, the risk of food poisoning by cross-contamination means that there is legislation requiring uncooked meats and cooked meats to be stored in ways to prevent cross-contamination.

The legislation in the latter case does not apply in non-commercial kitchens. The risk of food poisoning in your own home is seen as something that legislation cannot affect (it would be impossible to monitor) whereas the risk of food poisoning in a public eating place is deemed to be such that there is legislation to try to reduce the risk as greater numbers of people are likely to be at risk of infection.

The difficulty in trying to teach about safety is that there are no absolutes other than in specific areas where safety standards are defined. The skill is to be able to assess the risks in terms of the people involved. To leave a toddler in a room with an open bottle of bleach is unacceptable, whereas if the bottle has a 'child-proof' cap on it then it may be more acceptable. But at what age can you expect a child to be able to open the bottle and make the risk unacceptable once again?

These examples illustrate some of the issues around health promotion related to specific illnesses where certain actions can help to reduce the risks. They also show how decision-making and actions may have a variety of influences on them and may explain why people do not always do what the 'health professionals' think is best for them. Later on we will look at the environment and illustrate some ways to investigate and evaluate safety risks in different contexts.

The Thirteenth Annual Report of the Home Accident Surveillance System highlights the fact that:

'There is no such thing as "absolute safety". To say that something is safe effectively means that the risks are known and deemed to be acceptable for the benefits conferred.'

Lifestyle risks

There are many risks to well-being that come from the way that we live. They arise from aspects of a person's life that include:
- work roles or lack of work
- the food that a person eats
- the physical activity that is undertaken.

In short, they relate to the day-to-day habits and philosophies that make up a person's lifestyle.

Diet

It would seem odd to talk of malnutrition in the western world or of people in the UK dying of malnutrition. There are, however, regular reports that say that this is happening. The reports tend not to talk of starvation and deficiency diseases, but of excessive consumption and heart disease. Here we will look at some of the information that is commonly available and its impact on health and social well-being. As such we will consider two specific issues of malnutrition: excessive eating and dietary lack of specific nutrients.

Is being overweight really bad for you?

The simple answer to this question, if insurance premiums are a guide, is no. Tables of ideal weights with respect to height have been published. These normally show an area representing ideal weight range with other bands for overweight and obese people. The implication being that people should strive to maintain their weight in the 'ideal' band. Insurance companies do not load premiums for people who are outside the ideal weight band unless they are well into the obese band. In other words, there is limited statistical evidence that being mildly overweight is life-threatening.

Research in the USA and the UK has indicated that there are greater dangers involved in the typical cycles of dieting followed by weight gain than in maintaining a constant 'overweight' figure. There are, however, indications that being overweight can exacerbate some skeletal problems and affect quality of life.

The level of saturated fat (where the fatty acids have no carbon–carbon double bonds) in the diet, especially where energy intake is in excess, contributes to the manufacture of cholesterol in the body. Studies have indicated that the level of cholesterol in the blood stream may be one of the contributory factors in heart disease and the narrowing of the arteries in atherosclerosis.

From these simple examples, it can be seen that malnutrition from excessive intake of food can affect health. Health promotion must, however, take into consideration a range of factors and the simple advice to go on a weight-reducing diet may be more dangerous than accepting a steady level of overweight.

Dietary lack of specific nutrients

It is difficult to see how a person in the UK could suffer from dietary insufficiencies. We can easily obtain food and health education about diet has been available in schools for many years. However, there is still a level of such malnutrition that falls into three broad areas:

- **Malnutrition through social deprivation** where the welfare state has failed in its support of a person who therefore has a general insufficiency. This can also be seen with addicts to alcohol or other drugs who fail to maintain a balanced diet.
- **Malnutrition caused by change** A common example is with young girls at puberty who have their iron reserves depleted during menstruation and do not adequately replace them, thus leading to iron-deficiency anaemia. A second example can be where a person has changed to a vegetarian or vegan diet and has not ensured a sufficient balance of protein to supply all of the essential amino acids. This is often compounded by a move to vegetarianism during adolescence when there is a considerable amount of growth occurring.
- **Malnutrition by default** It is possible to be eating a balanced diet according to the published tables but still be malnourished. This usually occurs when research has shown that recommended daily intakes of micro-nutrients do not meet the needs for those nutrients. In the UK the recommended daily amounts (RDAs) for vitamins were once based on a figure that was twice the amount below which a person developed the deficiency disease. It is now thought that some vitamins, in particular vitamins C and E, have important roles as anti-oxidants in preventing some diseases. It may be that the RDAs will be increased in the future. (One eminent biochemist, Linus Pauling did recommend up to 6 grams per day of vitamin C compared with the RDA of 50 milligrams.)

It is thought that the antioxidant vitamins help to mop up free radicals formed in the body. These highly reactive chemicals can cause significant amounts of damage at the biochemical level within cells. Links have been postulated to cancer and atherosclerosis.

What constitutes an ideal diet?

The key term to remember is a 'balanced' diet. The diet is balanced to an individual's needs. These needs are met by sufficient of the seven classes of nutrient in proportions to maintain the individual.

In reality, most people think of the word 'diet' in relation to weight reduction. In this case the skill is to make an imbalance between the energy intake and that required for metabolism. If the balance shows a deficiency of energy intake than the extra requirements come from reserves of fat. It is not easy to determine the metabolic requirements as they vary from individual to individual.

The requirements are based on a person's:
- size (surface area)
- sex
- age
- amount of thyroid hormone
- state of well-being (fever, drug regime, emotional state).

All of the above contribute to the basal metabolic rate. On top of this there are other factors, such as:
- level of exercise
- food intake (it takes energy to digest food)
- the environmental temperature.

The total metabolic rate consists of the sum of the basal metabolic rate and all of the other factors. Guidance on weight reduction must take all these things into account and ensure that reducing energy intake does not remove other specific nutrients that are essential in a balanced diet. A simple dietary rule is to reduce on high fat and carbohydrate items and increase exercise but this should be done slowly and with advice from a doctor.

Exercise

The knowledge that exercise can help in weight reduction is useful but it also has other beneficial side effects. In particular, exercise increases cardiac output, improves muscle tone and improves the efficiency of the respiratory system. There is also a psychological benefit in being physically fit. That does not mean, however, that everyone should take up running marathon races.

In improving the various systems, the effect is to make them work more efficiently. The resting heart rate drops along with the respiratory surfaces becoming more effective for gas exchange. This means that the heart and lungs do not become stressed under exercise and that exercise can be sustained for longer periods.

The more efficient supply of oxygen to muscles means that they can work *aerobically* and so make a better use of stored glycogen (the carbohydrate energy stores in muscle). Muscles that are poorly supplied with oxygen work *anaerobically* producing lactic acid as a by-product which causes cramp.

Specific exercise can also have an effect in remodelling bone and joints to cope with the extra stresses. This method is used by physiotherapists in their work.

As with diet, any new exercise programme needs to be monitored and, where there may be some risk, checked with an appropriate professional. Most regimes advise starting slowly and building up the exercise over a period of time. A measure of what level of exercise is appropriate can be made by monitoring the pulse before, during and

Exercise is good for you

after exercise to ensure that the rate does not rise too much and that it returns to normal reasonably soon after stopping the exercise. The success of the regime would be shown by the ability to work at the same level for longer or to work with increased loads (for example, to run at the same speed for longer or run faster over a fixed time period).

The impact of social policies on health and social well-being

This section expects you to examine social policy decisions and analyse their effects upon the health and well-being of individuals. We shall look at two vital services to dependent people in their own homes and examine what happens when decision makers change policy and how these changes affect the lives of the recipients of the services.

The meals-on-wheels service

The meals-on-wheels service constitutes one of the most important and major forms of community support to the dependent (the elderly or those with a physical disability) wishing to live in their own homes. Providing food for the sick and elderly has a long history. The first meals-on-wheel service was organised by the WVS (now the WRVS) towards the end of the Second World War and taken up by local authorities after 1962.

In 1970, the Ministry of Health argued that the service could only provide a significant contribution to the nutritional needs of the recipients if the service was provide on at least five days a week. However, nutritional needs are not the only objective of the meals-on-wheel service. The opportunity for social contact for the housebound is vital, the average time spent by those delivering the service was approximately five minutes with each client. During this time the client and the person delivering the meal talked, brought messages from relatives, took orders for shopping to be delivered later and also listened to the dependent person's problems. The overall service, therefore, provide a number of important services – nutrition, social contact and surveillance.

The person who delivered the meal was often the only contact the housebound person had with the outside world. The service not only provided food but also improved the morale of the dependent person. In addition, the provision of the meal also helped to sustain and encourage the client to maintain other less demanding self-care activities.

Recently, many local authorities in an effort to save costs decided to deliver meals which can be microwaved. Each recipient is given a microwave, and once a week a supply of meals are delivered. The dependent person is expected to cook the meal him or herself. This change in social policy has had a detrimental affect on the health and well-being of the housebound person. The new meals may be nutritional and cost effective but the social contact has been reduced to one visit a week and therefore invaluable surveillance has also been reduced.

Activity 8.21

A local authority because of funding problems decided to change it admission policy to residential homes for the elderly. It has changed it policy from one of only allocating people a place within their own local community to placing a client in the first vacancy that arises. This means that the elderly person could be placed in a home miles away from his or her locality.

What would the effects of this change in policy be upon the elderly people's health and well-being in the residential home and what would the effects be upon their relatives and friends.

The home care service

Home care services (commonly manifested in the traditional 'home helps') are also vital to some people living in their own homes. Many social policy decisions have affected the development of this service which in turn has had detrimental effects upon the well-being of clients. Since 1948, local authorities have had the power to charge for home care services but many never choose to do so. However, now almost all authorities charge for these services. What effect has this change in policy had upon the elderly recipients of the services, especially those on low incomes or state benefits?

When charges are introduced many elderly people cancel the service. Those who cancel are not necessarily those who needed the service least; in fact those who cancel are in many cases those who are most dependent and receive only their old age pensions. Those who organised the service felt that over half who cancelled would suffer considerable hardship as a result. Many clients expressed grave concern about the loss of the service and had no idea how to replace the vital support they had been receiving. For those clients that felt they had no option but to keep the service and pay for it, how did they manage their small pensions? Many in fact cut down on food and heating to pay for the home help.

The two service examples above give some insight into how social policy decisions at local level may have a very serious affect on the health and well-being of individuals.

Activity 8.22

Your local social services department has decided to cut creche provision for single parents who go out to work. What would be the implications for the health and well-being of the parents and the children as a result of this policy decision?

Review questions

1 How are the attitudes we hold shaped?
2 What two groups in society have a major influence on the process of socialisation?
3 What is meant by the term 'culture'?
4 Explain what is meant by the term 'peer group'?
5 What is the distinction between sex and gender?
6 What does the term deviance refer to?
7 Why may certain illnesses be seen as deviant by western society?
8 Why may the concept of health change over time?
9 List as many environmental factors as you can which may influence the physical and psychological devilment of children?

Assignment 8.1
Understanding individuals and society

This assignment develops knowledge, understanding and portfolio evidence for element 4.2, **Analyse how individuals function in and are influenced by society**, and element 4.3, **Investigate the effect of socio-economic factors on health and social well-being**.

Your tasks

1 Select one person that you know, perhaps a relative, and discuss with him or her the socialising effects that his or her education, work and religion has had on his or her development.

2 Explain how the role of women in the family has changed over the past 100 years and discuss the possible changes that might occur in the future.

3 Discuss how societies definition of 'health ' has changed over the past 50 years.

4 Choose two different groups in your locality and explain potential conflicts which exist between the norms and values of such groups.

5 Explain how the values promoted by health and social care workers may differ from those of clients.

6 Describe how the following demographic characteristics are used in assessing the health and social well-being of the population:
   a disease
   b crime
   c life expectancy.

7 Describe the inter-relationship between:
   a social class and health
   b geographical location and disease.

8 Write a report assessing the possible impact of the removal of child benefit for families who are receiving state benefits on:
   a the health
   b the employment status of the mother
   c the housing of the family.

6 Recommend two ways in which the health and social well-being of the population could be improved.

228

9   The provision of health and social care services and their changing nature

What is covered in this chapter

- The statutory provision of health and social care services and facilities
- The classification and variation of health and social care services and facilities
- Why variations in classifications have arisen
- The relationship between statutory entitlement and the resourcing of services
- Access to care
- Origins and development of health and social care provision
- Funding health and social care
- The effects of demographic changes
- The role of the independent sector in influencing care provision

These are the resources you will need for your portfolio for element 5.1:
- A summary report on five local health and social care services and facilities, covering statutory, non-statutory and informal provision, which:
  - describes the extent to which there is statutory entitlement to the services and facilities
  - describes variations in classification and explains why any difficulties occurred
  - describes the major forms of resourcing and relates them to the classification services and facilities
  - describes how clients might access these five services in detail and whether there are particular routes of access for the different services.

These are the resources you will need for your portfolio for element 5.2:
- A report which describes in outline:
  - how services and facilities have changed in your country
  - three effects of recent government policy on the structure and funding of health and social care services
  - ways in which demographic characteristics affect priorities for health and social care, supported by three examples.

Finally:
Your written answers to the activities, review questions and assignments in this chapter.

The statutory provision of health and social care services and facilities

Within a welfare state the expectation is that the state will provide for the health care needs of the individual. In an ideal world that would be the case but to do this would require infinite resources. Instead there are certain services to which you are entitled and others which may be made available at the discretion of the purchaser or by paying for them yourself. This divide is present within the statutory services and has meant that charities are still necessary within a welfare state.

Entitlement to a service comes as a result of legislation which identifies something that is a statutory right and that the statutory sector must make provision for. This does not mean that the service must be provided by the statutory sector; it may be provided by the independent sector but paid for by the statutory sector. In some cases the entitlement to a service may mean a fee has to be paid by the client, with provision being made for those unable to pay.

Each local authority can make its own decisions regarding what charges, if any, to make for a number of services (section 17 of the Health and Social Services and Social Security Adjudication's Act 1983). The government encourages authorities to recover the full economic cost of providing home care and day care costs where possible. However the charges should not cause hardship to the client and should take into account the client's ability to pay.

Although the government's care reforms encourage people to live in their own homes there is no absolute right to equipment to enable them to do so. People can approach social service departments directly for advice on, and the provision of, aids to daily living and other types of equipment. Such aids as wheel-chairs, bath aids, aids to eating and dressing are usually provided free or on loan. More expensive pieces of equipment such as hoists, lifts and ramps are, however, subject to payment. The local authority may contract out the provision of some specialist equipment services such as the services for deaf people or those with sight problems.

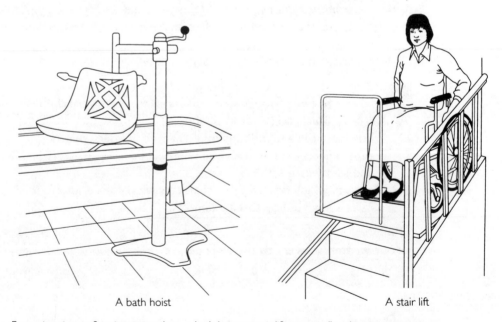

A bath hoist   A stair lift

Expensive pieces of equipment, such as a bath hoist or stair lift, are usually subject to payment

The provision of residential care also has to be paid for, but people who need such support will receive financial assistance with the cost of independent sector residential care through local authority social service departments. The local authority must pay the full fees for anyone placed in a residential or nursing home who needs help with the cost. The social services department will usually collect a means-tested contribution from the client towards the cost.

Most health care services are free but such services as dentistry, provision of glasses and prescriptions are subject to a charge.

People have a statutory right to services provided by the National Health Service (NHS) and local authorities. However just because the services are provided on a statutory basis does not mean that the client is entitled to the services if the authority feels that, after assessment, they are not appropriate services (see Chapter 11). There is no statutory right to services from voluntary, independent or private organisations such as Barnardo's, MIND, SCOPE, MENCAP, Age Concern or many of the small local organisations.

Increasingly, the statutory services are *purchasers* of services, and many independent organisations are *providers* of services (see Chapter 10). This means that some statutory services may be contracted out by the local authority to independent organisations.

Statutory services
NHS	*Local Authority*
Hospital services	Day care
GP services	Residential care
Community nursing	Domiciliary services
Nursing homes	Aids and adaptations
Accident and emergency services	Meals on wheels
	Approved social workers (mental health)

Non-statutory services
Local Authority	*Private/Voluntary/Independent*
Luncheon club	Residential care
Transport	Nursing homes
Holidays	Home help
	Meals services
	Specialist adaptations
	Aids to daily living

Activity 9.1

Investigate, through looking at local literature, the health and social care services to which you are entitled. Also identify services that are not part of statutory requirement but that are provided by the statutory services. If possible, discuss with a care provider any changes in the last 20 years.

The classification and variation of health and social care services and facilities

It seems to be part of all bureaucracies that systems for classification have to be developed. It is also an unfortunate problem that when classification systems are drawn up there are inevitably people who do not fit easily into any one class.

Classification systems to identify different groups needing care are based on a variety of criteria:

- age (e.g. children, adults, elders)
- needs (e.g. mental health, learning ability, physical ability)
- care type (e.g. acute health care, chronic health care)
- social care (e.g. priority services)
- level of care (e.g. primary, secondary, tertiary)
- care setting (e.g. domiciliary, day care, residential, hospital)
- service (e.g. physiotherapy, osteopathy, criminal justice services, foster care)
- locality (e.g. community health services, mental health, etc.).

This list is discussed in more detail on pages 233–4.

The classification systems are often used to define boundaries for funding. Difficulties can occur when a person fits into more than one classification being used, or does not fit easily into any one of them.

Difficulties also occur when funding is based on criteria that are not defensible for an individual. Should a child in need of a transplant because of failing kidneys be treated differently from an elder in a similar situation? Should the health funding for the elderly be focused on tertiary (long-term) care rather than surgery?

Activity 9.2

For each of the following situations describe the possible services that the individual being described might need. Wherever possible use any locally defined classification system.

- A 44-year-old woman suffering from multiple sclerosis who is unable to walk and has a two-year-old child.
- A 30-year-old man with Alzheimer's, disease in an advanced state.
- A 14-year-old mother who is addicted to crack cocaine.
- An 80-year-old who has had a series of strokes, but is otherwise fit.

Classification may be linked to needs other than those for which the person requires care. Hospitals normally separate children from adults so that they can more readily provide for the emotional and developmental needs of the children. Young offenders are treated in different ways to older offenders with the expectation of reducing the risk of them continuing to offend.

Variations in the classification of services

Why have variations in classification arisen? The basic answer to this is historical. You will have seen that the various caring services have different origins. The client groups may have been defined by an original charity, for example, or by a perceived common need. More recently, classifications have developed in an attempt to make what is perceived to be the best use of resources.

There is no straightforward classification system of health and social care services and facilities. How services are classified depends on the perspectives taken, whether you look at the service from a manager's viewpoint, a care worker's viewpoint or the viewpoint of someone receiving the services.

Services may be classified as follows:

According to age

Child	Health visitor services
	School health service
	Child guidance services
Adult	Acute medical services
	Dental services
	GPs service
Elderly	Home help services
	Chiropody services
	Consultant geriatrician

According to needs

Mental health needs	Psychiatric day centre
	Community services
	Hostel accommodation
	Speech therapy services
Learning disability needs	Specialist teacher services
	Diagnostic services
	Rehabilitative services
Physical disability needs	Day care services
	Hostels

Type of care

Acute health	Emergency health services
	District general hospitals
	Nursing home
Chronic health care	Geriatric hospital
	Home help services
Social care services	Residential care
	Day care services
	Paramedics service
Priority services	Ambulance service

Level of care

Primary	School health services
	Home nursing services
	GP services

| Secondary | Acute hospital services |
| Tertiary | Super specialists hospital services, e.g. neuro-surgery, open heart surgery |

Care setting

Domiciliary	Nurses
	Home helps
	GPs
Day care clinic	Day hospitals
	Day centres
Residential care	Nursing homes
	Hostels
	Long stay hospitals
	Community homes
Hospital	Acute care
	Long-term care

Service being supplied
Physiotherapy
Chiropody
Probation hostels
Church work (voluntary visiting)
Substance abuser centres
Psychiatric day centres

Locality

Locality planning is a popular option for may health authorities and local authorities, particularly in rural areas. It is a means of adapting services to the needs of local communities, and replaces the centralised services which have developed in most areas. The idea is to provide services closer to people's homes. Every community has its own sense of being, and natural centres where it conducts its ordinary business.

Locality planning taps knowledge of local need through local people. Priorities and solutions to problems are locally, and not centrally, derived. It depends on consumer involvement and public representation. Therefore, locality planning is not just about the physical siting of resources, but represents a major change in the philosophy of care delivery. (See *Access to care*, page 237)

Case study

Joan's fall

Joan is a 70-year-old who has broken her leg in a fall in the high street; she also suffered a cut to her arm. She was rushed to hospital for emergency treatment. Her leg was put in plaster by doctors in the emergency department. She was seen by the duty social worker to discuss how feasible it was for her to return home.

As she lived alone it was agreed that she should be admitted for two or three days so that domiciliary care services and community nursing services could be organised.

On her discharge Joan agreed to a care plan which included: a home help; meals on wheels service; and district nurse to support her in her home. She received regular visits from her GP and attends the out-patients department at the local hospital for physiotherapy and a local authority day centre for company. She is being observed until her wounds and leg are healed.

Activity 9.3

Read the case study of Joan and list the services she agreed to receive to help in her rehabilitation.

1 Place them under the headings used above. Did they overlap?
2 Did the classification help make it easier to understand the services she was offered?
3 Find out which services Joan would have received free and which she might have been assessed to contribute towards payment.

Why variations in classifications have arisen

The increasing pressure on health and care resources this century has led recent governments to ask the question as to whether services should be available free to the whole population or only to those on a low income. The Beveridge proposals in the early 1940s put forward the concept of universality. Services available to all were not thought to be socially divisive and avoided the problem of stigma associated with some services. Universal services increase the chances of the service reaching those in most need.

However, over the years since 1950, experience has shown that the universal approach is expensive to provide although relatively cheap to administer. This situation has led many to question this universal approach and develop a more selective approach that would allow concentration of scarce resources to those who most need them. This has led to positive action so that services are directed to populations that need them. Health clinics have been built in areas, for example, where people have not got access to transport or cannot afford it.

We can see from Activity 9.3 that classifications are not mutually exclusive but overlap to some extent. People may be classified because of their age and be in receipt of services usually associated with that age group, i.e. a health visitor attending a family with young child or a consultant geriatrician supporting an elderly person.

The relationship between statutory entitlement and the resourcing of services

The resourcing of services is largely controlled by central government. There is direct resourcing of health care through the NHS. Social care is most often the responsibility of local authorities, who receive an allocation of money from central government, and also raise money through the council tax. The NHS and Community Care Act 1990 requires local authority social service departments to manage the funds available for community care. This is done by assessing two criteria: need and wealth.

It has been the philosophy of governments in Britain for a number of years to reduce public spending on health and social care. One way of achieving this is to induce individuals to make their own provisions for care via private insurance schemes, or rely upon charities.

Charities are under great strain, as they have to deal with increasing numbers of individuals who need assistance. While they receive some help from central government and local authority grants, they must increasingly rely on public generosity, which is also waning.

Of course some fortunate individuals will always be able to pay for their own health and care requirements. In fact, having significant personal resources puts such individuals well out of reach of the NHS and Community Care Act. They do not need to be assessed for need or for wealth. These individuals are the only ones to have genuine free choice in health and social care services.

Private insurance for health and care is used elsewhere in the world, particularly the United States, and has been found to be an unsatisfactory means of providing health care. Some common problems include increased spending on health care as unnecessary investigations and treatments are provided, without resulting in improved health generally. In addition, insurance payments often fall far short of the true cost of treating serious illnesses, leaving sick people in great debt. It has been argued that the encouragement of private medicine and care in Britain has been at the expense of resourcing statutory services.

Entitlement to care

Entitlement to care is very carefully controlled by government as to make it obligatory

Beds blocked by funding crisis

by Linda Steele

Bed blocking and granny dumping. Catchy or insulting the jargon may be but it all amounts to the same thing – a shortage of resources and human misery.

Hospitals have warned that beds are 'blocked' by elderly and disabled patients who cannot be discharged because community care services are not available.

Patients needing long-term care are caught in the crossfire of the local government and community care funding crisis, and health-service underfunding and the closure of continuing care NHS beds.

In some cases, this has meant 'granny dumping', with distraught families trying to insist on continuing NHS care because they can neither care for dependent elderly relatives at home nor afford private nursing homes.

In other cases, patients have found themselves placed in private nursing homes, where they often have to pay. Elderly people, robbed of the belief that free health care is a cradle-to-grave right, have watched as their savings are eaten away.

The crux has been a distinction between medical care, provided free by health authorities, and social care, means

tested and organised by local authorities. Sometimes, the distinction is so fine and the pressure on resources so great, that health and local authorities can't agree who's responsible.

In a celebrated case, the Health Ombudsman ruled that the NHS had a duty to provide long-term care to a profoundly brain damaged man whom a Leeds hospital had discharged to a private nursing home, leaving his wife to foot the bill.

The Government has stepped in, not to increase the number of beds or fund care adequately but to end the right to free, long-term NHS care.

Source: *Unison Magazine*, April 1995

to provide the care can have massive cost implications. The NHS and Community Care Act recognises this in that it is the right of an individual to have a care plan. There is no entitlement to the care identified in the plan. However, once a service has been provided it is illegal for social service departments to withdraw the service without a reassessment of the client's situation. The High Court has ruled that services cannot be taken away without reassessment. However, it also ruled that local authorities can take resources into account when drawing up care packages and care plans. This ruling may put paid to the myth of needs-led assessment (see Chapter 11) as authorities can take into account whether they can afford the provision of a service when drawing up care plans with clients.

Access to care

Having established something of the organisation, structure and staffing of the caring services, it is important to look at how people can make use of the services offered. There are basically three ways that a person can be referred to the care services:

- **self-referral** – where people seek help themselves, which may involve support from family members
- **referral through professionals** – in this case a doctor, social worker, nurse, teacher or other professional may assist the person to request care
- **compulsory referral** – where the person in need of care is taken into care by an authorised care worker for his or her own (or others') protection.

Self-referral

This is often the first route for most people receiving health and social care. Within the health service this may be by simply turning up at the GP's or dentist's surgery. The first point of contact can also be through a health visitor. Within social care, referral may be to an area office, a patch office or direct to a care facility, such as a day care centre or a nursery.

In all cases, the initiative is with the person requiring care or a friend or relative making the initial contact, for example, a spouse of a person who is behaving oddly who seeks professional help.

Self-referral at the GP's surgery

Referral through a professional

Unless admitted to hospital as an accident or emergency case, the only way that a person may voluntarily receive hospital treatment is by referral from another professional, normally a GP. Where a GP diagnoses, or suspects, ill-health that requires specialist treatment, the patient is referred to an out-patient clinic, or admitted direct to a ward if the case is urgent.

In social care, an example of referral by professionals might be when a teacher in a school suspects child abuse and refers the case through to the duty social worker. Under the Children Act 1989, all schools should have a named person who makes this referral. Another example might be referral through the police who have given a 'warning' to a child who has committed an offence and who they feel should be referred to social services.

Activity 9.4

Discuss with colleagues the different scenarios that can lead to people seeking care and identify the people who might assist them.

Issues relating to access

It is clearly the responsibility of health and social care organisations to promote access through effective marketing. This means publicising the services in a positive way, and ensuring that information about the services reaches individuals who are most likely to make use of them (see Chapters 14 and 15). It also means de-stigmatising services, and generally making people feel good about using them.

However, many public sector care organisations have been notoriously poor at marketing. There are several reasons for this:

- Marketing is a dirty word in public sector services.
- Many public sector organisations do not employ marketing experts.
- There is often a conscious attempt to demarket services – that is, limiting access to them because of financial constraints.

The last reason is an important one. In reality, many health and social care organisations dare not actively promote access to their services through fear of not being able to respond to the genuine levels of need in the community.

Origins and development of health and social care provision

The formation of the National Health Service

The National Health Service (NHS) came into existence on 5 July 1948 as a direct result of the National Health Services Act 1946. The legislation was preceded by an influential report from the British Medical Association on health insurance and the Beveridge Report on Social Insurance and Allied Services. The minister who piloted the legislation through Parliament and oversaw the formation of the NHS was Aneurin Bevan, Minister of Health 1945–51.

It is important to recognise that the legislation built on a series of earlier plans arguably started in 1808 with the County Asylums Act. Subsequent legislation included the 1848 Public Health Act, the 1867 Metropolitan Poor Act, the 1911 National Insurance

Act and the 1929 Local Government Act. In other words, there had long been a recognition of the weakness in the pattern of health care services and their availability to all.

The 1946 Act brought the health services, and in particular the hospitals (most of which had previously been controlled by charities or voluntary organisations) under the control of the Ministry of Health. It expanded the provision of the National Insurance Act, which had provided for general practitioner care for working people, to cover access to health care for all, free at the point of delivery. Prior to the 1946 Act the funding for this care had been by private insurance through, for example, friendly societies. After the Act the funding came from general taxation, national insurance contributions and charges made to private patients. The Beveridge Report that had preceded the Act made the assumption that there was a fixed quantity of illness in the community, which the introduction of a health service, free at the point of consumption, would gradually reduce. (Funding of the present services is considered later in this chapter.)

'Stuffing their mouths with gold'

One of the major difficulties in the setting up of the National Health Service was to get the agreement of doctors and consultants. Clearly for the service to work, there needed to be co-operation from the medical profession. Members were, however, divided in their views:

- At one extreme were the consultants who were able to command high fees for their work and feared that they would lose money and autonomy within a national service. They were at the top of their profession and had the greatest power.
- At the other extreme were General Practitioners working in areas of poverty and unemployment. In such areas the opportunities to collect payments were limited and most insurance schemes were for people in employment. For these practitioners the contracts under the NHS would provide opportunities to plan health education and provide higher levels of care. There was still a fear of the loss of the highly prized professional autonomy.

In order to persuade the consultants to join the NHS, the Minister of Health allowed them to maintain their private practices and to make use of NHS hospitals for consultancy and practice. In this way they were not becoming part of the NHS, but were working within it while maintaining their work outside. The accusation was made that in order to form the NHS the Minister had had to 'buy off' the opponents in the medical profession by 'stuffing their mouths with gold'.

The legacy of these concessions to doctors still exist, although the funding arrangements in terms of purchasers and providers now make the distinctions more blurred.

The government had effectively nationalised the health services in an attempt to provide fair access to all. The Black Report in the late 1980s indicated that, after 40 years of the NHS, this provision was still not being made. In part, the recognition of this has been evident from the number of changes in the management of the NHS over the years. We will looking at these changes in an attempt to identify some of the underpinning issues.

The structure set up at the inception of the NHS (Figure 9.1) was in place for almost 26 years. However, weaknesses began to appear almost from the start. In particular, there were three problem areas that were highlighted in the 1960s:

- The Gillie Report in 1963 recognised the greater emphasis being placed on primary health care teams and the integration of health and care services.
- In 1967 the poor quality of care given to certain patient groups was highlighted.
- The administrative control of the NHS was becoming ever more cumbersome. In particular, the need to provide balanced packages of care for all people in the community was being distorted by demands from acute specialties (surgery and general medicine) being favoured over long-term geriatric and psychiatric provision.

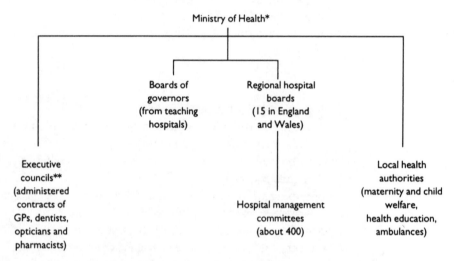

*Later the Department of Health and Social Security (1968)
**Executive council members appointed by local professionals, local authorities and the Ministry

Figure 9.1 Structure of the NHS 1948-74

National Health Service Act 1973

As early as 1962 the weaknesses of the tripartite structure had been identified, and in 1968 and 1970 the government produced papers proposing reforms in the NHS. It was another three years until the National Health Service Act 1973 was passed and 1 April 1974 when it to come into operation. The new structure in England from 1974 to 1982 is shown in Figure 9.2.

The structure in Wales was similar, with the Welsh Office combining the functions of a central government department and the regional health authority.

In Northern Ireland there were four health and social services boards linked to the DHSS (Northern Ireland). Each board was split into several districts and was responsible for personal social services as well as health services.

The three main aims of the reorganisation were:

- **The unification of health services under one authority.** This was not total as GPs maintained independent contractor status and some postgraduate teaching hospitals retained separate boards of governors.
- **The co-ordination between health authorities and related local government services.** To this end, the area health authority boundaries were to a large extent

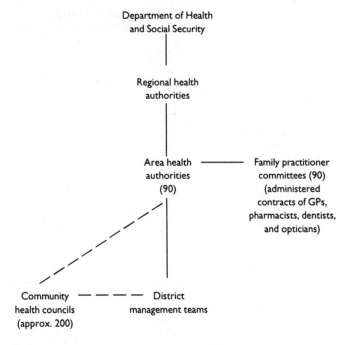

Figure 9.2 *Structure of the NHS 1974–82*

the same as local authority boundaries. Joint consultative committees were set up between the two types of authority to discuss the delivery of services and common issues.

- **Improvement of management.** Job descriptions were provided for different personnel and a key feature was the introduction of multi-disciplinary teams and consensus management. It is no coincidence that the management structures borrowed ideas from the private sector as they were devised with the help of the management consultants from that sector.

All of the changes reflected the need to pursue national priorities at local level and a movement of resources towards neglected groups such as the elderly and mentally ill

The new structure meant that by 1977 16,400 extra administrative posts had been created to cope with the bureaucracy. The decision-making procedures were long indeed, meaning that the costs of reorganisation were high and staff morale in all areas was low.

As early as 1979 the then Conservative government produced proposals for reform which were revised and finally published in July 1980. In essence these proposed the removal of one management tier by amalgamating the functions of District Management Teams and Area Health Authorities within a new body, the District Health Authority. In 1981 the proposals were extended to give Family Practitioner Committees a level of independence with the status of employing authorities.

Health and Social Security Act 1984

The Health and Social Security Act 1984 encompassed these changes and recognised the structure that had been in place from 1982 (Figure 9.3 overleaf). In Wales the structure was similar to England, again without a specific regional health authority. In Northern Ireland the Health and Social Services Boards were retained.

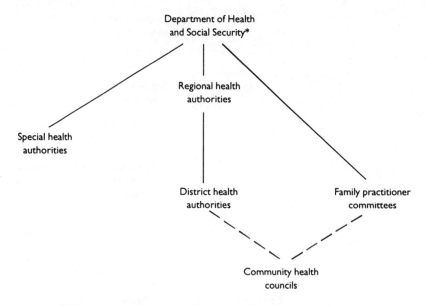

*The DHSS became the Department of Health in 1988

Figure 9.3 Structure of the NHS 1982–90

One important effect of this reorganisation was the loss of boundary links with local authorities in England and Wales, and hence integration of health services and personal social services became more difficult.

From 1982 increased emphasis was placed on devolving management of districts down to **units,** each with a general manager. These could be made up of a physical entity such as a large hospital or group of hospitals, or a more diverse unit such as a 'community health unit'. The latter would have responsibility for services such as district nursing, health visiting, chiropody, community psychiatric nursing, etc.

It is these units (hospital or community-based) that have more recently become self-governing trusts.

Activity 9.5

a What different units cover your health area?
b What services does each offer?

The structure of social services

The Social Services Committee, established by the 1970 Local Authority and Social Services Act has responsibilities in four areas:
- childcare under the various children's acts and adoption acts, including the 1989 Children Act (see below)
- provision and regulation of residential accommodation for older people and people with disabilities under the 1948 National Assistance Act and the 1984 Registered Homes Act
- welfare services for older people, people with disabilities, those who are chronically ill, and statutory powers under the various mental health acts

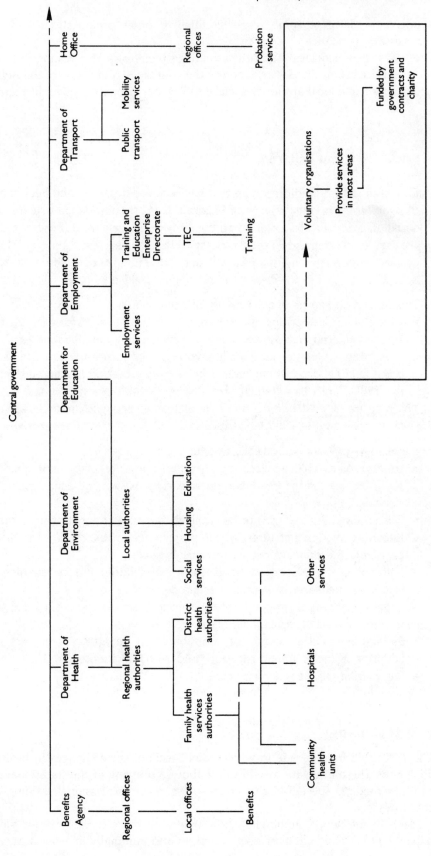

Figure 9.4 Relationships of organisations involved in health and social care

- power to delegate some responsibilities to other organisations and to provide necessary assistance.

The ways in which local authorities manage their roles and responsibilities through social services committees varies across the country. An example of the organisational structure for one local authority social services department is given in Figure 9.4.

Case study

> ## Social care and children
>
> One area of local authority care that has received attention and been the subject of significant legislation is care of children. It is no coincidence that many early charities, that are still working, had their roots in working with children. Children are very vulnerable and so their protection has been seen as a priority. The care of children is governed by many laws. Since 1969, for example, there have been at least 20 Acts passed by Parliament relating to children.
>
> This legislation can be broken down into two areas:
> - where public authorities can intervene in children's cases, for example the 1980 Foster Children Act and the 1969 Children and Young Persons Act
> - those Acts which do not initially involve public authorities but define the position of children within families, for example the 1973 Guardianship Act and the 1987 Family Law Reform Act.
>
> This mixture of legislation has more recently been brought into focus and replaced in most cases by the 1989 Children Act.
>
> Social services have responsibilities to children as follows:
> - Supervision of children placed in day care – nurseries, playgroups, childminders, etc. This includes the need to register such provision and define the acceptable standards.
> - Preventing children having to be received into care or appear before the courts.
> - Receiving into care children whose parents are unable to care for them. Legislation describes appropriate circumstances.
> - Initiation of court proceedings in respect of children and looking after the interests of children subject to certain court orders.
> - Supporting the best interests of children in their care, providing accommodation for them and maintaining them.
> - Supervising children placed for adoption. Many departments also act as adoption agencies and arrange for children to be adopted.
> - Supervising children in foster care.

Developments in technology

The 1990s will be a decade in which recent technological changes in health care will accelerate. These innovations will bring about a blurring of the traditional boundaries between medical specialists and create pressure on professional training and career structures.

Many of the new technologies allow treatment to be carried out on a day or out-patient basis. The potential of laser treatment and minimally invasive surgery (keyhole surgery) to reduce post operative illness will have an effect on the number and type of hospital beds needed. Other growth areas include genetic screening and therapy, and organ transplantation.

> **New technologies in the health services**
> Laser technology
> Key hole surgery (minimal invasive surgery)
> Transplants
> Genetic screening
> Computers and telecommunications
> Biochemical diagnostics

Many other technological changes such as computer and video-phones will allow many treatments to take place in primary care centres and perhaps patients' homes in the near future.

Funding health and social care

Health care funding

When the NHS was first formed one of the important aims was to improve the health of the nation. One of the tenets of the provision was that while initial costs would be high there would be a reduction in costs later as health improved and demand for health care decreased.

Activity 9.6

a Table 9.1 (overleaf) details the cost of the National Health Service. Use these figures to plot a graph of NHS costs in actual and inflation-adjusted terms.

b Why have the costs in real terms increased? Consider issues such as life expectancy and advances in medical techniques, amongst others.

In 1992–3 the total gross expenditure of the NHS in the UK was 29.3 billion and was funded as follows:
- 80.8 per cent from general taxation
- 13.9 per cent from National Insurance contributions
- 3.9 per cent from charges to patients
- 1.4 per cent from capital sales.

The major charges to patients include:
- attending a person involved in a road traffic accident and for their initial out-patient treatment
- accommodation and services for private patients
- non-emergency NHS treatment of overseas visitors
- for drugs and appliances on prescription by a doctor or dentist
- dental treatment.

Initially, health services funding was provided to hospitals directly from central government through the structures then in place. The way funds were allocated was not

Table 9.1 The cost of the National Health Service

Year	Total (£m)	Total (at 1949 prices £m)	Year	Total (£m)	Total (at 1949 prices £m)
1949	437	437	1969	1,791	875
1950	477	477	1970	2,040	929
1951	503	466	1971	2,325	950
1952	526	499	1972	2,682	997
1953	546	452	1973	3,054	1,054
1954	564	459	1974	3,970	1,171
1955	609	477	1975	5,298	1,229
1956	664	489	1976	6,281	1,271
1957	720	509	1977	6,971	1,258
1958	764	515	1978	7,997	1,288
1959	826	549	1979	9,283	1,324
1960	981	623	1980	11,914	1,434
1962	1,025	628	1981	13,720	1,498
1963	1,092	655	1982	14,483	1,479
1964	1,190	695	1983	16,381	1,584
1965	1,306	728	1984	17,241	1,581
1966	1,433	769	1985	18,412	1,602
1967	1,556	816	1986	19,690	1,670
1968	1,702	861	1987	21,488	1,737
			1988	23,627	1,797

Source: OHE (1989) and C. Hamm, *Health Policy in Britain*, 3rd Edn. (Macmillan, 1992)

controlled directly by demand. While there were constraints on spending and demands for planning of provision, the provision was controlled by the individual units in consultation with district and regional authorities.

More recently the NHS and Community Care Act 1990 has divided the functions of providing funds for health care from the provision of care. The purchaser–provider relationship was introduced with the idea of freeing up the marketplace and introducing a level of competition. The aim, of course, being to reduce the costs of health care.

The purchasers are able to purchase health care from any provider, whether NHS, private or voluntary. The providers lose the 'automatic' funding of current provision and have to look at costs and quality. The concept of customer care becomes more important.

All care has to be paid for and there must be a limit on the money available. All care agencies have to predict expenditure, and do so, rather like insurance agencies predict risk. However, there is never enough money available to provide all the services people would like. In social care this tends to mean that statutory services are provided and decisions are made to provide only some of the 'optional' services defined in enabling legislation. In health care it is often the non-urgent treatment that is delayed. Advances in medical care mean that funding decisions become even more complex. Is it better to provide kidney transplants and save life, or carry out plastic surgery on burns victims and improve quality of life?

Activity 9.7

Old should be spared 'inhumane' treatment, says study

Call to curb surgery on terminally ill

Chris Mihill
Medical Correspondent

SOME old and sick patients are suffering needlessly because operations are carried out without a realistic hope of success, a report published yesterday says.

The report, produced by the royal medical colleges, says of such operations: "Surgery should be avoided for those whose death is inevitable and imminent. A more humane approach to the care of these patients should be considered."

It also blames a shortage of facilities, unsupervised surgery by junior doctors and a lack of research, for causing post-operative deaths.

The inquiry, which looked at 1,400 of the 18,000 adult deaths within 30 days of surgery from April 1991 to March 1992 in England, Wales, Northern Ireland and the Channel Islands, identifies four problems:

● Lack of an operating theatre reserved for emergencies;

● Inadequate intensive care facilities, leaving some operations for old and sick people little chance of success;

● Emergency operations at night on old and sick patients, by unsupervised doctors in training grades;

● Poor standards in the appointment of locum doctors.

Some 7,000 consultants were invited to take part in the investigation, but 24 per cent declined to do so, often because they could not find the case notes or other medical records.

Professor John Blandy, chairman of the inquiry, said: "There are roughly 3 million operations per annum in this country and about 18,000 deaths — a rate of 0.6 per cent — almost entirely restricted to the very old and the very sick."

The death rate has remained unchanged since a previous survey. "The vast majority of operations for the vast majority of patients are safe," Prof Blandy said. "However, this report is an effort by anaesthetists, gynaecologists and surgeons to see if they can't do better."

Prof Blandy said some of the large-scale desperate operations on very sick patients were carried out to reassure relatives that everything possible was being tried, but it some cases it was difficult to understand why they had been done.

He said patients, as well as health districts placing contracts, should ask questions about the surgical facilities available in hospitals.

The report says it "is no longer acceptable" for trainees to work alone without suitable supervision and direction by consultants.

Some patients are being given far too much fluid while they are unconscious and unable to pass urine. This can build up until it damages the heart and lungs, says the report.

Some examples of "hopeless" operations given in the report included that of a 74-year-old woman with a head injury who was operated on although she appeared lifeless. She later died from broncho-pneumonia.

A 68-year-old man with inoperable spread of cancer in the brain was recommended for surgery, and later received a second operation the same day to relieve fluid pressure in the brain. He died soon afterwards.

A senior registrar operating on an 80-year-old woman with a perforated duodenal ulcer also discovered she had womb problems. He carried out a hysterectomy, but the patient died from a heart attack. "There was no justification for this hysterectomy," the report said.

The report of the National Confidential Enquiry into Perioperative Deaths 1991/1992; 34-35 Lincoln's Inn Fields, London WC2A 3PN; £9.00.

Source: *The Guardian*, 8 September 1993

Read the article above.

a What are your views on the issues?

b How might medical decisions be affected by funding issues?

Case study

> ### Controlling access to care: shepherding the resources
>
> There are many demands on resources in the NHS. One of the ways in which these demands can be managed is to consider the value added to a patient's quality of life. This can lead to a purely numerical system for determining the benefit of carrying out an operation.
>
> It would be clear to say that it would not benefit the patient greatly if a kidney transplant were carried out on an 87-year-old man with terminal cancer and with an estimated life expectancy of a month. The improved quality of life and the risk of dying under the anaesthetic would indicate the unreasonableness of carrying out the operation.
>
> More difficult decisions need to be made where the risk of the operation means that life expectancy is not improved although quality of life may be.
>
> There have been cases where access to care has been conditional on the patient changing his or her lifestyle in some way. An orthopaedic surgeon may insist that a patient lose weight before carrying out a hip replacement. The logic for this is that the reduced weight will make the operation easier and will improve its long-term success. It is not an unreasonable request.
>
> Of more concern is the insistence that a person give up smoking before being treated for an unrelated illness. There was a case of a person who was refused access to an investigation for heart by-pass surgery unless he gave up smoking. He subsequently died of a heart attack. In this case the argument was almost the same as the one put forward at the start of this case study: the operation had a reduced chance of success; continued smoking would recreate the problem, thus making the original cost a waste of money!
>
> The difficulty with all of these decisions is that it is easy to theorise and make pronouncements about general situations, but the needs of individual patients are real, not theoretical.
>
> In the end, to be efficient, funding has to look at cost benefits. In terms of immunisation it is cheaper in the long run to provide rubella vaccine to all women before they have a chance of getting pregnant than it is to provide care to a damaged child for its lifetime. Similarly, the cost of providing domiciliary support for an Alzheimer's disease sufferer and his or her carer is less than providing full-time residential care. It could be argued, however, that in the latter case the cost is in the carer's loss of quality of life.

The population changes in the UK over the next half century mean that, as people live longer, the cost of care will increase, whilst the workforce is decreasing. Legislation already recognises this problem as the NHS and Community Care Act 1990 requires local authorities to assess need, but does not require them to meet all of the assessed need. Greater demands are now being made on the relatives of people needing care. The cost of caring for these carers has yet to enter the equation.

Case study

> ### Care in the community: Alice's tale – the long bereavement
>
> Alice had been a professional with 15 people working under her. She had responsibility for care of several hundred children. She and her husband moved to

a large house in the country before they both retired with the aim of following their joint interests in gardening.

About two years after she retired, friends and family began to notice small changes. Alice was constantly talking about her old job as if she were still there. She still remembered the grandchildren's birthdays, but the presents didn't reflect the fact that they were growing up. She started to forget what she had said and so often repeated herself. Everybody put it down to the delayed reaction following her retirement from a job she had enjoyed and done well.

Her GP gave her a check up and initiated treatment for high blood pressure. He continued for the next two years to repeat prescriptions and gave infrequent check-ups. People close to Alice didn't notice much change other than she was starting to slow down and needed more time to think.

Four years after her retirement, her forgetfulness started to show more clearly. She needed prompting to recognise her daughter, visiting her after a long absence. She called her son by her brother's name. Alice's husband started to become concerned when what he had not noticed as major changes were pointed out to him. The GP arranged for an appointment with a geriatrician.

The next six months showed a sharp decline in Alice's health. She became very forgetful and also very angry towards her husband. She became incontinent, especially at night, and so her husband's work load increased with all the extra washing.

Eventually a care plan was agreed, with Alice attending a day centre three days a week and going into residential care one week in four. Also domiciliary support would be provided to help wash and dress Alice on two days a week.

Over the period of time before the next six monthly review Alice deteriorated. It became more difficult to get her into the car and take her to the day centre. She became incontinent during the day, putting an even greater work load on her husband. Also, for financial reasons, it was decided to reduce the residential weeks to one in five. Alice's husband is awaiting the review of her case under the Care in the Community legislation.

Clearly he is coping, and making a limited use of the social services resources. The care plan originally agreed needs urgent review, but because he can cope and Alice's needs are being met there is likely to be little change – possibly more domiciliary support and collection from home by ambulance as she will soon find it impossible to travel by car. It is unlikely that full-time residential care will be available because Alice's needs are being met by care in the community.

Care in the community is working for Alice. But for her husband it is not. He retired with plans for his garden – it is a wilderness. He looks forward to the respite care time to get basic housework done. He is unable to go out as Alice cannot travel far by car and when he goes anywhere with her, it has to be somewhere that can cope with Alice's needs. Like many people in his situation he will be alone for Christmas. His only conversation will be with relatives and friends over the telephone. He could be with family but refuses to allow them to 'ruin' the young grandchildren's Christmas by taking them away from home.

Alice has Alzheimer's disease. She cannot talk, feed herself or in any way care for herself. The personality her husband married is no longer there, it has died and only the living body remains. He and his family know the meaning of the other name for the disease – 'the long bereavement'.

Activity 9.8

Read the case study above and answer the following questions:

a What are Alice's needs? How are they being met?

b What are her husband's needs? Which voluntary organisations might provide support for him?

c Investigate provision in your area that might be made available remembering that Alice and her husband live seven miles from the nearest town.

Alzheimer's disease: some facts

- Over 600,000 people in the UK suffer from Alzheimer's disease.
- Every day 42 more people develop the disease.
- It affects one in every 20 people over 65, and one in five over 80.
- It can affect people as young as 40.
- Alzheimer's disease is on the increase simply because the advances in medicine mean that people are living longer.

Private health care

The Act of Parliament that formed the NHS has been described as a structure based on compromise. Many health professionals, in particular doctors, were unhappy at the thought of giving up their private practices. They were concerned, in part at least, that their freedom to charge for their services outside the NHS should be maintained. In fact, so strong was this feeling that in order to bring doctors into the NHS, agreement was made to enable doctors to work both with the NHS and in private practice.

Private health care can occur both within NHS-owned institutions, with the client paying for the services, or within totally separate 'private' health care facilities. With the current move towards a mixed economy of care and the concept of purchases and providers, the distinction becomes blurred. Purchasers (e.g. district health authorities) are free to purchase care from any provider, not just those within the NHS. So NHS patients may receive treatment in 'private' establishments.

Is free health care for all possible?

The economic argument must be that total health care provision for all is impossible. It is clear that if all the renal dialysis units are fully utilised then a new patient cannot be accommodated. To buy a new dialysis machine would be possible, but the money would have to come from somewhere. Would it be reasonable to have a single machine for one patient, especially if not buying the machine would pay for several hip replacement operations, or more incubators for premature babies?

With any provision, the funding must be insufficient. The costs of the NHS represented almost 12 per cent of public expenditure in 1950 and almost 15 per cent in 1988. Any increased government funding must either be from increased taxation or from reductions in other areas.

Another issue has to be the increased complexity and cost of health care. As knowledge and techniques improve so people can be treated for more and more things. Often, it is the emotive areas that point up these issues. In 1967 abortion was legalised up to the 28th week of pregnancy. This time limit was partially fixed by the then current knowledge that no child born prior to that date was able to survive. Developments in technology now mean that some children born at 24 weeks can now survive. The monetary cost is high and the potential for physical and mental impairment is high, but public expectation is that the provision must be made available. At the same time, the developments open moral and ethical debates.

Management issues

The NHS and Community Care Act 1990 attempted to use market forces to improve management of care provision. It also helped to rectify a problem that had occurred when people in need of further care were discharged from hospital. In the past people have occasionally been discharged into the community without their needs being met and without referral to the social services. Now the requirement for the DHAs, trusts and local authorities to work together in assessing care need should reduce the risk of people 'dropping' through the system. In the next few years we will see how effective these measures have been.

Activity 9.9

The costs to the health services of treating a person with lung cancer are high. It is possible to reduce the incidence of the disease by stopping people from smoking.

a Consider how the different strategies for service delivery could be used to cope with the issue of lung cancer.

b What care does a sufferer need and what are the benefits of prevention to the nation?

Who receives care?

The principal exogenous input to social welfare policy is the structure and size of the UK's population. The structure of the population refers to such variables as age, social class, gender, family and household status, marital status, employment or health status and religion. Estimates of current and future population structures form the basis for health and care policy planing. Population structures can therefore affect health and social care priorities.

Mortality trends would seem to indicate potential for people to live longer, particularly those over 65 years of age. However, people may live longer but do they have a gain in quality of life? If people are expected to live longer but also as they grow old become dependent, what effect does this have on the health and social care services?

Activity 9.10

What effect upon health and social care services will the trend for elderly people to live longer have? List the services that you think will be affected most and explain why? Changes in family structure also affects planning. Marriage is now less popular than for some centuries – this unpopularity is also linked to a falling in fertility. However, the relationship between marriage and childbearing is becoming weaker and weaker. Marriage is been replaced by cohabitation with no foreseeable decline or increase in the birth rate. The rise in single parents might indicate that childbearing is becoming a matter for woman alone. All of these changes have implications for household and family structures.

Activity 9.11

Access data in your school or college library and find out the percentage of single parent families in your locality. Is there any differences in the percentages in different wards in your local authority? Why should these differences occur?

Independent of changes in the family the population of the UK will age considerably in the decades to come. The timing of this ageing is also linked to the baby boom in the 1960s and the later decline in fertility. In the UK the most rapid rise in the number of those over pensionable age is expected between 2000 and 2030 with a rise in the number of those over 80 years of age coming some years later.

Access to health and social care is not simply about the procedures of achieving treatment or care. There is the very important issue of who receives care and whether access is equal to all groups in society. The introduction of the welfare state hoped to remove the inequalities of access to care. One of the tenets was access to all, free at the point of delivery. If access to care is equal for all who need it then there should be no inequalities and the health of the general population should improve.

The Black Report in 1980, which looked at inequalities in health, highlighted issues of differing mortality and morbidity levels related to social class. It emphasised the significance of broad social, economic and environmental influences on health. It argued that attention needed to be paid to factors such as housing, income support and nutrition if class differences in health were to be reduced. The issues are discussed in more detail in Chapters 1 and 8.

These issues were at the heart of the development of the welfare state and the legislation that went before it. The three prongs of health care, social care and welfare benefits were intended to reduce the differences between social classes in terms of access to health and social well-being. The evidence is that in many ways the divide is just as great today as it was in 1946.

The effects of demographic changes

Demography is the study of population. It consists of two primary aspects: structures and processes.

- **Structures** examine how the population is made up. For example how many individuals over 70 or how many single parent families live in a particular area.
- **Processes** examine the rate of change of variables such as births, deaths, and migration.

There is a regular flow of statistical information from census returns, surveys, and registration of births, deaths and marriages. The demographic scientist identifies trends and makes projections. These trends and projections are major factors in resourcing health and social care. The trend toward an increasingly large dependent elderly population is one of the factors the government uses in promoting private care and insurance schemes. They claim that the taxpayer cannot and will not support the needs of older people.

Activity 9.12

Using nationally produced statistics work out the proportions of people in the following categories in the UK:

- those under 16
- those over 16 and under 60
- those over 60.

Do this for the most recent data available to you and also for data that are 10, 20 and 40 years old. How is the population changing?

The three categories shown in Activity 9.12 represent potential wage earners (>16,<60) and others who may take more in terms of services than they contribute to the cost.

The results of Activity 9.12 will indicate some of the trends in the population in terms of:

- birth rate
- length of life.

Other statistics would show the increased incidence of 'costly' diseases such as cancers and heart disease. In earlier times treatment was limited. Now it is available but often at a high cost.

If you consider the costs to the caring services of the increased life expectancy, improved treatment of disease and dysfunction, and the decreased birth rate then it will become clear that potential costs will increase whilst the number of taxpayers will fall along with the number of workers available to provide care. This demographic time-bomb is already seriously affecting the structure of the welfare state in the UK.

Government control

The demographic information is worrying. If you expect to need to use the caring services in the future then you expect the government to be able to provide. There are two extremes in terms of this provision. The first would be to make each individual responsible for the payment for care. This would require an increased use of private insurance systems. The second extreme would be for government to increase taxation to pay for the caring services. In both cases the costs would be met by the population. In the first case the costs would be met by the individuals (through insurance); in the second the costs for older people and children would largely be met by taxpayers. As the population ages a greater burden would fall on the smaller number of taxpayers.

Government has to try to resolve the dilemma. Much of the most recent legislation has been to ensure that entitlement can be paid for through the statutory provision but that non-statutory services are, at least in part, paid for by the client. There has also been some encouragement through taxation for individuals to take out insurance related to potential care needs.

It is important to recognise that whilst the solutions may vary according to the political party in power, the demographic time-bomb will not be affected by party politics. The future problem will not go away whichever political party is in power.

Government control also arises as a result of political dogma and ideology. As almost all funding for the services comes from government (local and national) there is an opportunity to use funds to support different aspects of the services. A party that believes in traditional family values might focus funding to encourage mothers to stay at home and rely on a partner to provide the family income. This would disadvantage single parent families. A party that believed strongly about equality of opportunity might fund services, such as child day care that would allow mothers, in particular, to retain paid employment.

The role of the independent sector in influencing care provision

The term *independent sector* refers to all non-statutory organisations which contribute to social care. The majority are not set up by government. Many are charities, and many are private businesses.

Many independent agencies act as a focus for fund-raising to provide for people with specific needs. The funds are then used to purchase the equipment or care required. Others, such as Anchor, provide specific residential or sheltered accommodation for older people around the country.

The traditional image of the independent sector is of well-meaning amateurs. This image is not true of the sector today. While some charities work with unpaid volunteers almost all of the larger ones and many others are staffed by salaried staff. The term 'independent' refers to the status of the organisation and not to the status of the workers.

Case study

The NSPCC

One example of an independent voluntary sector organisation is the National Society for the Prevention of Cruelty to Children (NSPCC). This organisation, formed in 1884, is in the interesting position of having statutory powers. It has the authority to take legal action on behalf of a child and has access to records such as the register of children at risk. To carry out its work it employs qualified social workers and works closely with the statutory social services and the police. Thus, a child may be referred to the NSPCC who investigate the case and work with the family. If there is a need for the child to be taken into care, then the case may be taken to court by the NSPCC or passed over to the local authority social services. The emphasis of the organisation is working with families and seeking to prevent their break up.

Volunteers in the independent sector

Volunteers also have a clear role to play in social care. There are a large number of people willing to take on work without pay to provide a variety of forms of care. This may be with the statutory or voluntary services. In many areas this may be co-ordinated by the local Council for Voluntary Services. The functions of this organisation are:

- **Co-ordination** It tries to bring together the various local voluntary organisations, in part at least to reduce the duplication of provision. It also acts as a pressure group for the constituent organisations.
- **Review** It constantly monitors local provision and seeks areas of unmet need. As part of this, it helps to form new organisations and seek funding for new projects.
- **Organisation** It co-ordinates and interviews volunteers. In doing this, it attempts to match people wishing to volunteer to a role that they are suited for. There is also a follow-up to monitor the success of the matching from the volunteer's and the agency's point of view. The agencies involved can be from the voluntary and statutory sectors.

Case study

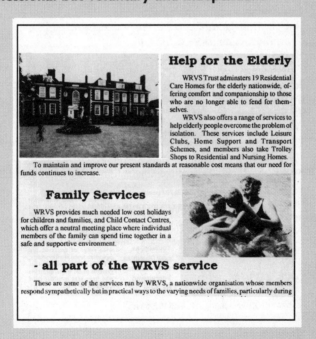

WRVS: Professional but voluntary and independent

Help for the Elderly

WRVS Trust adminsters 19 Residential Care Homes for the elderly nationwide, offering comfort and companionship to those who are no longer able to fend for themselves.

WRVS also offers a range of services to help elderly people overcome the problem of isolation. These services include Leisure Clubs, Home Support and Transport Schemes, and members also take Trolley Shops to Residential and Nursing Homes.

To maintain and improve our present standards at reasonable cost means that our need for funds continues to increase.

Family Services

WRVS provides much needed low cost holidays for children and families, and Child Contact Centres, which offer a neutral meeting place where individual members of the family can spend time together in a safe and supportive environment.

- all part of the WRVS service

These are some of the services run by WRVS, a nationwide organisation whose members respond sympathetically but in practical ways to the varying needs of families, particularly during

The term voluntary in the title of the Women's Royal Voluntary Service defines a non-statutory organisation, but does not imply a lack of professionalism. Many of the workers are unpaid volunteers but the range of their work is phenomenal, as the advertisement indicates.

Table 9.2 (overleaf) shows the range and commitment of just one of the many voluntary organisations. The support of the statutory services can be measured in manpower, in the donations of money and in materials, but this does not reflect the true value of the organisation in its unquantifiable support for individuals and families by the simple fact that it is there.

Table 9.2 Statistics of selected WRVS activities, 1992

Family welfare
Mother and baby/toddler clubs	96
Family and drop-in centres	25
Toy and pre-school libraries	45
Playgroups	40
Welfare clinics	137
Social clubs for the disabled	108
Stroke clubs	63
Riding for disabled groups	5
Disabled people on holidays	271
Elderly people on holidays	1,705
All-day clubs for the elderly	133
Afternoon/evening clubs for the elderly	1,574
Social clubs in part III accommodation	18
Trolley shopping in OP homes	788
General home support – people helped	4,890
Escorts – people helped	4,156
Laundry service – people helped	1,513
Prescriptions/pensions collected – people helped	5,341
War widows/pensioners visited	1,049
Books on wheels – recipients	35,585
Community service orders	47
Court canteens	241
Prison canteens	91
Prison shops	3
Visitors centres in prisons	13
Court and prison children's play areas	16
Crisis support – people helped	2,702
Social transport – passengers	122,462
Social transport miles	1,488,803

Hospitals
Number of hospitals	959
Canteens	644
Trolley shops	647
Static shops	233
Number of members working in hospitals	32,138
Blood donor sessions assisted at	2,400

Other hospital activities:
libraries, magazine and newspaper distribution, visiting, shopping, flower arranging, hairdressing transport, messenger service, hospital radio, letter writing, interpreting, general clerical/administrative tasks.

Table 9.2 is not exhaustive. Did you know:
• That the WRVS delivered 15 million meals on wheels to more than 120,000 housebound/elderly people in 1992?

- That the WRVS run 15 residential homes for the elderly?
- That 7500 under-privileged children and adults had WRVS holidays in 1992?
- That the WRVS emergency teams responded to over 200 incidents in 1992?

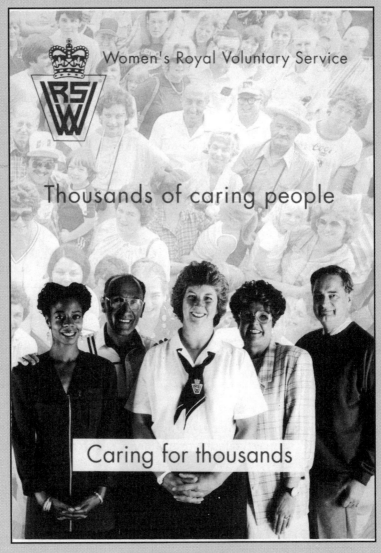

Women's Royal Voluntary Service

Thousands of caring people

Caring for thousands

Source: All information kindly provided by the WRVS

Activity 9.13

Contact your local WRVS and identify just what they do in your area. Personal experience is that they are always ready to accept volunteers and the work can be enjoyable – you don't even have to be a woman!

Private enterprise in the independent sector

Increasingly, many health and care services are being provided by private companies. Privately owned independent services are having a significant impact in areas such as residential and nursing care services, nurseries, private medicine, home care services, and hospital support services. The government has encouraged competition among independent organisations for work previously done wholly within the public sector. Competition is fierce. Within many care markets, and geographical areas, there is an oversupply of private services, driving prices down. This is, of course, the aim of the exercise – to reduce costs. We shall discuss more fully in Chapter 10 how this new split into **purchaser** (the statutory authority) and **provider** (the independent organisation) works.

Review questions

1 Define 'contracting out' of care services.
2 Give five examples of services that are likely to be contracted out by a statutory authority?
3 Identify the ways in which health and care services may be classified.
4 Why have variations in classification of services arisen?
5 How does resourcing affect access to services?
6 Identify the differences in the National Health Service in England, Wales and Northern Ireland.
7 What is a health service unit?
8 Describe key legislation affecting the operations of health services and social services.
9 Explain the effects of demography on the provision of care services.

Assignment 9.1
Investigating health and social care agencies

This assignment provides knowledge, understanding and portfolio evidence for element 5.1, **Investigate the provision of health and social care services and facilities.**

Your tasks

1 Select five local health or social care services, ensuring that you cover statutory, non-statutory, and informal provision. This task may provide a useful opportunity for students to find out about each other's work placements.
2 For each of your selected services, you will write a report, using the following format:
   – An introduction describing the service. Who runs it? Where is it? Who uses it? Do users have a statutory entitlement?
   – Describe what classification systems are used in the service – do users select the service because of their age? Their needs? Their label or diagnosis? Their degree of dependency? Where they live? The special skills of the service staff? What sorts of difficulties, if any, arise because of the systems of classification used?
   – With reference to the classification systems used, explain how the systems used are a consequence of how resources are allocated.
   – Describe how clients can access the service. How does the service either promote or restrict access?

Assignment 9.2
Development and change in health and social care services

This assignment provides knowledge, understanding and portfolio evidence for element 5.2, **Explain why health and social care provision develops and changes.**

Your tasks

1 Prepare a report detailing the basis of health and social care services specifically in your own country (England, Wales, Northern Ireland, or Scotland). Ensure that you identify the relevant legislation underpinning the services. How has the provision of these services changed over time?
2 With reference to your report in 1 above, describe three effects of recent government policy on how health and social care services are funded and structured.
3 Explain how demographic characteristics have affected the health and social care provision described above. Provide three examples to support your explanation.
4 Describe how the independent sector has influenced the development of services in your country. Provide examples of how independent organisations have influenced statutory provision through raising funds and by organising pressure groups.

10 The organisation of health and social care planning and provision

What is covered in this chapter

- The structure of health and social care
- The role of purchasers in meeting the needs of their population
- How provider services are changing to meet the demands of purchasing and providing

These are the resources you will need for your portfolio for element 5.3:
- a short report which:
  - describes the role of a local purchaser
  - describes the changes required of a local provider in meeting the needs of the purchaser
  - includes examples of different agencies involved in health and social care
- your written answers to the activities, review questions and assignment in this chapter.

The structure of health and social care

Introduction – The move towards a mixed economy for care

Since 1983 (The Griffiths Report) it is has been recognised that there was weaknesses in the general management of the National Health Service (NHS). Accordingly, the Griffiths Report recommended that general managers should be appointed at all levels in the NHS to provide leadership, introduce a continual search for change and cost improvement, motivate staff and develop a dynamic management approach.

There was also a recommendation that management be streamlined at the centre with the establishment of a Health Services Supervisory Board and an NHS Management Board within the then Department of Health and Social Security (DHSS), with the chairperson of the Management Board being drawn from outside the NHS and civil service.

Further change was instigated in 1989 with the government White Paper *Working for Change* which proposed the creation of competition between hospitals and other service providers.

- It introduced the concept of a distinction between **purchasers** and **providers** of health care. District health authorities (DHAs) would have the responsibility for purchasing services for patients, using funds based on the population (taking into account factors such as age, sex, etc.). Hospitals would then have to contract to provide services. The aim was to make the providers more responsive and more efficient as money would follow patients. DHAs could purchase services from public, private and voluntary providers. An example might be for a DHA to purchase one hundred tonsillectomy operations from a local hospital. The money for these would be paid to the hospital, be it NHS or in the private sector.

- Hospitals (and any other units) would be able to opt out of health authority control and become **self-governing NHS trusts**.
- DMUs or **Directly Managed Units,** usually hospitals, are managed directly by the District Health Authority.
- Family Practitioner Committees (FPCs) were to become **family health service authorities** (FHSAs) which would be accountable to the regional health authorities rather than directly to the Ministry of Health. An FHSA would have a general manager together with four health professionals, five non-executives and a chairperson.
- At the same time as health care trusts were able to move towards direct control of their own affairs, there was also a move to take some of the purchaser roles from the DHAs. GP practices with a large number of patients were to be able to receive funding directly from the regional health authorities to purchase a defined range of services for their patients. (These are known as **fund-holding GP practices**.) The services they could purchase include outpatient services, diagnostic tests and in-patient and day-care treatments for which it was possible to choose the time and place of treatments. Part of the funding also formed a budget for prescriptions.

By the middle of the 1900s about 50 per cent of the population will be covered by GP Fund-holders. GP Fund-holders are in effect small, purchasing authorities.

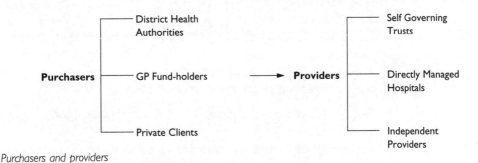

Purchasers and providers

Activity 10.1

Find out how many Self-governing Trusts operate in your locality. What services do they provide. (Remember Self-governing Trusts are hospitals as well as community services.)

National Health Service and Community Care Act 1990

Local authorities have a long tradition of provision of health care. Over the years most of these responsibilities have been removed until only personal services and environmental health services remain. A White Paper in 1988 called *Caring for people,* had proposed that local authorities be given the lead in planning community care. They would be required to prepare community care plans with the DHAs/trusts. Thus, areas of personal social services were becoming linked more strongly to health issues. The NHS and Community Care Bill 1989 received Royal Assent in 1990. As with most legislation relating to care, there was a phased introduction with one of the earliest effects being the formation of 56 hospital trusts in April 1991, with a further 95 hospital and service trusts in 1992. Also in April 1991 300 fund-holding GP practices were established.

The local authority responsibilities were phased in more slowly with planning for 'community care' being required in 1992 and responsibility being taken from April 1993.

Summary of the NHS and Community Care Act 1990

The principal areas covered by the Act are:

- community care plans
- assessment and care management
- purchasing and contracting
- complaints procedures
- inspection units
- specific grant for mental illness.

The implementation targets to be completed by April 1991 were:

- complaints procedures in place
- inspection units set up to evaluate public, private and voluntary care provision, to ensure a consistency of approach and to improve quality control
- the specific grants for mental illness and drug and alcohol services to be available – these were to ring-fence money for these areas so that it could not be diverted to other services
- community care plans to be written
- contracting procedures to be in place – bringing in the purchaser–provider relationships
- assessment procedures to be set up
- case management procedures to be in place.

By April 1992, the developments of 1991 were to be continued, with the following additional target:

- community care plans and planning agreements between local authorities and District Health Authorities and Family Health Service Authorities to be in place.

And by April 1993 with the following additional targets:

- assessment procedures for all clients looking to local authorities for support to be working
- payments and charging mechanisms to be in place
- funds for 'Care in the Community' to be transferred to local authorities
- contracting arrangements to be implemented.

Source and further reading: Community Care in the Next Decade and Beyond: Policy Guidance (HMSO 1990).

Social services departments are responsible for meeting social care needs, for example by the provision of residential, day and domiciliary services. The Act also places upon them the added responsibilities of:

- publishing annual community care plans in consultation with housing authorities, health authorities, representatives of community care service users and the independent sector

- the assessment of people's need for support and care, in collaboration with users, carers and other support agencies designing packages of care
- purchasing residential and nursing home care for appropriate clients.

The development of such functions implied major changes in the organisation of social service departments which are discussed later in this chapter. The NHS has shared in these changes through the NHS and Community Care Act 1990 which separated **purchasers** (health authorities and GP Fund-holders) from **providers** (NHS Trusts and GP Fund-holders) and created an internal market. However, despite fundamental changes in other areas of the postwar welfare state, the founding principals of the NHS are currently still in place – it is still predominantly free at the point of delivery and funded by the nation as a whole through central taxation.

Objectives of recent changes

One of the objectives of the recent changes in the organisation and management of the public sector has been the control of the cost to the taxpayer. Funding to the NHS by the government is now in two ways:

- open-ended funding for most of the primary care services provided by family practitioners
- cash-limited allocations to DHAs for expenditure on hospital and community health services and FHSAs for a limited range of expenditure.

Cash limited allocations are distributed to DHAs on a 'capitation' model which uses death rates and the age structure of the local population to calculate how much funding the DHA should get. This money is distributed through the RHAs.

Activity 10.2 ───────────────────────────────────────

Visit your local library and gain access to the local health authority strategic plan. Find out what services are provided under the following headings: primary, secondary, and tertiary, care.

──

The structure is still evolving. The number of Regional Health Authorities was reduced in 1994 to eight (from 14) in England. The role of the RHAs is also altering to becoming more focused on the purchaser aspects and administration.

The number of health service trusts has risen rapidly and there are now very few directly managed units under the control of the District Health Authorities. The DHAs are now coming together with the Family Health Service Authorities to take on a powerful position of purchasers of care. This emphasises the split between the purchaser and provider roles.

Ironically it will also make the role less clear for fund-holding GPs as their numbers increase. Whereas the FHSAs and the DHAs undertook both roles when they had direct control of units and GPs, they now fall firmly in the camp of the purchasers. The fund-holding GPs now have the role of providers of primary care and purchasers of care at other levels.

Case study

Fund-holder GPs and access to care

Early experience of the implementation of the NHS and Community Care Act 1990 has meant that several hospitals have completed their contracts before they have completed the financial year. Newspapers have highlighted the fact that in some hospitals routine surgery was only available to patients of fund-holding GPs. What has happened is that the hospitals have contracted with the district health authority to carry out a certain number of the routine surgical operations. Once that number has been achieved, there is no more funding available to carry out more.

This means that people still requiring such operations will have to wait until the next financial year. It may well be a problem at the district level where the original number was determined. It may also be that the hospital had charged more than others and so was allocated fewer operations.

The situation is complicated by the fact that the hospital can still accept contracts to fill the empty places but the only funds available are from fund-holding GPs. These doctors contract with hospitals to carry out routine procedures for their patients and have some control over with whom and when the contract will be carried out. This explains the newspaper headlines highlighting queue jumping by the patients of fund-holding GPs.

Activity 10.3

In your own area, establish who delivers health care. Identify where they fit within the structure of the NHS (see Figure 10.1) and whether they are part of a trust.

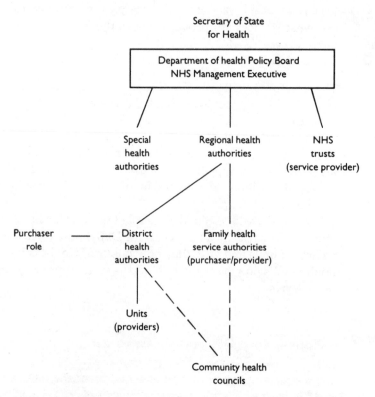

Figure 10.1 The structure of the NHS

The role of social services in health and care planning

The Social Services Committee, established by the 1970 Local Authority and Social Services Act, has responsibilities in four areas:
- childcare under the various children's acts and adoption acts, including the 1989 Children Act (see below)
- provision and regulation of residential accommodation for older people and people with disabilities under the 1948 National Assistance Act and the 1984 Registered Homes Act
- welfare services for older people, people with disabilities, those who are chronically ill, and statutory powers under the various mental health acts
- power to delegate some responsibilities to other organisations and to provide necessary assistance.

The ways in which local authorities manage their roles and responsibilities through social services committees varies across the country. An example of the organisational structure for one local authority social services department is given in Figure 10.2 (overleaf).

Case study

Nursing care

Mr Jackson who is 90 years of age has become very infirm and is in need of nursing home care. His local authority purchases a place for him in a local nursing home. His local authority is responsible for paying for general nursing care needs and the cost of incontinence services.

Mr Jackson's District Health authority and GP Fund-holder is responsible for purchasing physiotherapy, chiropody and the provision of specialist nursing services that he needs.

The professionals involved in care

Activity 10.4

a Make a list of all of the key personnel involved in delivering care, both health and social care. Identify if they are providers or purchasers of care.
b Where might each be based?

In your health care list, you should easily have identified: doctors; nurses; physiotherapists; occupational therapists; speech therapists; radiographers; dentists; dental hygienists; opticians; pharmacists and ambulance personnel. You may have thought of health care assistants, nursing auxiliaries, porters and the many people who work in catering, cleaning and administration. The list could go on.

In your social care list you should have included: social workers; residential and day care staff; home helps (domiciliary support workers); probation officers and nursery nurses. Again this ignores many of the administrative roles but shows something of the range.

The relationships between health care and social care operations are shown in Figure 10.3 (overleaf). We will take each area separately and look at the personnel involved, their roles and how people access the services.

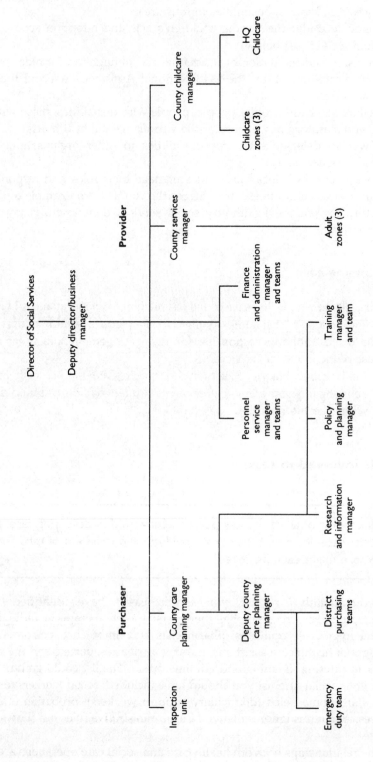

Figure 10.2 The structure of a typical social services department

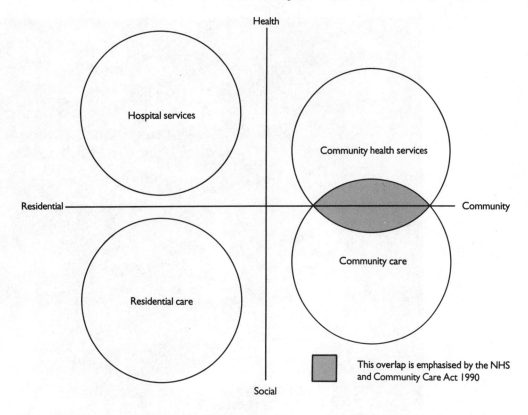

Figure 10.3 The relationship between health care and social care

Hospital and specialist services

Hospitals are traditionally seen as places where people who are too ill to be cared for at home are taken for treatment. They are also the places where people go for 'operations', or where they go for help from a specialist on an out-patient basis. They are staffed by specialist doctors who concentrate on a small area of medicine.

The roles of other sectors in planning and providing care

So far we have only considered the roles of the statutory sector (NHS and Statutory Social Services). Both the voluntary and private sectors play a vital role in the delivery of care.

Whereas in the past a statutory provider of care could reasonably expect to receive funding to provide care within an area there is now a requirement to view the voluntary and private sectors as potential providers of care. This has brought in an element of competition which has made the statutory sector look at issues around quality.

The voluntary and independent sector has also been active in the provision of health and social care services on a contractual basis. It does not really matter to a patient if the care is provided by the statutory, voluntary or private sector, so long as the care is appropriate and meets the needs of the patient. In the days of little competition it was not unusual to hear of people waiting for hours to see specialists or being given little

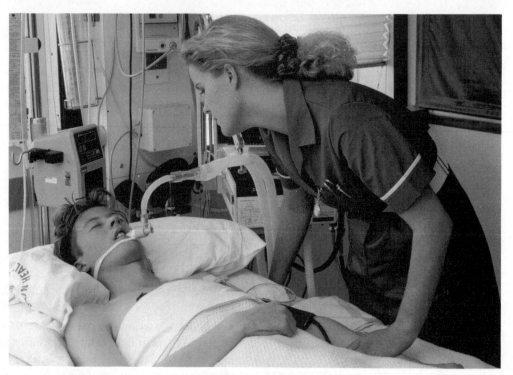

Some of the personnel involved in delivering health and social care

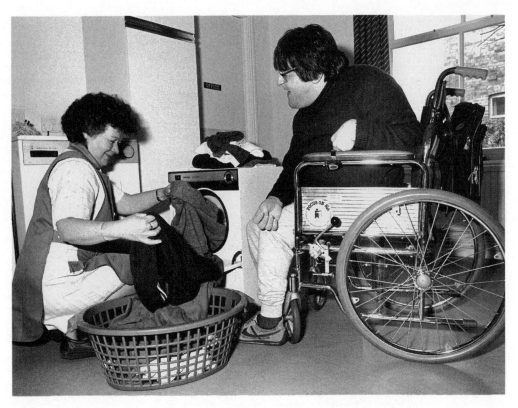

Listening to a client

support by carers. Now the service providers have developed quality standards stating clearly the level of service a client can expect. There is clearly a level of accountability to the client for the service quality.

The role of purchasers in meeting the needs of their population

The District Health Authorities are responsible for planning and assessing the health needs of the population living in their area; almost all have produced strategic plans and consultative documents. They are a major influence in the internal market of the NHS. The DHA is accountable to the Regional Health Authority (RHA). The RHA monitors the performance of the DHA who works closely with other agencies such as GPs and Family Health Service Authorities (FHSAs) in drawing up its purchasing plans. These plans must include a statement of priorities, statements about how improvements in service are to be achieved and monitored and the range of services to be funded. DHAs also have overall responsibility for services not provided by self-governing trusts. In these cases, they agree contracts with providers for a particular standard and level of service.

The National Health Service Management Executive (NHSME) was set up to manage the self-governing trusts who are accountable directly to the Secretary of State for Health. The NHSME has regional offices to deal directly with the self-governing trusts. This structure is shown in Figure 10.4 (overleaf).

Under the GP fund-holding schemes, GPs receive a budget which covers the cost of running their practices. This fund also allows them to purchase drugs, non-emergency

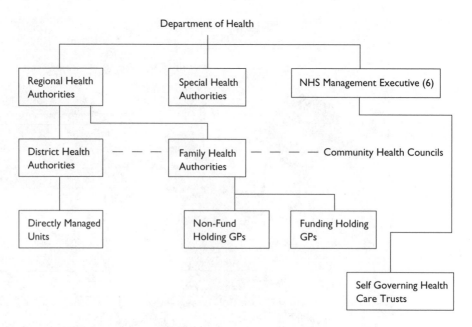

Figure 10.4 The National Health Service 1995

hospital services and also some community health services. Those GPs who are fund-holders are in effect purchasing authorities who can contract with other health providers to give a service to patients on their list.

Multi-agency schemes

Health authorities have powers to make payments to local authorities and other agencies to purchase services such as personal services and housing. These funds are known as 'joint finance'. They are used to support people already in the community or to support their transition from hospital to community. *Multi-agency* refers to any arrangement where joint funds are used to pay of the care of groups or individual clients.

Multi-agency examples

Sheffield Health Authority and Sheffield Social Services Department has established a multi-agency strategic planning group whose role is to prepare multi-agency strategies for drug and alcohol services and recommend an annual investment plan for the services. Other multi-agency services are provided for people with HIV/AIDS covering counselling and advice, social care, health care and housing services, and HIV prevention and health education. A variety of agencies is involved.

Source: Sheffield Community Care Plan 1995/95

Other multi-agency plans involve the independent or voluntary sector. For example, the Family Welfare Association (FWA) in Wandsworth developed a three-year programme to provide services for families and individuals with long-term mental health problems.

The services provided include day care and social work assessment and counselling. A number of social work counselling sessions take place in GP practices.

Assessing the needs of the local population

One of the main challenges facing purchasers of social care provision is to assess and map the needs and demands of the local population. Many authorities argue that it is futile to map needs when they have not got the resources to meet them. Although the NHS and Community Care Act 1990 placed emphasis on a needs-based service recent court cases have began to erode the concept of a needs-led service by allowing authorities to provide only services within their resources.

All local authorities and health authorities have to publish an annual community care plan whose purpose is to report progress with implementing the government's community care reforms. The other aim of the plan is to describe the plans for the provision and development of community care services for the locality.

How provider services are changing to meet the demands of purchasing and providing

The NHS and Community Care Act 1990 urged local authorities to consider changes in their structure to separate the provision of services from the purchasing arm of the agency. The purchaser – provider split was seen as essential to identify the true costs of provision and to ensure that there was no favouritism in the market for contracts. Another reason for this split was to weaken the influence of those who provided the services and so hopefully move the power to the users rather then the providers. Many social services moved to an organisation which recognised this split (see Figure 10.2). This structure allows social service departments to purchase services from a range of agencies both statutory, voluntary and independent in the community. This system's intention is to improve the quality of services, involve the user (client and family) in the planning process, increase choice and obtain better value for money.

In 1991, the Department of Health expected that these changes in the way local authorities managed services would provide the following benefits:

- give the client choice
- needs-led planning
- needs-led budgeting
- individual assessment and care packages which were needs-led
- improved value for money
- improved services
- develop a mixed economy of care
- develop service specification and standards
- development of monitoring of the quality of service.

Contracts

Social service departments have used contracts to buy services for clients for many years. Children placed in private or voluntary children's homes were placed there under a contract of some kind. The voluntary organisation or private agency agreed to provide a service (look after the children, feed them, house them and in some cases offer therapy) and in return the local authority would pay a fee. Standards were usually inspected by either the authority's social workers or government inspectors.

Any contract agreed by either a health authority, social service department or GP fund-holder must comply with certain specifications. These specifications set out what the agencies want for the client or group for which the contract is intended. The specification sets minimum standards relating to quality of inputs and outcomes. For example, the contract may specify the qualifications of staff, who the users must be, a complaints procedure, care practices, equal opportunities, and involvement of clients and users. These specifications form the basis of a legally binding contract.

Authorities usually print all the specifications in one publication and in many cases advertise for agencies to apply to provide the service. This procedure is called *tendering*. It has been used for residential care, domiciliary care and meals on wheels services, among others. Open competitive tendering allows everybody to make a bid to run the service. The WRVS has recently won the tender to provide the meals on wheels service in Derbyshire.

Types of contract
Spot contracts for individual clients – in this situation providers remain independent agents and may accept or reject a contract in any given situation. **Block contracts** are those where the provider is given a contract for a group of clients.

Health authorities are encouraged to use block contracts which give the provider a fixed payment for services given.

Standards of care are enforced by inspection units of local authorities and health authorities. These units increase the pressure for explicit standards which can be inspected and measured.

Client involvement

Associated with the accountability and quality issues has been the need to involve client choice in the delivery of care. The Children Act 1989 made it clear that the needs and wishes of a child needed to be listened to and used in making decisions about care needs. The NHS and Community Care Act 1990 also identifies the importance of client choice.

The effects have been for individuals to be given much more information about the options available for care. They have become much more involved in planning care. The care organisations also monitor the quality of their services by using questionnaires to elicit client views. One of the effects of all of this is to empower clients to make decisions about care rather than have care thrust upon them. Since 1987 patients in the health service have been able to gain access to their medical records if they were held on computer and from 1991 if they are held on manual systems. The introduction of the Patient's Charter in 1992 was an attempt to make the public sector more responsive to the consumer.

The emphasis on the customer comes over very strongly in the various charters (see the Patient's Charter below) produced nationally and by individual trusts. These set out the expected level of care and attention that a person should receive. They also highlight the systems for complaining if the provision does not meet the minimum standards. It is a requirement that the units monitor compliance with the charter standards. Results of this monitoring have to be published, in part at least to enable purchasers of the care to determine where the 'best' treatment is available.

In some respects these processes are compatible with the ideals of the original National Health Service with more care being available and so provision for all, free at the point of delivery coming closer. The reality is that in a broad sense it works but there are areas where facilities have been threatened with closure on economic grounds with an increased risk to potential patients.

The Patient's Charter

The first nine national standards:

1 **Respect for privacy, dignity and religious and cultural beliefs:** practical arrangements should include appropriate meals and private rooms for confidential discussions with relatives.
2 **Arrangements to ensure everyone, including people with special needs, can use the service:** an example is the provision of access for people with wheelchairs.
3 **Information to relatives and friends:** there must be arrangements to inform relatives and friends of progress, subject to the patient's wishes.
4 **Waiting time for an ambulance service:** for an emergency ambulance this must be no longer than 14 minutes in an urban area and 19 minutes in a rural area.
5 **Waiting time for initial assessment in an accident and emergency department:** the standard requires immediate assessment of the need for treatment.

6 **Waiting time in outpatient clinics:** each patient should be given a specific appointment time and seen within 30 minutes of that time.
7 **Cancellation of operations:** this should not happen on the day of arrival in hospital. If an operation is cancelled twice then it should be carried out within one month of the second cancellation.
8 **A named qualified nurse, midwife or health visitor responsible for each patient:** the standard says that this should be the case.
9 **Discharge of patients from hospital:** before being discharged a care plan should be made to meet any continuing heath or social care needs. Arrangements should be made with agencies to undertake this care before the patient is discharged.

273

From 1 April 1992, these first nine standards were increased by the requirement for local standards relating to:

- waiting time for first outpatient appointments
- waiting times for treatment after assessment in accident and emergency departments
- waiting times for transport home where a doctor identifies a medical need for the transport
- signposting of hospitals internally, for visitors
- ensuring all staff in contact with the public wear name badges.

These extra standards can also be increased by locally agreed standards.

Moving into purchaser-only roles

Historically, all statutory agencies have been the providers of health and care services. The moves over the last few years have been toward purchaser-only roles. Internal departments within statutory agencies will have to compete with the independent sector in order to continue to exist. For this reason, many internal departments are developing arm's length relationships with their organisations.

Example

Most hospitals have pathology laboratories. Pathology laboratories are where tissue samples are examined for disease, and where post-mortem examinations are often carried out.

The total market for pathology services is comprised of those services presently within NHS hospitals, and a newly flourishing private sector. It is highly unlikely that all of these pathology services can remain viable in a competitive market. Many are likely to close.

Increasingly, one may find a small hospital in the Midlands sending pathology specimens to a laboratory in Scotland, or the other way around. Pathology consultants may not have the personal relationships with local colleagues which they presently enjoy. Pathology services will go out to the lowest tender, which may not be the hospital's own department.

Many pathology consultants have been sent for training in management and marketing, in order to prepare them for the competitive market.

Example

Increasingly, local authority social services residential homes are unable to compete with the 'lean and mean' private sector. Their wage bills are higher, and the management is sometimes relatively complacent. Many authorities do not have the money necessary to bring their own homes up to the standards of the private sector, although they are required to do so. Consequently, some local authority homes are closing. Others have formed independent trusts. It is evident that social services departments are moving toward a purchasing and inspection role only. They cannot afford to stay in the provider market.

> **Wishful thinking**
> On his return to Earth after his famous moon walk in 1967, American astronaut Neil Armstrong was asked what occupied his thoughts most while in space. He replied that he had been hoping that the contract to produce the millions of electronic components used in the mission had *not* gone to the lowest tender.

This rapidly changing commercial environment into which care services are moving has not had all negative consequences. Concepts such as customer care and marketing have increasingly higher profiles. Marketing in particular is helping to shape services more to meet consumer needs. It has also been recognised that this new environment needs trained and qualified managers to lead the industry into increasing competitiveness. Care services are investing in management education, such as the BTEC Higher National Diploma in the Management of Care. This is a comprehensive and demanding two-year course, which is linked to Level 4 NVQs in Management.

Review questions

1 What are purchasers?
2 What are providers?
3 What roles do the independent sector have in providing care?
4 What is meant by 'joint finance'?
5 What types of contracts do local authorities use to 'buy in' care?
6 What are the advantages of purchaser-only roles?
7 What are the disadvantages of purchaser-only roles?

Assignment 10.1
The organisation of health and social care provision

This assignment provides knowledge, understanding and portfolio evidence for element 5.3, **Investigate the organisation of health and social care planning and provision.**

Your tasks

1 In your own community, identify an organisation which purchases care services. Describe the ways in which they procure services on their clients' behalf. In order to find out, you may have to interview someone from the organisation and/or collect and read some of the organisation's written documentation.
2 With reference to the organisation identified above, select one organisation with whom the purchasing organisation has a contract to provide care services.
   a Find out from the purchasing organisation why that particular provider was successful in obtaining the contract.
   b Find out what the provider had to do in order to achieve the contract. For example, did it need to cut cost? Market more effectively? Employ consultants?
   c Summarise your findings.

11 The planning of care and interventions for individual clients

What is covered in this chapter

- The care planning cycle
- The range of practitioners in the care planning process and the main focus of their work
- Types of intervention – their nature and purpose
- Interventions – their nature and purpose in relation to client needs
- Ways of encouraging greater involvement of client and carers in care planning and changes in practice necessary for this process.

These are the resources you will need for your portfolio for element 6.1:
- A report which:
  - describes the care planning cycle and illustrates this by reference to one client's needs
  - identifies five different practitioners who might be involved in care planning and the extent to which they are working alone, with other professionals or with the client
  - explains two interventions which are commonly available including their relationship with client needs, with two examples of each
  - explains ways of encouraging greater client and carer involvement in care planning and interventions
  - describes two recent changes in practice in care planning and interventions.
- Your written answers to the activities, review questions and assignment in this chapter.

The care planning cycle

Definition of terms used in care planning

There are a number of important terms used within the health and social care delivery system that you should know:
- care planning
- care management
- care manager
- assessment
- key worker.

Care planning
Care planning is the process of negotiation between the assessor, client, carers and other relevant agencies to establish the most appropriate methods for meeting the needs of clients, within available resources, and incorporating them into individual care plans.

Care management
Care management is any strategy for co-ordinating and reviewing services delivered to clients in a manner that provides for continuity of care.

Care manager
The care manager is the person who undertakes all, or most, of the 'core tasks' of care management, assessment, monitoring and review. The care manager is not usually involved in direct service delivery or provision. The assessor or care manager will usually arrange for others to deliver the agreed services.

Activity 11.1

Mrs Temple has asked you to explain what the role of the care manager is and also to explain the difference between that role and the role of the key worker.

Assessment – the principles
Before examining the process of assessment in detail, it is necessary to consider the basic principles of the subject. An assessment carried out by a social worker, nurse or care worker is primarily an assessment of a person, their abilities, expectations and aspirations.

- Any assessment must be with the explicit consent of the client and, if appropriate, carers.
- The client should understand the process and agree to the assessment unless there is a clear statutory mandate for intervention, for example under the Mental Health Act or Children Act.
- Care should be taken to clarify with clients when the partnership is based on consent and when it is based on legal authority.
- Any subsequent intervention should be based on the views of all relevant carers and family.
- Any services offered should be based on negotiated agreement with all concerned. This includes statutory, voluntary and private sector services
- Clients should have the greatest possible degree of choice in the services they are offered.

Assessment is the process of objectively defining needs and determining eligibility for services. The word assessment is preferred to the medical term diagnosis as it more accurately reflects the process involved.

Assessment is a joint process involving the client, carers and other agencies. Assessment embraces the client's 'physical environment, health, abilities, financial needs, formal and informal networks, culture, language, religion, emotional and psychological needs, their personal perceptions and wishes'.

Assessment is more than the completion of forms. It encompasses a variety of processes from responding to a straightforward request for a meals-on-wheels service, through to a highly complex gathering of information about the total health and social care needs and preferences of users and their carers.

Essentially, care planning is a process by which professionals from various disciplines and agencies, in conjunction with clients and carers, share their knowledge and expertise about the client's situation in order to clarify their understanding of the causes which prevent the client from achieving the lifestyle to which they aspire. For example, clients who suffer from a disability that prevents them from carrying out an activity such as making their beds or cooking a meal may need help to enable them to become more independent. However, the assessment of human need cannot be considered in isolation from the particular resources available to meet them. Statements about the need for warmth, food, shelter and companionship must be translated into terms that enable plans to be drawn up to respond to the deficiencies that occur.

The process of care planning must therefore involve a broad appreciation of the client's situation as well as a recognition of the contribution that the health and social care services can make in meeting diverse needs. A great deal of care planning in the past has involved trying to fit identified need into the services available. If services were not available then the need was not usually identified.

Key worker

The key worker is the person who has the most contact with the client and is usually involved in health and social care service delivery to the client, for example a social worker, a home care worker or a community nurse.

Activity 11.2

What does the process of care planning involve?

Types of assessment

There are two main types of assessment:
- self-assessment
- observation.

Self-assessment

Self-assessment reinforces the importance of the client's own views. It actively promotes the participation of the client and carer and their assumptions of responsibility within the process. This method also enables professional staff to have an understanding of the client's perspective. One example of self assessment is when a client fills in a form, from which they can see if they are eligible for a service. Some welfare benefits fall into this category. This method of assessment has some disadvantages:

- it favours the more able and articulate
- it allows difficulties to be concealed
- the reliability of the assessment will vary with the self-knowledge of the client.

Self-assessment reinforces the importance of the client's own views

Observation

Observation methods of assessment tend to be associated with health care rather than the social care field. The findings of observation assessments should be treated with caution as they may not be typical of every situation in which the client may function. Clients behave in different ways in hospital than in their own home. The place where an assessment is conducted may have a material effect on the outcome. As a rule, assessment is best undertaken in the normal environment of the individual. However, contrast between behaviour in different settings can help to reveal the client's needs. Care should be taken not to expose the client to any unnecessary disruption.

Individuals do not exist in isolation from their social situation, so it is rarely possible to isolate needs from their social context. One of the tasks of assessment is to define the scope of the social network that it is necessary to explore in order to have an understanding of the client's needs and, as a consequence, where any services are best targeted. However, due to constraints on time, the assessor has to set a limit on the number of people, places and activities that are deemed to be significant to the assessment of the client's needs.

Activity 11.3

1 Obtain as many DSS pamphlets as possible and discuss with your class colleagues how many of them call for a claimant to assess themselves.

2 Arrange an interview with a representative of your local social services department and find out how many referral situations fall into the self-assessment category.

Levels of social care assessment

A number of 'levels' of assessment have been developed which enable specialist and complex assessments to be targeted to those clients and their families who need them most. Specialist assessment staff will usually see all referrals to the social service department in the first instance. Following an initial assessment, where there is a need for a continued service or where specialist help is needed (childcare or mental health), the referral is passed on to staff with experience and qualifications in those fields.

- **Level 1.** This is usually the initial contact that a client has with the social services department. At this stage the assessor collects basic information from the client, on the basis of which a decision is made as to whether the client's needs fall within the remit of the department or another agency, such as the health services. At this stage, such requests as bus pass renewals or car badges (orange car badge scheme for the disabled) can be met immediately. Other requests for more detailed assessment are passed on to specialist staff (childcare, mental health, domiciliary care or occupational therapy, for example).
- **Level 2.** This is for the client whose needs cannot be met at level 1. The outcome of action at this level might be:
  - giving advice or immediate counselling,
  - redirecting the client to another agency more appropriate to their needs,

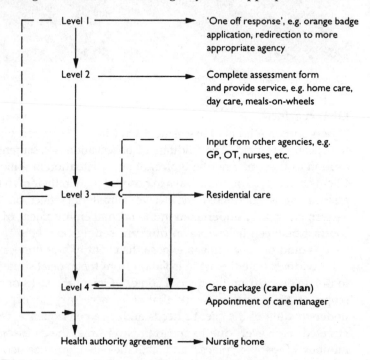

Figure 11.1 The assessment process for a client living in the community

    – the collection of information so that a more complex assessment may be made in the client's home, if they wish.

- **Level 3.** Assessment at this stage results from the client's need for a more detailed assessment of their health and social care needs and will involve personnel from other agencies. Assessment at this level attempts to change the focus from assessing for one specific service to building up a profile of the client, their environment and support networks. After consultation with all involved, a care plan is drawn up and resources made available to meet such a plan.
- **Level 4.** Assessment is carried out at this stage if it is clear that the client has very complex needs, has been assessed for residential care or is to be rehabilitated from hospital to community.

Assessment check-list

- Has the assessment been negotiated with the potential client? Is the client aware that they are being assessed or do they think the discussion is an informal one? Has the assessor explained their role and why they are there?
- Has the appropriate setting for the assessment been chosen? It is important that both the assessor and client are comfortable and at ease.
- Have the client and carer been empowered to take part in the process, taking into account their ethnic, cultural or communication needs?
- Does the client have access to someone who can speak on their behalf if appropriate?
- Have any differing perceptions of need been clarified and, if so, have they been recorded?
- Does the client know if they are eligible for the service they have requested?
- Have the client's needs been prioritised and have objectives been set for each of those needs?
- Has the client seen and agreed the written record of the assessment?
- Does the client know when they may request reassessment?
- Does the client understand how to complain if dissatisfied?
- Does the client know that they may decline assistance if they wish unless there is statutory intervention?

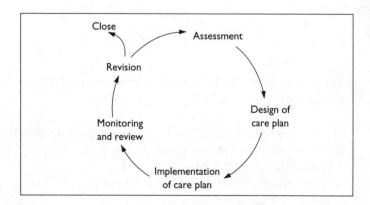

Under the National Health Services and Community Care Act, social services departments have a legal duty to assess a client's needs. Collaboration with other services in this task is essential, the aim being to secure the most cost effective package of services that meets the client's needs, taking account of the client's and carer's own preferences. To achieve these objectives the following processes are observed:

- assessment of the client's circumstances including support required by any carers
- design of a care package in agreement with clients, carers and other relevant agencies to meet identified need, to be delivered within the care resources available and to include help from willing and able carers
- implementation of the agreed package
- monitoring and review of the outcome of the package by users and carers.
- revision of service provision if necessary.

The function of care plans

Personnel engaged in the delivery of care plans are well aware that success in planning care can only be achieved if time is spent developing a sound assessment system to identify individual needs. Care staff are often involved on a one-to-one basis with individuals and have a unique opportunity to assess needs within the context of the family and the community. The client's family and other carers should be involved in identifying solutions to problems rather then having decisions made for them.

Health and social care workers are members of a multi-disciplinary team sharing responsibility for the planning and delivery of care. Before considering the care planning process in detail it is necessary to consider how care staff identify the needs of people and their families.

The function of assessment is an integral part of the problem-solving process. It is a continual process of gathering and interpreting information to provide a basis for choosing and adapting service delivery plans. Assessment of need allows the health and social care worker to understand a client's needs and priorities, and agree objectives for any intervention. It is important in this process that the individual client's own interpretation of his or her problems and needs is identified, recorded and considered. Remember that all the relevant people; clients, carers and families, should be involved in meeting the client's needs and identifying solutions to problems.

Activity 11.4

Explain the function of care plans.

The range of practitioners in the care planning process and the main focus of their work

Health and social care delivery plans are based on the following principles:
- Assessment should be carried out for and with people not to them. Assessment is primarily focused on the individual.
- Assessment should occur in the climate of a charter of rights and a clear complaints procedure for both carers and clients.

Clients should understand that one function of assessment is to make decisions about the allocation and use of scarce resources. The basis of any decision-making should be described to the client clearly.

As many health and social care workers as appropriate, taking client confidentiality into account, should be involved in the assessment process so that the outcome is enhanced, in terms of both quality and provision of services. Professionals draw on their specialist expertise when assessing the needs of clients. If they work in isolation their response may be limited to what they personally know or can deliver.

Assessment should be holistic and those involved should be properly equipped to give information on how the client's needs might be appropriately met. To offer an assessment from a holistic perspective, professionals must work together effectively for the benefit of the client, sharing their skills and resources.

Staff should have up-to-the-minute knowledge about services which are currently available and also understand the potential of these services to be tailored to specific needs.

Multi-disciplinary assessment requires the assessor to understand the inter-relationship of the client's needs and strengths, and the roles and functions of colleagues who are involved in the assessment process.

A review should be undertaken as an evaluation of the assessment process and its outcomes, and in recognition of the changing needs and preferences of clients. The principles and process outlined above imply a shift towards a problem-solving approach, which for many workers involves a significant change from traditional practice.

Activity 11.5

List the principles of care planning.

The care manager

The care manager is the person who undertakes all, or most, of the 'core tasks' of care management in a social care assessment. The care manager is not usually involved directly in providing any service for which the client has been assessed. The care manager can be from any profession, but is usually employed by the local social service department.

The role of the care manager is:
- to assemble and co-ordinate services to meet the assessed needs of individuals in conjunction with service users and within agreed criteria and budgetary limits,
- to co-ordinate comprehensive assessments of individual needs in conjunction with staff of the social services department and other organisations and with the applicants for services,
- to devise, agree and record individual care plans with clearly identified priorities within County policy and available resources and in conjunction with service users and, where appropriate, their carers,
- to make recommendations to the care management co-ordinator regarding expenditure on individual care plans,

- to amend the care plan and negotiate changes to provision of care required within the allocated budget,
- to negotiate with service providers. This will include costing and prioritising services to be provided and preparing and agreeing with the service user specifications of the service required,
- to monitor, evaluate and sustain the provision of care in line with the care plan,
- to review care needs in conjunction with the service user at intervals agreed in the care plan and review the provision of services,
- to monitor needs and make recommendations as appropriate for the development of services,
- to provide and undertake training.

(**Source:** Community Care in Lancashire Case Assessment and Care Management October 1992 Paper 1)

Types of intervention – their nature and purpose

Preventative care

From the moment of conception everyone makes use of the caring services. Even before birth care is given to foetuses. This is often to avoid the need for more complex care in the future. In the same way immunisation of young children prevents the need for medical care related to the disease for which immunity is achieved. Similarly early health education provides strategies for preventing ill-health in later life. This model targets a large population at low cost in an attempt to prevent a later more expensive need for care.

Interventionist care

There are times when the carer has to intervene to deliver care. An example of this is the prescription of drugs to support the body's own defence mechanisms in fighting disease. An extreme example in social care is compulsory admission to care. The interventionist model empowers an outside agency to become involved when the need for care is evident. This model can produce dependency, relying on care givers to intervene, and take over. It can also impose a level of social control with the need for intervention being determined by the care providers rather than the care receivers.

Activity 11.6

Explain the differences between preventative and interventionist care. Give two or three examples of each.

Remedial care

If dependency after intervention is to be avoided then remedial care is needed. This is a time for enabling the client to work towards a situation requiring the minimum of care. The client's need for care is reduced. An example occurs where the NSPCC works with a family. The initial care may be an interventionist act to deal with the immediate needs.

However the NSPCC's aims are to work with the family members and enable them to progress together away from the need for care. This second stage represents the remedial stage for care.

Multi-disciplinary care

Approaches to care delivery can also involve a variety of agencies. This has been legislated for in the NHS and Community Care Act in which there is a requirement for health and social services to work together in assessing the need for care.

This approach has the benefit of reducing the risk of people being discharged from one form of care without another agency continuing to monitor and provide care. A multi-disciplinary approach also allows the various professionals involved to exploit their individual strengths and reduces overlap in provision.

Holistic care

So far we have focused on care delivery for specific needs. Another approach which builds on the multi-disciplinary approach is to switch the focus to the total mental and physical state of the client, not just the present problem. This approach recognises the inter-relationships of body systems, the psychological and social states of a person. This was touched on in the case study of the Starlight Foundation in Chapter 8.

Many professionals and lay people may be involved in the assessment and delivery of a care plan. Let us take an example of a particular client now living in their own home.

Case study

John is a very elderly and confused gentleman. He has lived alone for many years in a very large house and has managed to cope on his own until his recent bout of flu three months age. Since his illness he has become more and more confused and, as a result, he fell down the stairs and broke his arm. He has no relatives or close friends living near (his daughter lives 20 miles away) and has difficulty getting out to get his pension every week or go to the local pub as he used to do three or four times a week. He is now so frail that he can no longer cook his meals or clean the house. He has recently developed leg ulcers. John is a very educated man but because his eyesight is poor he can no longer read his books.

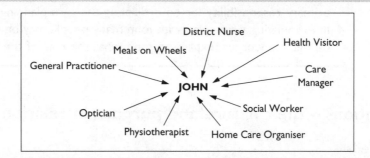

Figure 11.2 The care team

Figure 11.2 illustrates the care team that would be involved in providing services for John.

- **The social worker.** The role of the social worker in this case would be to enable John to accept the services of the home help and meals-on-wheels. The social worker would also discuss with John how he could make new friends, develop carer networks, get to the pub etc. The social worker would also liaise with the library service to supply John with either talking books, tapes or large-print books. The social worker will also provide emotional support through counselling.
- **The physiotherapist.** The physiotherapist will provide John with a rehabilitation service to enable him to keep the use of his arm and help him build his muscles during the period in which he has his arm in a plaster cast. *Rehabilitation* consists of enabling the client to achieve maximum recovery of function, and thereby to lead as active, full and independent a life as possible. If John does not make a complete recovery from his fall then the physiotherapist will teach John to cope despite the persistent residual effects of his disability.
- **The general practitioner.** The general practitioner is the leader of the primary care team and carries prime responsibility for the health and well-being of John. The GP may have referred John to the social services department in the first instance.
- **The district nurse.** The district nurse will oversee the dressing of the ulcers on John's leg. The district nurse herself may do this task or she may oversee a health care assistant doing this task for John.
- **The optician.** The optician will examine and test John's eyesight and prescribe new glasses if necessary.

Activity 11.7

Read John's case study again and write down your responses to the following questions.
1 At a care planning meeting how could you make sure that John's views are represented?
2 John has asked you to explain what the role of a care manager is in the new assessment process. Give the principal aims of the care manager.
3 Which of the statutory health and social care agencies, since April 1993, has the primary responsibility for co-ordinating the care planning process with John?
4 In formulating a care plan with John many people may be involved. One of these will be the key worker. Explain to John what the role of the key worker will be.

Interventions – their nature and purpose in relation to client needs

Client needs

It is most important that the client's own interpretation of his or her problems and needs is identified and considered before any intervention is discussed or planned. However, perceived need may bear little relation to the level of impaired functioning itself. Perception of need can be crucially affected by the attitude and motivation of the client and the degree of support they have from their friends or relatives. Any intervention should reflect the following areas of client need:

- physical need
- emotional need
- social need
- psychological need
- cultural need
- identity needs.

There are two models of care assessment that you may encounter:

- Maslow's hierarchy of needs
- activities of daily living.

Maslow's hierarchy of needs

This is a useful starting point, first put forward in 1943. Maslow suggests that human needs are arranged in a series of levels; a hierarchy of importance.

The hierarchy ranges through five levels from the lowest level, physiological needs, through safety needs, love needs, esteem needs, to the need for self-actualisation or fulfilment at the highest level (Figure 11.3).

The needs shown at the bottom of the pyramid are the basic, essential requirements for any individual. The more complex needs shown in the middle of the pyramid only come into play when the basic needs have been taken care of. The theory also implies a thinning out of needs as people progress up the hierarchy. Maslow assumes that for an individual to be functioning at his or her highest potential, all the needs shown should be considered and provided for.

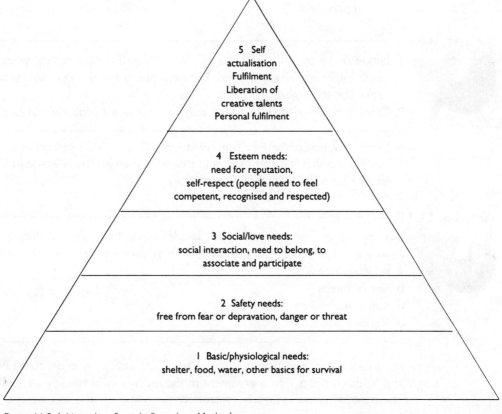

5 Self
actualisation
Fulfilment
Liberation of
creative talents
Personal fulfilment

4 Esteem needs:
need for reputation,
self-respect (people need to feel
competent, recognised and respected)

3 Social/love needs:
social interaction, need to belong, to
associate and participate

2 Safety needs:
free from fear or depravation, danger or threat

1 Basic/physiological needs:
shelter, food, water, other basics for survival

Figure 11.3 A hierarchy of needs (based on Maslow)

- **Basic/physiological needs.** These include homoeostasis (the body's automatic efforts to retain normal functioning such as satisfaction of hunger, thirst, the need for oxygen and to regulate body temperature. It also includes the need for sleep, sensory pleasures, maternal behaviour and sexual desire. If people are denied any of these, they will spend time seeking to meet these needs. For example, if water is not readily available then a person's energies will be directed to obtaining a supply.

Activity 11.8

Read a selection of daily newspapers and note any situations in which you think that people might spend a lot of time and energy looking for food and water.

- **Safety needs.** If physical needs are met, our next concern is usually safety and security, freedom from pain, threat of physical attack, protection from danger or deprivation and the need for predictability and orderliness.
- **Love/social needs.** These include affection, sense of belonging, social activities, friendships, and the giving and receiving of love.

Activity 11.9

Read the sections in Chapters 2 and 8 on socialisation. Discuss with your class colleagues what it means to not have all or any of your social needs met.

- **Self-esteem needs.** These include self-respect and the esteem of others. Self-respect involves the desire for confidence, strength, independence, freedom and achievement. Esteem of others involves reputation, prestige, status, recognition, attention and appreciation.

Activity 11.10

1 List as many situations as you can in a residential care setting where self-esteem needs might not be recognised. For example, not allowing residents to chose when to retire for the night.
2 Discuss how self-esteem needs may be met in a residential establishment.

- **Self-actualisation/self-fulfilment needs.** This is the development and realisation of one's full potential. To function at this level then all the needs identified in the model should be considered and provided for.

Activity 11.11

List some examples of need under the following headings and discuss with your class colleagues at which of the five levels of Maslow's hierarchy these needs could be met:
a religious needs
b sexual needs
c nutritional needs
d learning needs.

Maslow's model has been used as a basis for assessing individual need in social care and health settings. The assessment of the individual is the key element in any process. The approach and skills are essentially the same for the assessment of any health or social care need.

Activities of daily living

Using this model the assessor starts with an examination of the everyday activities that people need to carry out every day. The list of activities to discuss with the client could be as follows:

- safe environment – Are you free from pain? Are you comfortable?
- body functions – Are you breathing comfortably? Passing urine and faeces regularly? Maintaining body temperature, etc.?
- nutrition – healthy diet, ability to eat, adequate and suitable fluids.
- personal cleaning and dressing – mouth, teeth, eyes, ears, skin, clothing, ability to dress or undress.
- mobility – Are you able to get out of bed or exercise?
- sleep – Sleep pattern, do you wake during the night?
- leisure and work – recreation, rehabilitation
- sexuality – ability to express feelings, ability to enter into meaningful sexual relationships
- religion – cultural needs of client, freedom to worship
- communication – ability to communicate verbally, express emotions, using smell, touch, taste, hearing, etc.

Activity 11.12

Identify a client that you have been supporting in your work placement. Observe their behaviour over a period of time.

1 Using Maslow's model, list the needs that you think are being met and those which are not. Explain your observations.
2 Repeat your observation using the activities of daily living model.

How motivated and able is the client for self-care?

Activity 11.13

A GP has referred six month-old Mary to the hospital as she has a dislocated shoulder. The GP believes she may have received this injury as a result of physical abuse from her parents. The health visitor states that she feels Mary's mother may be aggressive towards the child. Mary's father has left home.

List the factual information and the information that is based on personal opinions (i.e. not based on fact or observed fact) in this case.

What information is necessary before intervention is discussed?

When gathering facts or taking a history of the client, it is very important that the assessor explains the reason for the interview so that the client is aware that the information they give will be purposefully utilised in planning their care. In gathering information, the worker is primarily concerned with establishing facts. What is the client's and carer's condition? What prevents them from functioning effectively? What aspects in their everyday life cause them most difficulty? How do they cope with dressing, cooking, cleaning, meals, walking and general household tasks?

To aid assessment, a certain amount of personal information from the client is necessary. However there must be a rationale for asking any particular question, and individual judgement should determine the relevance of particular questions in each situation. Simple needs, such as a request for meals-on-wheels will require less investigation than more complex one such as a request for support after discharge from hospital after a serious accident. The assessment process should be kept as simple, speedy and informal as possible. Exploration of areas other than those about which information has been volunteered, should only be undertaken with the consent of the client.

The broad areas that should be covered in a comprehensive assessment include:
- basic biographical details of the client. These include date of birth, gender, marital status, ethnic origin, physical or sensory disability, address, telephone number, household composition, next of kin and GP,
- how motivated and able the client is for self-care. This includes basic activities such as eating, dressing, bathing, mobility, shopping and cooking,
- abilities, attitudes and lifestyle. Perceived needs derive from aspirations and expectations of life as much as from any disability itself. A client's ability to cope depends as much on their personal resources and motivation as on the extent of their disability. Two people with similar problems will manage differently and need different levels of support,
- personal history (if relevant). Information relevant to personal resources and how clients have coped with similar situations is very useful in determining how the client may handle the present problem,
- race and culture. It is important that the assessor takes account of and understands racial and cultural differences, their differing perspectives and the impact of racism,
- physical or mental health. It is not usually the task of a social care professional to assess a client's physical or mental health. However, the assessor must be able to decide whether the client needs to be seen by a health specialist,
- contribution of relatives, friends and neighbours. Where a client is supported by, or is dependent upon, relatives or friends, the assessor should be in a position to gauge their contribution to any care package. To achieve this the assessor will need to take

account of: the status of the carer and their relationship to the client; the care they provide; their physical or mental health; their other commitments; the emotional or physical stress they may be experiencing; their future capacity or willingness to care and their wishes and preferences,

- need for care services, housing, finance and transport,
- risks arising from any health, behavioural, family, social or environmental hazard. The assessor must remember that social service departments have a duty in law to protect as well as support individuals. The right of social care staff to intervene is confined to childcare and mental health legislation and the National Assistance Act, where the client may be deemed a danger to themselves or others. However, the assessor must be alert to other risks occasioned either by environmental hazards (gas fires which may be left on by confused elderly people) or behaviour (psychotic episodes). The assessor has to weigh risks to the client against those faced by carers or the wider community in arriving at a balanced judgement,
- other needs such as leisure, employment or education. Under the NHS and Community Care Act all the community needs of the client must be considered. These considerations extend beyond health or housing needs to such areas as education, employment and leisure.

Activity 11.14

Mr Jones has been referred to the social services by a neighbour because she thinks that he needs meals-on-wheels. Mr Jones agrees with his neighbour but he does not think he needs any other help. When the assessor arrives to see Mr Jones it is obvious that he could also be helped by the support of a home help.

What course of action would you take?

Clients' perceptions of the process

Facts about people are never straightforward. A client may say that they cannot bath themselves, but there may be no physical reason for not doing so. It may be that they are depressed or afraid they might fall when getting into or out of the bath. It is very important therefore to understand the client's perception of their problem. How they feel about a situation is just as much a fact as whether they can or cannot carry out a task. Each fact is a meaningless piece of information until it is compared with others to build up a picture of the client and their needs.

The assessor needs to ask themselves:

- What do these facts mean?
- What is it like to be this client?
- What can the client do for themselves?
- What support can family, friends, neighbours or carers give?
- What aspects of the client's needs or functioning are outside the assessor's competence and who else should be involved in the assessment process?

Ultimately, the assessor is responsible for defining the client's needs and planning interventions. They have to define, as precisely as possible, the cause of the client's difficulty, remembering that the same apparent need may have a number of different causes. For example, a child refusing to go to school may be suffering from fear of bullying, loss of confidence or depression, or it may be a consequence of some breakdown of relationships within the family. The proper identification of the cause of the problem is the basis for selecting the appropriate service to support the client.

What can the client do for himself?

The assessor cannot discard their own personality, prejudices and assumptions. The assessor should instead try to display judgement and integrity by being aware of their own reaction to disability and human needs. However, the assessor is a product of society and will inevitably make judgements based on life experiences unless they receive the appropriate training to help them not to do this.

Ways of encouraging greater involvement of client and carers in care planning and changes in practice necessary for this process

Health and social care delivery plans must be viewed in the context of the government's proposals for community care legislation (the National Health Service and Community Care Act 1990). The White Paper *Caring for People* emphasised two points:

- that social service departments are expected to identify the needs of the population they serve
- that carers' needs must now be considered.

New assessment strategies are seen as a way of challenging the health and caring services to rethink their approach to arranging and providing care. This change will only occur when it is founded upon a common set of shared values which includes respecting the rights of clients and guaranteeing an equal opportunity to service provision irrespective of gender, race or disability. Other values include the right to independence, privacy, dignity, choice and fulfilment.

The fundamental aim of community care is to promote the independence of the individual so that they are able to live as normal a life as possible.

Power

Traditionally, power resides with the providers of a service, who control services and make decisions about how they are delivered. Working with clients and empowering them to negotiate their own care plan through the assessment process should:

- not make assumptions
- recognise the differing interests involved in the process
- recognise the need for negotiation
- help and support clients to regain control of their situations
- recognise people's own abilities and experience
- give accurate, honest information to the client, family and carers
- provide choice for the client
- shift influence from those providing to those using or purchasing the services. This is implemented by adapting services to meet individual needs rather than fitting people into existing services. This, in fact, shifts power into the hands of the client and away from the professional service provider.

Activity 11.15

Imagine you are a car driver and list the people that you think have power over you when you use your car.
Did your list include:
- the police
- traffic warden
- school crossing warden?

The planning cycle

Setting priorities with the client

When each relevant fact about the client's situation has been obtained, the next step is to come to some agreement with the client about priorities. The facts must be clear in the mind of the assessor so that all significant details can be identified and fitted into a pattern. Having collected the relevant facts the assessor is ready to draw together all the issues and make an assessment of the presenting problem on the basis of information, observation and facts. The purpose of assessment is not only to identify the nature of the needs and difficulties that people experience, but also to discover the reasons for those difficulties in order to form the most appropriate response.

> Remember, account must always be taken of the client's and carer's wishes and preferences.

However, before the assessor prioritises client needs they should first discuss which of those needs are of most concern to the client or family. What is perceived as important by the client should be addressed first unless there are specific reasons not to. Giving the client full opportunity to make decisions about their own future can be time-consuming for those involved. It may be far easier, though less effective in the long-run, to adopt an authoritarian approach. Although certain needs may seem to the assessor to take priority, it is essential to bear in mind those needs which the client is most motivated to address.

Some needs are easy to distinguish between, for example:

- immediate needs, such as a health crisis needing the support of medical or nursing staff,
- immediate short-term needs, such as home care following discharge from hospital or respite care,
- long-term needs, such as home care or residential care for dependent clients.

Most clients and carers face the prospect of an assessment interview with anxiety. The interview may induce a sense of failure to manage their own affairs. People who have been active and independent may resent their move towards dependence. In such cases it is not unusual for clients or carers to give vent to their anger and frustration on the assessor. The worker must be prepared for such eventualities and to spend time discussing with the client their feelings about asking for help. The ideal place in which to make an assessment of a client is in their own home. Usually the health and social care worker has the advantage of being able to do this, although assessment is also carried out in many other situations such as hospitals, residential establishments, schools, clinics or day centres.

The advantage for the client of being assessed in their own home is that they can operate in a situation in which they are most confident and competent. Their capabilities and limitations in their everyday setting can also be observed at first hand. Their interaction with other members of the family, with carers and friends can be noted.

Activity 11.16

Mrs Smith is 90 years old and lives alone. She has some family but they have lived in America for many years. Mrs Smith has difficulties with cooking her meals and getting in and out of bed. She is able to wash herself, but cannot get in or out of the bath. She is unable to collect her pension or shop. She would like to go out to the pub occasionally. However, she is most concerned about her cat which seem to be suffering from some illness. In fact, she is so worried about the cat that she is not eating. Mrs Smith wishes to get the cat to the vet immediately.

Copy the grid in Figure 11.4.

How would you support Mrs Smith so that she could continue to live in her own home?

People usually have strong views about their personal situation. Clients may superficially appear to have the same needs, but each person will see their situation in a different light. One may see it as a challenge to be overcome and another may suffer depression and despair dealing with the same circumstances. One person who has a foot amputated may become very depressed and not wish to leave the house, while another person in the same situation may view the loss of a foot as a challenge. Why do you think people react so differently to the same situations? Each person involved in the

Problems	Solutions
Cannot cook meals	Arrange for home care service to cook meals Arrange meals-on-wheels Saturday and Sunday
Cannot bath	
Cannot shop or collect pension	
Wishes to go to pub	
Wants her cat seen by vet	

Figure 11.4 Assessment grid

process may set very different priorities to meet apparently similar needs. The assessor may have to reconcile potential differences between carers, client and other agencies involved. The important thing to bear in mind is that the client's aspirations must be appreciated.

Agreed statement by clients and carers

The first stage of assessment should lead to an agreed statement which will include:
- the definition of needs in order of priority
- identification of the potential abilities and strengths of the client
- the objectives to be achieved and the time scale involved
- the means by which the objectives will be measured
- any needs to be met by other agencies
- points of differences between the client and assessor.

Case study

Mr Jones is 89 years old. Mrs Jones has died and Mr Jones now lives alone. After discussion with Mr Jones, his needs and the services available to meet those needs were identified as shown in Table 11.1.

Table 11.1 Mr Jones's needs and possible services

Mr Jones's needs in order of priority	Mr Jones's potential abilities and strengths
Home help Meals on wheels Visit to day centre to meet new friends	Overall good health Willing to learn to cook and how to clean house
Objectives and time scale	**How objectives will be measured**
Help him to learn to cook (to be done at day centre) eight weeks. Make new friends (at day centre and locally) 12 weeks	Cooking. Preparation of meal Make friends. Discussion with Mr Jones as to how he perceives his relationships.

Involvement in designing the care plan

Care planning is a means of identifying the most appropriate ways of achieving the objectives set by the assessment process. These ways of achieving objectives are set in the context of an individual care plan (ICP) (see Table 11.2 overleaf).

Design and delivery of care plans will vary according to the complexity of the client's needs. If the client's needs are simple and can be met with a single service, say a home help for a few hours each day, then the care plan's objectives may be quickly accomplished.

On the other hand care plans are sometimes very complex, possibly involving the co-ordination of services from various agencies. These agencies should be identified and involved in the determination of the final care plan as early as possible. For example, a child who is exhibiting behavioural problems at school may need help from a number of different agencies, such as the school education welfare service, a child psychologist, a social worker, the school teaching staff and his or her family.

During the assessment process the client's needs will have been prioritised. The care plan should reflect this order of priorities. As previously mentioned, one aim of most care plans is to promote the independence of the client. Unless the client feels that the options proposed for their care are relevant, it is unlikely that they will be able to use the services positively and so enhance their quality of life. People like to feel in control of their lives as far as possible. This is achieved when people are able to make decisions for themselves, based on available information about alternative or complementary services. The strengths and abilities of the carers can be utilised, but the assessor must remember not to exploit the goodwill of family/carers. Care planning that enables clients and carers to utilise their own resources is usually the most effective intervention.

Table 11.2 Care plan for a 55-year-old widower discharged from hospital following a stroke

Identified Needs	Objectives	Helping factors	Hindering factors	Time scale	Resources needed	Action by whom	Action taken
Unable to reach toilet	Provision of equipment	None	Access to property	Immediate	Commode	Hospital social worker	
Support on hospital discharge	Convalescence rehabilitation support	Available support services	No support network volunteer	8 weeks review	Home care meals on wheels	Home care organiser	
Loss of function arm/leg	Restore function	Good prognosis	Client's loss of confidence	4 months review	Physiotherapy aids/equipment	Physiotherapist Co-operation of home care organiser	
Adaption of home	Ensure home suitable to need	Option of sheltered housing	Outcome of rehab. programme	6 months review	Adaptions to house	Occupational therapist and social worker	

How much does it cost?

A number of services offered to clients or their carers may be subject to charges. An assessment of the client's ability to pay may, therefore, be needed. The client should fully understand the implications of this charging policy, and no care plan should be finalised until the client has been advised in writing of the charges involved. However, no charges can be levied for the assessment or care planning process itself.

Are the services available?

Once the wishes of the client or carer and the cost of the services have been ascertained, they have to be reconciled with available resources. This will usually be done by the person who carries out the assessment. A conflict may arise between the needs of the client and the availability of services. In this case clients should be informed of this conflict of interests. If they are dissatisfied or wish to complain they should be advised of the local complaints procedure.

The final stage of the planning process is to finalise the agreements with all the agencies and parties to the plan.

Keeping records

Records can potentially perform many functions. At the simplest level they provide an account of the care worker's contact with the client, while on another level records can assist in providing information to facilitate planning of services. Without some form of record, the information gathered quickly becomes inaccessible.

Confidentiality of information

This is a principle common to all health and social care organisations. Before any information is shared with other agencies, carers, families or friends, the client's (or if appropriate, the carer's) permission must be obtained. If the purpose of sharing is made clear, then consent is more likely to be given.

Users, carers and other agencies all have a right to know what use will be made of the information they provide. Information should not normally be shared without the consent of those who give the information and should only be shared on a 'need to know' basis. Although all agencies are urged to work more closely together, this closer partnership should not lead to laxity regarding confidentiality.

All data stored on computer about identifiable, living people is controlled by the Data Protection Act. Individuals are, in most circumstances, entitled to access.

Activity 11.17

1 Can you think of any circumstances under which people may not be entitled to have access to information about themselves which is held on computer?
2 Find out what information about you is held by your school or college on computer and how much you are entitled to see.

Implementation of the care plan

The aim of implementing the care plan is to achieve the objectives set by the assessor and the client or carer. Only one person should be responsible for implementing the care plan and this person will be accountable to both the client and agencies involved. If possible the person who drew up the care plan should also be responsible for implementing the objectives, as he or she will have the benefit of having established a relationship with the parties concerned.

The role of the person responsible for implementation can be summarised as follows:

- Agreeing the scope of the client or carer participation. All recommendations and inputs should be geared to support the client's or carer's contribution to the care plan. A successful care plan is one that enhances rather then undermines any arrangement that may have operated before the assessor's intervention. Clients should play as active a part in meeting the care objectives as their abilities will allow. The client may require a considerable amount of reassurance and persuasion to accept support. If a client is unable to participate or represent themselves, someone should be appointed to speak on their behalf.
- Agreeing on the speed of the implementation of various objectives. Once the care plan has been finalised, how it is implemented and the pace of implementation should be negotiated with the client and carers. How this is carried out may be a determining factor in the acceptance of the plan by the client.
- Checking the availability of services. The assessor's role is to confirm the availability of the agreed services. If any negotiated service becomes unavailable or subject to charging arrangements it should be re-negotiated with the client.

- Revising the care plan. The care plan should be revised in the light of any changes that have been made during implementation. The reason for any such changes should be recorded. For example, if an agreed service becomes unavailable, the fact should be recorded and brought to the attention of the assessor's senior manager. All parties to the care plan (client, carers and other agencies) should be told of any change in the plan.

Case study

> Robert was a seven year-old boy with learning difficulties. He had been soiling since he started nursery school at the age of three. Prior to this, he had been toilet-trained. He was prone to constipation. He had been seen several times at the local hospital and been admitted for an in-patient stay to clear his bowel. Robert's parents accepted his soiling as a permanent problem.
>
> Robert was being made fun of by his peers at school because of his soiling and constipation. He complained of 'tummy ache'.
>
> Solutions to help Robert:
>
> - A community nurse to help with a bowel-training programme. The nurse agreed the following with Robert's mother:
>   - Three enemas a fortnight to be given regularly for a three-month span. This was to ensure that Robert's bowel was cleared at frequent intervals.
>   - Introduction of more bran into Robert's diet to build up over a period of weeks.
> - A behaviour programme. Robert's mother was asked to check his pants on an hourly basis during the day so see if he was clean. When he was clean he was praised and given a cuddle by his mother.
>
> Over a period of time the programme became more successful. The soiling reduced and Robert gained more self-confidence.

Monitoring, evaluation and review

Monitoring the care plan

Monitoring is a proactive form of surveillance which supports the achievement of the objectives set in the care plan. As a result of the monitoring process the objectives may be adapted to the changing needs of the client. How the monitoring is carried out will depend on the scale of intervention.

The purpose of any monitoring should be discussed and explained to the client and any others involved in the delivery of the care plan. Monitoring will be undertaken by a number of individuals:

- the client
- the carer
- neighbours, friends and relatives
- the key worker
- service providers
- quality assurance and inspection units.

Monitoring involves a number of tasks:

- **Monitoring the objectives of the care plan.** The aim of this is to see that the objectives of the care plan are achieved. Each member of the team delivering services is observed to see if they are keeping to the agreed objectives. Progress is measured against the criteria or performance indicators defined and agreed in the care plan.
- **Co-ordination of inputs into the care plan.** The more agencies and individuals involved in the delivery of care, the more important the role of the monitor becomes. Any changes in the pattern of care must be co-ordinated in such a manner that the continuity of care is not interrupted.
- **Ensuring that agencies and individuals are carrying out their roles according to agreed specifications.** Make sure that the care given to the client is of an adequate quality.
- **Fine tune the care plan.** The monitor should be alert to any changes in the needs and preferences of the clients or carers. Any new needs should be identified and minor adjustments made to the care plan. Any major changes identified should only be sanctioned by a full review of the case involving client, carer and all agencies involved.
- **Contribution to the review process.** Monitoring provides the evidence on which care plans are re-evaluated and should be recorded in a systematic way. Any review should record progress, or lack of progress, in achieving the agreed objectives. A monitoring programme will also provide evidence of any difficulties that might point to the need for a early review.

Reviewing the care plan

Care plan reviewing is the process by which changing needs are identified and service delivery is adapted accordingly. The review process should help to determine whether the objectives that were set have been achieved. Reviewing is needs-based, focusing on the needs of the client or carer, and not on the services available to meet any identified need. The views and preferences of the client must be the focus of reviews which should be held at regular intervals as appropriate.

The scope of the regular review will depend upon a number of factors, the complexity of need and the level and complexity of services delivered.

The review should be held at an appropriate venue suitable to the client. The client's home should be considered if the client so wishes.

Normally the review will take the form of a meeting of all concerned parties, but in some cases consultations by telephone or letter may be appropriate. Large-scale review meetings may be intimidating to clients or carers and if they are necessary their purpose should be clearly defined. They should be chaired and a full record of the proceedings should be made. Client or carers should be clearly informed that they may be represented or accompanied by a third party. Large-scale reviews should only be contemplated if:

- needs have changed
- new arrangements have to be agreed
- there has been a lack of co-ordination between agencies or individuals involved in the delivery of care.

Purposes of the review

- To review the achievement of the care plan objectives. The perception of the client should be the starting point for any review. Their view of what progress has been made in achieving the objectives of the care plan is most important. The views of the client or carer can then be measured against the views of the agencies or the individuals delivering the services.
- To examine the reasons for success or failure. The reasons why the objectives have been met or not should be discussed and analysed so that lessons can be learned and objectives reviewed. Was the objective partly achieved? Was the objective understood by all involved, the client and workers? Was the appropriate support offered to allow the objective to be achieved?
- To evaluate the quality of care provided. The review situation gives an opportunity for the formal evaluation of the quality of services delivered. The reasons for any shortcomings or failure can be discussed and explored.
- To re-assess current needs. The review also allows the opportunity to consider whether any new needs have arisen since the original assessment. A client's needs will constantly change and the assumption should be that the care plan will change to meet those new needs.
- To re-appraise eligibility for services. The review will give the multi-disciplinary team the opportunity to decide whether the client's eligibility for services has changed. The level of service delivery may need to be adjusted and this should be explained to the client and reasons given.
- Revise the care plan objectives. The review gives the opportunity to re-evaluate the objectives set at the original assessment. The short- and long-term objectives can be examined and any changes made. The client should be as fully involved in this process as they were in the original assessment
- To redefine the service delivery requirements. Any changes in the care plan may require the client to agree to a new care plan contract and, if appropriate, new levels of charges.
- To set a date for the next review. The dates of the next review should be set taking into account the complexity of the care plan and the client's wishes.
- To record the findings of the review and circulate these to all parties. The findings of the review should be recorded and a copy given to all parties, including the client or carers.

The focus of the review should not be on the services provided, but on the needs, views and preferences of the client and their carers. The outcome of the review should be an enhanced understanding of the needs of the client and their perceptions of the services provided. This should lead to a redefinition of the objectives of future intervention and an allocation of responsibility for their achievement.

Review questions

1 How would you assess a client's cultural needs?
2 What is the function of the initial assessment process?
3 Why is the monitoring process such an important aspect of the care plan cycle?
4 In drawing up a care plan how would you ensure the independence of the client?
5 What is the purpose of the review process in the care planning cycle?
6 Give two examples of how you would assess the cognitive needs of a five year-old child.
7 Give an example of how in the assessment process you would display respect and value for the client's identity.
8 What is meant by the term 'cultural needs'?
9 How could you monitor freedom from discrimination in the care planning process?
10 How would you ensure that a client's religious needs were met?

Look back at the case study on pages 285–6. Now answer these questions.

11 Explain the processes involved in the monitoring of any services which might be offered to John.
12 As John's social worker, it is your responsibility to interview him to assess his individual needs. Which interviewing technique should you use?
13 When you are reviewing the care plan with John and other agencies, you should use secondary and primary sources of information. Give one example, from the case study, of each source of information.
14 From the details in the case study, identify one social need that John may have.
15 There are four principal objectives of a care plan for promoting independence. Give two examples.
16 What broad issues would you want information on in order to be in a position to make a comprehensive assessment with John of his situation?

Assignment 11.1
Assessment and review of the needs of a disabled child

This assignment develops knowledge, understanding and evidence of element 6.1, **Investigate the planning of care and interventions for individual clients.**

Scenario
Mary is a very physically disabled, wheel-chair bound, seven year-old girl who lives with her father who moved to this part of the country due to a change of job. Mary's

mother lives many miles away. She still loves Mary and wishes to continue to have a say in her future. Mary's present accommodation is a large Victorian house in a suburb of a large city with good health and social care support services. The local education authority's policy is to integrate all children with a disability into mainstream education.

Planning

In implementing any care plan for Mary remember that the following principles of assessment should be adhered to:
- Assessment should be with the explicit consent of Mary.
- Mary must understand the assessment process. If there is a statutory mandate for intervention (non-school attendance, for example) this should be explained.
- The client should always understand when the assessment partnership is based on consent and when it is based on legal authority.
- Any intervention must be based on the views of all relevant carers and/or the family.

	Need	Possible support
Physical needs		
Social needs		
Cultural needs		
Emotional needs		
Cognitive needs		
Behavioural needs		
Identity needs		

Figure 11.5

- Any services offered to Mary should be based on negotiated agreement with all agencies.
- Mary should have the greatest possible degree of choice in the services that are offered.

Assessment

1 Using a copy of the grid on page 305 (Figure 11.5), identify how you would attempt to meet Mary's needs.

2 Using a copy of the following grid (Figure 11.6), set objectives for Mary's care plan which can be monitored and reviewed by all the supporting agencies. Identify:
   - the agencies or individuals from which Mary might obtain support
   - the objective of such support
   - the likely time scale of any support offered.

3 What processes would you employ to help empower Mary within the care planning process?

4 Present your assignment to a group of your colleagues and discuss ways in which you could monitor and review your care plan.

Presentation and review

The presentation of the assignment should be in written form using the grids suggested and supported by any other information requested in the tasks.

	Support from	Objective	Time scale
Domestic abilities			
Self-care			
Social needs			
Intellectual needs			

Figure 11.6

12 Practitioner promotion of health and social well-being and the client's influence over health and social care provision

What is covered in this chapter

- Practitioners involved in promoting health and social well-being
- Practitioner creation of environments conducive to health and social well-being
- Practitioners who protect the public from potential risks
- Legislation and the restriction of the liberty of individuals
- Ethical dilemmas experienced by practitioners.
- Clients' perceptions of the continuum of care
- Support services available to clients receiving care
- Ways in which clients and their carers can take control of care services
- The involvement of clients in the improvement of services

These are the resources you will need for your portfolio for element 6.2:
- A report discussing two ethical dilemmas which practitioners may face when they are balancing the needs of different individuals and groups.
- A summary description of the way in which relevant legislation may restrict the liberty of individuals for their own or others' health and social well-being.
- A summary describing the range of practitioners who work in services which:
  - promote health and social well-being
  - create environments conducive to health and social well-being
  - seek to protect individuals from risk.
At least three examples of practitioners should be given for each of the above.

These are the resources you will need for your portfolio for element 6.3:
- A project report comparing at least two clients with health and social care needs and how they experience care and feel able to influence the provision. The report should look at:
  - their perceptions of their care
  - the extent to which they perceive a continuum of care
  - the support which has been offered compared with that which is potentially available
  - whether the clients feel they have been in control of the care which is available.
- A summary of how one health and social care service in the local area is attempting to improve its service, and the student's own recommendations on how it could be improved day-to-day based on the clients' perceptions.

Finally:
- Your written answers to the activities, review questions and assignment in this chapter.

Practitioners involved in promoting health and social well-being

The function of maintaining and promoting health is qualitatively different from that of preventing specific illnesses. It is founded on a positive definition of health as 'a state of complete physical, mental and social well-being and not merely the absence of disease and infirmity' (World Health Organisation, 1961). This approach emphasises the subjective nature of feeling 'well' and the ability of the individual to participate in social and economic life. The last 15 to 20 years have seen an unprecedented explosion of interest in the participation of people in their own health care. These developments have been supported by the World Health Organisation whose 1978 Declaration Of Alma Ata recognised the right and duty of individuals to participate in their own health care. The government's White Paper *Promoting Better Health* (1987) attempted to raise standards of health care, placed more emphasis on health promotion and disease prevention and aimed to provide patients with more information with which to make choices. A further White Paper, *The Health of the Nation*, in 1992 put forward a strategy for improving the general health of the population by identifying priorities which set targets for health and encouraging collaboration between agencies. Five key areas were selected for action:

- Coronary heart disease and stroke (CHD)
- cancer
- mental illness
- HIV/AIDS and sexual health
- accidents.

For example targets were set:

- to reduce mortality in people under 65 years of age by 40% by the year 2000 or
- to reduce pregnancy by 50% in the under 16 age group by the year 2000.

In recent years government strategies seeking to prevent health problems have had three main elements:

- Education, which seeks to inform and persuade individuals to adopt healthy lifestyles or reject habits which may harm their health such as drinking or smoking;
- Clinical prevention, which includes services to monitor health and detect illness at an early stage. For example, screening clinics to detect cervical and breast cancer and immunisation programmes against measles, rubella and mumps;
- Intervention at the social and environmental level, which involves authorities in taking up social policies to tackle the causes of ill health.

One principle which is central to the concept of health promotion is the creation of a healthy environment and there is much evidence to suggest that health promotion has been successful in Britain over the past decade. This is evident in the reduced prevalence of smoking, greater participation in exercise and changes in diet. The increase in self help groups is also a healthy sign. Who are the people who have brought about this change in attitudes? In one sense all care workers are concerned with prevention. Caplan (1961) identifies three kinds of health prevention:

- *primary*, which is designed to prevent the occurrence of a problem,
- *secondary*, which involves the detection of illness and
- *tertiary*, which involves after care concerned with containing an established condition as well as with rehabilitation and readjustment.

The Family Health Service Authority (FHSA)

The Family Health Service Authority which replaced the Family Practitioner Committee in the early 1970s is responsible for providing information to the public and developing health promotion activities over and above their existing responsibilities for screening programmes for cervical cancer. FHSAs are now involved in co-ordinating the call and recall of women for breast cancer screening and also in encouraging GPs to give priority to health promotion.

The Primary Health Care Team (PHCT)

The PHCT involves a wide range of professionals, nurses, health visitors, midwives, social workers and the general practitioner. The White Paper *Promoting Better Health* (1987) removed the restriction on the type and number of staff that GPs could employ at their surgeries. *Promoting Better Health* encouraged a GP-led service and as a result GPs were able to employ *practice nurses*. At the moment GPs cannot employ health visitors or district nurses, but they may be able to in the future.

The health visitor
The National Health Service Act 1946 established the preventative and social aspects of the health visitor's work. The role of the health visitor is that of a 'health educator' and social adviser who acts 'as a common point of reference and a source of standard information, a general advisor on health teaching, a common factor in family welfare'. The majority of the health visitor's work is with families and young children, advising and mobilising resources. While one-to-one teaching is part of the health visitor's work he or she is also expected to be involved in group teaching , for example, with classes of expectant mothers, mother and toddler groups, obesity clinics, clubs for the elderly and health education and promotion in schools. Health visitors focus on the healthy rather than those who are ill; their work is concerned with the prevention of illness rather than treatment. Health visitors visit clients on their own initiative, without needing a specific request for help. They also work as part of a multi-disciplinary team involving the GP, district nurse and care staff. To the health visitor health promotion may mean exploring with a young mother how to budget for nutritious and affordable food for the family, or explaining why the children ought to be immunised.

The district nurse
The district nurse is an important member of the community care team and is responsible for assessing, implementing and evaluating the nursing needs of patients living in their own homes. Because of their relationship with patients and their carers they have an important role to play in health education. They also promote good health in the community by helping to raise awareness of health issues, teaching, advising and helping patients to become as independent as possible in their own homes.

The community midwife
The first thing to remember about midwives is that they are **not** nurses, they are independent practitioners responsible for the care of the mother through pregnancy and for some time after birth. The community midwife provides a service to all childbearing women during pregnancy and for up to 28 days after the birth. The midwife works closely with the GP and health visitor in providing a health education service to the mother. Education is a vital part of the role of the midwife, who may provide information on breast feeding and general care of both the mother and her child.

The general practitioner
The general practitioner has a health prevention role which has widened over the past decade. Almost all GP practices include ante-natal, post-natal and family planning clinics. In many practices other preventative services are offered: screening clinics for

the pre-school child; hypertension and coronary risk clinics; and well woman clinics. New working arrangements introduced for GPs in 1990 place emphasis on the provision of information to patients and the extension of health promotion activities to include advice on lifestyle and general health education. Health promotion activities now include detection of risk factors for disease, advice and counselling on the maintenance of good health, chronic disease management and tertiary prevention.

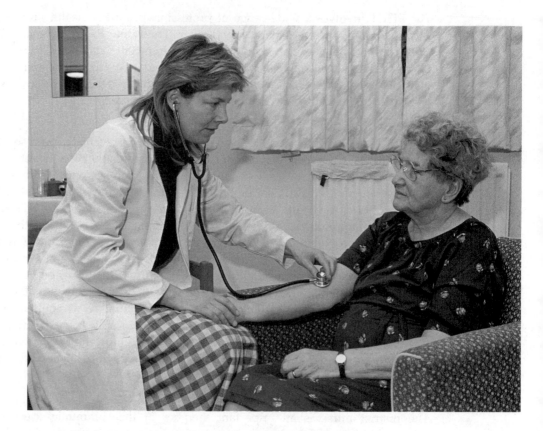

The practice nurse

The practice nurse holds clinics for people with chronic conditions and offers health promotion at the GP's surgery. To the practice nurse health promotion can mean offering advice to diabetic patients on how to look after their feet and eat the right diet. The practice nurse can also be involved in well woman and well man clinics as part of the health promotion role. They also conduct routine health checks, checking blood pressure and urine specimens and offering general health advice on such issues as weight, smoking, alcoholism, asthma and diabetes.

The health facilitator

Health facilitators are usually employed by FHSAs and District Health Authorities (DHAs). Their primary role is to develop health promotion activities and provide advice to primary health care teams. The health facilitator does not perceive him or herself as an 'expert' but as a person who encourages and empowers others to define their own health needs. Most health facilitators are female with a nursing background but some have qualifications in social work, counselling or management. Health facilitators usually have a specialist area of expertise in which they work, for example HIV or asthma. They work to empower individuals to develop quality health services in all areas of primary care, which covers all the services provided by GPs, dentists, pharmacists and opticians as well as services provided by chiropodists and speech therapists.

The occupational health nurse

Occupational health nurses work in factories, large companies, the NHS and local authorities providing a preventative health service to the firm's or company's employees. In larger organisations they will work as part of a team of doctors, safety officers and other nurses and social workers. Occupational health nurses provide clinics, health training, counselling and information packs on such issues as stress, diet and blood pressure for employees.

The chiropodist

The chiropodist treats patients' feet; their patients have a number of footcare problems. Chiropodists treat the existing problems of their patients and also provide preventive services through health education and health promotion projects. They give talks on foot care and also advise on appropriate footwear to prevent foot problems.

The dietician

The dietician's primary role is to draw up food plans for those who are ill and anyone who needs a special diet for any reason. Dieticians work in hospitals, the community and industry. The health education role of the dietician consists of encouraging individuals, groups or communities to eat a healthy, balanced diet. Devising new ways to influence eating habits is also part of their health promotion remit. Dieticians often work with groups in the community, such as groups of elderly people or mothers and toddlers.

The dental hygienist

The dental hygienist helps individuals to keep their teeth healthy. They work under the supervision of a dentist and are an important part of the dental health education team.

Practitioner creation of environments conducive to health and social well-being

The influence of the local environment on the health and social well-being of individuals and groups has long been recognised. In the 19th century the health needs of those living in growing cities prompted major programmes to improve water supplies and sewerage. These changes were a major factor in the decline of infectious diseases. Today some environments pose specific health risks; asbestos, lead and badly designed buildings can all damage health.

Today there is a growing awareness that current modes of economic and social development are unsustainable because of their harmful effects upon the environment and the individual. In Britain a wide range of legislation regulates activity which affects the environment, for example, health and safety in the workplace and food hygiene.

A number of agencies are responsible for the regulation and enforcement of legislation which relates to the environment; The Health and Safety Executive, The National Rivers Authority and local authorities.

Environmental health officers

Environmental health officers (EHOs) are employed by the local authority. Their role is to deal with physical factors in the environment, such as noise or pollution, which may be a health risk. Their responsibilities are broad-ranging and include food safety and hygiene, housing problems, noise, pollution and home safety. The EHO can either advise or take legal action on behalf of individuals affected by noise or pollution. Some EHOs extend their role by advising people on home safety or promoting fitness. The educational aspect of the EHOs work is becoming more and more important. In some authorities they give lectures and talks and organise exhibitions.

Environmental protection unit

A number of local authorities have an environmental protection unit whose role is to survey air quality and respond to complaints about domestic and industrial air pollution such as lead, smoke and sulphur dioxide. A number of city authorities have in operation air pollution warning schemes to alert those with respiratory conditions to the high levels of atmospheric pollution.

An adequate and safe supply of water is necessary for health and social well-being. Pollutants such as lead and nitrates contaminate water and are a risk to health. The National Rivers Authority and the local authority Drinking Water Inspectorate share responsibility for monitoring drinking water quality. Since the privatisation of the water industry in 1993 the National Rivers Authority has had power to issue consents for discharge into waterways, to impose conditions and to prosecute unauthorised discharges.

Housing

Housing and the urban environment both have a significant impact on health and on the general quality of life. Lack of basic amenities such as running water and sanitation are not conducive to health and social well-being nor are conditions such as damp, cold or noisy environments. Inadequate housing design also contributes to accidents in the home and can restrict domestic activity. Women suffer disproportionately from poor housing because they often spend more time in the house than men.

Safe outdoor play space reduces the chance of road accidents among children, and access to appropriate shops promotes healthy diets.

Leisure and recreation

Leisure activity covers all the different ways people chose to spend their free time. Leisure activities can include pursuits such as walking and games or just watching others play sport. Exercise has various health and social well-being benefits. It may help people live longer, protect against heart disease and lower blood pressure. In older people exercise reduces the risk of joint instability and bone fractures and also has beneficial effects on mental health. All leisure activities contribute to health and social well-being and the overall quality of individuals' lives.

Leisure opportunities can be provided by individuals themselves in their own homes, television for example, or in the community by private and local authority agencies.

Practitioners who protect the public from potential risks

Essentially, clients should have the same choices and rights afforded to all of us in everyday life. That means that the client's perception of his or her problems and preferred responses to those problems should be encouraged, listened to, acknowledged, and recorded. Options, rather than solutions should be presented to the client, and the differences between the options should be fully explained. Any risks should always be fully explained, but only in exceptional circumstances should the right to take risks be removed from the client. Such a situation should only arise when it is deemed that the client cannot make a reasonable assessment of the risks, for example, in a case of mental illness or severe learning disabilities. In such a case, the client's rights would be legally protected by the Mental Health Act.

Independence

An electronically-controlled wheelchair

We often talk of independence, but perhaps *inter*dependence better describes the relationship that most clients would wish to establish with a care service. For many, the care service becomes an important part of their lives, and the support offered should be emotional as well as practical. Care workers are often not allowed sufficient time to meet other than urgent practical needs. Therefore, it is important that clients are encouraged to develop relationships with their carers, and that these relationships are based on mutual respect. Such relationships will be dependent on the carer's ability to promote and acknowledge the individual's rights and choices. This may entail sensitive areas, such as the right to have sexual feelings, and to express these in activities and relationships. Particular attention is drawn to this area, because in the past, many clients of care services have been denied such rights.

Activity 12.1

In groups, discuss how you would support a client in making choices in an institutional setting such as a hospital or a residential home. How might your activities create conflict within the work setting?

All of the ways in which individuals may differ, which were discussed above, are areas in which tolerance must be developed and individual rights and choice must be actively promoted and supported. This requires good interpersonal skills.

Effective interpersonal skills are particularly important in dealing with challenging behaviour. Service users may be angry or aggressive and the care worker will need good rapport and listening skills to calm the situation down. However, care workers need to be careful not to expose themselves to dangerous situations, and may need to call on the support of others, including the police, where necessary.

What if a client is not capable of exercising choice? If a client is not capable of exercising choice because of a mental disability their rights to choice are not diminished. First, communication may be other than verbal. A client's choice may be determined by observing the client's behaviour toward different options. An individual's delight or dissatisfaction is often clearly observable. A thorough understanding of the options available should always be attempted, using a variety of methods, if necessary. It may be necessary for the client to actually experience different options before making a choice. For example, a trial period in a residential home may be allowed before a decision about admission is reached.

When it is believed to be impossible for the client to comprehend, it may be necessary to use a client representative or advocate. It is not accepted practice for the care worker, manager, or care agency to make decisions alone for such a client, because there may be a conflict of interests. The client's needs may be in conflict with the agency's or worker's needs. A suitable representative for the client in such a case may be a relative or a friend. Such an arrangement should be formal and recorded. Where a friend or relative is not available or willing, it may be necessary to use an advocate for the client. Advocates are non-professional volunteers, preferably trained, who will get to know the client very well, and advocate the opinions that they believe the client would express if they were capable of understanding the options open to them.

Advocacy schemes are formal, and advocates should be trained and supported. Advocacy schemes have not generally been adopted by care organisations as widely as they should be.

Restriction of clients' rights

Many of the criteria for the restriction of clients' choice and rights are established in law. Two notable examples are the Children Act, which establishes statutory obligations to remove and protect children in certain circumstances, and the Mental Health Act, which provides for compulsory treatment and detention. Common Law also allows for certain decisions to be made in situations of risk to life or property.

The removal of an individual's rights and choice is a legal and formal decision, often taken only by professionals issued with the legal authority to do so. When such decisions are made, they will be incorporated into the care plan for the client, and all care workers will be made aware of their responsibilities. When a client's rights or wishes are denied for whatever reason, this should be explained appropriately to the client, and recorded in a file, or reported to the appropriate worker. Such action can never be casual or informal.

Sometimes, a client's wishes may be denied because of the impact they would have on others. All of us are sometimes restricted in our activities in relation to others. The same applies to users of health and social care services, and this becomes particularly important in communal situations, such as residential homes and hospitals.

Protection of children

The purpose of compulsory admission to care is to protect people unable to protect themselves. One of the most vulnerable groups in society is children, and so there has been much legislation relating to children in need of care. This has been brought into some sort of logical order with the Children Act 1989.

Children playing at the Patmore Centre

In summary, compulsory care and supervision can come about as a result of:

- A care order, which places the child in the care of the local authority to safeguard and promote the child's welfare. The authority shares parental responsibility and must work with the parents. The order lasts until discharged by the court or the child reaches the age of 18 years or marries.

Where the care is in dispute courts are required to make or approve arrangements taking the child's needs as paramount. To safeguard the needs of the child the court appoints an independent social worker to act as guardian ad litem (GAL). The GAL prepares a report based on local authority records, interviews with carers, parents and others to assist the court in reaching a decision.

- A supervision order, where the child stays with his or her parents but is supervised by a social worker or probation officer. The parents retain parental responsibility. Orders last for one year and may be extended for up to three years.
- An emergency protection order (EPO). When a child is likely to suffer significant harm a court may grant an EPO which lasts for a maximum of eight days (extendible by a further seven). Care is passed to the local authority. The child, parent or carer can apply to the court for the order to be discharged after 72 hours.

The police can also remove a child into protection for a maximum of 72 hours but they must allow reasonable contact with parents/carers in the child's best interests.

- A child assessment order, which requires a child to attend for medical, psychiatric or other assessment. This remains in force for seven days.
- An education supervision order is made where a child of compulsory school age is not being properly educated. Supervision is by the education authority and the order lasts for one year.

It must be emphasised that all of these orders are made as a result of placing evidence before a court and the order is made by the court.

Case study

The story of John: A child in need of care

There has often been a view that children are placed in care at birth for the purpose of adoption. There is always a flood of offers to adopt an abandoned baby. The reality of care under the Children Act is very different and many decisions have to be made to enable children to access care. John's story is typical of many cases and is based upon a real person, though modified sufficiently to protect the people involved and for their confidentiality to be protected. This scenario gives an indication of the people and agencies involved, and their roles in protecting and assisting young people.

John was the youngest of six children. His mother had been diagnosed as schizophrenic. Her first husband, and father of four children, had died of a heart attack. At the time of John's birth his mother was living with her third husband. The neighbours had noticed that the children appeared to be well cared for, although they did not always go to school and at times appeared to be left in the care of the oldest child (a 12-year-old). The school had also reported the sporadic attendance of the children to the Education Welfare Officer.

On visiting the home, the Education Welfare Officer (EWO) noticed that the mother's drugs were left on the kitchen work-surface and that her level of anxiety and actions gave cause for concern. With the mother's permission, the EWO contacted the family GP who arranged for her admission to a psychiatric hospital. John's father refused any help and insisted that he could cope with the children. However, after a week a neighbour contacted the NSPCC because he had heard one of the children crying for over an hour during the Saturday evening and when he called round discovered that John's father was working overtime to earn enough money to support his children. He had impressed on the oldest child that nobody should know that he was out or they would all be taken away to children's homes.

The NSPCC social worker called and worked hard to find ways in which the family could stay together and be provided with support. This included setting up regular after-school care for the children, along with counselling and guidance. It was during the after-school care that carers noticed disturbed behaviour from three of the younger children. Observing and listening to them convinced the carer that the children may have been abused either physically or sexually by one or the other of their parents. This was reported to the social worker.

The evidence was significant enough for the social worker to call a case conference and see an emergency protection order as it was thought that all of the children were in danger. A care order was later sought and granted by the court. After many weeks of work with the children in care, and with both parents, it was decided that in the best interests of the children they should be placed for adoption. This decision had come about as a result of the father's prosecution and conviction for assault and the mother's requirement for long-term mental health care.

At this point the care of the children was transferred to the local authority social services. This was no reflection on the NSPCC, but shows the way in which the various organisations co-operate. Under the Children Act the needs of the children are paramount and one of those needs was thought to be to stay together. Another need was for them to be removed from institutional care and placed within a family environment.

It was not possible to find one family prepared to adopt all the children and so the decision was made to split the children up. At the same time the arrangements for the care had to be agreed with the court. The judge agreed the details and made a recommendation that the children should meet up on at least two occasions a year.

Eventually, all the children were adopted. John, being the youngest, was easiest to place and eventually ended up with his 12-year-old sister who, after a long search for adoptive parents, was placed with John's new family.

The actual incidence of abuse in Britain is unknown. Registrations of child abuse record only the reported cases, and no records at all are kept of cases of abuse of the elderly. Children on the at risk register are more likely to come from large families or from parents who had children very young. Marital problems, debt, unemployment and criminal records are typical characteristics of families where abuse occurs.

Table 12.1 Total children registered with social services departments between 1988 and 1990

Reason for registration	Number	(%)
Physical injury	2,786	29
Sexual abuse	1,732	18
Neglect	693	7
Emotional abuse	240	2
Failure to thrive	114	1
Neglect, physical and sexual abuse	20	
Neglect and physical abuse	107	1
Physical and sexual abuse	56	1
Neglect and sexual abuse	30	
Total abused	5,778	60
Grave concern	3,848	40
Accidental injuries	2	
Total registered	9,628	100

Source: Adapted from Creighton, S., *Child Abuse in England and Wales 1988–90* (NSPCC, 1992)

Activity 12.2

a Why do you think that the true incidence of abuse in Britain is unknown? List your reasons.

b Discuss and compare your reasons with those of your class colleagues.

Protection of the elderly

With more people living into old age and being cared for at home, professionals are beginning to recognise the strain carers are under when looking after elderly people. This strain can lead to ill-treatment of an elderly person. Recently some data has become available on the prevalence of abuse of the elderly. Bennett (1992) suggests that between 750,000 and 2 million people over 60 years of age had been abused by a close member of the family at the time of the survey. The person most likely to abuse is the immediate carer, although other family members or visitors to the household may also be responsible.

There is no legislation comparable to the Children Act to protect the elderly from abuse. The law expects that if an adult has been abused they themselves must take appropriate legal action. As much of the abuse of elderly people comes from their relatives or carers, the old person may be either frightened or reluctant to report the matter to the police. One option the abused person has is to ask the courts to stop the abuser from going anywhere near them. This is called an injunction and, if it is granted by a Judge or Court, it can prevent the abuser from coming near the abused person or their home or locality.

Activity 12.3

Identify services that are available in your locality to support elderly people suffering from physical abuse.

Helping and supporting those in need

Legislation and the restriction of the liberty of individuals

The 1948 National Assistance Act placed a duty on local authorities to provide residential accommodation for older people who were unable to look after themselves. It also gave them the power to remove people in need of care and attention to a suitable premises on the recommendation of a named medical officer to prevent injury to the health of, or serious nuisance to, others. The local authority has to make an application under Section 47 of the Act, supported by a medical officer (community physician), for the compulsory removal from their home of those who are suffering from grave chronic disease or who, being aged, infirm or physically incapacitated, are living in insanitary conditions, and are unable to devote proper care and attention to themselves, and are not receiving this from other people.

These compulsory powers are used in approximately 200 cases each year. Much of the debate surrounding this section of the act is amongst doctors and social workers and focuses on the ethical desirability of compulsory removal of people from their own homes.

Protection for those who are mentally ill

A compulsory referral may also be made under the 1983 Mental Health Act. Section 2 of the Act lays down procedures by which a person, unwilling to receive treatment for a mental disorder, may be compulsorily admitted to a suitable hospital for assessment. Application can be made by either the patient's nearest relative or a social worker who has been authorised to act as an approved social worker. The application must be supported by two doctors, one of whom has previous acquaintance with the patient. The detention can last for up to 28 days.

An emergency admission for up to 72 hours can be made on an application supported by only one doctor. Within this 72 hour period a second medical opinion can be added and the detention extended to 28 days.

There is provision within the act for courts to hear objections from nearest relatives to compulsory admittance. There is also the option for courts to refer people convicted of a criminal offence to be admitted and detained in a specified hospital such as Broadmoor special hospital. Crown Courts can also impose restrictions on discharge.

Criminal justice services

Society has ways of making us follow the rules that it has set to maintain an orderly community. The criminal justice system deals with the formal rules for social control which are enforced by people such as the police or the army. The criminal law is concerned with protecting society through laws dealing with deviant behaviour, which is seen as threatening social order. Deviance is behaviour which is seen as deviating from accepted norms or standards. Not all deviance will be dealt with by the criminal justice system; only that which breaks the law of the land.

A number of people are involved in operating the criminal justice system – the judge, the probation service, the police, solicitors and barristers.

The Criminal Justice Act 1988 created Young Offenders Institutions where those who are between the ages of 15 and 20 can be detained if they fail to respond to non-custodial penalties or if they have committed a serious offence.

The Criminal Justice Act 1993 allows courts to impose fines unrelated to the person's ability to pay. Another protection for the public is the court's ability to impose a probation order on people over 16 years. Special conditions may apply, such as attendance at a day centre or medical treatment. This order is only made if offenders agree to the sanction and they are placed under the supervision of a probation officer for between six months and three years. A supervision order is another way of protecting the public. The agreement of the offender is not necessary. A supervision order can prescribe where a person lives or oblige them to participate in a certain activity.

Courts can also grant injunctions at their discretion, provided that they can be effectively enforced. For example, a battered wife may be granted an injunction to stop a spouse or partner from living in the home.

Protection from infection

Many infectious diseases are preventable, but prevention depends on achieving high levels of immunisation. Despite an increase in immunisation in this country whooping cough and measles are on the increase in many cities.

Immunisation is carried out primarily by GPs. Health visitors have a responsibility for monitoring immunisation levels, identifying children who have not been immunised and alerting GPs, or immunising opportunistically themselves. Many Health Authorities have a target level for immunisation of about 95 per cent for diphtheria, polio, tetanus, pertussis and MMR (measles, mumps and rubella). Girls are also immunised against rubella at about age ten to protect their unborn children if they become pregnant later in life. The government has given a high priority to improving take-up rates for the main childhood vaccination and immunisation programmes.

Could my child become
infected with HIV,
the virus that causes AIDS?

A mother who has the virus
can pass this to her baby before
or during birth, or sometimes by
breastfeeding.

Playing, hugging and everyday
contact with someone who has
HIV is perfectly safe.

HIV is the Human
Immunodeficiency Virus

FOR FREE AND CONFIDENTIAL
ADVICE PHONE THE 24 HOUR
NATIONAL AIDS HELPLINE ON
0800 567 123

Health
Education
Authority

Screening

Concern over various aspects of the arrangements for cervical cancer screening led the government to issue guidelines to Health Authorities in 1988 urging them to:

- introduce computerised call and recall systems,
- invite all women between 20 and 64 for screening,
- to recall all women every five years.

However, many women, up to 60 per cent, still ignore their screening appointments. The main reason for this situation is fear, lack of information and impersonal computer invitations. The objective of breast screening is to ensure that all women between the ages of 50 and 64 are called for screening at three-yearly intervals. There are doubts however, as to whether screening will significantly reduce the number of deaths from the disease. There are some in the care professions who argue that the screening programme may do more harm than good by causing unnecessary mastectomies and emotional distress.

Ethical dilemmas experienced by practitioners

Who's problem?

When using compulsory powers, either under the Mental Health Act or the National Assistance Act, we must ask the question for whom is the situation a problem? People's behaviour is often seen as problematic, socially disruptive or a nuisance to those around them. The behaviour of the mentally ill or of elderly dependent people is seen as deviant and an embarrassment. Their behaviour may cause anxiety, fear and anger in others; for example when a confused elderly person does not eat properly or occasionally leaves the gas taps turned on. Relatives and neighbours may feel that they are unable to control the elderly or mentally ill person. The relatives may resort to legal controls not because the person is a danger to themselves or others but because the carer or relative or neighbour feels anxious. This anxiety may be transferred to social workers and doctors, who may then take action in situations where they would not do so if pressure from relatives was not so great.

Health promotion activities raise a number of important issues regarding the kind of ethical questions which might arise. Services, such as health promotion, which are proactive give rise to ethical questions concerning personal freedom and choice. In order to be proactive professionals have to intervene in the lives of people who may view themselves as perfectly healthy. Do the benefits outweigh the costs? For example, many feel that vaccination can do more harm than good. Vaccination of children is now a matter of parental choice. This led to a low take-up of whooping cough vaccine in the 1970s because of the reported dangers of certain types of vaccine.

Activity 12.4

The following situation was reported in a national newspaper. A woman and her children were removed by a GP from his list because she would not agree to have her children vaccinated.

1 Do you think that a GP should have the legal right to do this?
2 Do you think that the GP was ethically right to do so?

Write down your answers and discuss them with your class colleagues.

Many professionals argue that there is evidence to suggest that intervention in the lives of those who are healthy can be justified by the potential reduction in the incidence of disease. The eradication of smallpox and the virtual disappearance of poliomyelitis point to the success of vaccination programmes. So some argue that if disease is to be eradicated then an infringement of personal freedom is justified. In this country there are a number of health prevention measures which are compulsory; for example, laws relating to the purity of water, which include the fluoridation of water. However, in such matters as screening there has been a marked reluctance to use force to secure compliance.

Clients' perceptions of the continuum of care

How do clients perceive care?

In the activity above, you were asked to consider the attitude of a GP towards their patient. How do you thing that the woman felt when she was told that she had been taken off the GP's list? She certainly was not in control of the process and she may have felt that the GP did not respect her as an individual. So how do patients perceive health and social care services? Many express dissatisfaction with nursing or medical care but by far the largest concern is about communication. Many patients are unhappy with the way the medical and nursing professions communicate with them. Poor exchange of information stems from a failure by carers to recognise the social and emotional needs of patients and clients. Many patients are unhappy with the inability of doctors to tell them what is wrong with them or their children, and the inability of doctors to take an active role in the clinical interview (Korsch *et al*, 1969).Other studies show that patients wish to know more about their illness and its treatment.

Activity 12.5

Think of the last time you visited your GP. How did you feel? Did you feel able to ask him/her questions? Discuss the feelings that you had with your class colleagues. Why do you think you behaved in the manner that you did?

Many people perceive professionals as being in a different class from themselves. This has been put forward as one of the reasons for the barriers in communication. Many people are afraid to ask questions of professionals and wait to be told, so they often fail to discover what they need to know. Middle class patients tend to spend more time in consultations with doctors and ask more questions. Some argue that patients perceive how their doctor wants then to behave and then they modify their behaviour accordingly (Cartwright and O'Brian, 1976). How can we improve communication with clients or patients? Ley (1976) suggests:

- giving instructions and advice and stressing their importance
- using language appropriate to the client
- giving specific detailed information rather than general statements.

These suggestions fall short of the concepts explored in the previous chapter when looking at care planning. Care planning emphasises the importance of treating each person as an individual, listening to them and involving them in exploring ways of changing their situation. Clients or patients should feel that they are in control of the situation, that they have respect from the person helping them and that they will be given all the information they need to make a decision about any services or treatment offered. Remember the client can always refuse help. It comes as a shock to many doctors when patients refuse treatment.

Continuum of care

The delivery of care to clients has been criticised many times in the past half century because of the division of responsibility between local authority and health services. This structure does not contribute to a continuum of care for clients. The National Health Service and Community Care Act 1990 is the latest attempt to overcome this problem. The care of individuals should be a team effort involving client, carers and all professionals who might be involved in service delivery. This system should make sure that there is a continuity of service, a smooth transition from one service to another and a sharing and flow of information upon which to make decisions.

Case study

Mrs Johnson

Mrs Johnson is 90 years old. She is an independent lady but has suffered a stroke at home. She was found by a neighbour who called an ambulance, and she was admitted to hospital. After a few days in hospital the care team held a conference to co-ordinate Mrs Johnson's care and treatment. The conference was attended by the doctor who was responsible for her medical treatment, the nursing staff responsible for her nursing care, the dietician who looked after her diet (Mrs Johnson was a diabetic), the physiotherapist to help her regain the use of her limbs and the speech therapist to help her learn to speak correctly again. The social worker was also present to liaise with community services when Mrs Johnson was well enough to go home or into residential care.

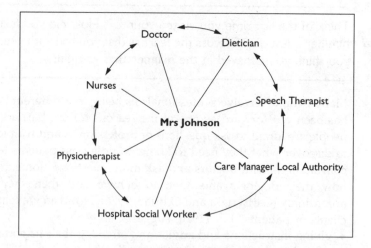

After some weeks Mrs Johnson was ready for discharge and a further case conference was held with staff from the hospital and the care manager from the local authority. A number of local authorities have agreed a protocol for hospital discharge, this requires hospitals to provide:
• written information to all patients regarding assessment and discharge arrangements,
• referral of all patients requiring a full needs assessment to the hospital social work service,
• completion of assessments within an agreed time scale,
• development of a care plan on completion of the patients' hospital treatment plans,
• identification of appropriate placements for patients within an agreed period of completion of the treatment plan (Sheffield's Community Care Plan 1994/95).

Mrs Johnson felt very strongly that she wanted to return to her own home although the doctor and physiotherapist did not agree. However, it was agreed

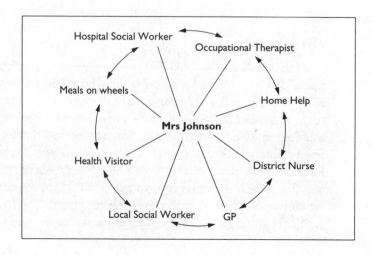

that Mrs Johnson's wishes should be adhered to and arrangements were made for her return home. The care manager called together all the people who would have some input into helping Mrs Johnson function as independently as possible in her own home. The hospital and local social worker, health visitor, occupational therapist, home help, meals-on-wheels, district nurse, GP and Mrs Johnson herself. The hospital social worker provided the link between the hospital and community services and was a person with whom Mrs Johnson could relate as they had built up a relationship in hospital. A care plan was agreed with Mrs Johnson.

Mrs Johnson's care plan

- She would receive meals-on-wheels seven days a week until she could cook her own meals again.
- The health visitor would advise her on general health problems.
- The district nursing service would provide a bathing service three times a week.
- The home help would cook Mrs Johnson breakfast and evening meals and help her get out of bed each morning.
- The occupational therapist would help her to learn basic living skills.
- The social worker would co-ordinate all these different services.

Mrs Johnson's health and social well-being improved for about six months. However, during the winter months she became depressed and expressed a wish to the social worker to go into a residential home.

A meeting of all the care workers that were providing services for Mrs Johnson was called with Mrs Johnson present. After discussion it was agreed that she should enter a residential establishment.

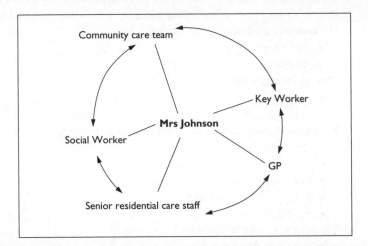

The social worker made arrangements for her to visit a number of establishments. After Mrs Johnson had decided on one establishment a member of staff and a key worker came to visit her in her home and discuss with her a date for admission. On admission to the home she was met by the key worker and introduced to other staff and residents. She was encouraged to keep her own GP although she was given the choice to do so or register with a GP who came into the home regularly.

This case study illustrates the number of people who may be offering services to support a client in hospital, the community and in residential care. It illustrates continuity of care, the need to inform all involved and the importance of monitoring and review. It also emphasises the need for a smooth transition from one care setting to another, and the need to fully involve the client such decisions. Mrs Johnson was supported by certain key workers during the transition stages; by the hospital social worker and GP from hospital to community care, and by the local social worker and GP from community to residential care. The holding of regular meetings involving Mrs Johnson ensured the smooth flow of information between different agencies and Mrs Johnson herself.

Support services available to clients receiving care

In Chapter 9 the services available to clients were discussed in detail and in Chapter 4 ways of supporting clients on an interpersonal level were illustrated. You should refer back to these chapters for a detailed description of services available to clients when receiving care.

Any service offered should reflect and promote social care values such as:
- the promotion of autonomy and respect
- the involvement of the client in the process
- privacy for the client
- the promotion of equality.

These values place the individual client at the centre of service planning and delivery.

Support in the home

Services in the client's own home should provide support with tasks to enable the client to live as 'normal' a life as possible by providing help with:

1 domestic and household tasks;
- cleaning
- laundry
- preparing meals
- shopping
- collecting pensions,

2 personal assistance with daily living activities;
- dressing/undressing
- washing
- bathing
- eating and drinking
- taking to the toilet,

3 emotional and social support;
- conversation/listening
- company
- reading, writing
- accompanying on outings
- helping to keep in touch with neighbours etc.

Any care in the home should be co-ordinated and provided with the assistance of other carers, neighbours or friends, and be delivered in a way that fosters independence and realises the care values discussed above. These services should be reliable, co-ordinated, flexible and sufficient to meet the client's needs.

Shaving a client

Ways in which clients and their carers can take control of care services

How can clients be encouraged to take control?

You have seen in the last chapter how in the care planning context clients are empowered to take control of their own situation. The case of Mrs Johnson also illustrated how this was done. There are many other ways in which clients can be empowered by giving them information and advice so that they can make appropriate informed decisions. Clients should be encouraged to take responsibility for their own lives which involves choosing which services they want and taking decisions about their lifestyle. This assumes that they will be able to take risks to maintain their freedom and independence.

Services should be delivered in a manner that respects the dignity and value of the client. Services which are offered should be appropriate to the client's situation, culture and lifestyle.

Information

Clients need information and knowledge of the services provided. The government encourages agencies to publish details of services available. In order to make informed choices clients must therefore have adequate information about services and also about complaint procedures. This information should be accessible to all and produced in appropriate languages and formats. The National Health Service and Community Care Act 1990 requires social service departments to provide 'information accessible to all potential service users and carers, including those with any communication difficulty or difference in language or culture, setting out the types of community care services available, the criteria for provision and services, the assessment procedures to agree needs and ways of addressing them and standards by which the care management system will be measured'. This is done by publishing a Community Care Plan annually and also by setting up consultation procedures with clients and carers. Booklets and leaflets are also used to provide information.

Advocacy

For those who request it, an advocacy service should be available. Carers have a duty to act on behalf of clients if they request it. Clients can be represented or accompanied by a person of their choice when meeting care staff. Advocates should be available from the same racial or cultural background as the client.

Voluntary organisations provide advocates for certain groups of clients, for example, Age Concern provide support for elderly people and MENCAP provide an advocacy service for those with learning difficulties.

The involvement of clients in the improvement of services

Many social services and health authorities have set up consultative groups as one way in which clients can influence services. Communication is at the centre of what most health authorities and health care trusts seek to do. These agencies do this by explaining the role of authorities and trusts to the local community and by listening to local voices and involving local people in the consideration of care and health service standards and priorities. This is done by involving user groups, special interest groups, local advisory groups, Community Health Councils and voluntary groups.

A number of authorities have developed new initiatives to encourage users of services to become involved in the planning and management of services. The Margin to Mainstream project, funded by the Rowntree Foundation, enables clients and carers to become involved in the organisation, management and delivery of services. This initiative gives people who use and provide services to come together to distribute funds, meet each other and organise workshops. The project supports a direct payment scheme which allows for community care finance to be paid to users who can, in turn, purchase and manage whatever services they wish. Other schemes under this project facilitate users' input into training schemes and develop ways in which clients can influence public policy.

Sheffield social services department has developed an Older People's Reference Group which meets every two months to consider day services, home care and residential care facilities. This group also plays a direct role in the preparation of strategic plans and is developing a Direct Payment to Users Scheme for older people to enable them to purchase the services which best meet their individual needs (Sheffield's Community Care Plan 1994/95).

Review questions

1 What are the five key areas put forward by the White Paper *The Health of the Nation* (1992) that were selected for action to improve the health of the nation?

2 What are the three strategies adopted by the government to prevent health problems in the population?

3 What is the Primary Health Care Team and who are its members?

4 What is a health facilitator and what do they do?

5 What does an environmental protection unit do?

6 Explain what is involved in the compulsory admission of a person to assessment under the 1983 Mental Health Act.

7 What kind of ethical issues do health promotion activities raise for those involved?

8 What do you understand by the term 'continuum of care'?

9 List the kind of support that is available to enable dependent people to live in their own homes.

10 List a number of ways that you think clients can be encouraged to take control of their own lives.

Assignment 12.1
The ethical dilemmas and influencing provision

This assignment discusses the ethical dilemmas faced by practitioners when balancing the needs of different individuals and groups. It then goes on to compares two clients' experiences of health and care services and how they feel that they are able to influence that provision.

This assignment provides knowledge, understanding and portfolio evidence for element 6.2, **Investigate methods for promoting and protecting health and social well-being**, and element 6.3, **Evaluate how clients experience and influence health and social care provision**.

Scenario

Mary, who left home when she was 16 years of age, is now 26 years old and has two children; two-year-old Rose and two-week-old Samantha. Mary lives in a rented flat in a very run-down house with no garden. The flat is damp and has no central heating. At about the time of Rose's birth her father, John, left the family home. Six months later Mary met her present partner, the father of Samantha.

Since Samantha's birth Mary has felt very depressed but refuses to see a doctor. She has done no housework and is not looking after Rose very well. She is breast feeding Samantha but does not cook for either her partner or Rose. Her partner Nick works driving heavy lorries and is away from home for four or five nights each week and is very tired when he does get home. He has, on occasions, hit Mary. Mary is beginning to express hostile feelings towards Nick and Samantha who she feels does not love her as she cries all night.

After a particularly heavy work session Nick came home to a cold house, no food and both Samantha and Rose crying, as they had not been fed for nearly two days. Samantha was suffering from a bad rash as she had not been changed for some time. Mary was in bed and was drunk. Nick tried to feed the children but Rose in particular was very disruptive and, in a fit of temper, Nick hit her and broke her arm. The next door neighbours called the police when they heard the noise.

When the police arrived they took the children to the local general hospital, as a place of safety, and arranged for a doctor to see Mary. She was later admitted to the psychiatric ward of the local general hospital. Later that day the staff made arrangements for her to have Samantha with her, but under strict supervision. Rose was placed in a local foster home until the Family Court could make a decision about her future. Nick was interviewed by the police who, after investigations and consultation with the local social services and health visitor, charged him with assault.

Nick visited Mary in hospital but his visit disturbed her very much. Nick became aggressive and abused both Mary and the staff. The hospital applied to the courts for an injunction to prevent Nick from coming near the hospital. Mary however, wishes to go home and live with her two children and Nick as soon as possible.

Your tasks

From the scenario above answer the following questions:
1 List the practitioners who will be asked to attend a case conference to discuss Mary and her children and recommend what course of action to take. Describe their roles.
2 List and describe the roles of at least three professionals who have a responsibility to protect individuals from risk.
3 List at least three practitioners whose role it might be to give health promotion advice to Mary.
4 List three practitioners who would be involved in creating an environment conducive to Mary's and the children's health upon her discharge from hospital.
5 What ethical dilemmas face the various practitioners, in particular the social worker and police, in balancing the needs of Mary, her children and Nick?
6 What legislation was used to restrict the liberty of Mary, the children and Nick?

Now do the following:
7 Make arrangements to interview at least two people who have had recent experience of the social care or health services.
8 Draw up a questionnaire which will illicit data to enable you to write a report comparing the two clients. Include:
   - their own perception of their care;
   - the extent to which they perceive a continuum of care;
   - a description of the support they were offered;
   - whether they felt they had been in control of the care that they were offered.

13 Health education campaigns: rationale, sources and methods

What is covered in this chapter

- The focus of health education campaigns
- The campaign messages conveyed to different groups
- Campaign content and objectives
- The sources of health education campaigns
- Promotional methods and their selection
- Identifying shortfalls in health education campaigns

These are the resources you will need for your portfolio for element 7.1:
- A project report based on three different sources of material which details:
  - how the objectives for the campaign have been identified and where these relate to national or local health targets
  - how the campaigns for different target groups have conveyed messages
  - how the main aspects for health promotion have been identified
  - the effectiveness of the health education material which has been identified.

These are the resources you will need for your portfolio for element 7.2:
- An analytical report based on a project which:
  - identifies two different sources of health education campaigns (you may use two of the three selected above) and gives examples of their campaigns
  - analyses the two sources and explains why they are promoting their messages
  - identifies the different promotional methods used by the campaigns and their relationship to the sources concerned
  - suggests a rationale as to why these particular methods were selected
  - identifies any shortfalls in the two identified campaigns.

Finally:
- Your written answers to the activities, review questions and assignments in this chapter.

The focus of health education campaigns

Caplan (1964) argues that communities must accept responsibility for their own health, and that the efforts of health and social care professionals should be orientated to identifying the sources of social and health ills, and acting to alleviate these causes. This necessitates the development of primary preventative programmes. Caplan's work had been mostly concerned with mental health, but the conceptual model he developed has been extended to all areas of health and social well-being promotion. He suggests that the prevention of ill-health can been divided into three types:

- primary prevention
- secondary prevention
- tertiary prevention.

Primary prevention

Primary prevention is a community concept. Its aim is to reduce the risk of ill-health for an entire population. Its goal, therefore, is to create an optimal living situation for all members of the population, so that they will be able to adapt constructively to whatever crises they encounter. Thus, the primary preventative programme will identify environmental influences that are harmful, as well as environmental forces that are useful for resisting adverse influences. Caplan's model identifies **supplies** that every individual in a population needs in order to remain healthy:

- Physical supplies, such as adequate shelter, food, the means to protect oneself from bodily harm, and opportunities for exercising the body. (These supplies are fundamental.)
- Psycho-social supplies – needs that must be satisfied through interaction with other human beings. This includes a sense of 'belonging', as opposed to isolation.
- Socio-cultural supplies – the expectations generated towards individuals because of their perceived place in the structure of society, often determined by customs and values in the culture. Those disadvantaged in this way by virtue of gender, class, race, creed, religion, health status, and age, are prone to difficulties in health and social well-being.

Examples of primary prevention programmes include:

- the provision of public housing
- the creation of the National Health Service (NHS)
- education programmes promoting a high-fibre diet, low-fat diets and the practice of safe sex (both to prevent unwanted pregnancies and to reduce the risk of HIV infection).

Activity 13.1

a Identify one example of each of the following:
- physical supplies
- psycho-social suplies
- socio-cultural supplies.

b Discuss within your class why each of your examples characterises the type of supply, and why it fulfils the definition of primary prevention.

Secondary prevention

Secondary prevention involves reducing the actual rates of health and social disability in a population, usually by efforts directed to lowering the prevalence of specific disorders.

While primary prevention is concerned with eliminating the factors that cause health and social problems within a community, secondary prevention is concerned with lowering the incidence rate through early detection and effective treatment of the disorder. Improving early detection procedures and encouraging individuals to make early referrals is usually accompanied by preparing the treatment agencies to deal with these problems.

For a promotional programme aimed at early referral there must be:
- information about where individuals can be referred
- no barriers between the referral agency and the community (to facilitate referral)
- the agency located close to or within the community from which referrals are sought
- no bureaucratic 'red tape' in dealing with referrals.

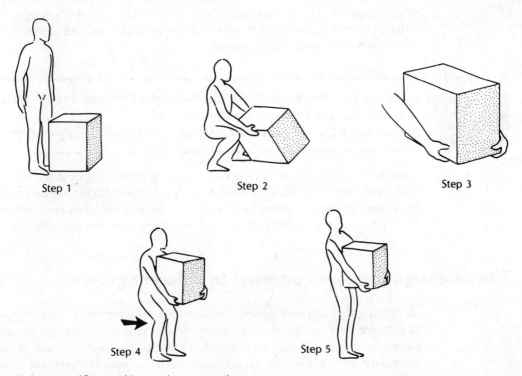

Safe steps to lifting an object – primary prevention

Examples of secondary prevention include:

- campaigns of information aimed at overweight individuals in relation to heart disease
- screening programmes, for example, cervical smears
- health and safety education in relation to lifting
- ante-natal services for parents-to-be.

The vast majority of promotional programmes aimed at health and social well-being are concerned with secondary prevention. It should be noted, however, that successful primary prevention programmes have secondary prevention impact. In addition, secondary prevention programmes may use more personalised communications. For example, the primary health care team will be directly involved in bringing health risks to the attention of vulnerable individuals.

Activity 13.2

a Choose an example from each of the three types of 'supply', where secondary prevention programmes have been used.
b Discuss the methods employed to lower the incidence rate of the problem you have identified.
c How successful do you believe your examples have been, and why?

Tertiary prevention

The focus of tertiary prevention is on individuals who have suffered or who are suffering from health or social disability. This focus is two-fold:

- services directly related to the needs of the affected individual (such as physiotherapy, occupational therapy, nursing and domiciliary services)
- programmes of public education and consultation about the nature of the problem (such as the fears of AIDS sufferers, or resettling individuals with mental health problems into local communities).

Activity 13.3

a Identify two illnesses and describe the range of services directly available to individuals experiencing these illnesses.
b How accessible are these services, and how do individuals get access to them?

It can be argued that each of the three types of prevention outlined by Caplan overlap with each other. All three types require the skills of marketing, and many health and social service organisations now employ professional marketers either within their agencies, or they contract professional marketing agencies to do the job.

The campaign message conveyed to different groups

Identifying the targets of health education can be complex. In primary prevention, the targets are often political or environmental in nature. While this concerns everyone, particular campaigns may be directed at key decision-makers, such as government. In secondary prevention, the target may be more specific: *potential* service users or patients. This requires the identification of an 'at risk' population. At risk populations

The message should get the attention of the target audience

are identified through comprehensive research. Much of this research is called *epidemiological research.*

Epidemiological research investigates the distribution and determinants of ill-health in the community. It seeks to answer questions such as where are people becoming ill, and who is most at risk. Epidemiological research provides essential information about ill-health in the community, and therefore is a rich and invaluable source for the health educator. In tertiary prevention, the targets are those already affected by ill-health and their carers.

It is important to have a profound understanding of the target group, and what sort of approach to take with them. The target group will determine:

- what is said
- how it is to be said
- when it is to be said
- where it is to be said
- who is to say it.

Image analysis

In designing a health and social well-being promotion campaign, it is necessary to determine the target group's current attitudes toward the topic, and this is established using image analysis.

Questionnaires are designed to determine:

- How aware the target population is of the topic.
- How favourably or unfavourably the topic is perceived by the target population.

The questionnaires will determine whether it is necessary to build awareness of the topic, and whether the topic suffers from being perceived negatively. These two criteria combine to determine the nature of the communication problem.

Activity 13.4

1 Identify a health or social well-being campaign in which the purpose has been to raise awareness.
2 There will be specific features of the campaign that will make you suspect that awareness had been identified as a problem. Describe these features.

How do you affect attitudes?

After determining whom the target audience is, and how they perceive the topic, it is necessary to decide what response the promotion campaign should elicit. There are three primary responses from which to choose:

- **Cognitive response** This seeks to put an idea about the topic into the person's mind.
- **Affective response** This seeks to change the person's attitude toward the topic.
- **Behavioural response** This seeks to get the person to literally 'do something' in relation to the topic.

> In designing the message which constitutes the promotion, the following should be remembered:
> - The message should get the attention of the target audience.
> - The message should hold the interest of the target audience.
> - The message should elicit the chosen response from the target audience.

A moral appeal on behalf of multiple sclerosis suffers

The message will undoubtedly make some sort of appeal. There are three types of appeal that a health or social well-being promotional message may make:

- **Rational appeal** This sort of appeal is directed at the audience's self-interest (such as effective stress management programmes in the workplace, reducing absenteeism and staff turnover).
- **Emotional appeal** This sort of appeal stirs up negative or positive emotions such as fear, guilt and shame. Emotional appeals aim to get people to do things (such as brushing teeth, attending annual health screenings, etc.), or to stop people doing things that they are presently doing (such as smoking, abusing substances, or overeating).

  Fear appeals, such as we have seen with anti-smoking campaigns, are effective only up to a point. If the audience anticipates too much fear in the message, they will avoid it. Positive emotional appeals, often involving humour, are successful at attracting audience attention, but may detract from comprehending the message.
- **Moral appeal** This is directed to a sense of what is right and proper. Moral appeals exhort people to support health and social causes such as a cleaner environment, improved race relations, and giving time or money to charitable causes.

  In looking at health promotion issues within the UK, it is clear that there has been a general campaign to educate people about the ways to avoid being infected with HIV. The difficulty has been to educate without causing panic and also without inducing a sense of complacency. The campaign is careful not to stigmatise sufferers, or create anti-homosexual beliefs.

Activity 13.5

1 In groups of three or four, think of as many examples as you can of health or social well-being promotional campaigns that have sought:
   a cognitive responses
   b affective responses
   c behavioural responses.
2 For each example, explain how the campaign attempts to elicit these responses.
3 We have given examples of rational, emotional and moral appeals. How many more examples of each can you think of?

Campaign content and objectives

Essentially, health and social well-being promotion is about attitude change. An attitude always has a focus. This focus may be a person, an ethnic group, a nation – almost anything!

Attitudes are a means by which we form impressions in order to generalise in comparing one thing to another. They are characterised from favourable, through neutral to unfavourable. Attitudes are not directly visible. They may only be inferred from interpersonal behaviour. Therefore, it is important that those engaged in health and social well-being promotion have some expertise in measuring attitudes before and after the promotional effort, in order to determine the degree of attitude change. This is easier said than done, as attitudes are difficult to assess. The right questions must be asked in the right way. In addition, people may be less than truthful when their attitudes are being assessed. For example, Sarason (1977) reports that professional people like doctors and lawyers are less than truthful when being questioned about job-satisfaction.

Social psychologists believe that attitudes and values change because of the introduction of inconsistency. The human mind has a strong need to remain consistent in its beliefs. This consistency is necessary in order to form a sensible view of the world around us. When ideas are presented which are inconsistent with present beliefs, there will be some adjustment. It is the responsibility of the health and social well-being promoters to carefully introduce the inconsistency, and to manage the message so that the adjustment is in the desired direction. For example, smokers damage their health. This is inconsistent with survival. The desired direction for the smoker is to give up smoking, in order to survive.

Although attitudes tend toward stability, they in fact change all of the time. Therefore, attempts at attitude change need to be sustained. Among the most effective ways to sustain attitudes changed in the desired direction, is the association of the message with credible, respected personalities, and the identification of the message with a positive perception that individuals hold of themselves or aspire to.

Politics of health and social well-being promotion

Health and social well-being promotional messages are not themselves value-free. They represent the beliefs of the people who promote the message, and these beliefs may not be universally shared. Messages may prove to be contentious, and provoke alternative messages to enter the marketplace. Some of these alternative messages may be financed by powerful lobbies and/or commercial organisations, such as sugar manufacturers, breweries or tobacco companies. The anti-smoking campaigns of ASH have been countered by organisations who believe that the right to smoke is an individual choice, and that our civil liberties are being threatened by the anti-smoking lobby.

In addition, the targeting and presentation of certain messages may be coloured by prevailing politics. For example, messages, which might best be targeted at particular groups, may not be due to sensitivities surrounding issues of equality. The AIDS awareness campaign had to be careful about targeting the homosexual community, so as not to portray homosexuals as being any more vulnerable to the disease than anyone else.

Case study

Tobacco advertising

Overleaf is the poster that British Transport Advertising (BTA) would rather you didn't see. Produced free of charge by the advertising agency Abbott Mead Vickers for a group of health organisations including ASH (Action on Smoking and Health), it has been judged as being too 'socially sensitive' by BTA, which receives considerable revenue from tobacco advertising posters. As Pamela Taylor from the British Medical Association (BMA) pointed out, 'it is amazing that running ads to promote cigarettes ... is not considered controversial. Yet it is considered controversial to point out the truth behind the effect of tobacco advertising on children.'

Source: ASH *Campaign News*, Spring 1992

Smoking kills 300 people a day.
Is the tobacco industry
advertising for new recruits?

Cigarette advertising reaches everybody, not just adults

The sources of health education campaigns

The process of health and social well-being promotion is often initiated through established organisations. The best known of these is the Health Education Authority (HEA), established in 1968 as the Health Education Council to promote health education in England, Wales, and Northern Ireland. In addition, the Department of Health have established budgets for health promotion, available to regional and district health authorities. Most district health authorities employ health education officers. Local government is actively engaged in health and social well-being promotion through its education, social services and environmental services departments. Many local authorities have developed active partnerships with district health authorities in promotional campaigns.

In addition, there are hundreds of charitable organisations dedicated to specific health problems, who provide significant promotional efforts. Similarly, commercial organisations such as pharmaceutical and health equipment supply companies invest considerably in health promotion as part of their public relations strategies.

Professional bodies and trade unions are also actively engaged in health and social well-being promotion.

Activity 13.6

Visit a local health centre, and examine the posters on display, and the leaflets available. Make written notes of the source of the poster or leaflet, and the message being communicated. Explain why you believe each promotional source has an interest in the message being communicated.

Promotional methods and their selection

How do you get the message across?

Selection of appropriate communication channels for the message is crucial. A communication channel is the means by which the message reaches its target

Charities

Pharmaceutical companies

Local authorities

Pharmaceutical companies

The Butter Council

Milk Marketing Board

Department of Health

Who promotes health?

audience. There are two primary communication channels from which to choose:

- personal
- non-personal.

Personal communication

Personal communication channels generally provide face-to-face contact, although telephone and postal correspondence is sometimes used. Personal communication allows the message to be individualised, and provides opportunities for feedback. Such interactive marketing is highly effective, but the information providers must be skilled in both presentation and interpersonal skills.

The effectiveness of personal communication channels is highly dependent on how the audience perceives the persons selected to deliver the message. Highly credible sources are the most effective, provided that they are perceived as having expertise, and as being trustworthy and likeable. Such individuals may be perceived as role models. Personal communication channels may be useful in primary prevention, for example, by establishing effective education programmes in schools, but they are particularly effective in secondary prevention, where networks of social workers, nurses and doctors working in the community may be mobilised as communication resources. The use of peers may also be effective. For example, ex-drug addicts have been highly effective in both getting the anti-drug message across, and in working directly with addicts in order to get them off drugs.

Non-personal communication

Non-personal communication uses no personal contact or feedback. It relies on print media (newspapers and magazines), electronic media (radio and television) and display media (billboards, signs and posters). Non-personal communication channels may be directed at a mass audience (large and undifferentiated) or at specialised audiences. It is important that the differences between **advertising** and **publicity** (or public relations) be understood.

Advertising and the media

Advertising includes:

- print and broadcast advertisements
- mailings
- producing magazines
- videos and films
- brochures and leaflets
- billboards
- symbols and logos.

The advantages of advertising lie in its being a highly public mode of communication. It is pervasive, with the message being repeated many times. It is also dramatic, making the most artful use of print, sound and colour. However, advertising carries on a monologue with the audience, allowing no opportunity for response.

Publicity

Publicity includes:

- press releases and information kits
- speeches
- seminars

Childhood diseases haven't died. Children have.

It's sad, but true.

Childhood diseases like Mumps, Measles, Rubella, Diphtheria, Tetanus, Polio and Whooping Cough can all have very serious consequences.

They can lead to blindness, deafness, paralysis, brain damage and even death.

Rubella can be especially serious for a pregnant woman, whose unborn child may be born deaf, blind or even brain damaged.

However, children don't have to be at risk.

Immunisation can protect against all these diseases and help to wipe them out.

So parents who don't immunise their children are taking needless risks.

The time to start your child's Immunisation programme is at the age of two months.

For more information and advice see your doctor or health visitor or just pop down to your local clinic.

They're there to help.

Remember, it's better for you to see your doctor before your child has to.

IMMUNISATION The safest way to protect your child.

Issued by The Health Education Authority and The Department of Health

A magazine advertisement used as part of a campaign for immunisation by the HEA and the Department of Health

343

- annual reports
- public relations.

An important part of the publicity and public relations approach to health and social well-being promotion is to keep the message in the news. Media coverage of events and human-interest stories may be more effective than directly pitching messages, especially when well-known personalities become involved. An example is the campaign to get ME (Myalgic encephalomyelitis) accepted as a genuine illness. Both television and newspapers carried stories about how the illness had changed the lives of sufferers, and the campaign used personalities such as Clare Francis in order to establish credibility. News stories are not perceived as obvious advertising, and have a higher credibility. The inclusion of the message in the story-lines of television programmes and films is also highly effective. It is far less expensive than advertising campaigns.

Clare's still in the swim

FORMER round-the-world yachts woman Clare Francis, 42, who has become a best selling adventure novelist, would like to reassure her public that she is still alive and kicking.

Because it has been well documented that she is one of an estimated 100,000 suffering from Myalgic Encephalomyelitis (a viral attack on the nervous system which causes intense tiredness and muscular weakness), Clare fears that people think she has sunk forever into a life of terminal inertia.

'Half the world think I'm at death's door, but I'm out doing things and leading a 95 per cent normal life. It takes a long time, but I'm nearly fully recovered,' says the petite, blonde former Royal ballet School pupil.

Indeed, at the five-storey Kensington home she shares with her 10-year-old son Tom, Clare is working on a fourth novel — which she says has an environmental theme — and celebrating the fact that her last novel, Wolf Winter, has just topped the best-seller list in Australia.

Since a specialist first diagnosed M.E. (her doctor had wrongly thought it was depression), Clare has been helping fellow sufferers through her presidency of the M.E. Action Campaign. David Puttnam has just joined as patron of the group, which has been lobbying to get the illness recognised and for more research into it.

But coping with the viral disease has not helped as far as relationships for the beautiful novelist, who was divorced in 1985 from her French husband Jacques Redon. Clare tells me: 'M.E. is a wrecker of marriages and I thought I was better off on my own. I severed a relationship when I got M.E. — it wasn't fair.'

Source: *The Daily Mail*, 28 February 1989

News stories are not perceived as obvious advertising

Using a promotion mix

Few campaigns of health or social well-being promotion would rely on only one means of communicating a message. Many campaigns would also seek to establish their influence in all three types of prevention. Therefore, a promotional campaign would develop a promotion mix. A strategy for a promotion mix would look like Table 13.1.

Identifying shortfalls in health education campaigns

It is important that health and social education campaigns be evaluated. If a campaign is not working, it is important to identify the reasons why, and adjust the campaign to increase effectiveness. Perhaps the campaign has not been reaching its target audience. Perhaps the campaign has reached the target audience, but left a confused or ambiguous messages.

Earlier, we mentioned three criteria for success of a health education campaign. It must attract the attention of the target audience, maintain its interest and elicit the desired response. It seems entirely reasonable that these may also be acceptable as criteria for evaluation. The different forms of appeal that may be made can sometimes result in unpredictable and surprising results.

Table 13.1 Health promotion campaign mix

	Primary promotion	Secondary promotion	Tertiary promotion
Target audiences	General public	People who smoke	Victims of smoke-related diseases
Response sought	Don't start smoking	Give up smoking	Co-operate with treatment
Type of appeal	Rational	Emotional/fear	Emotional/ rational
Communication	Ads/publicity	Ads/publicity/personal	Personal
Channel/ Choice of media	Print, broadcast, video press, billboards	As Primary plus warnings on packets	Leaflets, information kits, counselling

The success of a health education campaign is analysed along two dimensions. Effectiveness is whether the campaign has achieved the results it set out to achieve. Efficiency is how well the results have been achieved in comparison with other techniques which might have been used. The ways of measuring effectiveness and efficiency depend entirely on the nature of the campaign. Large national campaigns would need to use major, national means of evaluation. Smaller, more localised campaigns, may be evaluated more simply.

A health education campaign encouraging children to be immunised, for example, may be simply measured by the numbers who have turned up for their immunisations. Other campaigns might be evaluated by continuing epidemiological studies. Epidemiology investigates the distribution and incidence of particular social or health problems. It is often epidemiological studies which provide the reasons for a health education campaign. By continuing or repeating the studies, the changes measure the effectiveness of the campaign.

Of course, not all health and care education campaigns can be so directly evaluated. Some campaigns challenge values and ways of thinking. These more subtle objectives may be evaluated through interviews and questionnaires. The results achieved through interviews and questionnaires can be very enlightening. These results may be compared to the objectives of the campaign, and valid conclusions may be expressed. The consequence of such information is that concrete recommendations may be made, which can result in improved effectiveness of the campaign, by focusing on the perceived shortfalls.

Review questions

1 How the audience perceives the person sending or giving a message will determine the effectiveness of the message in a health education campaign. How does the kind of person sending the message affect the way the audience perceives the message?
2 What kind of responses may a health education campaign elicit in an individual.
3 There are four kinds of appeal that a health education message may make to an intended target group. Name all four and explain how they function.

4 Explain the differences between primary, secondary and tertiary prevention in a health promotion campaign.

5 Give an example where personal communication would be an effective communication channel, and explain why.

6 Identify one example each of health education advice targeted specifically at the following age groups:

   a children
   b adolescents
   c adults
   d elders.

7 Identify one example each of health education advice targeted specifically at the following activity groups:

   a smokers
   b substance abusers
   c obese individuals.

8 Identify one example each of health education advice targeted specifically at gender groups:

   a men
   b women.

9 For your examples in **6**, **7**, and **8**, identify how the messages differ for each group in their style of presentation.

10 Explain the role of epidemiological research in health education.

Assignment 13.1
Looking at health education campaigns

This assignment provides knowledge, understanding and portfolio evidence for element 7.1, **Investigate health education campaigns.**

Your tasks

Select three different health education campaigns, each aimed at different target groups.

1 Write a description of each campaign, identifying its target group and its objectives. Identify where any of these campaigns relate to either national or local health objectives.

2 For each of the three campaigns, analyse the methods of promotion used in relation to the respective target groups.

In this chapter, we have explained the varied aspects of health education. A campaign may intend to reduce the incidence of a specific disease, through both primary and secondary prevention. On the other hand, the campaign may attempt to support and aid those already affected (tertiary prevention). The campaign may be environmental or political in nature, or aimed at changing our living practices from unhealthy to healthy.

3 Write a report in respect of the three campaigns described in above, which explains what the main aspects of each campaign are, and why you believe these were chosen by the health educators.

4 Using evidence from the campaign organisations or from the government (local or national), explain why the campaigns have been effective or not, as the case may be. Provide examples of material from the campaigns to support your explanation.

Assignment 13.2
Examining campaigns in detail

This assignment provides knowledge, understanding and portfolio evidence for element 7.2, **Investigate the reasons for, sources of and methods used in health education campaigns.**

Your tasks

In this task, you will examine two of the campaigns selected above in more detail.

1 Clearly identify the two campaigns you have chosen and describe the source of each.

2 Analyse each of the two organisations in detail, and what their interests are in promoting a health education campaign.

3 Identify their sources of funding.

4 Describe the different promotional methods used by each of the source organisations, and explain why you believe they were chosen. Justify your views.

5 Identify any shortfalls in each of the campaigns, which may have interfered with their achieving their objectives? Describe these in detail. If you cannot identify any shortfalls, explain how the source organisations may have averted them.

14 The effectiveness of health education campaigns

What is covered in this chapter

- The objectives of health education campaigns
- Aspects of well-being promoted by campaigns
- Designing an interview schedule
- The evaluation and analysis of health education campaigns
- Concluding an evaluation
- Examples of health education campaigns and how they could be improved

These are the resources that you will need for your portfolio for element 7.3:

- An evaluation which uses a structured interview technique to assess the success of one campaign aiming to improve the health and well-being of the population. The evaluation should include:
  - a description of the aim of the campaign, related to researched information of the perceived needs of the target group (under investigation)
  - the structured interview format showing how this relates to the area of research
  - records of interviews with at least six individuals from the target group
  - clearly reasoned conclusions and recommendations based on evidence obtained from the interviews.
- Your written answers to the activities, review questions and assignment in this chapter.

The objectives of health education campaigns

All health education campaigns should have clearly stated aims and objectives. These specify what the campaign is hoping to achieve: what results are desirable. Objectives should be quite specific, and achieved within a specified time period.

It is important that objectives can be evaluated, so the way in which they are stated is important. They should be as measurable as possible. Objectives should also be realistic and obtainable. Objectives are about *why* the campaign is being conducted – not how.

Failure to establish achievable and relevant objectives can mean that much time and energy is wasted in conducting a campaign.

Objectives can be divided into three categories of outcomes:

- What the clients needs to *know*.
- How the clients should *feel*.
- What the clients should *do*.

Aspects of well-being promoted by health education campaigns

There are many issues involved with educating for health. Some health campaigns are aimed directly at individuals. The aim is to change individuals' lifestyle choices and behaviour. Other campaigns may be aimed at society in more general terms, attempting to change the environment in which we live.

Health is a complicated combination of our own choices and behaviours, and the environment in which we live. Both individual and environmental (or political) objectives are valid to pursue. Smoking is a good example (see the case study on page 353). The various campaigns to reduce smoking have focused on both individuals (smoking is bad for *you*) and on environment (limitations on advertising, smoke-free areas, etc.).

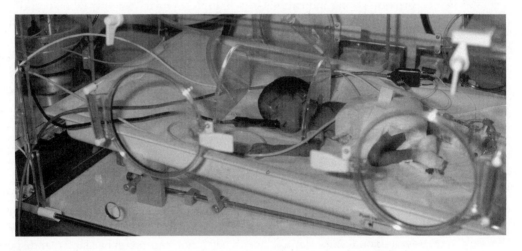

One in ten infant intensive care beds are filled by babies affected by parental smoking

Health education campaigns need to inform individuals about the ways in which their lifestyle choices can affect their health. They need to provide information, change values and attitudes, and ultimately influence individuals to make different choices.

Health education campaigns also need to raise awareness of social and economic conditions which contribute to health problems and actively work towards a change in political policy-making.

Some campaigns attempt to achieve their objectives through one focus or the other. In reality, probably both are required in order for the campaign to be successful. Successful health education campaigns work on both individual choices and political policy. For example, exercise is encouraged for individuals in order to promote health. Cycling is an excellent way to achieve this exercise. Individuals should be encouraged to 'get on their bikes' more often. Cycling also reduces pollution, as hopefully less car journeys are made. In that way it benefits the health of all. However, in order to provide a safe environment for individuals to cycle in, cycle paths and routes need to be established. This requires political action.

Aspects of well-being targeted by health education campaigns are often established by assessing needs. Needs are often determined by using objective data. This means collecting information about the present nature of a health problem in the community.

What grounds exist for instigating a health education campaign? Who are the 'at risk' groups?

The concept of well-being can be somewhat subjective, so information should be obtained from as many sources as possible in order to get as wide a picture as possible. An effective way of obtaining information is by using questionnaires.

Designing an interview schedule

Obtaining information from the public is important in assessing both the need for and effectiveness of health education campaigns.

Some campaigns require large-scale surveys. These are expensive and time-consuming. Often, health education professionals will conduct a 'pilot survey' this is a smaller scale, less formal means of obtaining information. The pilot survey can provide strong indications of what questions to ask and who should be questioned.

Interview schedules are important in establishing the need for health education, and also for evaluating the effectiveness of a campaign. Some interviews are done face-to-face or on the telephone. It is important that the same questions are asked in the same way, and that the answers are accurately recorded.

Self-evaluation is also often used. Here, the individual completes a questionnaire in his or her own time and returns it to the interviewer.

Designing an effective interview schedule to assess the need or effectiveness of a health education campaign is a very skilled activity (see Chapter 15).

The evaluation and analysis of health education campaigns

How is it possible to measure the success of a health education campaign? In relation to large-scale campaigns, sophisticated research is often required. However, the concept of evaluation is important. A health education campaign has stated and specific objectives. Evaluation is the process by which an assessment is made on whether or not the objectives have been achieved. What parts of the campaign seemed to work, and what parts did not? How could the campaign be improved?

Not achieving objectives may be due to:
- the objectives being unrealistic
- not identifying possible sources of resistance
- not using appropriate methods.

Evaluation is important because:
- It draws attention to errors that may be avoided in the future.
- It corrects problems and results in better communication or targeting.
- It justifies the use of resources that went into the health campaign.

Just as campaigns depend on stating specific objectives, evaluation must ask specific questions in relation to these objectives. The aims of health education campaigns are to result in changes in:
- attitudes
- knowledge
- behaviour
- awareness

- public policy
- health status.

For each of these categories, measures may be made before and after the health education campaign to provide information on both overall effectiveness and specific areas of difficulty that persist.

Activity 14.1

For each of the six categories of evaluation above, identify specific measures that can be obtained.

Concluding an evaluation

The purpose of health education is *changing* both the public policies and individual practices which affect health. A campaign may be based on initial research which had established a *need* for health education. From the initial research, specific objectives will have been stated. It is against these objectives which the campaign must be assessed in an evaluation. The conclusions of the evaluation must indicate whether each objective was met or not.

Health education is time-consuming and costs money. It is important that the effectiveness of individual campaigns are assessed. To run a campaign for two years and then evaluate it only to find it did not work, is an expensive mistake to make. Evaluation should not be seen as activity which follows a health education campaign, but rather an on-going activity. Evaluation should be designed into the programme at the start, and begin when the programme begins.

When evaluating a health education campaign, the enquiry should be in respect of the original objectives, and provide information on both the validity of the objectives, and the methods (or process) used in the campaign.

An evaluation will conclude with definite clear statements about how the campaign may be improved with respect to its objectives.

Examples of health education campaigns and how they could be improved

In this section, we have provided further discussion of four key areas on which major health education campaigns have focused in recent years. We have referred to them previously in Chapter 8. Following each example, we have provided questions for discussion that relate to evaluating the effectiveness of the health education campaigns. The questions relate to the earlier sections of this chapter.

Example 1: smoking and health

If smoking is so bad for people why does the government not ban it? This would seem to be a legitimate question to consider in a discussion of health education.

Look back at pages 217 and 218 (*Smoking and health* section in Chapter 8). If you have not already done so, do Activity 8.17.

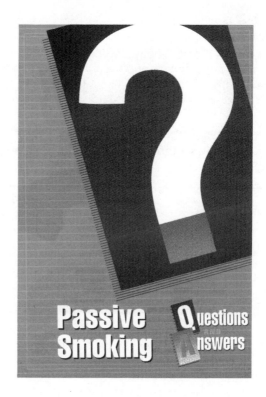

Should tobacco be banned?

Case study

Smoking in health and social care facilities

In recent years many local authority social services departments and many hospitals have completely banned smoking from their premises. The bans not only include staff, but also include service users. It is believed that as professionals promoting health and social well-being, care workers should provide no-smoking role models, and that care facilities should not cater to the needs of smokers. In many cases, the ban has been extended to, for example, hospital grounds. Consequently, there has been a growth in incidents involving secretive smoking. Small fires have started in toilets and closets. One individual's hair caught on fire outside of a hospital from a carelessly thrown cigarette out of a ward window by a patient, terrified of being caught.

Users of social and health care facilities are often under great stress when using the facilities. Many have smoked for many years, and declare that it is their greatest pleasure. Both patients groups and public sector trade unions have argued that a policy should certainly discourage smoking, but not ban it altogether. It would be reasonable, they claim, to have special rooms for smokers. This would avoid sick and elderly patients from sneaking a smoke on a fire escape outside in freezing weather. This dilemma is an example of the complexity of implementing the Care Value Base.

Activity 14.2

Before any discussion of the case study above, have a secret ballot in class on whether or not any smoking should be allowed in health and social care facilities. Then have a class discussion, or even a more formal debate on the topic: Smoking should be completely banned in all health and social care facilities. Follow the discussion or debate with another secret ballot. If the results are different from the first ballot, discuss the possible reasons why this is so.

What would some of the consequences be of a ban on smoking?
- People would live longer, healthier lives.
- There would be a reduced demand upon hospital facilities. Currently the cost to the NHS of treating tobacco-related diseases is £437 million per year.
- If people live longer, they would draw their pensions for longer, and so pension contributions for working people would go up or the value of pensions would drop.
- People working in tobacco-related industries would be unemployed and be drawing unemployment benefits.
- The country would lose the benefit of the revenue from taxes on tobacco. In 1990–91 this amounted to over £5,500 million.

The last figure is the crucial one when considering the action that governments might take. Banning the use of tobacco would cost the Exchequer over £5 billion per year. This figure alone is perhaps enough to ensure that any campaign to ban smoking will almost certainly fail at present.

As smoking may not be banned for some time, what must be the focus of any health promotion? The answer is to a large extent the provision of education to inform people so that they can make choices. The shock tactics of anti-smoking campaigns are less effective as people become almost immune to the messages.

Tobacco advertising

Another course of action could be to identify the targets for the tobacco company advertising and concentrate resources on stopping those people from smoking. It is important for tobacco companies to recruit a new smoker for every one that dies. For example, a recent target group for tobacco company marketing in the USA appears to be young people.

Case study

Old Joe Cool

In the USA the tobacco company, R J Reynolds, produce a brand of cigarettes called Camel featuring a cartoon character called Old Joe Cool.

In December 1991 the *Journal of the American Medical Association* contained details of a survey that showed that Old Joe Cool was recognised as easily as Mickey Mouse. The survey showed that the Camel character was recognised by 30 per cent of three-year-olds and 90 per cent of six-year-old children.

The effect of the campaign has been that the market share of the critical pre-18-year-old market for Camel cigarettes has risen from less than 1 per cent to 33 per cent.

The United States Health Department took the unprecedented step of asking the tobacco company to withdraw the advertisements in March 1992. The company refused to stop their successful advertising campaign.

In the UK, there are voluntary restrictions on campaigns geared towards young people and so such a campaign should not occur. However, in 1992 it was reported in the press that Benson & Hedges were using a puffin in their tobacco advertisements. The anti-smoking lobby, including many MPs, condemned this campaign as 'an outrageous theft of a symbol associated specifically with children' (it is used as a logo for Puffin Books).

- It is estimated (September 1991) that 10 per cent of youths aged 11–15 smoke regularly. This was an increase over the 1988 figures.
- It is estimated that illegal sales of tobacco to under-16s are worth £90 million a year to the tobacco industry.

Source: Action on Smoking and Health

There is clearly a difficulty in getting the message over about smoking and health. Both the health promoters and the tobacco companies try to use the mass media to get their differing messages across. Legislation and voluntary codes of practice have made it more difficult for tobacco companies to advertise but they have found ways to gain publicity and keep brand names in the public eye. The budgets for tobacco advertising are huge compared with those for health promotion.

Activity 14.3

1 Examine a variety of newspapers and magazines. Look at tobacco advertisements, articles on sport and photographs, and make a list of ways that tobacco companies manage to get their products mentioned and seen.
2 Discuss with your class colleagues what the message is that the tobacco companies are trying to put over.

Activity 14.4

Evaluating campaigns against smoking

1 Using the information available here, and also that obtained from other leaflets and booklets, try to identify what the objectives are of campaigns to stop people smoking.
2 In what ways are campaigns to stop people smoking seeking to achieve their goals (e.g. reducing incidence of disease, changing individuals' practices, etc.)?
3 How might the effectiveness of campaigns to stop people smoking be evaluated in respect of achieving the desired objectives?
4 In your view, how effective have these campaigns been? You need to support your conclusions with evidence.
5 How might campaigns to stop people smoking be more effective?

Example 2: other forms of drug abuse

Look back at pages 219–21 covering alcohol, illegal drugs and solvent abuse. If you have not done activities 8.18, 8.19 and 8.20 do those now. This will enable you to do the next activity which evaluates campaigns against substance abuse.

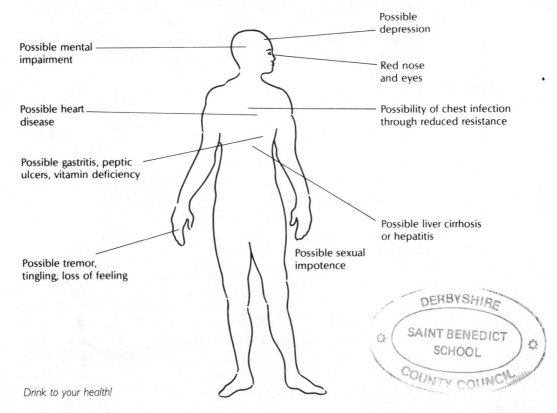

Drink to your health!

Activity 14.5

Evaluating campaigns against substance abuse

1 Using the information available here and from other leaflets and booklets, try to identify what the objectives are of campaigns to stop people abusing drugs?

2 In what ways are campaigns to stop people abusing drugs seeking to achieve their goals (e.g. reducing incidence of disease, changing individuals' practices, etc.)?

3 How might the effectiveness of campaigns to stop people abusing drugs be evaluated in respect of achieving their objectives?

4 In your view, how effective have these campaigns been? You need to support your conclusions with evidence.

5 How might campaigns to stop people abusing drugs be more effective?

Example 3: HIV and AIDS

Look back at the material on HIV and AIDS on pages 221 and 222. This will allow you to recap on the background and current situation regarding HIV and AIDS.

Health education and HIV

The difficulty in assessing the risk of the spread of HIV is in knowing how rapid the spread will be from the high-risk groups to the population in general. The major thrust of the campaigns has been to give information about the virus and advocate the use of barrier methods to stop the spread. This clearly affects the spread by sexual intercourse. The use of the word condom has re-entered everyday language. There has been a strong message that carrying condoms is a sensible precaution that does not imply immorality.

Hygiene precautions when dealing with vomit, blood and faeces have been emphasised. The use of rubber gloves is now seen as essential and the safe disposal of any potentially contaminated material is emphasised – the same precautions taken by

A cartoon from one of the HEA's leaflets on STDs

health care practitioners who wear disposable gloves whenever there is a risk of contamination. The barrier methods only work to prevent transmission if they are used on all occasions. The implied message is that all contacts must be treated as if they were infected.

A second part of the campaign has been to screen blood and blood products to reduce the transmission via that route. Blood donors have been questioned and those in high-risk groups have been asked not to donate blood. Even so, all blood is treated as potentially contaminated.

> In Edinburgh increasing numbers of babies infected with HIV are being born to mothers who have been injecting drugs. Of these children, about a third will be dead within two years. A third possible way to reduce the spread would be to introduce schemes which reduced the need for intravenous drug users to share needles. This could reduce the spread but is often seen as an encouragement to drug use and so needle issue and exchange schemes are not seen as priorities and are sometimes positively opposed.

An interesting point when considering health promotion is in a knock-on effect from the message that barrier methods (condoms) should be used during sexual intercourse to prevent the spread of HIV. This has resulted in a marked decrease in the reported cases of sexually transmitted diseases, such as gonorrhoea and syphilis. This result was particularly evident in the male homosexual group although it was noted in all groups.

The campaign had therefore reached people who were likely to be the carriers of the disease in the heterosexual population. People who become infected with a sexually transmitted disease (STD) normally do so through sexual intercourse with an infected partner. The greater the number of partners the greater the risk of infection and of passing it on. The decrease in the reported cases of STDs meant that either people were having fewer partners (unlikely) or that they were using condoms. The more partners a person has the greater the risk that one of them will be infected with HIV so an increased use of condoms in this group would decrease the rate of transmission into the general population.

Activity 14.6

Evaluating campaigns against the spread of HIV and AIDS

1 Using the information available here and from other leaflets and booklets, try to identify what the objectives are of campaigns to stop the spread of HIV and AIDS.

2 In what ways are campaigns to stop the spread of HIV and AIDS seeking to achieve their goals (e.g. reducing incidence of disease, changing individuals' practices, etc.)?

3 How might the effectiveness of campaigns to stop the spread of HIV and AIDS be evaluated in respect of achieving their objectives?

4 In your view, how effective have these campaigns been? You need to support your conclusions with evidence.

5 How might campaigns to stop the spread of HIV and AIDS be made more effective?

Example 4: lifestyle risks

There are many risks to well-being that come from the way that we live. They arise from aspects of a person's life that include:

- work roles or lack of work
- the food that a person eats
- the physical activity that is undertaken.

In short, they relate to the day-to-day habits and philosophies that make up a person's lifestyle.

Diet and Exercise

Look back at pages 222–6; this material provides the background you need on diet and exercise.

Stress

Look at the section on *Stress* in Chapter 7. If you have not done Activity 7.11 then attempt it now.

The long- and short-term effects of stress are shown in Figures 14.1 and 14.2. These illustrate only some of the physical and psychological symptoms associated with stress.

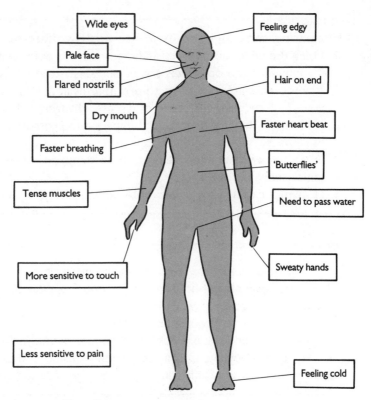

Figure 14.1 The short-term effects of stress

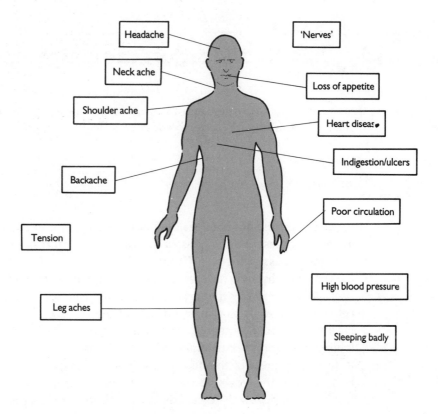

Figure 14.2 The long-term effects of stress

Activity 14.7

Evaluating campaigns to promote healthy lifestyles

1 Using the information available here and from other leaflets and booklets, try to identify what the objectives are of campaigns to promote healthy lifestyles.
2 In what ways are campaigns to promote healthy lifestyles seeking to achieve their goals (e.g. reducing incidence of disease, changing individuals' practices, etc.)?
3 How might the effectiveness of campaigns to promote healthy lifestyles be evaluated in respect of achieving their objectives?
4 In your view, how effective have these campaigns been? You need to support your conclusions with evidence.
5 How might campaigns to promote healthy lifestyles be more effective?

Review questions

1 Describe the characteristics of health education campaign objectives.
2 Provide examples of how campaigns may focus on changing individual behaviours, and on political or environmental action.
3 How are 'at risk' groups identified?
4 How can interviews provide valuable information for health educators?
5 Why is it important to evaluate health education campaigns?
6 What aspects of health education campaigns are subject to evaluation?

Assignment 14.1
Evaluating health education campaign effectiveness

This assignment provides knowledge, understanding and portfolio evidence for element 7.3, **Evaluate the effectiveness of a health education campaign for a target population.**

Your tasks

Using one of the examples of health education campaigns in this chapter, or one of your own choosing, describe the aims of the campaign. You may use the campaigns you studied for the assignments in Chapter 13.

1 Explain how the aims have been determined, with reference to research which has been done to identify the target group of the campaign. You will need to use reference materials to give you details of the research.
2 Design a structured interview to be used with individuals from the target group. This interview should seek to evaluate:
   a their awareness of the health education campaign
   b how much their own behaviours have been changed as a result of the campaign.
3 Use this interview with at least six individuals from the target group, and keep careful records of their responses.

4 Write a report which includes:
- A summary of your findings from the interviews.
- Clearly stated conclusions based on your findings, indicating whether or not the campaign appears to be achieving its objectives.
- At least two clear recommendations about how the health education campaign you selected may be improved. Your recommendations should be linked very clearly to your findings.

15 Research methods

What is covered in this chapter

- What is research?
- Ethical issues
- How research is carried out
- Qualitative research techniques
- Quantitative research techniques
- Sources of information
- Sampling methods

These are the resources you will need for your portfolio for element 8.1:

- A report which includes a short examination of two research studies into health and social well-being, one quantitative and one qualitative, identifying the different aspects of two processes in each and briefly describing:
  - the nature of the research process
  - the different stages of the research process
  - how the research stages are inter-linked.
- Your written answers to the activities, review questions and assignment in this chapter.

What is research?

Most people associate 'research' with activities that are substantially removed from day-to-day life, pursued by gifted people who are often academics. However, research can be, and indeed is, a stimulating and satisfying experience for many people with an enquiring mind.

> Research can be defined as 'an attempt to increase available knowledge by the discovery of new facts through systematic scientific enquiry'. Research in the health and social care field concerns itself not only with health and social care practice, but also with health and social care education and management.

To carry out research in an objective manner you need to think critically. For example, many of us take for granted that authority figures like social workers, policemen and women, doctors and government leaders usually provide us with factual information and that they are also equipped to make decisions about our everyday lives. What happens when such authority figures disagree, for example, when two doctors disagree on a diagnosis? We must ourselves then seek the relevant information in order to make our own decisions.

In the past, people believed that the earth was flat and that the sun revolved around the earth. How reliable are today's theories? In order to evaluate the claims of others we must use critical thinking; take nothing for granted. Just because something is in print does not mean that we have to believe it. To be critical you should examine definitions, the premises on which people build arguments, and think through the logic with which their arguments were developed. Every time your are asked to evaluate or analyse an argument, report or finding you should:

- be sceptical
- examine the definitions of terms used
- examine the assumptions of the arguments
- be cautious about drawing conclusions from the evidence
- consider alternative interpretations of the findings.

The purpose of research

Research projects have a number of different purposes. The most common ones are:
- to review existing knowledge
- to describe some situation or problem
- to construct something novel
- to explain.

The first two in the list above are the most common forms of student research project. Research at this level may have a practical outcome of value to the organisation, an objective increasingly being favoured by employers and workplace providers.

Ethical issues

The research process involves a series of decisions that must be made by the researcher before observing even a single subject or asking one question. A commitment to research at whatever level raises a number of ethical issues. These must be taken seriously as an integral part of a health or social care professional's responsibility. The general public and users of social care or health services have a right to expect adherence to a recognised code of conduct from the researcher who wishes to undertake research.

Social care researchers, when they undertake to carry out a research project, enter into a personal and moral relationship with the people that they are studying. The more sensitive the topic to be studied the more problematic the relationship becomes. If there are potential consequences for the participants then the relation of researcher to participant need careful thought. If the issue to be researched is a sensitive one (eg looking at staff rolls which could be used by management to promote, redeploy or even make staff redundant) the range of methods that can be used is restricted. Research on sensitive issues is frequently open to misinterpretation by those who see opportunities to exploit the findings.

Before you embark on any research project in health and social care, you should ask yourself:
- What are the aims and purpose of my research?

- Am I presenting any unnecessary risks or inconveniences to clients, staff or anyone else? (No person should be hurt or put at risk by the completion of the research or publication of the report.)
- Does my work respect confidentiality and anonymity? How will I be able to keep confidential the identity of participants?
- Am I competent to undertake the project?
- How much support do I need?
- For what do I intend to use the research findings?

All those involved in the research process, staff, clients and carers, are entitled to information on these points. It is part of the research code of ethics to explain the research to all the people involved in it. One of the most important safeguards is that the subject must always have the right to refuse or to discontinue participation at any time, even after having agreed to take part.

Informed consent is important – researchers must provide enough information so that participants are able to make informed decisions about their participation. Informed consent should mean that you have provided respondents with relevant information concerning the nature and value of your research and its likely dissemination. Researchers should not proceed to gather data until they have received the subjects' unequivocal consent.

Keeping confidential the identity of individuals may prove difficult at times, people may be identified by the description of the job they do or their disabilities. For example, the manager of a residential unit may be identified if his or her role is discussed because an establishment tends to have only one such manager. Likewise, a user may be identified by his or her disability, for example if there is only one client who uses a wheel-chair. Remember, other people have to live with the consequences of what you write and your conclusions.

Activity 15.1

Louise has been given permission by the manager of a residential care establishment to carry out research involving the use of a questionnaire to be given to elderly residents. There are two male residents and 20 female ones. The manager has not spoken to the residents or obtained their permission.

a What issues should Louise address before she begins her work? For example, what information should she give the residents to enable them to make an informed decision as to whether to take part or not?

b What issues of confidentiality should be addressed?

How research is carried out

How people actually carry out research depends on a number of factors. One important factor in choosing a research method is the theoretical perspective or beliefs held by the researcher. There are two schools of thought:

- *Interpretivists* see the social world as different from the natural world. People inhabit the social world and they are viewed as unpredictable, they may not behave in the same way in the same situation twice. Over the period between two sets of research the same people will have changed – they will be older, possible more tired or have the flu on the second occasion. The researcher may carry out the research with different people who will all have different experiences and values – every five-year-old or 85-year-old is different from their contemporaries. It is, therefore, difficult to study people objectively in social situations. They do not always behave in an objective way and may bring experiences and feelings to situations which cannot be repeated. Interpretivists use qualitative techniques (see below) to collect information.

- *Positivists*, on the other hand, believe that there is no difference between the natural and social world. The researcher is regarded as the collector of neutral facts by standing back from his or her own values and beliefs. Positivists tend to use quantitative techniques (see later in this chapter) to collect information and argue that these techniques are more 'scientific', reliable and open to checking by other researchers.

Practical restraints, such as time or finance available may also influence the method or methods to be used.

Qualitative research techniques

Qualitative research, often called *fieldwork* or *participant observation*, involves first-hand, face-to-face participation by the researcher in naturally occurring situations, such as observing children in a playgroup or observing activities in a dining room in a residential home. This type of research tends to be narrow in scope, concentrating on small groups and their views of the world. The researcher does not manipulate the subjects of the research or their situations to assess their causal significance. Unlike survey research, field research does not involve asking standardised questions to large, representative samples of people.

Observation research

Modern social science and all good practitioner research is rooted in observation. Researchers observe the behaviour of people in certain situations – in residential homes, in football crowds, therapeutic groups and small communities. The main virtue of observation is its directness – behaviour can be studied as it occurs. The researcher does not have to ask people about their behaviour – people are simply watched as they do and say things. Data collected by observation will usually describe the observed phenomena as they occur in their natural settings. Observation research is part craft and part art. Anyone can observe, but it takes practice and careful planning to observe and record a scene accurately and then to analyse perceptively what happened of significance. Most practitioner research, social work, nursing and medicine aims at changing practice.

Activity 15.2

1 In your class group, appoint two people as observers. Give them the task of observing and recording what happens in normal class conditions for the next 30 minutes.
2 At the end of 30 minutes ask each observer to report on what they observed.
3 Discuss any differences in what they have reported and why. (Despite observing the same group, they may have reported different aspects of what happened.)

Observation can take many forms. It includes observation of the most casual experiences as well as the most sophisticated devices such as one-way-vision screens and video cameras. In some cases, the individuals may not know they are being observed, while in other situations the researcher will disclose themselves to the person being observed. In *participant observation* situations, the researcher becomes part of the situation which is being studied. Thus a person carrying out research in a playgroup may work as part of the team and record observations in the normal course of work.

Activity 15.3

Discuss with your class colleagues the ethical problems you might encounter in observing a group of four-year-olds in a playgroup, or alternatively observing the activities of psychiatric patients in a hospital ward.

It takes practice and careful planning to observe and record

Non-participant observation is that in which the researcher is 'outside' the working team and takes no part whatever in the activities to be observed. This type of observation is usually carried out in one of two ways:
- continuous observation where the researcher attempts to obtain the whole picture of a specified time period
- activity sampling in which activities are recorded at random time intervals.

Observation as a means of increasing one's knowledge is basic to the investigation of almost any phenomenon. In a research project one of the first decisions the observer must make is the setting. The setting is chosen with the goals of the research project in mind. For instance, if the researcher wants to study football supporters, a suitable setting would be the football ground or the supporters' club. In these settings the researcher is likely to see football supporters interacting openly and frequently. The researcher must think of an unobtrusive way to record observations in an organised manner.

Many observers try to blend with others in the settings they are observing. They may dress and act as if they belong to the group so as not to influence the interactions by their presence. Sometimes an observer also participates in the activities of the group to get a feel for the meaning these activities have for the people involved. For example, a researcher wishing to observe the activities of a local gang may join the gang and take part in them. The observer must remain alert and flexible. Keeping track of the interactions of even a few people can be very demanding.

Activity 15.4

1 What dangers are inherent in joining a group and taking part in its activities as a research method?
2 List the reasons why this method might be a good idea; then list reasons why it may not be such a good idea.

Observable behaviour

Non-verbal behaviour

Non-verbal behaviour or *body language* is 'the body movements of the individual, which consists of motor expressions which may originate in various parts of the body'. It has been said that more human communication takes place by the use of gestures, postures, position and distances than by any other method, even speech. Researchers have found that over 65 per cent of communication is done non-verbally.

Extralinguistic behaviour

Words constitute only a small portion of verbal behaviour. The impact of a message is only about 7 per cent verbal (words only) and about 38 per cent vocal (including tone of voice, inflection and other sounds). Behaviour such as rate of speaking, loudness and tendency to interrupt constitute a fruitful source of data generally referred to as *extralinguistic behaviour*. The vocal characteristic of pitch, for example, can accurately measure emotional states so that a high-pitched voice might indicate nervousness.

Linguistic behaviour

The researcher can observe how the members of a group interact verbally. For example, they may observe how members release tension in the group by making jokes, laughing or showing satisfaction. Members may give opinions, disagree, agree or show antagonism by deflating others' status, for example, by asking what a person's qualifications are or what experience a person has.

Spatial behaviour

This type of behaviour relates to an individual's attempts to structure the space around him or her. For example, people tend to move towards, move away from, maintain

closeness and maintain distance from others. Social space is deemed to be between 1.22 and 3.6 metres and public space anything over 3.6 metres. Spatial behaviour may also be considered as a type of non-verbal behaviour.

Activity 15.5

1 List two situations where it is appropriate for people to maintain closeness and two situations where it is not so appropriate. Give you reasons for each example.
2 Why do you think that observers may only see what they want to see? How would you overcome this problem in designing a research project?

Recording observations

The researcher can use check-lists to record the behaviour observed. You must give a lot of thought as to how you are going to record data. You should do this well before you start observing. You may want to record events, i.e. event sampling. *Event sampling* is just a simple count of the number of times an event occurs within a given time frame. For example, when studying children's activity within a group, you may want to count the number of times the children play with a particular toy.

Table 15.1 Record of number of times children played with a doll

Child	Number	Total
Girls		
Mary	///	3
Joan	////	4
Rebecca	/////	5
Joanna	/	1
Boys		
John	/	1
Jack	//	2
Samir		0

Recording this kind of event is simple and straightforward, but how would you record the physical behaviour of people in a group? You could use what is called a *sociogram*. Groups vary in their cohesiveness; every group has a 'preference structure' or a network of likes, dislikes and indifferences that links its members to one another. The sociogram (sociometry) was devised to enable relationships within groups to be more reliably detected than by direct observation. The essence of the technique is to ask individuals to indicate those other group members whom they most like or most dislike. A diagram (the sociogram) which summarises this information is then constructed.

Activity 15.6

1 Choose a small group for study, taking into account the following:
 • The person carrying out the experiment should be independent of the group. If you have relationships with the group members, they may be less likely to reveal their true feelings about the rest of the group. If it is not possible to find such a group, this difficulty must be recognised and taken into account.

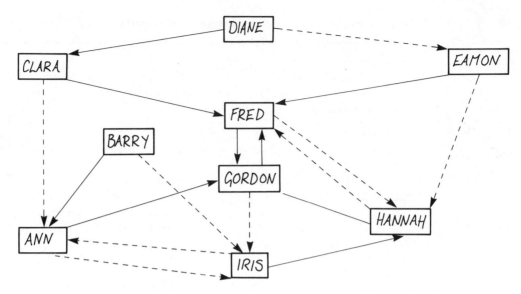

Figure 15.1 Example of a completed sociogram

- It is best to carry out this experiment with a group which is, to some degree, compelled to remain as a group, such as a class, tutorial group, sports team, people attending a day centre or residents in an old people's home.
- The ideal size of a group should be between 6 and 10 members. If it is larger than this it becomes difficult to represent in diagrammatic form.

The names of the group members should be listed and a copy of the list given to each group member.

(**Note:** It is important that you do not choose your own class to carry out this exercise.)

2 Each group member should be asked to make, privately and without consultation, two choices:
- one positive choice (e.g. Who would you like to sit next to? or Who are you most friendly with?)
- one negative choice (Who would you least like to sit with? or Who are you least friendly with?).

    These choices should be marked with some appropriate symbol (e.g. + or −) on the list of names of the group.

3 A chart should then be constructed to show each member of the group. From the data you have collected, illustrate positive relationships with a unbroken line and negative relationships with a broken line (see Figure 15.1).

Action research

Research carried out by a practitioner, social worker, teacher or nurse which focuses on questions about the researcher's profession is often called *action research*. In action research the focus of the researcher is usually a local 'one-off' situation in which the researcher wishes either to solve a problem or to evaluate the effects of a specific change involving people who are part of the situation, such as the effect of a new meal regime in a residential home. The action researcher does not attempt to hold anything constant

Table 15.2 Advantages and disadvantages of observation

Advantages

The use of video equipment allows several people to observe a situation thus ensuring greater reliability

Minimal interference in a natural system, for example a researcher observing children in a playground

Can observe non-verbal as well as verbal behaviour

Disadvantages

Participation by observers may make the situation atypical. The researcher's activity affects the group's behaviour

There may be ethical problems of confidentiality, permission, etc.

Observer may record events later and thus has to rely on memory

Selective perception is bound to operate; no one can observe everything, groups are too complex and there will be too many bits of information in even the simplest interaction

Observers may also only see what they want to see

but observes, in a systematic manner, how the people in the system cope with a local problem or how they adjust to an imposed change. Usually after the results of action research have been analysed some change for the better is implemented.

Example

> The researcher wishes to observe how both residents and staff cope with a new admissions procedure or how residents would cope with a change in regime in a home. In such situations, the researcher documents both staff and resident reaction to the changes, besides documenting the admissions process or the change in the regime.
>
> Action research has the disadvantage of being applicable only to the specific situation which is studied; it allows for no generalisation. For example, the researcher cannot generalise or say that in every home staff and clients will react in the same way to a change in the regime as they did in the residential establishment where the research was carried out. The results apply only to the situation where the research was carried out.

Activity 15.7

A researcher comparing the activity of children in two separate playgroups may have difficulty in duplicating the research with the same groups. List as many reasons as you can why this may be so.

Quantitative research techniques

Observational methods of data collection are suitable for investigating phenomena that can be observed directly by the researcher. However, not all phenomena are accessible to the researcher's direct observation. The researcher must, therefore, collect data by asking people who have experienced certain phenomenon to reconstruct them. To do this the researcher can conduct a survey using the personal interview, the postal questionnaire and the telephone survey.

The difference between quantitative and qualitative research is reflected in the language that researchers use. Quantitative researchers talk about testing hypotheses, while qualitative researchers talk about exploration, plausibility and low evidential value.

Activity 15.8

Which of the following are examples of quantitative research:
a the census?
b opinion polls?
c observation of people at work?
d market research in the high street?

Experimental research

The classic experimental design is usually associated with research in the biological and physical sciences. We talked about the positivists' attitude to research earlier in this chapter; experimental research is their main method. The main difference between experimental research and most other methods is that with the former the research situation is manipulated by the researcher. This type of experiment allows the researcher to control the process in order to prevent bias or error creeping into the research. Classical experiments are usually associated with studies in a laboratory rather than with the study of group behaviour or, say, the attitudes of residents in a hostel or voters before an election.

Experimental researchers usually test the effects of a single factor, such as a drug, temperature or teaching or social work method, upon two groups. Most classic experiments are based on the principle of an *experimental group* and a *control group*. The control group is used, for example, to see if the effect of the drug being used on the experimental group might not take place anyway, i.e. the effect might not be caused by the drug as it is seen in both groups to the same extent.

The groups must be as similar as possible in all respects except that the experimental group receives the input of the factor, such as the drug or teaching method, whose effect is to be studied. This factor is referred to as the *independent variable*.

Examples

> 1 A study of the effect of a particular drug on a group of individuals would need at least two groups selected for their similarities, i.e. age, sex, weight, illness. One group would be given a placebo, for example, a tablet or pill made of chalk which would not affect the individual in any way, while the other group would be given the drug to be tested, the independent variable. The two groups are observed for any changes as a result of taking the drug. Differences in the groups could then be attributed to the drug taken, the 'experimental factor'.
>
> 2 An ideal test to determine whether smoking causes lung cancer would be an experiment in which one group of people (subjects) was made to smoke, say, 40 cigarettes a day for ten years, and a second group of subjects, matched in all

respects to the first, were prohibited from smoking. If the first group subsequently developed cancer, one could conclude with reasonable confidence that smoking (the independent variable) has a direct affect on the incidence of lung cancer (the dependent variable).

Activity 15.9

1 How would you design a research test to find out if drinking alcohol was a factor in causing bad driving?
2 Working in small groups, discuss and list as many situations as you can think of in the health and social care field where experimental research might intrude on the rights of the individual.

It is clear that experimental methods have only limited applications in social research because they are impractical and may involve too great a restriction on human rights. Why then do we need to discuss this type of research?

The classic experimental design helps us to understand the logic of all research designs. The experimental researcher starts out with a hypothesis (see Chapter 16 for more detail about how to formulate a hypothesis) – a question or statement that the researcher want to test or provide an answer to. In the case of looking at the effect of alcohol the hypothesis may be 'the higher the alcohol level in a person's blood the more likely he or she is to think he or she can drive through a space smaller than the width of the car'. The experiment is treated as a model against which other designs can be evaluated. It also allows the researcher to draw causal inferences and observe, with little difficulty, whether or not the independent variable caused the changes, i.e. did the smoking cause the cancer or the alcohol the driving incident?

Table 15.3 The advantages and disadvantages of experimentation

Advantages

Can usually be repeated again and can contribute to the build up of a body of data

Theoretically, the most objective method likely to counteract experimenter bias

Disadvantages

In the social science field it is difficult to select and keep two similar groups constant

Surveys – descriptive research

A survey is usually carried out when the researcher wants to obtain statistical data from a large number of people. A survey is designed to obtain information from people in their natural environments. This is called *descriptive research*, i.e. the results will give a description of something, for example what certain groups think about capital punishment, sex outside marriage, or divorce. A survey may ask people about their attitudes, beliefs, plans, health, work and so on. Any human issue can be the subject of a survey.

The researcher approaches a sample of individuals presumed to have undergone certain experiences (e.g. students, residents of a home for the elderly or drug addicts). The responses obtained constitute the data upon which the research hypothesis is examined.

The best known example of survey research is the national census that is conducted every ten years. Every member of the population takes part in the this survey. Other examples are the opinion polls taken before elections when people's voting preferences are measured.

Example

One example of a major survey, that most people who work in the health and social care field will be aware of, is Townsend's work, *Poverty in the United Kingdom*, published in 1979. This survey was based on a representative sample of over 6,000 people from 2,500 households. The survey gathered data on wealth, income, work and use of social services, and was carried out between 1965 and 1968. It took ten years to analyse the data gathered.

There are a number of issues that you should think about before you embark upon a survey:
- How are you going to carry out a pilot study to test your questionnaires, interview content or method so as to identify any errors or design faults in the questionnaire or interview?
- How are you going to select your sample?
- How many people are you going to have in the sample?
- How are you going to record and analyse your data?

These issues are discussed in more detail later in this and the next chapter.

Survey research is not a new method. It began to be an important research tool during the 1930s, but its use only became truly widespread with the development of the

Table 15.4 The advantages and disadvantages of the survey

Advantages

When the research is concerned primarily with social characteristics and with information that lends itself to numerical presentation, survey research is the best way to operate

Results are valid (a concept that will be discussed later); validity is not a question of 'more' or 'less', something is simply valid or not.

Can measure attitudes, values and beliefs

Relatively inexpensive

Disadvantages

Emphasis on scope rather than depth

Interviewers may reveal biases and influence respondents answers

Even trained interviewers are not necessarily going to get over this problem as personality factors intervene, for example 'trust', an intuitive judgement made by the interviewee, can be 'taught' to interviewers

computer. This enabled rapid, accurate compilation and analysis of vast quantities of data to be quickly and easily performed. Before the development of the computer, the analysis of even simple data could take many months or years to complete.

Questionnaires

Methods such as observation are adequate for certain survey situations, but if the researcher wants to find out what a person thinks, or what he or she did last week, or why he or she reads a certain newspaper, one must ask questions and rely on the answers. Questionnaires are a standard technique used in social research. They are used to assess peoples attitudes and opinions.

The main distinction between the personal interview, discussed below, and the questionnaire is that in the latter respondents may record the answer themselves. The postal questionnaire is regarded as an impersonal survey method but under certain conditions this might be useful.

Questionnaires have to be carefully designed so that the respondent has no difficulty in understanding the questions and in knowing exactly how to record the answers. There are many difficulties to be overcome in designing a good questionnaire, for example:

- the layout of the questions needs to be addressed so that they are clear and unambiguous
- the content of the questions needs careful vetting to ensure that nobody, for example, someone from an ethnic group will be offended by the questions – questions must not be racist or sexist (see Chapter 16)
- the language used must be comprehensible and at the correct level for the target group, for example young children.

The use of questionnaires allows you to ask the questions that you want answers to. They enable you to collect data in a standard form, allowing you to analyse it (see page 388). With a questionnaire you can collect information quickly and it allows a large group of people to be questioned.

Table 15.5 The advantages and disadvantages of questionnaires

Advantages

Cheaper than other methods

Generally quicker than other methods

Avoids the problems associated with the use of interviewers (interviewer bias, attitudes of interviewer, sex of interviewer, etc.)

People tend to be more honest and less embarrassed at answering personal questions (in self-administered questionnaires)

People can take their time and consult documents to clarify answers

Disadvantages

Non-response (people may not respond) – a response rate of about 20–30 per cent is not uncommon for postal questionnaires

Questions must be simple and easily understood with the help of printed instructions

Answers have to be accepted as final. No opportunity arises to probe beyond the answer given

Mail questionnaires are inappropriate where spontaneous answers are required

There is no opportunity to supplement the respondents answer by observational data

Activity 15.10

In small groups, each select one of the disadvantages of the postal questionnaire. Discuss why it might be important to be aware of the problems caused by the disadvantages. For example, why might it be important to probe beyond the answers give in some situations? How would you encourage people to return their completed questionnaires?

Interviews

The personal interview is the method most used in social surveys to collect data even though it introduces various sources of error or bias (see page 389). It is the best method to use where the questionnaire is long and/or complex.

A *personal interview* is a face-to-face interpersonal role situation in which the interviewer asks respondents questions designed to obtain answers pertinent to the research being carried out. The interviewer may use an interviewing schedule which lists the questions to be asked and makes provision for recording the answers. Interviewing conducted by researchers has the same pattern as that used by curious non-researchers. The major difference is that the answers the researcher receives are usually carefully recorded and reviewed in terms of concepts and theories relating to the research. The interview allows the researcher to probe the intensity of an individual's feelings about a given social phenomenon, his or her definition of it and how it relates to other area of his or her life.

The schedule-structured interview

The most structured form of personal interview is the schedule-structured or highly-structured interview, in which the questions, their wording and their sequence are fixed and are identical for every respondent. The respondents in this situation do not have the opportunity to enlarge on any of their answers.

This type of interview is based on three crucial assumptions:

• that the respondents have a sufficiently common vocabulary so that the interviewer and respondent have the same understanding of the words used in the question

- that all the questions are phrased in a form that is equally understood by all the respondents
- that the sequence of the questions must be the same for all the respondents.

The semi-structured interview

In the semi-structured interview the respondent will have opportunities to answer outside the structure of the interview schedule. With little or no direction from the interviewer, respondents are encouraged to relate their experiences, to describe whatever events seem significant to them and to reveal their opinions and attitudes as they see fit. The interviewer has therefore a great deal of freedom to probe various areas and to raise specific queries during the course of the interview.

Example

'Do you think that people who kill policemen should be hanged?'
In a semi-structured interview, both those people who answer 'yes' and those who answer 'no' may be asked why they gave that answer. In a structured interview they cannot do this.
Interviews may, however, consist of structured and non-structured elements.

Table 15.6 The advantages and disadvantages of personal interviews

Advantages

The interviewer may get all the sample to respond to the questions
The interviewer can ask the respondents to explain their answers
The interviewer can see if the respondents understood the questions

Disadvantages

They are time-consuming and may cost a lot if you have to pay the interviewer
Difficult to interpret the data
Need to train interviewers
Personal interviews may intrude unnecessarily into people's lives

Sources of information

Primary sources

Primary sources are usually the first publication of a work, article or paper. Primary sources contain the original data collected in carrying out research, such as measurements from laboratory experiments, data from field observation, archive data, information gathered by questionnaires and interviews. Any results from your own research would be a primary source.

Secondary sources

Secondary sources are generally in the form of indexes and classifications of primary sources, such as text books, subject abstracts and monographs. This type of data varies from the highly quantitative statistics to the more qualitative documents, such as autobiographies, log books or diaries. These sources will suffer from the problem that they were collected for purposes other than the researcher's present work and will suffer also from the biases and inaccuracies of the author.

Major sources of secondary data are technical publications, books and journals, official publications, trade association data and computer databases.

Secondary data has considerable attractions for research students, particularly those in the social sciences and especially if they are engaged in short research projects. Secondary sources are more quickly available than primary sources and they exist in considerable quantities. However, before you use secondary sources you must evaluate how reliable the information contained in it is. You should ask:

• Who collected the data? If, for example, you were conducting a survey on the effects of cigarette smoking, how reliable would a survey carried out by cigarette manufacturers be? Similarly how would you treat a report on the side effects of a drug if the report was published by the drug company who manufactured the drug?

• For what purpose was the data collected? How was it collected? Was the sample size large enough for the results to apply to your research?

> *If possible, always go to the primary source of data.*

Example

Michael Howard, the Home Secretary, announced in 1995 a national fall of 5.5 per cent in recorded crime – the largest reported fall in 40 years. In Greater Manchester crime was reported as falling 12 per cent in 1994. However, in South Yorkshire the crime rate rose by 5 per cent. Were people in South Yorkshire more likely to be the victims of crime?

Researchers have looked at these figures to try an explain the differences. They found that crimes had been reclassified, which in turn affected the figures. Some police forces no longer record crimes such as malicious telephone calls, vandalism, deception, minor criminal damage and assaults. This lack of recording could have accounted for the fall in reported crime in some areas.

In South Yorkshire the Chief Constable, concerned about reports that some of his officers were not reporting crime, found that there was an above average number of reports of damage to houses where the damaged was valued at £20 or more. Those houses where the damage was valued at under £20 were not reported in the crime statistics. The Chief Constable stopped this practice and this could account for the rise in crime in South Yorkshire.

Activity 15.11

Choose an area of study such as residential care, day care, or out-patient departments. Using the resources in your school or college library make a list of primary and secondary sources of information or data for your chosen subject.

Tertiary sources

This category of data includes sources which facilitate the location of primary and secondary sources; it includes, for example, handbooks, bibliographies and encyclopedias.

Sampling methods

Selecting a sample

At first glance, it sounds a very simple exercise to select a sample. We sample things every day; for example, people sample wine or food in a supermarket. In practice, good sampling is a far from easy matter. For example, to be fully comprehensive and accurate a survey should be completed by everyone to whom it applies. If you wish to find out about how users of a cinema feel about it, in the ideal situation you should ask every user. This would, however, take too long and would be very expensive. You must therefore question a *sample* of the users.

How large should the sample be?

Activity 15.12

Asking your friends in a pub about drinking would be likely to give you a biased set of answers. Discuss with your class colleagues why this would be so?

The size of the sample will depend on what you want to do with the results. If you want to generalise, then you must interview as large a sample as possible. If you only interview six mothers who use a day nursery on a Friday, you cannot state that their views represent those of the users on the other days of the week. If you want to generalise about users of the day nursery, you must interview all users or a sample of those who use it every day.

Activity 15.13

a If you wanted to find out how people in your locality feel about their local councillors and it was only possible to interview people in the high street one morning at 11 a.m., which groups of people might be missed out on any day?

b How would you go about getting a fully representative sample?

The size of the sample is important but to believe you have a good sample is not just a matter of knowing how large the sample is, it also depends on how well you have chosen the sample. The principles underlying all sample design are:

● to avoid bias in the selection procedure

● to achieve the maximum precision for the resources available.

The goal of science is to find uniformity's or 'patterns' in nature. Obviously scientists cannot examine all instances of the data they are studying. For example, the botanist cannot look at all plants, or the social scientist all juvenile car theft. A poor sample can be disastrous – it can provide misleading information and result in errors. Even if researchers cannot observe all of the population, for example all people with an experience of hospital admission, they will wish to be able to generalise to all similar cases from the data they collect. The problem is how can the researcher be sure that the sample studied will be representative or similar to the rest of the people (population) who were admitted to hospital at some time?

A *population* may be a group of people, students, people over 65 years of age, residents of a home, shoppers or home owners. The specific nature of a population depends on the purpose of the investigation or research. The first step is to define the population to be sampled. This task is not as easy as it sounds. No sample of a population is perfectly representative; the smaller the sample, the more unrepresentative it will be. If you wished to interview students in your college or school about their attitude to a particular issue, could you interview every student? Would you chose five from every class or form? If you decided to do this, how would you select them? Would they be representative of the rest of the students? Similarly, if you wished to interview people who used a meals-on-wheels service, would those who received meals on Monday be representative of people who received them at weekends?

If you are going to generalise from your results to the general population then you must choose your sample according to the rules of statistical theory. It may be wrong to select, say, volunteers, friends or people who happen to be at hand.

Finally, the idea of sampling is not new and it is economical. It is obviously cheaper to collect information from 100 students than from 1,000. Sampling also saves labour and time.

Random sampling

Random does not mean 'haphazard'; it means the very opposite. It implies a very careful pre-selection plan. A random method of selection is one which gives each of the *units* (people) in the population to be studied a calculable probability of being selected. Each member of the population to be studied has an equal chance of being selected for the sample.

How might we draw a random sample? First, as already mentioned, you need to define the population which you wish your sample to represent.

Example

> If you wish to study students at your particular college, you first need to define what you mean by a student:
> - Who is included in the population?
> - Do you want to include full-time and part-time students?
> - Do you wish to include Youth Training trainees?
> - Do you wish to include students over 65 years of age?

When you have clarified the target population, you need to locate or complete a list of all of its members, say every full-time student under 65 years of age (a *sampling frame*). If you do not have such a list then random sampling cannot be used and other methods will be more suitable. Many lists are suspect and do not list all the population. A telephone directory is not an adequate listing of people in a town because it will not include people who cannot afford a telephone or those who wish their telephone number to be unlisted.

Assuming that you have a list (sampling frame) of all the members of the population you wish to study, how do you select your sample? There are a number of methods of probability sampling.

Simple random sampling

Simple random sampling is the basic probability sampling design. It gives each of the known (N) sampling units of a population an equal chance of being selected. To ensure that this happens one of the following methods may be used.

The lottery method

Each member of the population is represented by a disk or a piece of paper with his or her name or a number corresponding to his or her name on the list. The pieces of paper or disks are placed in a box, mixed well and a sample of the desired size is drawn. Every member of the population has an equal chance of being selected.

Table of random digits

The random number tables were devised to meet the two criteria of random selection:
- each number has the same chance of being selected
- each number is independent of the others.

The procedure is simple. Each member of the population is listed and numbered. A number is selected from a table of random digits. Each number that appears in the table of random digits corresponds to the numbering of a sample unit in the list. That sampling unit is selected for the sample. The process is continued until the desired sample size is reached. Random numbers can also be generated by computer.

Example

> You have a population of 100 students and you want a 10 per cent sample. You list all the students serially and give each one a number from 1 to 100. Randomly decide where to start in the table of random numbers (Table 15.7). Select one column and one row at random. For example, suppose you chose the 13th vertical column and the 9th horizontal row. The point on the table is numbered 17. Thus, the first number is 17. You therefore identify that person and number on the list of your sample. You next read down the column and find the next number which

> is 13; that person is also included on your sample list. You continue down the column until you have selected ten numbers (17, 13, 69, 55, 88, 80, 72, 75, 92, 18). The ten chosen people will be a random sample of the population you wish to study.

Table 15.7 1,000 random digits (part of)

1	36	45	88	31	28	73	59	43	46	32	00	32	67	15	32	49	54	55	76	17
2	90	51	40	66	18	46	95	54	65	89	16	80	95	33	15	88	18	60	56	46
3	98	41	90	22	48	37	80	31	91	39	33	80	40	82	38	26	20	39	71	82
4	55	25	71	27	14	68	84	04	99	24	82	30	73	43	92	68	18	99	47	54
5	02	99	10	75	77	21	88	55	79	97	70	32	59	87	75	35	18	34	62	53
6	79	85	55	66	63	84	08	63	04	00	18	34	53	94	58	01	55	05	90	99
7	33	53	95	28	06	81	34	95	13	93	37	16	95	06	15	91	89	99	37	16
8	74	75	13	13	22	16	37	76	15	57	42	38	96	23	90	24	58	26	71	46
9	06	66	30	43	00	66	32	60	36	60	46	05	(17)	31	66	80	91	01	62	35
10	92	83	31	60	87	30	76	83	17	85	31	48	13	23	17	32	68	14	84	96
11	61	21	31	49	98	29	77	70	72	11	35	23	69	47	14	27	14	74	52	35
12	27	82	01	01	74	41	38	77	53	68	53	26	55	16	35	66	31	87	82	09
13	61	05	50	10	94	85	86	32	10	72	95	67	88	21	72	09	48	73	03	97
14	11	57	85	67	94	91	49	48	35	49	39	41	80	17	54	45	23	66	83	60
15	15	16	08	90	92	86	13	32	26	01	20	02	72	45	94	74	97	19	99	46
16	22	09	29	66	15	44	76	74	94	92	48	13	75	85	81	28	95	41	36	30
17	69	13	53	55	35	87	43	23	83	32	79	40	92	20	83	76	82	61	24	20
18	08	29	79	37	00	33	35	34	86	55	10	91	18	86	43	50	67	79	33	58
19	39	29	99	85	55	63	32	66	71	98	85	20	31	93	63	91	77	21	99	62
20	65	11	14	04	88	86	28	92	04	03	42	99	87	08	20	55	30	53	82	24
21	66	22	81	58	30	80	21	10	15	53	26	90	33	77	51	19	17	49	27	14
22	37	21	77	13	69	31	20	22	67	13	46	29	75	32	69	79	37	23	32	43
23	51	43	09	72	68	38	05	77	14	62	89	07	37	89	25	30	92	09	06	92
24	31	59	37	83	92	55	15	31	21	24	03	93	35	97	84	61	96	85	45	51
25	79	05	43	69	52	93	00	77	44	82	91	65	11	71	25	37	89	13	63	87

Systematic samples

Using the simple random sampling method, each member of the population under study is given a number, and then a subgroup is taken for study. For example, if we wished to study a subgroup of your school or college, every student would be given a number, and then the subgroup, say a particular class or students of a particular age or hair colour, would be taken for study.

Systematic sampling consists of selecting every 10th, 20th or 30th (Kth) person (sampling unit) of the population after the first person (sampling unit) is selected at random from the first K sampling units. So if you wished to select a sample of 100 students from a population of 1,000 at a college, you take every 10th student ($K = N \div n$, where K is the interval of selection, N is the total population and n is the sample. (So, $1{,}000 \div 100 = 10$). The first selection must be chosen by the random process.

Suppose the fourth person was selected, the sample would then consist of students numbered 4, 14, 24, 34, 44, 54 and so on.

Stratified sampling

This method can only be used when there is detailed knowledge of the population under study. It is usually used when there are variations in the sample. Stratified sampling is used primarily to ensure that different groups of a population are adequately represented in the sample. For example, if you knew that the student population was made up of 20 per cent female students and 80 per cent male, a simple random sample might not give you a representative sample of these groups. You may find that all females have been selected. The survey would then tell you little about the male population.

The answer to this problem is to draw from each group a random sample proportionate to the size of the group; you will then be sure of having both male and females in your sample.

Non-probability sampling

If a list of a population is not available this type of sampling may be used. In non-probability sampling, there is no way of specifying the probability that each unit has been included in the sample; there is no assurance that every unit has some chance of being included. The major advantages of this type of sampling are convenience and economy.

Convenience sampling

A convenience sample is obtained when the researcher selects whatever sampling units are conveniently available. Thus you may select only students in your class or the first 100 people you meet in the street who are willing to be interviewed.

Purposive sampling

Sometimes this method is referred to as *judgement sampling*. The researchers attempt to obtain a sample that appears to them to be representative of the population they wish to research. The chance that a particular person will be selected depends on the subjective judgement of the researcher.

Quota sampling

The aim of this method is to try and select a sample that is as closely as possible a replica of the population to be researched. For example, if it is known that the group to be researched has equal numbers of male and female, the researcher selects an equal number of both. If it is known that the group or population has only 20 males then the researcher would select an appropriate percentage.

Activity 15.14

A large college is to open a new creche. The Principal is to hold a wine and cheese party after the official opening and at this party the Principal wishes to invite representatives of each of the sectors in the college in proportion to the numbers working in each sector. There is only space for 50 people at the party. How many will be chosen from each of the following sectors:

Sector	Numbers working in the sector
Health and social care department	50
Engineering department	78
Business and finance department	60
Building supervisors staff	20
Catering staff	26
Admin./clerical	100

Review questions

1 List the most common purposes of research.

2 Carrying out a research project raises a number of ethical issues. What questions should you ask yourself before you embark on any research project? Explain your answers.

3 Explain what is meant by qualitative research.

4 Explain what is meant by action research and discuss its advantages and disadvantages.

5 Outline the differences between experimental and observational research. Give an example of each.

6 Explain what is meant by primary and secondary data. Give an example of each.

7 **a** Identify appropriate examples of the main advantages of using the following data collection techniques:
  - structured questionnaire
  - observation.

  b In which situations would you use these methods?

8 Define what is meant by the following sampling methods:
  a random?
  b stratified?
  c quota?

Assignment 15.1
The interview

This assignment provides knowledge, understanding and portfolio evidence for element 8.1, **Investigate the research process.**

One of the major tools of the social scientist – the in-depth interview – is also a favourite of the average person in the street. Everyone at some time or another has used this technique to learn about a subject of interest. The researcher starts by asking a general question and following up the answers with increasingly specific questions until he or she has acquired 'an understanding' of the topic.

Ordinarily, an in-depth interview will last about 1 to $1\frac{1}{2}$ hours. You must carry out about five to ten such interviews to obtain some notion of the kinds of information that may be pertinent to the research problem. However, because your time is limited, your assignment is to carry out four 30 to 45 minute interviews.

You will be required to word process this assignment and present it in that form for assessment.

Your tasks

Planning

1 Choose an area to study. Read and analyse two research studies on the subject – one should be a quantitative study and the other a qualitative study. Identify the different research processes in both of these research studies.

2 Choose a subject for the interview – one that people usually have strong feelings about, such as child abuse, abortion, euthanasia, hanging or the government. Read as widely on the subject as you can before you begin to design any questions.

3 Think of a few neutral questions, say six, that will put the person you are interviewing at ease and that will lead him or her into your chosen subject.

4 Think of some more specific questions to follow that will give you a greater insight into the interviewee's feelings on the subject.

5 Decide whom you will need as respondents. For example, if your chosen subject was abortion, you might consider interviewing:

- rank and file respondents – people in the street
- participants in positions of authority – ministers of religion, MPs, councillors, teachers
- so-called 'well-informed people' – members of organisations for and against abortion, politicians, radio personalities, etc.

The interview

6 Depending on whom your are interviewing, talk to respondents about their feelings on the subject matter. Write down their answers as nearly verbatim as possible (i.e. in the interviewees' own words, not in a summary form by you).

7 Read over each interview before embarking on the next. Watch for points that you will want to follow up in this and subsequent interviews.

Presentation

8 By the time you have finished your interviews, you should have some interesting information concerning the topic you have chosen to investigate. Read your interviews and make notes concerning points you wish to make and the questions you wish to use in your report.

9 Write a report including the following:

- a brief statement stating the topic of study and explaining what aspect of that topic you intend to study
- a brief list of questions you asked in the order in which they developed, from the introductory ones to those that are more focused
- an explanation of why and how you selected participants; your sampling technique
- an explanation of why at least two other sampling techniques were not thought more suitable to use
- a discussion of your findings and the supporting evidence, taken from interviews, to back them up
- a discussion of the pertinent areas or hypotheses for further study
- a discussion of the problems you encountered in carrying out the interviews and any suggestions you have for surmounting them in the future
- a list sources of information and a bibliography.

16 Planning and producing health and social care research findings

What is covered in this chapter

- Defining a research problem
- Designing questionnaires and interviews
- Forms of response
- Analysis and interpretation of data
- Basic statistics
- Presentation of data
- Production of the final report

These are the resources you will need for your portfolio for element 8.2:
- You will need to undertake at least one piece of research into health and social well-being and /or related services and facilities using quantitative and qualitative methods of analysis. This may be achieved either within one piece of research combining both, or with two difference pieces of research. The research questions should be of interest to you and be ones which you can obtain reasonable answers to in the time and with the resources available.

These are the resources you will need for your portfolio for element 8.3:
- You should present your final substantial research project, or two or three smaller pieces of research. Evidence should contain both quantitative and qualitative methods of analysis where these are combined in one piece of research. Alternatively, you should present two pieces of research, one which uses quantitative and which uses qualitative methods of analysis.

Finally:
- Your written answers to the activities, review questions and assignments in this chapter.

Defining a research problem

A research project is a major undertaking and planning is necessary if you are not to waste time and effort. The first thing you will need to consider is the purpose of your research. Are you going to:
- review existing knowledge,
- describe something new, or
- explain some situation or event?

A good definition of a research problem aims to develop a realistic plan of action with clear objectives which take account of:
- resources, and
- constraints

and has a high probability of being achieved. One way to achieve this is to look at a broad subject area that you are interested in. For example, if you are interested in unemployment there are a number of major areas that you could look at (see Figure 16.1).

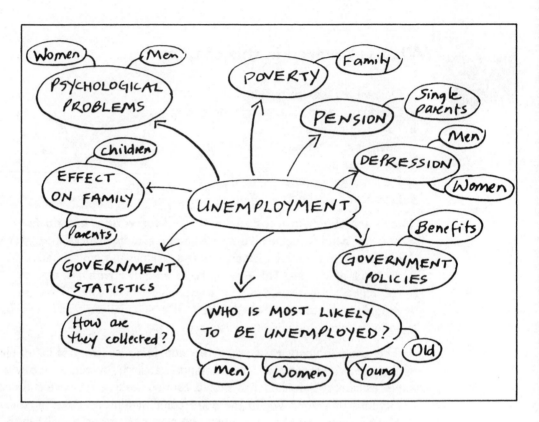

Figure 16.1 Some possible research questions

One way to link up ideas based upon a single concept, such as unemployment, is to produce a diagram like that in Figure 16.1, write down all the ideas that you can think of relating to unemployment and how they interact with each other.

When you have drawn a map of ideas like that shown in Figure 16.1 you can see that there are many aspects to unemployment. For example, you could look at the psychological aspects of unemployment, in particular what psychological effects it might have on men compared to women.

When you have finally agreed on an area of interest to study the next step is to develop a hypothesis.

Hypothesis

Not all research projects need a hypothesis, but you *must* have a clear idea in your mind of what you are planning to do. You may want to analyse a general problem (see below). However, let us assume that you want to carry out a piece of research that needs a hypothesis. A *hypothesis* is a proposition that can be tested, or the naming of the phenomenon which is to be tested. Any idea or theory which makes provisional predications is called a hypothesis. For example:

- All social care students are female.
- All engineering students are male.
- Sports enthusiasts are less likely to smoke than people who take no part in sports.

The view of the issue that the researcher holds has an impact on the formulation of the hypothesis. You may believe that all social care students are female but if you are to set out to prove it you must have an open mind and keep an objective approach to the research design. You set out to support or contradict the hypothesis.

The difference between problems and hypotheses

A few examples will help clarify the distinction between problems and hypotheses, and how hypotheses are constructed and expressed.

Problems are general questions. For example:

- What causes inflation?
- Who uses a playgroup?
- What types of student pass examinations?
- What causes football violence?
- Who becomes a leader in a group?
- What causes child abuse?
- What is the gender make up of engineering students?

The researcher can then generate a hypothesis based on a general question.

Examples

1 From the general question, 'Who becomes a leader in a group?', a hypothesis about how leaders develop in a group could be expressed as follows:
'As inter-group conflict increases, those people who are more aggressive and who are able or articulate are given power by the group.'
The researcher will then devise a strategy to observe behaviour in one or more groups to support or contradict the hypotheses.

2 'What causes child abuse?' The researcher may feel that those who have suffered abuse as a child are likely to abuse their own children. The hypothesis could be formulated as follows:
'Individuals who have experienced violent and abusive households are more likely to grow up to become child abusers than individuals who experience little or no violence in their childhood.'

Hypotheses can be derived from theories, observation, intuition or a combination of these. Ideas and background to any potential idea can be obtained by consulting bibliographies, indexes, abstracts, professional journals and statistical sources. It does not matter if your research findings do not support your hypotheses. Unexpected findings often are the most interesting.

Research problems are intellectual stimuli calling for an answer.
Hypotheses are tentative answers to research problems. Hypotheses should be clear, value-free and amenable to testing.

Activity 16.1

Generate a hypothesis based on the following general question:
Does having a certain number of GCSEs indicate whether students can obtain a GNVQ at Advanced level?

Planning

Once you have agreed on an area to study your next step is to look at what you need to do to complete your research, in effect a *research action plan*. How much time have you got to complete the work? Your tutor will have given you some idea of this – can you complete what you want to do in the time given? How much reading will you have to do? Are the books, journals and papers readily available or will the school or college librarian have to get them from another source? How long could this take?

If you have decided that your research needs interviews, how many people do you need to interview? How do you select your sample? Where are they? Have you time to interview as many as you would like? If not, what are you going to do about it? If you are going to use questionnaires, how long will it take you to design them?

How are you going to analyse your results? How long will it take you to write up your report? How accessible is your college computer resource – do you need to book a computer in advance?

When drawing up you research action plan you will need to answer all of these questions.

> **Summary of research aims**
> Before you construct a questionnaire or an interview you must carry out some background reading and research into the subject of your research. This will give you some ideas of the questions that you should be asking. You should read books, journals and leaflets to gain some general ideas about your project. It might also be useful to read other research papers which involved questionnaires, and other publications and statistics relevant to your area of study.
> If you want to draw up tables and graphs from your data you will need to ask questions which allow for only a limited number of answers. This will allow easier analysis of the results.

Designing questionnaires and interviews

Gathering and collecting data

When the researcher has formulated a hypothesis he or she has to decide how to gather or collect data. In the social sciences the most widely used methods are:
- the questionnaire
- the personal interview
- observation.

The foundation of all questionnaires is, of course, the question. Instead of observing what people do, would you get more relevant information if you asked people what they are doing or asked them their views on what they are doing? A questionnaire is simply a list of questions which provides a relatively fast, effective and cheap method of obtaining information.

The personal interview is a face-to-face, interpersonal situation in which the interviewer's questions are designed to obtain answers which are relevant to the research hypotheses. The interview can be tightly structured, with the interviewer asking questions from a prepared questionnaire or it can be open with scope to ask further questions in order to probe the respondent's feelings more deeply (see *Types of interview*, below).

Sometimes the researcher may make use of the self-administered questionnaire (see page 394).

A good questionnaire requires a lot of thought and planning You must ask yourself:
- What questions am I going to ask?
- Who am I going to ask?
- How am I going to record the answers?
- What am I going to do with the results?

Types of interview

There are two main types of interview:
- the structured interview
- the unstructured interview.

Structured interviews

The structured form of interview is one in which the questions, the wording and their sequence are fixed and identical for each respondent. Any variations which appear in the responses can be attributed to the actual differences between the respondents and not to variation in the interview.

Structured interviews provide an objective exercise and the tendencies toward bias are less than with observation or unstructured interviews. A major advantage is that the information can be easily coded and analysed.

It is important to give a lot of thought to the design of the questionnaire, as structured interviews are only as good as the questions asked. It is also important to frame the questions in a language that the respondents will understand:
- avoid woolly generalisations
- avoid bias that might encourage the respondents to give an answer that you want them to give.

Example

Question 1		Code
How often do you watch soaps on television?		
Never	☐	1
Every week	☐	2
Two or three times a month	☐	3
Once a month or less	☐	4
Question 2		
How much money do you spend on cigarettes each month?		
Less than £50	☐	1
£51–80	☐	2
£81 or more	☐	3
Question 3		
Do you go to the cinema? Yes/No		1　　2

If your answer is no, is it because:		
You don't like what's showing?	☐	3
You prefer to watch it on video?	☐	4
It costs too much money?	☐	5
You are worried about the cigarette smoke?	☐	6
Other reasons please state:		7

There are many problems with framing questions for structured questionnaires. Some questions may be unclear, or use words that the respondent may not understand.

Leading questions

These questions encourage the respondent to say 'Yes', therefore, the following two questions are biased:

- Do you think that women should not work until their children are old enough?
- Don't you agree that there is too much violence on television?

The following is a more subtle example of a leading questioning situation:

Interviewer	What brand of soap do you use?
Respondent	Pearly pink
Interviewer	Why do you like Pearly Pink soap?
Respondent	Ah...um...I have never really thought about it.
Interviewer	Well try to give me an answer. (Pause) Is it because of its smell?
Respondent	Yes, it's got a nice smell.

The interviewer writes down that the respondent liked the soap because of its smell. But perhaps the respondent was not prepared to admit that they liked the soap because it was the cheapest brand on the market or was helping get rid of their facial spots.

Questions which presume

These questions presume that the respondent has done the actions defined in the question:

- When did you last go to a pop concert?
- How many cups of coffee have you had?

Double questions

These are questions with more than one part:

- Do you think that the college should spend less money on books and more on sports facilities?
- Do you think that there is too much violence at football matches and that this is responsible for the lowering of standards in society?

Activity 16.2

Compare the following two questions. Which question expects the answer 'yes' and which the answer 'no'?

a Do you think people should be free to provide the best medical care possible for themselves and their families, free of interference from the state?

b Should the wealthy be able to buy a place at the head of the queue for medical treatment, pushing aside those with greater need, or should medical care be allocated only on the basis of need?

Unstructured interviews

The least structured form of interviewing is the unstructured, or non-directive, interview in which respondents are given no direction from the interviewer. They are encouraged to relate their experience and to reveal their opinions and attitudes as they see fit. It allows the respondents to express their opinions as well as answer the questions. The respondents can let you know their real feelings about the subject of the question and, therefore, tend to answer more freely and fully.

Example

> Your task is to discover as many specific kinds of conflicts and tensions between children and parents as possible. The four areas of possible conflict we want to explore are listed in question 3. The first two are to allow you to build up a rapport with the respondent.
> 1 What sort of problems do teenagers have in getting along with their parents?
> 2 What sort of disagreements do you have with your parents?
> 3 Have you ever had any disagreement with either parent over:
> staying out later? ☐
> friends of the opposite sex? ☐
> dating? ☐
> smoking? ☐
> drinking? ☐

Activity 16.3

1 When interviewing, do you think that there are situations when the respondent might feel inhibited?
2 Discuss with you class colleagues the effect on the outcome of an interview that the following scenarios might have:
   a a white interviewer and a black respondent
   b a male interviewer and a female respondent.

The principles of interviewing

The aim in interviewing is to get the desired information. This can be done by following a few simple guidelines:
- The person you are interviewing needs to feel that the interview will be pleasant and satisfying.
- Interviewers should present themselves as being understanding and easy to talk to.
- The people being interviewed need to feel that the study is worthwhile.
- The interviewer also needs to overcome the respondent's suspicions.
- The interviewer should explain in a friendly manner the purpose of the study and the confidential nature of the interview.

How can you put people at ease?

- Tell the respondent who you are and who you represent, and explain to them what you are doing in a way that will make them interested in your research.
- Tell the respondent how and why they were chosen to be interviewed. Any instructions should be brief.
- Create a relationship of confidence between yourself and the person you are interviewing.

Types of question

There are basically two types of questions:
- factual questions
- opinion or attitude questions.

Factual questions

Factual questions elicit objective information. The most common type of factual questions obtain information such as sex, age, marital status, education or income of respondents.

Example

At what age did you get married?	
16 years	☐
17 years	☐
18 years	☐
19 years	☐
20 years	☐
21 years	☐
Over 21 years	☐
Please tick the appropriate box.	

Other factual questions could elicit information about a respondent's social environment, for example, 'How may people are living in your household?'; or their leisure activities, for example, 'How often do you go to the pub?'

Opinion or attitude questions

Opinion or attitude questions are more difficult to construct. Before we examine how to develop an opinion or attitude question, we must first examine the difference between an 'attitude' and an 'opinion'.

An *attitude* is the sum total of a person's prejudices, ideas, fears and convictions about any specific topic. *Opinions* are the verbal expression of attitudes.

Activity 16.4

Which of the following are opinions and which are attitudes?
a John says he likes Liverpool Football Club.
b Mary refuses to allow her son to marry an Irish girl.
c Jim is convinced that anyone over 65 years of age should not work.
d Peter says that a woman's place is in the home looking after children.
e Jim refuses to allow his wife to go out to work after the birth of their first child.

To obtain data about factual matters or attitudes, you can ask two types of question:
- closed questions
- open questions.

Closed questions

In closed questions respondents are given a set of answers from which they are asked to choose one that closely represents their views (see Example 1).

Closed questions are easy to ask, quick to be answered and their analysis is straightforward. Answers can be more elaborate than open questions (see Example 2).

Examples

1 Managing is a man's job.
   - Strongly agree   ☐
   - Agree   ☐
   - Disagree   ☐
   - Strongly disagree   ☐

2 Do you feel that you are really part of your class group?
   - Really a part of my class   ☐
   - Included in most ways   ☐
   - Included in some ways, but not in others ☐
   - Don't feel that I really belong   ☐
   - Don't fit in with any class   ☐

   Please tick the appropriate box.

Open questions

Open questions are not followed by any kind of specified choice – the respondents' answers are recorded in full. For example, the question 'What do you personally feel are the most important problems the government should try to tackle?' is an open question. The virtue of this type of question is that the respondents can express their thoughts freely, spontaneously and in their own way.

What type of questions should you use?

In which situations should you use the different type of questions? The following points should be considered:

- **The objectives of the questionnaire** Closed questions are suitable when you want to find out if the respondent agrees or disagrees with a point of view. If you want to find out how the respondent arrived at this view, an open question is more appropriate.
- **How much does the respondent know about the topic in question?** Open questions give you the opportunity to find out how much the respondents know about the topic. Obviously, it is futile to ask any questions that are beyond the experience of the respondent.
- **Communication** How easily can the contents of the answers be communicated by the respondent?
- **Motivation** How motivated is the respondent to answer the questions?

How to encourage people to complete and return questionnaires

With all surveys there is the problem of people who may refuse to fill in your questionnaire or simply forget to do so. This makes your results less accurate. If your response rate is low, what can you do to improve it?

There are various methods that you can use to improve the response rate, including:

- **Follow-up** Write or telephone the people who have not responded.
- **Length of questionnaire** The shorter the better, as longer questionnaires tend not to be answered.
- **Who gave out the questionnaire** If the respondents know you or the college, then they are likely to reply. However, where questions are of a confidential nature this may not be the case; in these instances you must stress confidentiality in your introductory letter.
- **Introductory letter** An appeal to the respondents to emphasise that they would be helping the interests of everyone seems to produce the best results.
- **Method of return** A stamped addressed envelope produces the best results.
- **Format of the questionnaire** A title that will arouse interest helps, as does an attractive and clear layout with plenty of room for hand-written answers.

The self-administered questionnaire

The self-administered questionnaire, as a method, is cheaper than others and avoids the problems, such as bias, associated with the use of interviewers. It may handed out to people or sent through the post, to be completed in the respondent's own time.

The self-administered questionnaire has some positive advantages. People are more likely to express less socially acceptable attitudes and feelings when answering a questionnaire alone than when confronted by an interviewer. The greater the anonymity the more honest the response. Aside from the greater honesty that they may produce, self-administered questionnaires also have the advantage of giving a respondent more time to think.

This type of survey gives no opportunity for the respondent to probe beyond the answer given. The questions should be simple and straightforward, and be understood with the help of minimal, printed instructions.

Forms of response

Rating

One of the most common formats for questions in social science surveys is the rating scale. Here, respondents are asked to make a judgement in terms of strength of feeling.

Example

> Old people should not be allowed to live on their own if they are very dependent.
> 1 Strongly agree ☐
> 2 Agree ☐
> 3 Disagree ☐
> 4 Strongly disagree ☐
> 5 Don't know ☐
> Please tick the appropriate box.

These responses reflect the intensity of the respondent's judgement.

Ranking

Ranking is used in questionnaires whenever the researcher wants to gather data regarding the degree of importance that people give to a set of attitudes or objects. For instance, in a survey on the quality of life of students, respondents could be asked to rank in order various dimensions they considered important to student life.

Example

> I would like you to tell me what you have found important in student life. Would you please look at this card and tell me which of these is most important to you as a goal in your student life, which comes next in importance, which is third and so forth?
>
> Meeting other students
> 1st rank
> 2nd rank
> 3rd rank
> 4th rank
>
> Academic life
> 1st rank
> 2nd rank
> 3rd rank
> 4th rank
>
> Sport activities
> 1st rank
> 2nd rank
> 3rd rank
> 4th rank
>
> Student's union
> 1st rank
> 2nd rank
> 3rd rank
> 4th rank

Ranking is a useful device in providing some sense of relative order among judgements. It is important particularly in the social sciences where a 'numerical value' cannot be applied.

The rank order method is an extremely easy method to use. One of the most basic assumptions is that attitudes towards various statements may be expressed along a continuum from least to most favourable.

Semantic differential measuring method

The semantic differential measuring method is one of the most adaptable yet, ironically, under-utilised scaling methods in the social sciences. This scale, with minor variations, is adaptable to any attitude measurement. The *semantic differential* measures a subject's responses to stimulus – words, concepts or phrases – in terms of bipolar (opposite to each other) adjective ratings. An example is shown in Figure 16.2.

With a list of such bipolar adjective scales, it is possible to measure the effect experienced by any person towards any statement.

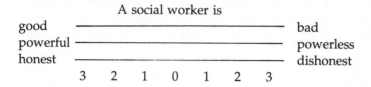

A social worker is

good	————————————	bad
powerful	————————————	powerless
honest	————————————	dishonest

        3   2   1   0   1   2   3

Figure 16.2 A bipolar adjective rating scale

Activity 16.5

Design a bipolar adjective scale to measure people's attitudes to the role of the police.

Analysis and interpretation of data

Validity

Validity is defined as the degree to which the researcher has measured what he or she set out to measure. Validity also provides a direct check on how well the questions fulfil their function, the determination of which usually requires independent, external criteria of whatever the questionnaire is designed to measure. Validity refers to whether the researcher is really measuring what he or she says is being measured. For example, a questionnaire asking home helps what they do for clients may not produce valid data indicating what they actually do in the clients' homes; the results may not be valid. The only way to find out what a home help actually does in a client's home is to observe him or her doing it. This data would be valid.

Do the questions asked in a survey actually measure the concepts the researcher intended them to measure? For instance, from the wording of a question, the researcher assumes that the respondent who agrees that 'all policemen are hostile' is indicating a distrust of the police. Undoubtedly, one of the most important questions that needs to be raised regarding any questionnaire relates to the validity of the questions, i.e. do the questions actually measure what they purport to measure?

Example

A measuring tape may measure in feet or metres, not in pounds or grams. You do not measure height by standing on a weighing scale.

Tests for validity

One of the common tests for validity is *face validity*. For example, if the concept the researcher wishes to measure is 'How satisfied is a person with his or her car?', the question 'Do you like your car?' has face validity because it is relevant to the concept in question and it is unambiguous. The answer that you will get from such a question will usually make sense. Face validity can be checked by discussing the questions in a questionnaire with respondents, who can give their opinions as to their validity (do they make sense?). For example, if you are constructing a questionnaire on the work of the district nurse, then asking members of that profession about the relevance of your questions would go some way to providing face validity.

The question you should, therefore, ask yourself is, 'Will the questionnaire look valid to the subjects who respond to it and to the personnel who make use of it?'

Reliability

Reliability should be distinguished from validity. It refers to consistency – to obtaining the same results again and again under similar circumstances. Will the same methods used by other researchers produce the same results? *Reliability* refers to consistency between independent measurements of the same phenomenon.

Many argue that in the social sciences 'true' answers do not exist. True answers may exist, but they may change over time. However, some sort of criterion is available which can be applied to the realm of 'factual questions' such as, 'Is bathing residents part of your job?' or 'Do you think that shaving residents is part of your job or someone else's?' Such questions would produce a true answer, if the researcher could find time to observe the member of staff at work. If another researcher asked the same staff the same questions the answers ought to be the same, i.e. show high reliability. If questions are poorly phrased and obscure, the respondent may answer differently to the same question on different occasions. The answers may reflect the respondent's current mood.

It is rare for researchers to obtain perfect reliability between independent measurements in the social sciences. Your questions may not be interpreted in the same way by the respondents the second time around.

Basic statistics

Statistics is a science that deals with the collection and analysis of numerical data. It can be divided into two main areas called descriptive and inferential statistics. *Descriptive statistics* are methods of summarising properties of data such as frequency, central tendency and variability. *Inferential statistics* are methods of generalising from properties of samples to properties of populations. For example, if after carrying out a survey of the work of staff in a children's home you find that staff give no choice of menu to children, could you infer that this would be the case in every children's home. You might be able to extrapolate (infer that it would happen in other establishments) that it would happen if your sample had been selected in a proper manner. You could not extrapolate if you had studied only one establishment.

Shapes of frequency distribution

One of the main reasons that we use statistics is to describe sets of numbers in a brief and understandable way. It is difficult to deal with information when it is presented in the form of large groups of numbers. It takes time to read through them and is difficult to see the wood for the trees. A way must therefore be found to present data in a manner that can be understood. One way to do this is to find out what the average is.

Mean (or arithmetic mean)

If we collect a large number of results we could split up the total range of values into a large number of small intervals and calculate the proportion of results falling into the intervals. If we mark in this proportion, at the midpoint of each small interval, and then join up the points we get a frequency distribution. For any given distribution researchers want some measure of the centre of the distribution. The most widely used is the mean.

The mean is the measure to which we usually refer in everyday life when we use the word 'average'. The *mean* can be defined as the value each item in the distribution would have if all the values were shared out equally among all the items. It is a measure of central tendency. For a sample, the mean is simply calculated by adding together all the values and dividing the result by the total number of values. The mean for a distribution is the sum of the scores divided by the number of scores. It is by far the most useful of all measures of central tendency and has the advantage of taking into account all the values in a distribution.

The formula for calculating the mean is:

$$X = \frac{\Sigma x}{n}$$

Example

Calculate the mean for the sample scores 3, 6, 8, 9, 10

$$X = \frac{\Sigma x}{n} = \frac{3 + 6 + 8 + 9 + 10}{5} = 7.2$$

Table 16.1 Age of residents in Summervale Residential Home

Resident	Age
Jack	65
Mary	66
Eamon	68
Joan	80
Mary	75
Joanne	76
Peter	70
Jose	86
Ken	90
Alice	88
Mark	94
Clia	98
Patrick	106
$n = 13$	Total ages 1062

Example

From the data in Table 16.1, the mean age for this sample is 81.69 years. This was calculated as follows:
List the numbers (ages) in a vertical column
Add the numbers (ages) together = 1062 years

Count the number of items (residents) making up the list to get n
As the list comprises 13 residents therefore $n = 13$
Divide the total (1062 years) by the value of n (13), so $1062 \div 13 = 81.69$.
Therefore, the mean, or average age, of residents is 81.69 years.

$$X = \frac{\Sigma x}{n} = \frac{1062}{13} = 81.69$$

This method is not as easy to use as the other two averages, the median and mode, and it takes time to calculate. Also it is not suitable to use with all sets of data. The mean may not be of the same value as any of the individual sets of data. For example, none of the residents in Table 16.1 was 88.5 years of age. If numbers in your data vary widely then the mean can mislead. For example, in Table 16.1 the youngest resident was 65 and the oldest was 106. Other measures can be used to give a more meaningful picture.

Activity 16.6

1 Calculate the mean of the following, 36, 21, 6, 18, 78, 90, 5, 67, 66.
2 Is the following set of data a suitable one on which to use this formula (the mean)?
30, 30, 30, 30, 30, 30, 56, 78, 30, 30, 30.

The median

The *median* is that value in a distribution such that exactly one-half of the scores are less than or equal to it, and exactly one-half are greater than or equal to it. The purpose of the median is to determine the exact mid-point of a distribution. The median measure of the central or middle point of the distribution is the value of the central result when the values are arranged in order of magnitude. If you want to obtain a figure that represents the central point then the median is a useful measure to use.

If we have an odd number of results then the median is simply the value of the middle result. If we have an even number as, in Table 16.2, then there is no single middle result, and we take the average of the two middle results. The two middle results are 80 years and 86 years $(80 + 86) \div 2 = 83$ years.

Table 16.2 Age of residents (in order of magnitude) in High View Residential Home

Resident	Age
Peter	70
Mary	75
Jack	78
Joan	80
Jose	86
Alice	88
Ken	90
Mark	94
Total (8)	661

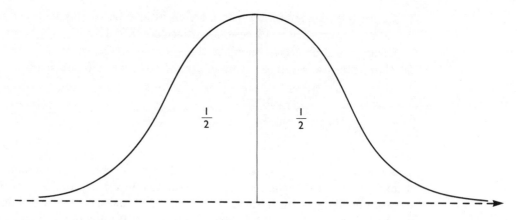

Figure 16.3 Frequency distribution showing the median

The median is sometimes a useful estimate of the middle of a distribution when the distribution is not symmetrical, i.e. when there is a long tail on one side and not on the other. An example of this would be salaries where most people have fairly moderate salaries, but a small number have very large ones. Most people would have salaries below the mean. This kind of distribution, which is not symmetrical, is called *skewed*. In this case, the median salary would be a sensible estimate of the middle of the frequency distribution of salaries. Half the individuals would have salaries below this and half above.

This method is less useful when we have many numbers but on the other hand it is not affected by extreme values. Would it be appropriate to use the median if you had the following set of figures – 24, 26, 31, 36, 37, 37, 38, 109, 140?

Activity 16.7

Calculate the median for the following values:
a 22, 33, 45, 46, 48, 89, 99
b 4, 6, 9, 23, 44, 44, 48, 78, 90
c 5, 5, 5, 5, 9, 9, 9, 9, 9
d 14, 15, 15, 16, 16, 16, 16, 18, 18, 18, 18.

Mode

Another measure of the middle of the distribution is the mode. This is the most popular value, or the value that occurs most often, i.e. the score that has the highest frequency.

In the following set of figures the number 11 occurs most often so it is the mode: 2, 3, 6, 7, 11, 11, 11, 11, 13, 15, 17.

The mode is a useful measure of the middle of a distribution when the variable the researcher is interested in is *discreet*, that is, confined to certain restricted values. For example, the mode would be useful as a measure of the number of children in a family in the UK. If the most frequent number of children in a family is, say, 2, then the modal value would be 2. One of the reasons that you might want to use the mode is when you want to indicate a 'normal' value or figure.

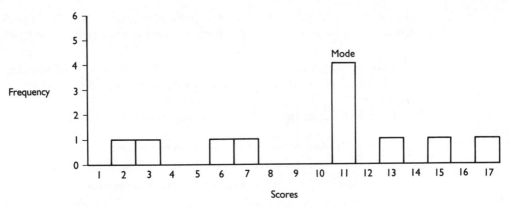

Figure 16.4 Frequency distribution showing the position of the mode for the above data

Choosing a measure of central tendency

> Use the mean when the scores in a distribution are more or less symmetrically grouped about the centre.
> Use the median when extreme scores may distort the mean.
> Use the mode when all that is required is an approximate value of central tendency.

Using statistics to help simplify and describe data is only the first step in analysing the results of a research study. The rest of the analysis is concerned not so much with the specific subjects that the researcher has tested (the sample), but with what those subjects can tell the researcher about a larger group (the population).

Frequency distribution

The data that we have been looking at so far have all been in 'sets' or 'groups'. In this section we shall be looking at the distribution of the 'sets' or 'groups' of numbers or values. Finding a single figure that indicates the location of a distribution is not easy. The distribution may be spread out over a wide range of values and to chose one to represent its location is like trying to find a single person who can represent one student in a college or one patient in a hospital. When data are purely quantitative, the simplest way is to count the number of cases in each category.

Example

> In an analysis of the census of students in a large college, one of the variables of interest was the number of males and females in each faculty. To summarise the data, we count the number of students in each faculty by sex. The results are shown in Table 16.3.

Table 16.3 Number of students by faculty by sex

Faculty	Engineering	Social care	Science	Art
Male	300	20	400	250
Female	20	200	100	200
Total	320	220	500	450

The count of individuals having a particular quality is called the *frequency* of that quality. The frequency for male students in the science faculty is 400. The proportion of individuals having that quality is the *relative frequency* or *proportional frequency*. The relative frequency of male students in the science faculty (of all students) is 400 ÷ 1,490 = 0.27 or 27 per cent. The set of frequencies is called the *frequency distribution* of the variables.

Table 16.4 is another example of a frequency distribution.

Table 16.4 Number of students by marks in examination

Marks	Number of students (frequency)
20-29	2
30-39	3
40-49	8
50-59	12
60-69	13
70-79	7
80-89	4
90-99	1
Total	50

An arrangement such as that in Table 16.4 is called a *grouped frequency distribution*. It shows the overall pattern clearly; in this case a bunching of observed values in the middle. This way of presenting information does not tell you what actual marks the individual students obtained.

Measures of dispersion

The median, mode and mean are single numbers which indicate the central tendency or location of that number on a scale. Each is incomplete as a descriptive measure, because it does not tell us anything about the scatter or *dispersion* of the values or set of numbers from which it is derived. In some cases these values will be clustered closely, as in Table 16.2, while in other cases they will be scattered as in Table 16.1.

The importance of dispersion can be see from a simple example. Say that we tested a sample of four light bulbs of type A, and found that the bulb life was (in turn) 20, 23, 25 and 26 months, assuming that each bulb was used for two hours daily. The mean life of the A bulb is 23.5 months. Next we tested four bulbs of make B and found that they lasted 4, 10, 25 and 55 months. The mean life for these bulbs is also 23.5. In such cases we need a way of specifying that the life of make B bulbs is more variable than make A.

If you were planning activities for adults attending a day centre and you were told that the mean age of those expected to attend was 25 years, it would be helpful to know the range of ages. Are those expected all within the range 20 to 30 years? If so, you could plan activities for this age group but if some 60-year-olds are expected some other activities might be more suitable. One way to specify the variability of data is to simply state the range.

The range

The *range* is the difference between the smallest and largest observation. The range is the simplest measure of variability and tells us about the interval between the highest and lowest scores in a distribution. It is calculated by subtracting the lowest score from the highest score. In the case of the B light bulbs, with a mean life of 23.5 months, the range is $55 - 4 = 51$ months. This wide range is because of the rather low and very high values at the extremes. This problem, however, can be overcome by working out the range between the lower and upper quartiles.

If we have a set of measurements or values arranged in order of size, the *lower quartile* is that value which has a quarter of the observations below it and three quarters of the observations above it. The *upper quartile* has three quarters of the observations below it and one quarter above it. If the quartiles fall between observations, they are given a value which is the mean of the number on either side of them. Below is an example of quartile positions based on the set of numbers for the A bulb:

20/23 25/26

The lower quartile falls between 20 and 23, so has a value of 21.5; the upper quartile has a value of 25.5. The *inter-quartile* range is therefore $25.5 - 21.5 = 4$ compared to the full range of 6. However, when we look at the set of data for B bulb the inter-quartile range is 33 (compared to the full range of 51 months). This shows that the inter-quartile value is less affected by extreme values than the range. The inter-quartile range gives a more reasonable indication of the dispersion in these two examples than does the full range.

Because the range takes account only of the two most extreme scores it is limited in its usefulness since it takes no account of how the scores are distributed. The problem of extreme scores can be overcome by using the inter-quartile range which uses the central half of the scores to calculate the range.

Standard deviation

The best measure of dispersion around the mean is the standard deviation (see Figure 16.5). Like the mean the standard deviation takes all the observed values into account. If there were no dispersion at all in a distribution, all the observed values would be the same. No value would differ from the mean. However, in real life the observed values always deviate from the mean; some a lot, some a little. The larger the dispersion, the

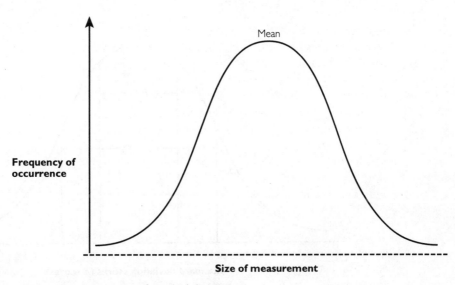

Figure 16.5 Pictorial representation of standard deviation

bigger the deviations and the larger the standard deviation. The *standard deviation* is calculated as follows:

- all the deviations (differences) from the mean of the set of numbers are squared;
- the mean of the squares is then calculated;
- the square root of this mean is the standard deviation.

Example

Let us look at what the standard deviation is for the following set of values 111, 114, 117, 118, 120 (mean = 116).

Value	111	114	117	118	120
Deviation from mean (116)	−5	−2	+1	2	+4

Note that if you take an average (mean) of the deviations they add up to zero − the negative deviations will always cancel out the positive ones. To overcome this difficulty each deviation is squared; this gets rid of the minus signs.

Deviation from mean (116)	−5	−2	+1	+2	+4
Squared deviation	25	4	1	4	16

The mean of the squared deviations is called the *variance*.

$$\text{Variance} = \frac{25 + 4 + 1 + 4 + 16}{5} = \frac{50}{5} = 10$$

To obtain the standard deviation we take the square root of the variance and the result is then the standard deviation.

Standard deviation of distribution = $\sqrt{10} = 3.16$

The standard deviation is therefore 3.16.

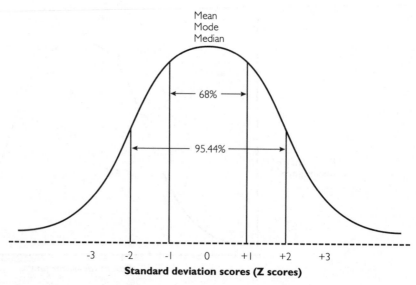

Figure 16.6 The normal distribution

If the standard deviation is large, then there is much dispersion around the mean. If the standard deviation is small, then the degree of dispersion is much less. The standard deviation does not in itself tell us much; on its own it is of limited value. It comes into its own when you have a number of sets of data and you wish to compare standard deviations.

A *normal distribution* has about 68 per cent of all scores lying within one standard deviation either side of the mean and approximately 95 per cent within two standard deviations of the mean. You can use these percentages to give you some idea of the proportion of the values you could expect to find within certain limits.

The normal distribution is a bell shaped curve as illustrated in Figure 16.6. The three measures of central tendency, the mean, mode and median all lie on the same point on the curve. The term 'normal distribution' does not mean that it is the typical or most often observed distribution. Normal is used in the sense that the bell shaped curve is a 'norm' or idealised version of a distribution against which you can compare the distribution of your data.

When you have a normal distribution you have 50 per cent of the observations on each side of the centre. The standard deviation is a way of showing how much your data vary from the mean.

Relationships between variables

One helpful technique when examining the association between two variables is to examine their joint distribution on a scattergram (see Figures 16.7 and 16.8). A *scattergram* is a plotting in which the position of each observation is designated at the point corresponding to its joint value on the dependent and independent variable. The *independent variable* is plotted on the horizontal axis and the *dependent variable* on the vertical axis. If the points that you plot bunch together like a thin tube (see Figure 16.7) the association between the variables is strong but if they bulge out at all sides like a balloon (see Figure 16.8), the association is weak.

Example

> You might want to investigate if there is a relationship between how many books a student reads and the student's age – see Figure 16.7. Age is the independent variable and so is plotted on the horizontal axis.

In Figure 16.7 there is a positive correlation between the two variables. Negative correlation is shown on the second diagram in Figure 16.9.

You might normally expect to find that the larger the discount on the disks the more (volume) that you might sell. However, the data in Figure 16.8 show that there is little relationship between the discount given and the numbers sold.

Presentation of data

Information or data can be presented in the form of:
- diagrams
- graphs
- pie charts
- tables.

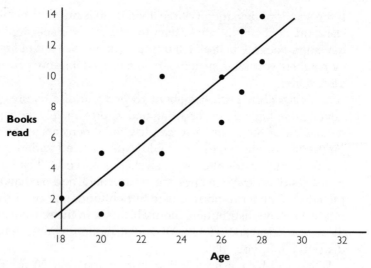

Figure 16.7 A scattergram

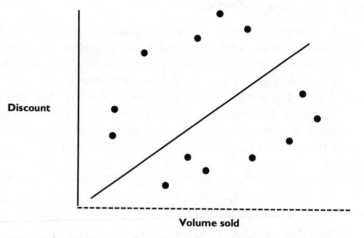

Figure 16.8 A scattergram showing the relationship between the volume of blank floppy computer disks and the size of discount offered

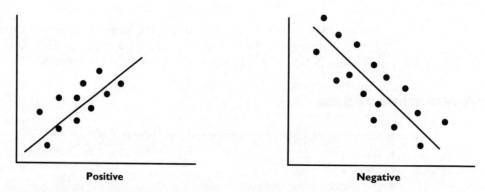

Figure 16.9 Example of scattergrams showing negative and positive relationships

Each of the four different methods helps you to present information in an understandable and logical way.

Diagrams

Diagrams are a way of presenting a lot of information in picture form. A good diagram will help you cut down on the amount of writing you would otherwise have to do to describe the information presented in it.

Graphs

A bar chart or graph shows the relationship between two variables; one is usually quantitative and the other qualitative. Information can be presented in a variety of graphical forms. Graphs can be used to show changes in a particular variable over a given period of time. The graph can be used to reinforce points made in writing.

Bar graphs

Examples of bar graphs are shown in Figures 16.10, 16.11 and 16.12.

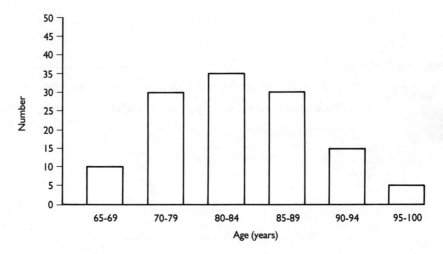

Figure 16.10 Bar graph to show the number of elderly people admitted to day care in Uptown Local Authority, by age, 1995

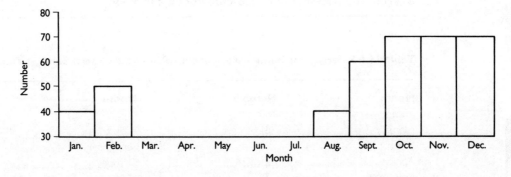

Figure 16.11 Bar graph to show the number of elderly people in residential care in Uptown Local Authority, by month, 1995

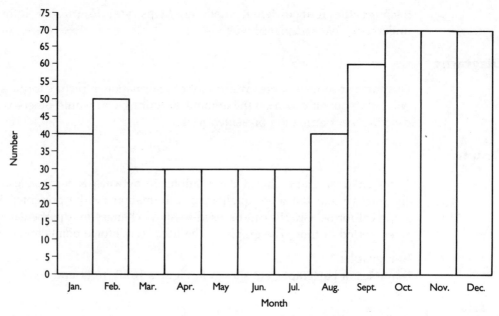

Figure 16.12 Bar graph to show the number of elderly people in residential care in Uptown Local Authority, by month, 1995

Activity 16.8

1 Construct a bar graph from the data in Table 16.5.

Table 16.5 Children on the child protection register at 31 March 1995, by age

Age	Number
1–4	200
5–8	67
9–12	100
13–15	75
16+	8

2 Look at the graphs in Figures 16.11 and 16.12. Although they give the same information, do they look different? Do they seem to be conveying the same message? Discuss the reason why they look as if they are giving different messages based upon the same data.

3 From the data in Table 16.6 construct a bar graph.

Table 16.6 Referrals for home care support to Downside Social Services Department, 1995

Month	Number	Month	Number
January	100	July	55
February	81	August	50
March	84	September	60
April	81	October	70
May	73	November	75
June	60	December	85

Line graphs

A line graph is another useful way to illustrate increasing or decreasing values. An example is given in Figure 16.13.

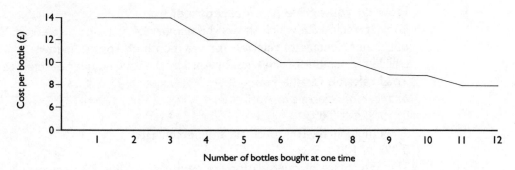

Figure 16.13 Line graph to show the advantages of buying wine in bulk

Activity 16.9

I Look at the graph in Figure 16.13 and consider the following questions:
  a What is the cost of one bottle?
  b What is the cost of five bottles?
  c What is the cost of seven bottles?
  d What is the cost of ten bottles?

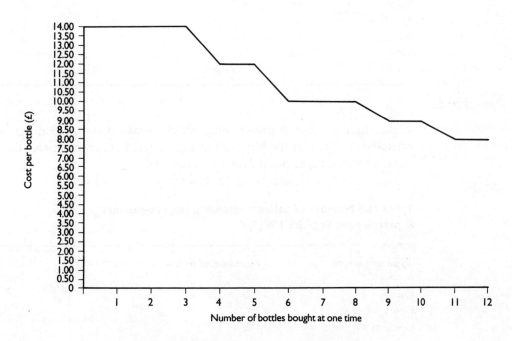

Figure 16.14 Line graph to show the advantages of buying wine in bulk

2 Compare Figures 16.13 and 16.14. Why does it look as if a bottle of wine is more expensive in Figure 16.14?

How do you arrive at a percentage?
Look at Table 16.6 which shows the number of home care referrals. We can work out the percentage of referrals for the month of April as follows:
Divide the number of referrals for April by the total number of referrals for the year:
Total referrals for the year = 874
Number of referrals in April = 81
81 ÷ 874 = 0.093
Then multiply by 100 to obtain the percentage:
0.093 × 100 = 9.3
The percentage of referrals for the month of April is 9.3 per cent.

Activity 16.10

Look at the information in Table 16.7. Copy the graph axes and draw either a bar chart or a line graph using the data in the table.

Table 16.7 Health care assistants by age

Age	Number	Percentage
Under 20	19	1.5
20–29	163	9.0
30–39	433	24.0
40–49	643	36.0
50/–59	418	23.5
60+	101	6.0
Total	1,777	100.0

Pie charts

A pie chart is a visual presentation which breaks down a total figure into different components. Look at the pie chart in Figure 16.15 which illustrates the percentages of patients attending as out-patients at a hospital.

The percentage figures were derived from Table 16.8.

Table 16.8 Number of patients attending the out-patients department at St Jack's Hospital

Type of patient	Number of patients
Adults	400
Children	200
Elderly 60–79 yrs	100
Elderly 80+	100
Total	800

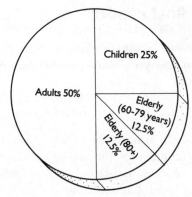

Figure 16.15 Pie chart to show the percentage of patients attending the out-patients department at St. Jack's Hospital

Activity 16.11

Construct a pie chart to illustrate the data in Table 16.9.

Table 16.9 Qualifications held by Uptown Social Services Staff

Qualifications	Number	Percentage of staff
Cert. Social Service (CSS)	86	9.9
Diploma in Social Work	180	20.7
Management	20	2.3
GNVQ	26	2.6
Other	23	3.0
None	532	61.5
Total	867	100.0

Tables

Tables enable you to show much more data than, for instance, a bar graph. Table 16.10 shows the response rate to a postal questionnaire which was sent to a sample of home helps (Group A) and a sample of auxiliary nurses (Group B) in a national survey.

Table 16.10 Response rates to a postal questionnaire

| | Group A | | Group B | |
	No.	%	No.	%
Questionnaires distributed	1,302	100.0	1,961	100.0
Questionnaires returned	1,170		1,482	
Uncompleted questionnaires	133		144	
Total analysed	1,037	79.6	1,338	68.2

From the data in Table 16.10 we can see that although Group B were sent more questionnaires (1,961), the percentage response (68.2 per cent) was lower than in Group A (79.6 per cent).

Production of the final report

There is no one way to organise a research report. Your tutors will also have their own ideas about how your final write up should look. The following headings are provided as guidelines.

1 Title

The title should indicate the nature of what you have been researching. For example 'A report on attitudes of further education students on smoking' or 'A survey of the workload of care assistants in four residential establishments for the elderly in Downtown Local Authority'.

2 Summary

It may appear strange that a summary of what you have done appears at the beginning of the report and not at the end. A summary (abstract) is written so that other readers can quickly see if the research is of interest to them before they read the main body of the report. The summary should be about 100 to 150 words long explaining what you did, your methods and results.

3 Introduction

In the introduction you should give the reader a general description of the research problem that you have looked at, why you are undertaking the work and what your hypothesis is. You can also give a clear picture of the aims of your research.

4 Review of the literature

You should give a review of the literature that you have read directly relating to you research. This gives the reader an overview of the field that you are studying.

5 Methodology

Under this heading you should describe your methodology, how you chose and sampled your population, how you developed your questionnaire, etc. You should provide enough information so that anyone reading your report could repeat your research if they wished.

6 Results

This section gives you the opportunity to present your results. To do this you can use tables, graphs or any other medium to present your data. Do not put your working calculations or computer printouts in this section; keep all this type of data for the appendix, if appropriate.

7 Analysis and discussion

This is where you discuss to what extent your results support or do not support your original hypothesis. This can be done by discussing your results and providing the evidence from these results to support (or otherwise) your hypothesis. You can also discuss your methodology and any problems that you have encountered, and what you could do to overcome them if you had the chance to carry out the research again.

8 Conclusions

Present any conclusions you have drawn from your results and any recommendations that you might wish to make based on these results.

9 List of references

You must give detailed references for all the sources that you have used in your report. There are a number of ways that you can do this. For example, if you have used quotes from Edwards & Talbot p.35 (1994) in your text then the reference could appear as:

Edwards, A., & Talbot, R. *The Hard-pressed researcher*, 1994 Longman.

If you quote from a journal then the reference could read:

Garnham, N., & Williams, R. (1980) 'Pierre Bourdieu and the sociology of culture', *Media, Culture and Society*, Vol. 2 No. 3 Academic Press.

Review questions

1 Give an example of the main advantage of using observation as a data collection technique.
2 In what situation would an in-depth interview be the most appropriate way to collect information?
3 What are the main disadvantages of the observation method of collecting information?
4 Explain what is meant by the term 'random sample'.
5 a Give an example of a rating scheme and why you would use it.
  b Devise a rating scale for a question of your choice.
6 Suggest two examples of how statistics may be misused.
7 Explain what is meant by the term 'measure of probability'?
8 Give two examples of a 'frequency count'?
9 What is meant by the term 'semantic differential'?
10 Give two examples of probes and prompts to support open questions.
11 Give an example of a situation in which you would use one of the following:
  a frequency count
  b mean
  c mode
  d median.

Assignment 16.1
Planning and data gathering

This assignment provides knowledge, understanding and portfolio evidence for element 8.2, **Plan research into health and social care and gather data.**

Your tasks

1 Choose an area of health or social care well-being, or health and social care services that interests you. You may want to find out your student colleagues' opinions on smoking or attempt to find out what users think of a particular service or facility.

2 Define your rationale for the research you want to carry out:

- *Research questions* What are you attempting to find out? (This is a study of the opinion of 200 students on what they perceive the effects of smoking to be on individuals' physical health.) Why do you want to research this particular subject?
- *Target audience* Describe the people to which you are going to present the completed report/research (e.g. colleagues, the wider public, teenagers, young children).
- Are there any links to previous work carried out in this field?

3 *Data collection:*

- Describe what is meant by primary and secondary data.
- Describe what type(s) of data you have used in completing your research.

4 *Research methods*

- Describe the different kinds of methods for obtaining data.
- Describe the methods you have used and say why the methods you did not use were unsuitable for your particular research project.
- Describe what is meant by quantitative and qualitative methods of analysing data.
- Describe in detail the method you have used and why. Outline how you selected your sample. State why methods you did not use were though unsuitable for your research.

5 *Appropriateness of research*

- Was the overall research as designed fit for the purpose?
- Bearing in mind your sample (type, size, etc.), what extent, if any, can the research you have carried out be generalised?
- What effect might your research have on those who participated?

6 *Ethical issues*

- What are the possible benefits of your piece of research?
- In carrying out your research, have you considered any effects of your work on the participants?
- Is confidentiality an issue for your research project?
- Did you keep in mind the rights of participants when designing your research?
- Were you aware of the effects upon the research of your background and culture?

Assignment 16.2
Surveying residents in a home for the elderly

This assignment provides knowledge, understanding and portfolio evidence for element 8.3, **Produce and present health and social care research findings.**

Scenario

You have recently taken up a post as junior research officer in a social service department. Your first task is to conduct a survey of residents in White Leas home for the elderly to find out some information about the residents.

The home has 50 residents and you have selected 25 from which to obtain data.

1 Describe three sampling techniques that you could use to obtain a representative sample of the population in the home.

2 The home has 40 female and 10 male residents. How would you ensure that you included male and female representatives in your sample?

3 The ages of the population you have selected are:

72, 74, 76, 72, 76, 76, 77, 76, 78, 72, 80, 77, 98, 72, 73, 74, 76, 79, 100, 87, 92, 72, 80, 82.

   a What is the number sampled as a percentage of the total population of the home?

   b Express the number of 72-year-olds selected as a percentage of the total population sampled.

   c Express the number of 76-year-olds in the sample as a percentage of the total population.

   d Draw up a frequency distribution table from the above data showing the frequency of distribution of residents in the home.

   e Calculate the range of the sample.

   f Calculate the mean age of the sample

   g Calculate and explain the mode of the sample population.

   h Calculate the mean average distribution of the sample population.

   i Calculate the standard deviation of the sample population.

Bibliography

Unit 1: Equal opportunities and individual rights
Littlewood, R. and Lipsedge, M., *Aliens and Alienists: Ethnic Minorities and Psychiatry* (Penguin, 1981)
National Occupational Standards for Care (Unit 0), Care Sector Consortium, 1992
Sacks, O., *The Man Who Mistook His Wife for a Hat* (Picador, 1985)
The Black Report, *Inequalities in Health* (DHSS, 1980)

Unit 2: Interpersonal interaction in health and social care
Bateson, J., *Do we need service marketing?* Marketing Consumer Services: New Insights Report (Marketing Services Institute, November 1977)
Biestek, F.P., *The Casework Relationship* (Unwin University Books, 1957)
Cowell, D.W., *The Marketing of Services* (Heinemann, 1984)
Gronross, C., *Strategic Management and Marketing in the Service Sector* (Swedish School of Economics and Business Administration, Helsinki, 1982)
O'Connor, J. and Seymour, J., *Introducing Neuro-Linguistic Programming* (Mandala, 1990)
Pease, A., *Body Language* (Sheldon Press, 1984)
Porras, J., *Stream Analysis* (Addison-Wesley, 1987)

Caring for Mary, a highly recommended video-based learning programme that addresses many of the interpersonal aspects of health and social care, within the context of the care value base (available only from Educare, telephone or fax 0114 2681075)

Unit 3: Physical aspects of health and social well being
A Manual of Nutrition (Ministry of Agriculture, Food and Fisheries)
Clare, A., *Psychiatry in Dissent* (Tavistock, 1980)
Clegg, A.G. and Clegg, P.C., *Man Against Disease* (Heineman) – unfortunately now out of print
Proposals for nutritional guide-lines for health education in Britain, prepared for the National Advisory Committee on Nutrition Education (NACNE, 1983)
Roberts, M.B.V., *Biology: A Functional Approach* (Nelson, 1986 [4th edition])
Simkins, J. and Williams, J.I., *Advanced Human Biology* (Unwin Hyman, 1987)

Unit 4: Psychological and social aspects of health and social care
Ahmad, W.I. (ed.), *Race and health in contemporary Britain* (OUP, 1993)
Argyle, M., *The Psychology of Interpersonal Behaviour* (Harmondsworth, Penguin, 1967)
Birren, J.E. and Renner, V.J., 'Research in the psychology of ageing: Principles and experimentation', in J.E. Birren & K.W. Sehaie (eds.) *Handbook of the psychology of ageing* (New York, Van Nostrand Reinhold, 1977)
Blau, Z.S., *Ageing in a changing society* (New York, Watts, 1981)
Bowlby, J., *Child Care and the growth of love* (Harmondsworth, Penguin, 1953)
Briggs, A., *Who Cares? Report of a door to door survey of people caring for dependent relatives* (Privately produced paper, Whitley Bay, 1981)
Coleman, J.C. and Hendry, L., *The Nature of Adolescence* (2nd Edition) (London, Routledge, 1990)

417

Collin, A., *Mid-life Crisis*, (Working paper No. 14 Dept. of Management Studies, University of Loughborough, 1977)

Cumming, E. and Henry, W., *Growing Old* (New York, Basic, 1961)

Department of Health, *The Health of the Nation: a strategy for health in England* (London, HMSO, 1992)

Erikson, E., *Identity: Youth and Crisis* (New York, W.W. Norton, 1968)

Erikson, E.H., 'Identity and the life cycle' *Psychological Issues* (1; 1–171, 1951)

Fitton, F. and Acheson, H.W.K., *Doctor/Patient Relationship: A Study in General Practice* (London, HMSO, 1979)

Fozard, J.L., Nuttal, R.L. and Waugh, N.C., 'Age related differences in mental performance', *Ageing and Human Development* (1972, 3, 19–43)

Freud, A., 'Adolescence' in A.E. Winder and D.L. Angus (eds.) *Adolescence: Contemporary Studies* (New York, American Books, 1968)

Freud, S., *Psychopathology of everyday life* (Harmondsworth, Penguin, 1914)

Friedson, E., *Profession of Medicine* (Dodds & Mead, New York, 1970)

Friedson, E., 'Dilemmas in the doctor-patient relationship', in *A Sociology of Medical Practice*, (eds.) C. Cox & A. Mead (London, Collier Macmillan, 1970)

Goffman, E., *Asylums* (Doubleday, 1961)

Gruen, W., 'Adult personality: an empirical study of Erikson's theory of ego development' in B.L. Neugarten *et al*, *Personality in Middle and Later Life* (New York, Atherton, 1964)

Hagan, J. *The Disreputable Pleasures* (Toronto, McGraw-Hill, 1984)

Hartshorne, H. and May, M., *Studies in the nature of Character* (New York, Macmillan, 1930)

Havighurst, R., *Human Development and Education* (New York, Longman, 1953)

Havighurst, R., 'Personality and patterns of Ageing' *The Gerontologist* (New York, 1968)

Hebb, D.O., *The Organisation of behaviour* (New York, John Wiley, 1949)

Holmes, T.H. and Rahe, R.H., 'The social readjustment rating scale', *Journal of Psychosomatic Research* (11, 213–1218, 1967)

Jewson, N. 'The disappearance of the sick man from medical cosmology' *Sociology* (10, 224–44, 1976)

Kelly, G.A., *The Psychology of Personal Constructs* (New York, W.W. Norton, 1955)

Laing, R.D., *The Divided Self* (Penguin, 1960)

Lay, P., 'Towards Better Doctor-Patient Communication' in *Communication Between Doctors and Patients*, edited by A. Bennett (Nuffield Hospital Trust, London, 1976)

Mares, P., Henley, A. and Baxter, C., *Health Care in Multiracial Britain* (Health Education Council, 1985)

Neugarten, B., 'Personality and ageing' in J.E. Birren and K.W. Shaie (eds.) *Handbook of the psychology of ageing* (New York, Van Nostrand Reinhold, 1977)

Parkes, M. *Bereavement; Studies in Grief in Adult Life* (Penguin, 1975)

Piaget, T.J., *The Language and Thought of the Child* (Routledge and Kegan Paul, London, 1959)

Riley, M.W., 'Social Gerontology and the age stratification of society', *Gerontologist* (New York, 1971)

Rose, A.M., 'A current theoretical issue in social gerontology', in A.M. Roise and W.A. Peterson (eds.) *Older people and their social world* (Philadelphia, Davis, 1965)

Sacks, O., *The man who mistook his wife for a hat* (Picador, 1985)

World Health Organisation, Report on the Primary Health Care Conference (Alma Ata, 1978)

Sorenson, R.C., *Adolescent Sexuality in Contemporary America: Personal values and Social behaviour, Ages Thirteen to Nineteen* (New York, World, 1973)

Young, A., 'The relevance of traditional medical cultures to modern primary health care', *Soc. Sci. Med.* (17, 1205–1212, 1983)

Zborowski, M., 'Cultural Components in Response to Pain', *Journal of Sociology*, issues 8–16–30 (1952)

Unit 5: The structure and development of health and social care services

Bennett, O.J., 'Elder Abuse in Britain', *British Medical Journal* (305: 998–999, 1992)

Caplan, G., *Principles of Preventative Psychiatry* (Basic Books, New York, 1964)

Cartwright, A. and O'Brian, M., 'Social Class Variations in Health Care in General Practitioner Consultations', in *The Sociology of the NHS* (Sociological Review Monograph No. 22 Ed. M. Stacy, University of Keele, 1976)

Charities Digest (Family Welfare Association, 1993) – an annual publication

Guide to the Social Services (Family Welfare Association, 1993) – an annual publication

Hamm, C., *Health Policy in Britain* (Macmillan, 1992 [3rd edition])

Korsch, B., Gozzi, E. and Francis, V., 'Gaps in doctor-patient communication: acceptance of advice in general practice', *New England Journal of Medicine* 280, 535–40)

Ley, P. and Spelman, M., *Communicating with the patient* (Staples Press, London, 1967)

Miliband, R., *Marxism and Politics* (Oxford University Press, 1977)

Moore, S., *Social Welfare Alive* (Stanley Thornes, 1993)

Ottewill, R. and Wall, A., *The Growth and Development of the Community Health Services* (Business Education Publishers Ltd, 1990)

Promoting Better Health, Department of Health (HMSO, London, 1987)

Sheffield's Community Care Plan 1994/95 (Family and Community Services Department, Sheffield)

Stoyle, J., *Caring for Older People: A Multi-cultural Approach* (Stanley Thornes, 1991)

The Health of the Nation Department of Health (HMSO, London, 1992)

Tossell, D. and Webb, R., *Inside the Caring Services* (Edward Arnold, 1986)

Townsend, P. and Davidson, N., *Inequalities in Health* (Penguin, 1991)

Walker, A. (ed.), *Community Care: The Family, the State and Social Policy* (Basil Blackwell and Martin Robertson & Co. Ltd, 1982)

World Health Organisation 1961 Constitution: Basic Documents (15th Edition, Geneva)

Unit 6: Health and social care practice

Care Management and Assessment: The Practitioner's Guide (HMSO, 1991)

Caring for People: Information Pack for the Voluntary and Private Sectors (Department of Health, 1993)

Community Care in Lancashire: Care Assessment and Care Management, Paper 1, 1992

Hall, J., 'Assessing People and Patients' in Hall, J., *Psychology for Nurses and Health Visitors* (Macmillan, 1988)

Langan, M., and Day, S. (eds), *Women, Oppression and Social Work* (Routledge, 1992)

National Health Service and Community Care Act (HMSO, 1990)

Payne, M., *Modern Social Work Theory* (Macmillan, 1991)

Swain, J., Finkelstein, V., French, S. and Oliver, M. (eds), *Disabling Barriers – Enabling Environments* (The Open University/Sage, 1993)

Witz, A., *Professions and Patriachy* (Routledge, 1992)

Unit 7: Educating for health and social well-being

Caplan, G., *Principles of Preventive Psychiatry* (Basic Books, New York, 1964)

I. Simmett, *et al*, *Promoting Health: A Practical Guide to Health Education* (John Wiley, 1985)

Ewles, L. and Simnet, I., *Promotion Health: A Practical Guide* (Scutari Press, London, 1992)
Open University, *The Good Health Guide* (Pan Books, 1980)
Sarason, S.B., *Work, Aging and Social Change* (Free Press, 1977)

Most of the statistics in Chapter 9 were obtained from published government sources. An abstract of such information is published annually by HMSO in *Social Trends*.

Unit 8: Research perspectives in health and social care

Clegg, F., *Simple Statistics: A Course Book for the Social Sciences* (Cambridge University Press, 1982)
Edwards, A. and Talbot, R., *The Hard-pressed researcher: A research handbook for the caring professions* (Longman, 1994)
Everitt, W., Hardiker, P., Littlewood, J. and Mullender, A., *Applied Research for Better Practice* (Macmillian, 1992)
Holman, R., *The ethics of social research* (Longman, 1994)
Moroney, M.J., *Facts from Figures* (Pelican, 1951)
Moser, C.A., *Survey Methods in Social Investigation* (Heinemann, 1969)
Oppenheim, A.N., *Questionnaire Design and Attitude Measurement* (Open University/ Heinemann, 1976)
Rowntree, D., *Statistics without Tears* (Penguin, 1983)
Townsend, P., *Poverty in the United Kingdom* (Allen Wall, 1979)

Useful addresses

This list is by no means exhaustive, there are many small support groups throughout the UK. Many of the organisations listed below have regional offices, check in your telephone directory or *Thomson's Directory*.

Look at the beginning of your local *Yellow Pages*, where there is a section entitled 'Yellow Pages and Disabled People' which explains how organisations for the disabled have been classified.

You will find many useful local addresses in *Yellow Pages* under:

- Charitable Organisations
- Counselling and Advice
- Social Service and Welfare Organisations
- Youth and Community Groups.

Community Health Councils exist to help users of the National Health Service. Look in your telephone directory under the name of your local health authority. Local social services departments and Citizen's Advice Bureaux also supply information.

Pharmaceutical companies, food manufacturers and the large supermarket chains all produce their own health promotion literature, as do organisations such as the Milk Marketing Board.

Action for ME
PO Box 1302
Wells
Somerset
BA5 2WE
01749 670799

Action on Smoking and Health
(ASH)
109 Gloucester Place
London
W1H 4EJ
0171 935 3519

Age Concern England
Astral House
1268 London Road
London
SW16 4ER
0181 679 8000

Alcohol Concern
Waterbridge House
32–36 Loman Street
London
SE1 0EE
0171 928 7377

Alzheimer's Disease Society
2nd Floor, Gordon House
10 Greencoat Place
London
SW1P 1PH
0171 306 0606

Arthritis and Rheumatism Council
for Research
Copeman House
St Mary's Court
St Mary's Gate
Chesterfield
Derbyshire
S41 7TD
01246 558033

ASBAH
Association for Spina Bifida and
Hydrocephalus
42 Park Road
Peterborough
PE1 2UQ
01733 555988

Association for Residential Care
The Old Rectory
Old Whittlington
Chesterfield
Derbyshire
S41 7QY

Asthma Research Council
St Thomas's Hospital
Lambeth Palace Road
London SE1

Banardos
Tanners Lane
Barkingside
Ilford
IG6 1QG
0181 550 8822

British Diabetic Association
10 Queen Anne Street
London
W1M 0BD
0171 323 1531

British Heart Foundation
14 Fitzhardinge Street
London
W1H 4DH

Carers National Association
20–25 Glasshouse Yard
London
EC1A 4JS
0171 490 8898

Centre for Policy on Ageing
25–31 Ironmonger Row
London
EC1V 3QP

Child Accident Prevention Trust
18–20 Farringdon Lane
4th Floor, Clerks Court
London
EC1R 3AU
0171 608 3828

Childline
Freepost 1111
London
N1 0BR
0800 1111

Child Poverty Action Group
4th Floor
1–5 Bath Street
London
EC1V 9PY
0171 253 3406

Commission for Racial Equality
Elliot House
10–12 Allington Street
London
SW1E 5EH
0171 828 7033

(Local community relations councils
can be found in your local telephone
directory.)

Contact-a-family
(links families of children with
special needs)
170 Tottenham Court Road
London
W1P 0HA
0171 383 3555

Cruse – Bereavement Care
126 Sheen Road
Richmond
TW9 1UR
0181 940 4818

Cystic Fibrosis Trust
Alexandra House
5 Blyth Road
Bromley
Kent
BR1 3RS
0181 464 7211

Department of Health
The Adelphi
1–11 John Adam Street
London
WC2N 6HT
0171 962 8000

Disability Alliance
1st Floor East
Universal House
88–94 Wentworth Street
London
E1 7SA
0171 243 8776

Disabled Living Foundation
380–384 Harrow Road
London
W9 2HU
0171 289 6111

Down's Syndrome Association
155 Mitcham Road
Tooting
London
SW17 9PG
0181 682 4001

Equal Opportunities Commission
Overseas House
Quay Street
Manchester
M33 3HN
0161 833 9244

Family Welfare Association
501–505 Kingsland Road
Dalston
London
E8 4AU
0171 254 6251

Gingerbread
(an association for one-parent
families)
16 Clerkenwell Close
London
EC1R 0AA
0171 336 8183

Haemophilia Society
123 Westminster Bridge Road
London
SE1 7HR
0171 928 2020

Health Education Authority
Hamilton House
Mabledon Place
London
WC1H 9TX
0171 383 3833

Health Visitor's Association
50 Southwark Street
London
SE1 1UN
0171 378 7255

Help the Aged
St James's Walk
London
EC1R 0BE
0171 253 0253

Hyperactive Children's Support
Group
c/o 71 Whyke Lane
Chichester
Sussex
PO19 2LD
01903 725182
(Tue–Fri, 9.30–3.30)

Institute of Race Relations
2–6 Leek Street
King's Cross Road
London WC1

Invalid Children's Aid Nationwide
Barbican City Gate
1–3 Dufferin Street
London
EC1Y 8NA
0171 374 4422

Kidscape
82 Brook Street
London
W1Y 1YG

Leukaemia Research Fund
43 Great Ormond Street
London
WC1N 3JJ
0171 405 0101

Low Pay Unit
9 Upper Berkeley Street
London
W1H 8BY

ME Association
Stanhope House
High Street
Stanford-le-Hope
Essex
SS17 0HA
01375 642466

Medic-Alert Foundation
12 Bridge Wharf
156 Caledonian Road
London
N1 9UU
0171 833 3034

MENCAP
(Royal Society for Mentally
Handicapped Children and Adults)
National Centre
123 Golden Lane
London
EC1Y 0RT
0171 454 0454

MIND
(National Association for Mental
Health)
Granta House
15–17 Broadway
Stratford
London
E15 4BQ
0181 519 2122

Multiple Sclerosis Society
25 Effie Road
London
SW6 1EE
0171 610 7171

Muscular Dystrophy Group of Great
Britain and Northern Ireland
Nattrass House
7–11 Prescott Place
London
SW4 6BS
0171 720 8055

National Association of Citizens
Advice Bureaux
Myddleton House
115–123 Pentonville Road
London
N1 9LZ
0171 833 2181

National Asthma Campaign
Providence House
Providence Place
London
N1 0NT
0171 226 2260

National Autistic Society
276 Willesden Lane
London
NW2 5RB
0181 451 1114

National Childbirth Trust
Alexandra House
Oldham Terrace
Acton
London
W3 6NH
0181 992 8637

National Childminding Association
8 Masons Hill
Bromley
Kent
BR2 9EY
0181 464 6164

National Children's Bureau
8 Wakley Street
London
EC1V 9QE
0171 843 6000

National Children's Homes
85 Highbury Park
London
N5 1UD

National Council for One Parent
Families
255 Kentish Town Road
London
NW5 2LX
0171 267 1361

National Council of Voluntary
Organisations
Regent's Wharf
8 All Saints Street
London N1 9RL
0171 713 6161

National Deaf Children's Society
15 Dufferin Street
London
EC1Y 8PD
0171 250 0123

National Eczema Society
163 Eversholt Street
London
NW1 1BU
0171 388 4097

National Meningitis Trust
Fern House
Bath Road
Stroud
Gloucestershire
GL5 3TJ
01453 751738

National Osteoporosis Society
PO Box 10
Radstock
Bath
Avon
BA3 3YB
01761 432472

National Schizophrenia Fellowship
28 Castle Street
Kingston-upon-Thames
KT1 1SS
0181 547 3937

NSPCC
(National Society for the Prevention
of Cruelty to Children)
42 Curtain Road
London
EC2A 3NH
0171 825 2500

Parentline UK
Endway House
The Endway
Hadleigh
Essex SS7 2AN
01702 554782

Parents Anonymous
(24-hr helpline for parents who fear
they may abuse their children)
9 Manor Gardens
London
N7 6LA
0171 263 8918

Parkinson's Disease Society of the
UK
22 Upper Woburn Place
London
WC1H 0RA
0171 383 3513

PHAB
(Physically Handicapped and Able
Bodied)
PHAB UK Ltd
12–14 London Road
Croydon
Surrey
CR0 2TA

Positively Women
(support for HIV+ women)
347–349 City Road
London
EC1
0171 490 5515

Relate
(National Marriage Guidance)
Herbert Gray College
Little Church Street
Rugby
Warwickshire
CV21 3AP
01788 573241

Release
(drugs and legal helpline)
169 Commercial Street
London
E1 6BW

RNIB
(Royal National Institute for the
Blind)
224 Great Portland Street
London
W1N 6AA
0171 388 1266

RNID
(Royal National Institute for the
Deaf)
105 Gower Street
London
WC1E 6AH

RoSPA
(Royal Society for the Prevention of
Accidents)
Cannon House
Priory Queensway
Birmingham
B4 6BS
0121 200 2461

Samaritans
10 The Grove
Slough
SL1 1QP
01753 532713

Scope
(for people with cerebral palsy)
12 Park Crescent
London
W1N 4EQ
0171 636 5020

Sense
(National Deaf-Blind and Rubella
Association)
11–13 Clifton Terrace
Finsbury Park
London
N4 3SR
0171 272 7774

Shaftesbury Society
(for the physically and mentally
handicapped, and the socially
deprived)
Shaftesbury House
2a Amity Grove
London
SW20 0LH

Shelter
(National Campaign for Homeless
People)
88 Old Street
London
EC1V 9HU
0171 253 0202

Sickle Cell Society
54 Station Road
London
NW10 4UA
0181 961 7795

Terrence Higgins Trust
(AIDS and HIV)
52–54 Gray's Inn Road
London
WC1X 8JU
0171 831 0330

Victim Support
Cranmer House
39 Brixton Road
London
SW9 6DZ
0171 735 9166

Voluntary Council for Handicapped
Children
8 Wakley Street
Islington
London
EC1V 7QE
0171 843 6000

Women's Aid Federation
PO Box 391
Bristol
BS99 7WS
01179 633494

Women's Health
52 Featherstone Street
London
EC1Y 8RT

WRVS
234–244 Stockwell Road
London
SW9 9SP
0171 416 0146

Index of legislation relating to health and social care

Index

427